ROMAN BUILDING

Materials and Techniques

ROMAN BUILDING

Materials and Techniques

Jean-Pierre Adam

Translated by Anthony Mathews

London and New York

Routledge is an imprint of the Taylor & Francis Group

Published in French as *La Construction Romaine: matériaux et techniques*

First published in English 1994 by B.T. Batsford Ltd

First published in paperback 1999 by Routledge
11 New Fetter Lane, London EC4P 4EE

© 1989 Éditions A. et J. Picard
English translation © 1994 B.T. Batsford Ltd

Typeset and printed by Colorcraft Ltd, Hong Kong
Bound in Great Britain by TJ International Ltd, Padstow, Cornwall

British Library Cataloguing in Publication Data
A catalogue record for this book is available from the British Library

ISBN 0–415–20866–1

CONTENTS

FOREWORD

Of all the kinds of architecture that have appeared and developed in the course of the last five millennia, Roman architecture is extraordinarily rich in terms of the buildings, monuments and structures which survive, and the variety of materials and means by which they were constructed. Much of our respect for Roman architectural achievement can be attributed both to this remarkable survival and to the incorporation of Roman theoretical and practical ideas into the practice of architecture from the Renaissance to the present day. In these circumstances it is surprising that there has been no modern study of Roman constructional and building techniques and it is this gap which Jean-Pierre Adam's book sets out to fill. It aims to provide a systematic study of building materials and the various types of building technique, in brick, stone and marble; arch and vault construction; carpentry; types and techniques of interior decoration; and methods of civil engineering for water supply, heating, baths and roads. Minor domestic buildings, workshops and shops are also considered.

The closeness of the relationship between the past and the present alluded to above is, to a great extent, due to two outstanding and complementary names, which, between them, unite theory and practice. They are Vitruvius and Pompeii, both of which have served as a major source of inspiration in the preparation of this book. Vitruvius is the most important writer on Roman architectural theory and practice whose work, *The Ten Books of Architecture*, survives in its entirety.

The subject matter of his influential survey ranges through architectural principles, the origin of building and the use of materials, the study of individual types of building such as temples, theatres, baths, harbours and town and country houses, and also includes a range of technical and engineering themes. Vitruvius' work was clearly regarded as important by successive generations of Roman architects, but it is still unclear how far his precepts actually reflected contemporary practice or were put into action within the Roman world in general. Certainly his writings are frequently turned to by modern scholars in their attempts to understand ancient structures, and to see how far they measure up to the principles laid down by Vitruvius. The latter would be easier to interpret if illustrations survived as well as the text; thus ample provision of photographs and line drawings is a key feature of Adam's book.

Illustration is where Pompeii plays a vital role as an exemplar of Roman practice. The destruction of the community in AD 79 and its burial in volcanic ash has ensured the survival of the town with a representative range of types of buildings and construction techniques current in the first century AD. Indeed it provides examples of buildings and other structures which span a period both before and after the life of Vitruvius. The main focus of research at Pompeii has been on the city plan, but not on the techniques of construction and the ideas and issues which influenced their choice. Pompeii offers an outstandingly good starting point and it has been one of the principal sources for this research. However, it has to be remembered that Roman buildings and monuments are visible all around the Mediterranean. For this study Jean-Pierre Adam has turned to sites other than Pompeii to provide examples of major imperial buildings, as well as those which employed marble and stone-block construction; all being aspects of Roman building poorly represented at Pompeii.

Jean-Pierre Adam acknowledges a great debt of gratitude to earlier scholars in this field. In particular he would like to single out A. Choisy, Giuseppe Lugli, Luigi Crema and J.B. Ward-Perkins, who, between them, have drawn attention to the most representative Roman monuments for studying techniques of construction. Finally, it is also appropriate to acknowledge the influence of the great student of Greek architecture, the late A. Orlandos. Considerable assistance on technical matters has been given by living craftsmen in France and Italy and elsewhere around the Mediterranean; a further illustration of the survival of long-established practices to the present day.

The selection, definition and etymology of technical terms are derived from different works or oral sources and are cited in the bibliography, rather than continually throughout the text. Photographs and line drawings have been chosen in order to provide a representative rather than definitive range. As far as possible the illustrations draw on actual examples, but where the remains are insufficient to be informative, Jean-Pierre Adam has relied on his own reconstructions, indicating any important details. Unless otherwise acknowledged in the captions, all line illustrations and photographs are by Jean-Pierre Adam.

It is a tribute to the interest already aroused by Jean-Pierre Adam's work that, even in the short time which has elapsed since its original publication in 1989, new research is continuing to advance rapidly our understanding of Roman buildings, the materials and techniques of their construction. Studies of the exploitation, characterisation and use of Roman marble, in particular, have been prolific in the intervening years. Progress in individual areas such as marble studies serves only to enhance the value of an original overview such as this, which seeks to bring together the many disparate elements that make up the overarching theme of this book.

In the collection and organization of the documentary material, this book would not have been possible without the constant help and support of Thérèse Adam, the author's wife, who, after many journeys around the Mediterranean, apparently became a remarkably competent *agrimensor*.

Michael Fulford
University of Reading
January 1993

1
SURVEYING

Wherever architecture and public works and rural and urban planning appear to be the result of systematic techniques,[1] surveying has been a necessary precondition. An indispensable step between the architect's plan and its realization, surveying holds the same intermediate position in the converse operation: that is, in the reconstruction of the plans of a monument or of a natural area, based on what survives. Three operations define the discipline of surveying and determine the methods and instruments used: the establishment of bearings, the measurement of distances and the estimation of heights.

While the Egyptian geometer is known to us both through administrative and funerary texts and through visual representations,[2] his Greek counterpart is familiar only through literature, the opposite of the Roman case for which, once again, sources abound.[3]

Even though we have no direct visual knowledge of the Greek geometers, through either depictions or actual objects, their high technical level is displayed, as is the potential precision of their instruments, by certain finds relating to parallel activities. An example of this is the Antikythera mechanism[4] and its remarkable mechanical construction.

The essentials of surveying are described by Hero of Alexandria,[5] who mentions in particular the complex problems of land surveying, such as the boring of a tunnel from both ends or the calculation of the distance between two remote points. Elementary operations such as alignment were not considered by him to be a problem or to be impossible to perfect.

To perform the measurements quoted in his treatise, Hero describes the use of angle-measuring tools, such as the *dioptra*.[6] There are no surviving examples or representations of this and so it can only be shown in the form of a drawn reconstruction (fig.1). Hero proposed some improvements to the basic form of this apparatus, allowing it to be used in astronomy: he added a gear mechanism and a second vertical disc, transforming it into a theodolite minus a lens. It is not known whether the Greeks thought of applying the principle of the *dioptra*,[7] consisting of a rule with a

1 Proposed reconstruction of the *dioptra* for carrying out horizontal angular measurements.

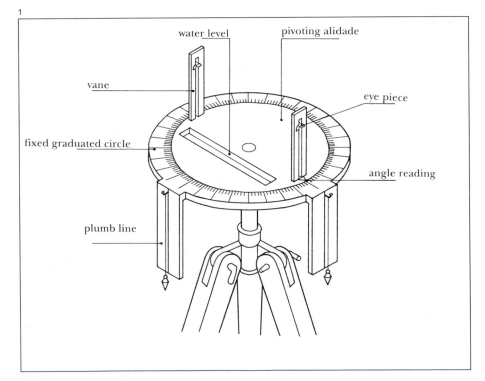

1

water level

pivoting alidade

vane

eye piece

fixed graduated circle

angle reading

plumb line

sight reference or vane at each end, to plotting directly on to parchment. Hero makes no mention of it but, since his purpose was to apply mathematical research to surveying and astronomy, his notes are only concerned with angle measurement.

For the simplest operations the equipment of the ancient surveyor hardly differed from that which remained in use in rural areas until the beginning of the twentieth century: the graduated rule or Κανών (canon), whose name has come to be applied to a level of academic standard, which is found used as both an instrument and a unit of measurement – the rod and the perch; the cord or σταθμη used for alignment or as a measure (it is the origin of the surveyor's old land measurement, the chain); the cross head, χύωμων, cited by Aristophanes as a precise instrument used to excess by Meton;[8] and the cord with two pegs, the τόρνος, for marking circles and arcs of circles on the ground.[9]

Finally, when considering the great achievements of the Romans, especially in the field of water supply, it must be remembered that, though they built on the research of the Greeks with a remarkable efficiency, the latter show no less evidence of some spectacular attainments, for example the channelling of water at Pergamon across particularly difficult terrain,[10] or the tunnel of Samos which was bored from the two ends, using the plans of Eupalinos.[11]

The Roman agrimensor is known mainly for the technical works his profession has left behind, including the fragments recovered from the surveying treatise of Frontinus. These texts, gathered in a collection entitled Gromatici veteres,[12] give precise information on the practical methods of the profession and the framework in which it evolved. However, for the interpretation of the written evidence, we can turn to the writings of experts whose

analyses are an indispensable complement, even a precondition, to the attempt to achieve a proper understanding.[13]

Fortunately, the surviving Roman archaeological material complements this theoretical expertise, as is still visible in the surviving constructions, and both elements are brought together in the following short practical study.[14] Two surveying tools will be used in the experiment: the groma[15] and the chorobates. The functions of these tools are complementary and are at the heart of standard surveying techniques used in the location of a building, a road or an aqueduct. In order to demonstrate the technical possibilities open to the agrimensor, whose range of techniques would be familiar to a modern surveyor, the experiment will be extended also to an exercise in land levelling, which is also part of the operations of land registry.[16]

In order to understand better the use of both the groma and the chorobates, it is necessary to remind ourselves of the nature of surveying work.[17] Alignment is the first and the most common of the operations; as the term indicates it facilitates the laying out of axes and boundaries, essential to all construction and public building works. Alignment, by the use of cords over short distances, or marker poles over longer ones, presents difficulties only on uneven ground; on a slope, the surveyor takes a series of inclined sightings, keeping the poles in the same vertical alignment. In addition the alignment has to be accompanied by measurement of the distance covered, and the method used is a series of stepped, horizontal sightings and measurements. Step-levelling was known to the agrimensor under the name of cultellatio[18]: the word has remained in French usage (though rare in English) as cultellation or cutellation.

The most elementary form of angle measurement, but also the most universal, is squaring off a baseline, which enables the vast majority of buildings, centuriations and square or rectangular *insulae* to be set out (fig.2). On the ground, two situations call for such a measurement: firstly the definition of a right angle starting from a known line marked by poles, described as raising a perpendicular; secondly, starting from an isolated point and joining up with a straight line, known as dropping a perpendicular. These different operations are usually completed by measurements of distances, which must always be horizontal for transfer to the map, the *forma*. Ranging a line and squaring off a baseline provide, by simple extrapolation, the solution to the majority of surveying problems. The instrument able to perform the two above-mentioned

operations must therefore be capable of taking in two axes of perpendicular sightings, dividing the space into four quadrants: this instrument, which is the present-day optical square or surveying square was in antiquity the *groma*.

Excavations at Pompeii have greatly contributed to our knowledge of this instrument as, of the two representations of the *groma* on funerary stelae (figs 3 and 4), one is from that city and, more importantly, the only *groma* ever recovered was discovered there by Matteo della Corte, in a shop on the via dell'Abbondanza.[19] The funerary stele, recovered from the necropolis of the Nucerian Gate, is that of the *agrimensor* Nicostratus, sculpted on a plaque of marble, measuring 55.2cm long, 33.1cm high and 4.3cm thick. The central text is framed on the right by the representation of two ranging poles and a cord (the lower right-hand corner is missing) and on the left by a *groma*, the cross of which is tilted forward so that it can be clearly seen.[20] If the funerary reliefs were the only available evidence, the use of this instrument would seem problematic, since the view through the plumb lines would be obstructed if the cross had the same axis as the foot.

Fortunately, the discovery of an actual *groma* at the house of the tool maker and seller Verus (via dell'-Abbondanza, Regio I, Insula 6, no. 3)[21] clarifies the actual appearance and the operation of this instrument (fig.5).

As the principle is that of squaring off a baseline, the functional part of the instrument is formed by a cross with four perpendicular arms of equal dimensions, making up the directional square; a plumb line is suspended from each of these arms. These four lines are the *perpendicula*, forming the two sighting planes. To avoid the obstacle of the base, the square is fixed by a pivot on to a positioning bracket, at the top of the base (or upright) of the

2   Timgad (Algeria), an example of the division of a city into square *insulae*. (L. Benevolo, *L'Arte e la citta antica*, Rome, 1974, p.237, fig.351.)

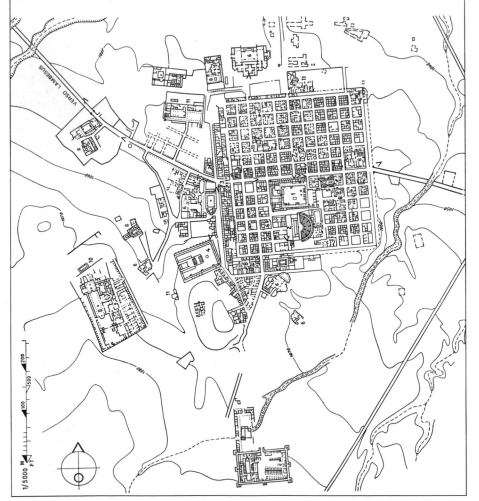

instrument. To enable the square to pivot easily, the arms have been made longer than the positioning bracket.

Finally the upright is provided with a point so that it can be fixed in soft ground; while on rocky ground it seems that the operator had to have a light easel or tripod available to keep the instrument standing without having to hold it all the time.[22] Setting up over a station took place in three stages: first the *mensor* secured the base of the instrument; then, swinging the positioning bracket, centred the square with the plumb line over the station to be fixed or an already existing one; and finally lined up the square on the principal axis or direction to be followed.

Aerial photography has made it possible to recover with great precision the traces of the centuriations laid down by the Roman legions,[23] particularly in arid regions or those not affected by later enclosure, and it can justifiably be concluded that the *groma* was, in such operations, the standard instrument of the military *mensores*.

The boundary stones recovered in Tunisia,[24] and more rarely in Italy, even illuminate the way in which the surveyor divided space. The *mensores* placed boundary markers at the intersection points along the two principal axes, *cardo (Kardo)* and *decumanus*, and on the right angles delimiting the centuries. On the surface of the markers they engraved the two horizontal 90° axes, the *decussis*[25] (fig.6), and on the vertical face (the markers could be cylindrical or square) their location in relation to the *cardo maximus* and the *decumanus maximus*. The difficulty in reconstructing these today comes from the fact that the markers have often been moved (it is enough for them to have been knocked over for the original orientation to be lost). Another problem is that the surveyor, who distinguished in his text right and left (DD and SD

respectively, *Dextra Decumani* and *Sinistra Decumani*)[26] did not observe a systematic polar orientation.

Joël le Gall,[27] studying the problems of orientation associated with the laying out of towns and centuriations, has established a comparative orientation table for 14 Roman survey plans (2 centuriations, 2 fortresses and 10 towns).[28] This table shows that the centuriation, but not the town, of *Augusta Raurica*, has an orientation strictly aligned to the cardinal points of the compass. The fact that the towns and the centuriations that border them, especially on rough ground, often have different orientations,[29] and the fact that the north–south and east–west axes are far from universally respected, prove that the surveyors essentially made a practical choice of orientation (fig.7). Religious requirements, to which the Romans attributed, along with the technique of surveying, an Etruscan origin,[30] were nothing but memories that were occasionally invoked only for the laying out of temples.

Based on the indications given on the boundary stones,[31] it is possible to

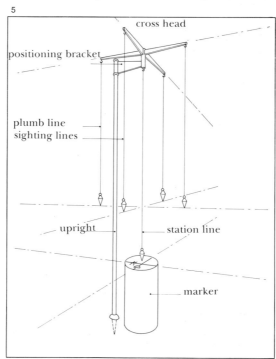

cross head

positioning bracket

plumb line
sighting lines

upright   station line

marker

3 Funerary stele of an *agrimensor* from Ivrea (Val d'Aosta), showing a dismantled *groma* and its plumb lines.

4 The stele of the Pompeian *agrimensor* Nicostratus; detail of the *groma*.

5 Reconstruction of a *groma* stationed over the centre point of a boundary stone.

6

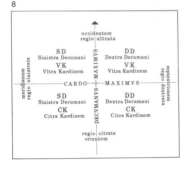

7

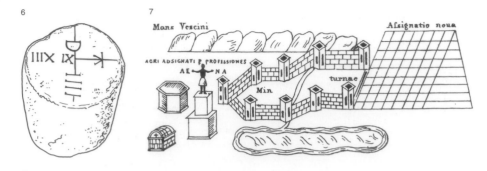

8

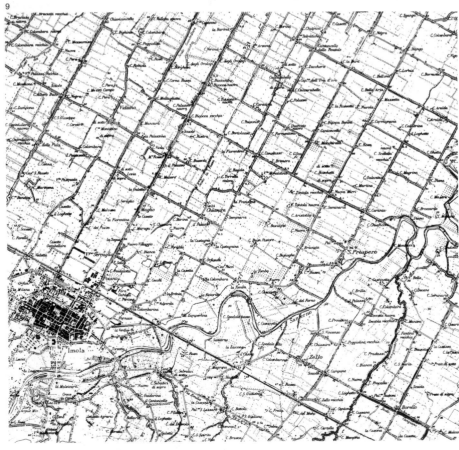

propose a reconstruction of the procedure for setting up the boundary of a centuriation (fig.8). To the initial letters of the position in relation to the *cardo* and the *decumanus* were added the numbers giving the distance of these reference points, measured in centuries. In the best examples, four markers defined 25 centuries, forming a square of 5 centuries a side called the *saltus*.[32] However elementary such operations may seem, they nevertheless constituted a remarkable achievement when the division of land extended over tens of kilometres or more (fig.9).[33] It is probable that the *agri-*

mensores, familiar with Pythagoras' theorem, periodically carried out cross-checks along the diagonal, which, for an *actus* of 120 feet square, would have had a value in the region of 170 feet (169.7). The same cross-check, applied to the diagonal of a century, had to come out at about 3400 feet (figs 10 and 11). The accuracy of the framework was ensured by the measurement of the two diagonals, which have to be equal to make a square (if there was a difference of value, the square *actus* or the century would be lozenges). The same check was of course applicable to rectangular areas.

In a commentary at the time of the publication of the cadastre of Orange by A. Piganiol, F. Salviat[34] clearly sets out the arrangement of three documents, A, B and C, describing the division of land between Montélimar and Avignon. Displayed on three walls of a room, these plans each had a different orientation when viewed straight, but when tilted downwards to the horizontal they returned to a common coherent orientation.[35] This particular example, due to the large area required by these documents and because of their being positioned on three walls, was a problem for the interpreter who did not have the key. It could possibly have led to them being understood as different topographical orientations,[36] while, as the study of F. Salviat shows, A, B and C constitute one homogeneous document in time and space. Returned to the horizontal the three plans could be read with a *cardo* oriented from east to west, and it could be presumed that the *agrimensor* had chosen for the orientation of the markers an identical west-facing position at the time of the initial survey.

In order to test the efficiency of the *groma* in a practical situation, the simplest thing was to make a life-size reconstruction of it, then carry out the linear and right-angle measurements for which it was designed (fig.12). The

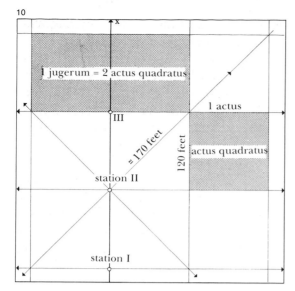

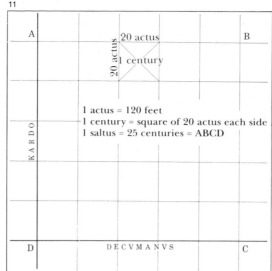

1 jugerum = 2 actus quadratus

1 actus

≈ 170 feet

120 feet

actus quadratus

III

station II

station I

x

A 20 actus B

20 actus

1 century

KARDO

1 actus = 120 feet
1 century = square of 20 actus each side
1 saltus = 25 centuries = ABCD

D DECVMANVS C

6 The boundary stone of a centuriation with *decussis* giving the orthogonal directions of the *kardo* K, and of the *decumanus* D, plus indications of distances. Diameter: 40cm; height: 78cm. (Museo della Civiltà Romana, room XLIII; JPA.)

7 The centuriation of Minturno, from a drawing in the *Gromatici veteres*.

8 The designation of the directions and the quadrants by an *agrimensor*, looking towards the west.

9 Map of the region of Imola (*Forum Cornelii*), crossed by the *via Aemilia* – the ancient centuriation system can still be seen in the modern road network.

10 The process of land division using the *actus* and the *jugerum* as units of length and area.

11 A diagram of square centuriation.

12 Aligning with the *groma* (Th. Adam).

instrument manufactured for this purpose was fixed on to a metal upright 190cm high (the height making it possible to sight through the lines), ending in a positioning bracket 18cm long, on which the cross-head could pivot, the arms of which were 61cm long.[37] The plumb lines, or *perpendicula*, for sighting and setting up were suspended from the ends of the arms and from their intersection.

The *groma* is set up by placing the upright near the chosen (or existing) point, at a distance not exceeding the length of the positioning bracket; then by rotating this, the setting-up line of the square is aligned with the bench mark of the station. The horizontality of the cross-head (at right angles to the upright) is checked by seeing whether one of the plumb lines is parallel with the axis of the upright. The apparatus can then be secured by a steady support (tripod) and, after first rotating the square to the required direction, sighting can be carried out. The disadvantage of this type of instrument lies, as the experiment amply showed,[38] in its great sensitivity to the wind, a disadvantage also underlined by Vitruvius in relation to the *chorobates*. However, the plumb lines are a great advantage since they enable offsets to be made at right angles even on very

rough ground thanks to their height and regardless of the eye-level or the size of the operator. In a very strong wind the operator conceivably resorted to using the arms of the square directly as lines of sight.

Site experiments have proved that the speed of setting up and the accuracy of the layout resulting from linear and right-angle measurements over short distances[39] was comparable to that obtained with modern instruments.

The opposite to laying out was planning or topographical recording, the natural consequence of the geometer's work. The existence of topographical documents, the most complex of which is undoubtedly the plan of Rome, the *Forma urbis*,[40] unfortunately fragmentary, provides evidence of the application of this technique in the preparation of detailed plans in urban areas. It would of course be particularly interesting to know what instruments and methods were used in this considerable work, recorded on marble, and also the type of records made in the field. In the absence of these details, it is instructive to employ the *groma* for this type of work, which supports the assumption, if it does not prove it, that the instrument was used for such purposes.

Since the instrument can only measure right angles, the procedure is the same as that undertaken by surveyors with an optical square and a chain, known as planning by offsets. In this, a straight line, the baseline, is laid out with poles at intervals linked by a cord. The recording is done by moving the *groma* along the baseline (from point A in the two examples shown in fig.13) and locating it at distances, either fixed or arbitrary, that are measured in order to plot them in *abscissa* on the recording sheet. From each of these stations two sightings are made: one aligned on the baseline AB and one at right angles along which

there will be one or several points to record. The distances from these points to the baseline are chained; these are the offset measurements, whose values constitute the ordinates. These measurements of distance are completed by vertical measurements (heights above the datum line), taken on the ground or the buildings themselves. The greater the number of stations, hence of measurements, the greater the accuracy of the final document, independent of that of the instrument, which depends on the quality of its cross-head. It might be thought that the risk of error would increase in proportion to the number of measurements, with a consequent loss of accuracy. In reality, the experiment shows that in working along a straight line the errors, sometimes positive, sometimes negative, occur in equal numbers and cancel each other out.

To assess the efficiency of the method the same process was carried out with the aid of an alidade and a plane-table (fig.14). The advantage of this procedure lies in the low number of stations: only two are required with the alidade as against fifteen with the *groma*; besides, the alidade, which works by radiation, covers an area of 360 degrees and enables a considerable number of points to be plotted (except when there are obstacles), while the *groma* can plot points only in four directions per station (two in the present case). However, setting up the ancient instrument, with a little practice and in the absence of wind, can be done very rapidly and the time taken to do the same survey is practically identical. As regards accuracy it is noticeable that, on a slight slope (22m baseline and 25m ordinate), the differences are not excessive: the most considerable angular variation on a wall less than 10m long is only about 10cm at one end.[41] It is worth noting that the plan done with the *groma* was

13 The different methods of plotting with the *groma*, with the aid of several baselines surounding or bisecting a piece of land.

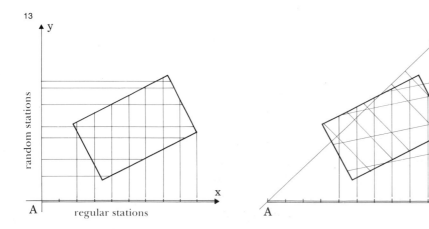

reproduced without the corrections of triangulation usually carried out.[42]

This experiment clearly showed that the method of planning by co-ordinates means that the *groma* has numerous operating possibilities in planning and laying out, such as the location of two positions for digging a tunnel from opposite ends. The *agrimensor*, when working on very uneven ground which rules out a rectilinear traverse over the obstacle, carried out a traverse with constant angular measurement[43] in the form of a series of alignments and off-sets, complemented by levelling with the *chorobates*, following the same route (fig.15). Naturally, in the course of the operation, all the distances and changes of direction must be noted in order to return to the two original points, in the simplest case of a tunnel with a straight gallery of constant level.

The completion of the tunnel of Samos, and its difficulties, have been referred to above, but the Greeks were not the only ones to encounter difficulties in boring tunnels, as is witnessed by an inscription at Lambaesis.[44] This text relates the story of the intervention of the military engineer Nonius Datus, stationed at Lambaesis and despatched to *Saldae* (Bejaia, formerly Bougie), to take over the planning and boring of an underground portion of the aqueduct designed to supply the town with water. The work was well advanced, but the two galleries, dug simultaneously from the two sides of the mountain to be crossed, had passed one another without meeting: '. . . the upper part of the gallery leading southwards deviated to the right and the lower part leading northwards likewise deviated to the right; as the accurate plan had not been followed, the two sections missed one another'. Nonius Datus resurveyed the angles and calculated the levels carefully, as a result of which the job was completed in four years, indicating

the extent of the work needed to bore a tunnel 428m long. Despite the absence of technical details, this text nevertheless suggests that a method of planning with the aid of the *groma* and the *chorobates* by rectilinear alignment and step-levelling was used, since it says: 'a precise line had been marked out over the top of the mountain from East to West'. From this it can be understood that the line did not go round the mountain but, as is always preferable when the relief allows, simply maintained the chosen direction over the surface, which made it possible, during the excavation, to maintain a true alignment consistently on both sides.

The technique applied here to a deep tunnel must also have been the one used in digging tunnels close to the surface. In this case boring was possible not only from each end but

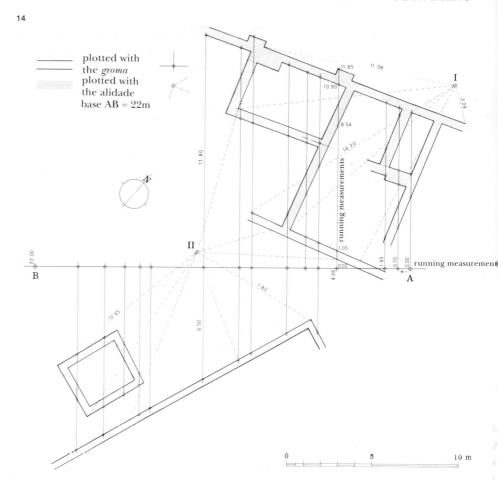

14 Comparative surveys of the same buildings with the *groma* and with the alidade. *Groma*: 15 stations on a single baseline AB and 51 points; alidade: 2 stations totalling 53 points.

also through open pits along the course of the tunnel (cut and cover). The gain in time would be appreciable since, in view of the relative narrowness of the tunnels, very few workers could work at the face. An example of this technique is the large tunnel at the fort of Euryale which is not very deep and links the outer bastions to the interior of the *enceinte*. Here ten digging pits can be counted along the course of the tunnel.

Infinitely more impressive is the canal of Seleucia-in-Pieria (Cilicia), dug during the reigns of Vespasian and Titus, as commemorated by the inscription engraved on one of the walls. Partly in a deep cutting (up to 50m

deep), this canal, designed to divert the course of a raging torrent, passes through two tunnels surviving in the rock. The steps leading down from the surface can still be seen, showing that the work, starting at each end, was carried out simultaneously at several different points along the course of the tunnel.[45] But the record should go to the *emissarium* (or artificial channel) of Lake Fucino (Lake Celano/Capistrano), planned by Caesar, begun in the time of Claudius and finished in 52, designed to transform a vast lake with marshy banks in central Italy into a fertile plain. The gallery, measuring 5679m, took eleven years and some 50,000 workmen to build and necessitated the boring of 42 ventilation and spoil evacuation pits.[46] A relief recovered from the channel, probably originally from the decorated outlet of the *emissarium*, shows two lifting machines with vertically positioned drums. With these a bucket full of rocks could be raised from the excavation at the same time as an empty bucket was lowered. Such mechanisms must have been in-stalled above the vertically-stepped pits to the right of the survey line. (See the illustrations in the chapter on aqueducts, below.)

Like numerous ancient cities, Pompeii has an urban layout in which can easily be detected a regular plan establishing small blocks of houses (*insulae*) separated by parallel roads in twos. This division, however, is only apparent in the areas defined at the same time as the line of the surviving wall, which is 3.2km long and was laid out in the course of the fifth century BC. The ancient town, confined to the south-western zone and including the Temple of Venus, the Civic Forum and the Triangular Forum, although integrated into the new plan, nevertheless preserved an irregular pattern of streets, even if the buildings found there, with the exception of the Doric temple, no longer belong to the Greco-Oscan period of the city.

15 Boring a sloping tunnel from two ends and planning the exits (points 1 and 14) by carrying out a series of right-angle measurements to bypass the obstacle. The sum of the off-sets must be equal to zero at the finishing point.

15

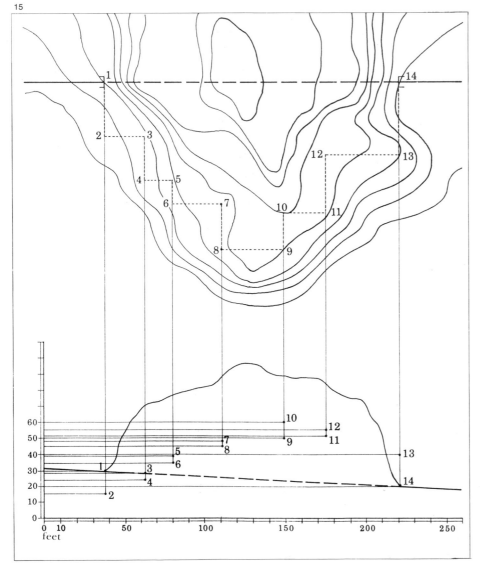

Pompeii was not a city on a plain but was originally a defensive establishment on a spur of lava, ending to the south with a small cliff at the foot of which flowed the Sarno. Any extension beyond this central core could therefore only take place northwards and eastwards, on a slope of Vesuvius with a significant difference in height from north to south (34m between the Vesuvius Gate and the Stabian Gate). To adapt to this topography, the new city was developed in a vaguely ellipsoidal plan, with the major axis east–west measuring 1270m and the minor axis north–south 730m.[47] The ancient city-centre was respected and outlined by two straight roads, the via Stabiana and the via della Fortuna,[48] defining a dihedron, beyond which a regular plan could be laid out. This, however, was not a simple rectangular grid but an adaptation to the slope of the ground. Six areas were defined, delimited by three roads, to which the nineteenth-century excavators gave the names in use today: the via Stabiana, now the *cardo*, via dell'Abbondanza and the via di Nola (extending the via della Fortuna) referred to as *decumanus minor* and *decumanus major* respectively (names that have today fallen into disuse).

It is interesting to note that the development of the city within this new plan took place quite naturally outwards from the ancient core, but in AD 79 the built-up area did not entirely fill the space defined by the city wall. After the Sullanian conquest, the western sector was sufficiently free of construction for the two biggest monumental complexes of the town to be laid out: the amphitheatre[49] (150 × 110m) and the Large *Palaestra* (141 × 106m).[50] Around these two complexes the individual blocks on the north and the west have revealed enormous gardens,[51] while the the first habitations discovered, such as the *Praedia* of Julia Felix (II,4) and the House of Octavius Quartio (II,2,2), were completed by green areas, filling the space defined by the streets. Looking at the general plan of the town, it is noticeable that the rectangular division of the *insulae* is found only in areas I, II, III and IV, that is less than a half of the total urban area. This subdivision was altered by numerous modifications made between the initial planning and AD 79, and in fact only the axes of the roads and not the façades of the houses respect the rectangular alignments.

By contrast, the care taken over the systematic organization of a space is shown clearly by the corrected arrangement of the Civic Forum.[52] This vast rectangular and very elongated space (154 × 46m) was flanked in the course of the second century BC by religious, civic and commercial buildings whose somewhat haphazard layout was in fact integrated into the orientation of the surrounding *insulae* without making a regular space in the centre. At the end of the second century, a two-storey portico of tufa, erected by the Quaestor Vibius Popidius,[53] formed on three sides – east, south and west – a rectangle which was completed to the north by the Temple of Jupiter, providing the axis of the whole complex. In order to link up and align the already existing structures to the new plan, outer walls and extra thicknesses, invisible to the visitor, made the back walls of the three porticoes parallel to the colonnades.

The complement to the *groma*, the *chorobates*, is known only from a description by Vitruvius.[54] In fact, being made of wood, there is little chance that this instrument would survive.[55] Fortunately the text is sufficiently explicit for a design and then reconstruction to be attempted.[56] Designed for the task of levelling, the *chorobates* takes the form of a long bench with vertical legs, with a channel on the top. On the side are reference lines, perpendicular to the table-top,

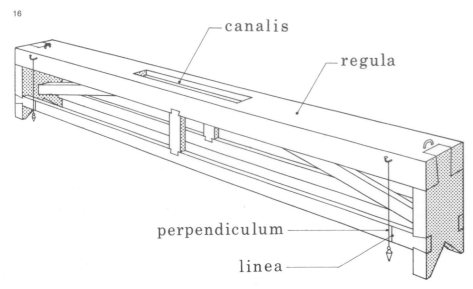

16

canalis

regula

perpendiculum

linea

16 Reconstruction drawing of
the *chorobates*, based on the
description of Vitruvius (VII,5).

17 The reconstructed
chorobates wedged into a
horizontal position.

17

which are aligned with plumb-lines
when the apparatus is wedged into
a horizontal position (fig.16). The
channel serves as a water level, useful
when the wind disturbs the plumb
lines. If the dimensions given by
Vitruvius – twenty feet long (nearly
6m) – are true, they are impressive, but
they do demonstrate the requirement
for accuracy demanded by the surveyor
charged with the laying out of aqueducts. Such an object must have been
very difficult to operate in the field
and impossible to position on only
slightly uneven ground. Besides, such a
long piece of wood must have had a

tendency to warp due to variations in
humidity.[57] It seems reasonable to
suggest, therefore, that instruments
of more modest proportions were also
in use.

This was certainly the choice made
for the construction of an experimental *chorobates*, and the dimensions
decided on demonstrated the relative
efficiency of an easily transportable
apparatus.[58] The instrument, 1.5m
long and 60cm high, was provided at
one end with a footing designed to
make it easy to prop up on the levelling supports (fig.17). As any piece of
ground is only rarely horizontal, the
instrument is set up by placing chocks
under one of the ends, flat ones at
first, until it is nearly horizontal, then
wedge-shaped ones, knocked in gently
until the plumb-lines and the vertical
lines incised on the instrument coincide; a cross-check can always be made
by filling the channel with water, level
with the top. Levelling can be carried
out by placing one's eye at the level of
the table, looking along the axis of the
instrument and sighting through the
two eye-holes.

Several procedures can be undertaken by the surveyor, the most systematic consisting in levelling in steps at
a constant height. The top of the
measuring pole need only be placed
along the sight line of the operator of
the *chorobates*. The difference in level
will always be equal to the known
height of the measuring pole, minus
that of the *chorobates* (fig.18). This
method can be used on long traverses
in order to simplify recording and
calculation. Since on gently sloping
ground this procedure is not always
possible, the height would be read
using a graduated pole, or as it is
known today, a levelling staff (fig.19).
Because of the lack of a magnifying
lens, the operator, when too far away to
read the staff, sights on to a sliding
marker on the staff, leaving to an
assistant the task of measuring the

distance between the marker and the ground.

An experiment using the two methods gave the following results:

1 Step-levelling at a constant height with a pole 148cm high (4 sightings) plus a sighting on to a known height of 131cm with the height of the instrument being 60cm. The difference between the starting point A and the finishing point B, 63.5m apart, was found to be 423cm.

2 Reading off a levelling staff using the *chorobates*, with three sightings, starting from the same station and over a distance of 51.3m, gave a difference in altitude of 340cm (fig.20). The same operation carried out with a theodolite gave 344cm.

One conclusion arrived at from these experiments is that it was in the surveyor's interest to carry out a restricted number of set-ups, allowing for the limitations of eyesight. However, it must be remembered that, because the apparatus may have been subject to warping, the normal result when wood is exposed to humidity, readings over large distances are the most susceptible to error.

The main levelling operations at Pompeii were those needed to lay out a water supply network in the Augustan period. The plan developed from the line of an aqueduct, not itself an independent water conduit but a branch of the aqueduct of Serino which supplied Naples with water and finished at Baia at the gigantic reservoir of the 'Piscina Mirabile'. In the city centre the problem facing the engineers was the building of watertight channels, strong enough to resist the force of the water caused by the considerable difference of level between the Vesuvius Gate, the high point of the city where the main water distribution tank was situated, and the quarters to the south which lay between 20 and 30m below. The following drops in height give some idea of the problem:

Great *Palaestra*: 24.5m; Nucerian Gate: 29.5m; Stabian Gate (lowest point): 34m; *Palaestra* of the Theatre: 29m; Marine Gate: 20m. The solution adopted (which will be analysed in the chapter on hydraulic installations) was the creation of a series of rises using columns supporting a tank, forcing the water-pressure to drop progressively. It was the location and estimation of the height of these columns that required the *surveyors* of Pompeii to level along all the routes taken by the water channels, in order to achieve at the end a final drop of least pressure. A check made along the course of the via Stabiana has, however, demonstrated that the first column was built too high and was therefore not very efficient since it raised the water practically back to its original height.[59]

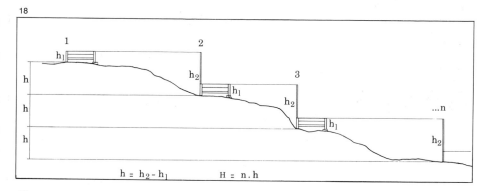

18 Step-levelling at a constant height, systematically sighting on to the head of the pole.

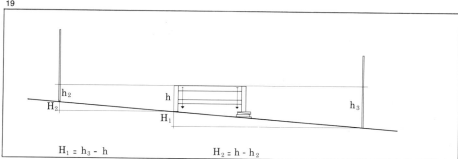

19 Levelling by backsights and foresights and measurement of the height of the point sighted.

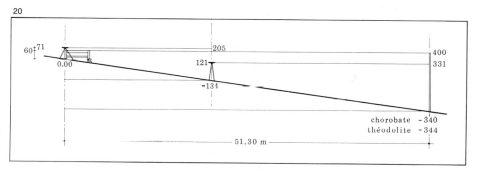

20 Comparative levelling carried out with the *chorobates* and the theodolite (the vertical scale is doubled).

2
MATERIALS

1 Stone

a Extraction

At the most basic level, the use of stone for building begins with the collection of surface stone fragments, rocks broken off by the action of weathering or vegetation or resulting from rockfalls at the foot of escarpments. These pieces, of varying sizes, can be used in the construction of drystone walls, the stability of which is guaranteed by the use of the largest and most regular blocks, made up of facings with an infilling of rubble. Sea or river pebbles make an ideal material because of their sizes and regularity, but their roundness means they cannot be used without mortar; it is therefore advisable to use a mortar of clay, though the two products do not always occur together naturally.

As well as this collection at source, a method still used up to the present day, architecture of quality demands the extraction from the ground of building stone that can be shaped to suit different requirements and fashions.

As with the collection of stones, extraction begins with the exploitation of surface outcrops, and numerous quarries did not go beyond this method of supply because of the abundance of rock in certain areas.[1]

The term quarry (carrière in French), referring to such a site, seems to originate in a shift of meaning of a word originally denoting a road passable for vehicles ('carossable' in French). It was probably the heavy cart designed to transport stones which gave to the source the name of the track leading to or from it. However, a derivation from *quadraria* referring to a place of squaring, i.e. stone-cutting, has also been suggested. This more appropriate etymology would seem to be confirmed by the French spelling of *quarrier* and *quarrire*, attested in the eighteenth century but which the *Encyclopédie* fixed definitively as *carrier* and *carrire*.[2] Be that as it may, it is stone alone that is referred to in *De Lapidicinis*, the title Vitruvius gives to his chapter where he deals with the places '. . . whence one obtains for building stone blocks as well as rubble stone'.[3] A last relic of the term is probably to be found in the medieval French word *lavier*, likewise meaning a quarry,[4] and in the phrase, *laver un bloc*, meaning to remove the rough outer surface in order to make a facing stone from it.

A builder looks for certain mechanical and aesthetic qualities from stone, and this led the Romans not only to select local material but also to import stone, sometimes from considerable distances. The physical qualities of a stone are judged by the stone-mason according to cutting hardness. This classification comprises six categories defined as: very soft, soft, semi-firm, firm, hard and cold. Thus in the first category are the cretaceous limestones or the sandstones and the less concretized volcanic tufas and in the last the marbles and granites.

In general, Roman architecture, particularly with its extensive use of rubble stone masonry, used local stone for the bulk of construction and imported only those materials intended for the noble and decorated parts (elements of the orders) or for facings. As usually only one type of stone was available in the immediate vicinity of a town or monument, its identification is relatively straightforward; the presence of marble slabs, on the other hand, calls for a complex investigation into geographical origin, bearing in mind the organized nature of the importation of this material in the imperial period.

Among the most frequently exploited or imported rocks that were highly valued are:

Marbles:

    Chemtou marble, yellow veined (Tunisia)

    Chios marble, grey-blue (island of Chios)

    'cipollino' marble, white-yellow veined (island of Euboea)

    Filfila marble, white (cap de Garde, Algeria)

    Lesbian marble, white-yellow (island of Lesbos)

    Parian marble, bright white (island of Paros)

    Pentelic marble, white (Mount Pentelikon, Attica)

    'Porta Santa' marble, polychrome veins, red-blue, violet, black, white (Iassos)

    Proconnesus marble, white and white-black veined (island of Proconnesus)

    Pyrenean marble, white (Saint-Beat)

    'Rosso Antico', red marble (cape Matapa, Peloponnese)

    serpentine marble, green (Thebes, Egypt)[5]

    Thasian marble, white, coarse-grained (island of Thasos)

Other rocks:

    alabaster, white (Thebes, Egypt)

    black basalt, green basalt (Upper Egypt?)

    grey granite, black granite (Aswan)

    pink granite (Aswan)

    red porphyry (Egypt)

    green porphyry (cape Matapa, Peloponnese)

The Italian peninsula itself possesses fine stones, the most famous being the marble of Carrara, which exists in two varieties – white 'Lunense' and grey-blue 'Luna'. The exploitation of this stone became an imperial privilege under Tiberius. Another Italian stone is the Roman travertine extracted from the Tivoli quarries.

The stones used to make rubble are innumerable and, as already noted, of local origin. At some sites, however, different stones, sometimes in large numbers, have been found and it is useful to list those found at the exceptional cases of Rome and Pompeii.

Rome: Seven kinds of volcanic tufa (Anio, Campidoglio, Cappellacio, Fidene, Grotta oscura, Monteverde, Peperino)[6] to which must be added travertine; i.e. eight varieties of building stone.

Pompeii: Hard lava, honeycomb lava or scoria, volcanic tufa (Nuceria, Pappamonte, giallo), calcareous tuff; i.e. six local rocks to which are added the imports.[7]

When several sources are available locally, builders have the freedom to use stones according to their qualities or appearance, for example using hard lavas mainly as paving stones or for foundations and tufas in the body of the masonry.

Vitruvius makes some observations relevant to this:[8] 'The stones which are not hard have the advantage that they can be easily cut and are good when used in covered places, but placed out of doors, the frost and rain turn them to dust . . .'[9] Further, he recommends stone from 'the territory of the Tarquins' (the region of Bolsena) which ages well, even the finest mouldings: '. . . one sees great and fine statues, small bas-reliefs and several very delicate ornaments representing roses and acanthus leaves which, notwithstanding their age, have all the appearance of having just been finished quite recently.' Finally, he advises, when using soft rocks and volcanic tufas, to '. . . take them from the quarry in summer and not in winter and to expose them to the air in a covered place two years before making use of them . . .' As a result of this precaution porous rocks lose moisture, called the quarry sap, and those not resistant to the weathering due to exposure outside can be rejected.

With experience, the quarry master recognizes in the field, especially in cuts made in the rock, the strata unsuitable for building stone. With surface quarrying, the first step is to remove a superficial layer, sometimes itself covered with earth, which is subject to weathering and plant infiltration and called the overburden.[10] The overburden may include a lower layer useful for producing pebble stones. The upper layer can therefore be distinguished by the term dirt bed.[11] Once the overburden has been removed and the quarry master has exposed the rock mass, exploitation can begin (fig.21).

The quarry master can sometimes make use of the natural strata to remove blocks that can be shaped and transported. Fissures may outline a volume of rock which is already detached, so that it can be extracted simply by forcing with metal wedges and crowbars. This method is only rarely possible, however, and work usually takes the form of cutting grooves into the rock to define blocks which, when extracted have a shape and size approaching those needed. This common process makes for both an economic use of material and a considerable saving in the time taken in cutting (figs 22, 23).

After exposing a vertical face (an operation usually assisted by a natural incline) and a horizontal face, the quarryman would cut, to right and left, incisions the same depth as the height of the block required, and then another marking the back face. These

21

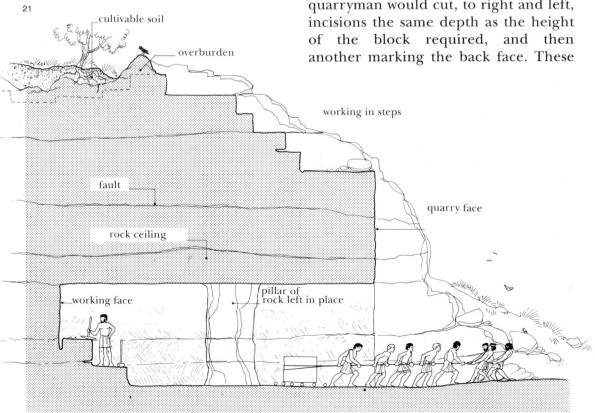

21 Diagram showing different types of quarrying.

narrow grooves, forming the undercutting, were made with a pick (*fossaria dolabra*)[12] which left concave furrows corresponding to the quarryman's hand movements. The grooves could be enlarged for access when the block to be cut out was of a considerable size. Thus at the quarries of Cusa (Selinunte) the grooves surrounding the column drums are 85cm wide at the top and 55cm wide at the base, enabling the quarryman to get in and work. A final groove was made under the block by forcing in metal wedges (*cunei*) with a mallet (*mallei*); the operation was made easier if a fault or a line of natural stratigraphy was encountered. When the cuts were deep enough it was sometimes possible to use a crowbar to finish detaching the block thus outlined in the rock mass. If wedges were used, one of them was struck very hard to cause a fracture as far as the back cut.

In some cases the quarrymen used wooden wedges, a technique common in certain quarries until the eighteenth century.[13] Very dry wooden wedges were forced into the cracks, then soaked with water and covered with wet cloths; the capillary action slowly caused the wood to swell, thus loosening the stone block.

Quarrying took place in steps, at least one course high. Depending on the duration of the quarrying operations and particularly if the vein of rock went down a long way, traces of ancient workings are relatively rare. What survive mostly are the steps, with deep drops, or vertical walls resulting from the continuation of quarrying downwards.

An example found in Sicily, though borrowed from the Greek world, perfectly illustrates this type of extraction. Quarries were opened there during the reign of Dionysus the Tyrant (405 to 367BC) in order to construct the formidable wall, 27km long, designed to protect the city of Syracuse.[14] (The wall enclosed an important extra-urban zone reserved for cultivation in the event of siege and never actually built on.) The quarries were never used for anything other than the provision of the stone required for the wall and were abandoned after it was built. On this site, quite exceptionally, the steps resulting from the extraction can be distinguished for several kilometres, showing clear traces of the preselection of blocks of uniform size, detached from the rock using outline grooves and wedges forced into the lower part.

Certain large, isolated monuments had particular quarrying operations associated with them which were not continued, owing to both their distance from any large settlement and the presence of other well-situated deposits near at hand. In Roman

22 Preparatory grooves in the quarries used for the walls of Syracuse.

23 Method of extraction of square blocks at the ancient quarry of St-Boil.

Gaul the most interesting example is provided by the Pont du Gard, the stones for which were extracted from the banks of the river a few hundred metres to the north of the building site.[15]

The two methods of extraction, using natural fissures and strata, and undercutting the edges combined with the use of wedges, were standard, and there is hardly an ancient quarry where the traces of these workings are not visible. It is still easy to imagine the great activity at many sites that were abandoned in the course of quarrying operations for a variety of reasons that cannot now be established with certainty. Numerous prepared blocks can be found in all quarries, not only at Syracuse where there is a whole host, but also at Barutel (quarries of Nîmes),[16] Saint-Boil (Saône-et-Loire),[17] Boulouris (Var),[18] Monte Lepino (near Segni), Gabii (Latium) and at Cerveteri.[19]

The extraction of blocks either for use in coursed masonry, or of manageable size intended to be split up (rubble stones) or shaped (mouldings, drums) was not the only task of the quarrymen. The desire for technical achievement, and the practical spirit that went with it, encouraged the Romans to extract from the rock large architectural pieces, not only in the form of rectangular blocks (for megalithic courses on monuments in the eastern empire and architraves), but also columns of all dimensions, usually of marble and granite. These columns are still visible in the Pantheon (granite), in the Temple of Venus and Rome (granite), at the Basilica Ulpia (granite and "cipollino") and at the Temple of Antoninus and Faustina ("cipollino" marble), to mention only examples in Rome.

Although the technical accomplishment is evident, given the scale of the majority of these works (12m high and 56 tonnes in the case of the Pantheon),

it also seems certain that mastery of handling and transportation made such grand achievements commonplace, and in the case of smaller pieces, facilitated the work of extraction and transport. A particularly spectacular demonstration of this comes from the depot of imported marbles in Ostia, where considerable quantities of materials have been recovered, waiting for delivery to the user. Among these blocks are several bundles of marble columns, still joined together in groups of four just as the quarrymen had extracted them from the rock (fig.24)

In quarries the sites corresponding to the removal of the shafts can be traced in the rock, as for instance at Chemtou (Tunisia) (fig.25) or at Aliki (Thasos).[20] Sometimes the columns themselves have remained in place, partially or totally detached, as in some quarries in Sardinia[21] or again at Aliki. In the Greek quarries of Selinunte (the so-called Cave di Cusa), which deserve a mention despite being earlier (sixth–fifth century BC), several column drums intended for the gigantic temple G are still visible at different stages of extraction. The work in the quarries here is as spectacular as the building of the monument itself, since the blocks were cut from the rock in a roughed-out form ready for use (fig.26).[22]

When considering the sudden abandoned state apparent at a number of places it is useful to make comparisons with modern-day sites of the same nature. For instance, the limestone quarries at the foot of Ventoux, near Malaucène (Vaucluse), abandoned for only two generations, illustrate that the quarrymen had left in place material with no thought of ever salvaging it and that the work of extraction was interrupted in different parts at different stages of progress. In studying another activity, woodworking, the author has been able to show through an investigation into water-powered

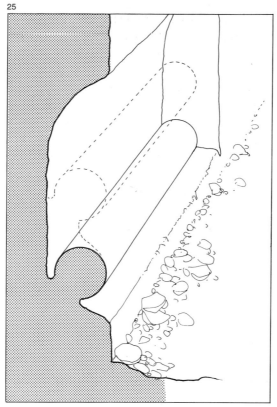

saw-mills, that numerous mills had been abandoned by their owner, on his retirement or death, leaving all the material and the tools in place, including logs that were partially cut and still under the saw. Now, in neither of the two examples mentioned above had a sudden catastrophe occurred to interrupt or destroy the local economy. The end had come quite naturally with a simple cessation of activity. This observation does not exclude other explanations for other situations, but it may moderate hasty conclusions which invoke a human or natural cataclysm to explain the interruption of work in progress at a quarry or building site.

When working in steps reached the lowest level at the foot of a natural incline, quarrying continued by descending vertically on one or more working faces, progressing in heights of courses, using the same method as before. Once the courses had been removed, a vertical cliff remained, the quarry face, in which the imprint of the courses can be clearly traced (fig.27). The tufa quarries in the area around Rome, where activity continued for centuries, are all similar and the regularity of the extracted courses means that their height can be ascertained – usually between 60 and 65cm – a simple choice of measurement from which it can be concluded that the blocks were 2 feet high (fig.28).

The vertical descent of a quarry

stopped when the rock vein came to an end due to a change in the subsoil; when, as frequently happened, an underground water level was encountered; or simply when lifting the material from the bottom of a very deep hole became a problem. When this occurred the rock mass was reached by means of tunnels (*fossae*), a much less productive process, for the obvious

24 A group of four columns, still joined, found in the port of Ostia.

25 The method of extracting column shafts in the quarries of Chemtou (Tunisia).

26 Drums intended for Temple G at Selinunte, still in the quarry at Cusa.

reason that the majority of the rock has to stay in place to provide support and roofing (figs 29, 30).

Depending on the type of rock, the cavities left by working look completely

27

28

29

27 Quarries at Gabii (Latium); the step workings become a vertical wall.

28 Quarry face in the tufa of the Anio Valley (Latium); the traces of cutting the rock in regular courses can be clearly seen. Note the overburden above.

29 Quarrying into the rock in halls and galleries; the tufa of the Anio Valley (Latium).

different. When the natural strata are approximately horizontal and are split by breaks which occur relatively closely (2m or less), the quarryman often digs low tunnels of average working height, taking care always to leave above him at least one, and usually two, natural strata, forming the quarry roof. In order to enlarge the workings, chambers are opened out, supported at regular intervals by rock masses left in place; these pillars are sometimes built of rubble stones to hold up a fissured roof.

Cutting underground used the same methods as in the open air. However, when the tunnel or chamber was low, the blocks extracted were of full height, and this was done by undercutting the front and the sides, with the final removal by forcing with wedges being necessarily decisive as it was the only way to get at the inaccessible back face.[23]

When the rock deposit was very deep and there were no lines of breakage or fracture, the work was in many respects easier as it was possible to open sizeable chambers, needing only widely-spaced pillars. Work at the rock face then proceeded in that same way as outside, in steps descending vertically.

More than tools for working wood, tools for stone become blunt and lose their edge. The quarrymen themselves saw to the maintenance and upkeep of their equipment, as they still do today.[24] All quarries of any size had a small forge where damaged metal pieces could be rehoned and sharpened. Traces of such activity are only uncovered when layers of debris and rock falls are removed, and generally consist of piles of cinders and hearth remains, often spread over different areas following the movement of the workings, as was probably the case at the quarries of Barutel[25] and Aliki.[26]

The distance between the extraction site and the building work was naturally of concern to the builders. A number of towns were fortunate enough to discover in their own subsoil the material or materials necessary for their architectural genesis – for instance Rome, Naples, Syracuse, Paris and Lyon, at least at the beginning. However, this was only rarely the result of a planned decision since Roman towns, in the peninsula as well as in many parts of the Empire, were only enlargements of earlier settlements built on sites chosen for their strategic or commercial value.

With the development of monumental building programmes and the demands of monumental decoration, quarries were opened almost everywhere where deposits of building stone appeared in any quantity, as far as possible with an eye to the proximity of a land, river or sea route for its exploitation. Special arrangements were made to obtain access to a working site, sometimes crossing very rough terrain as was the case for the marble quarries of Pentelikon and Carrara.

As the marble quarries on the slopes of Mount Pentelikon were quite high up, the transport of the blocks, as at Carrara, was achieved by means of a descent road that has been located and exposed for most of its route towards the plain.[27] This road, paved with marble and laid out almost in a straight line, in fact formed a slipway, comparable to the runways used by Alsacian timber-sledges. Holes dug in the rock on both sides of the road at regular intervals were sockets for heavy wooden bollards around which the quarrymen wound the ropes designed to brake the descent of the sledges loaded with marble (fig.31). At Carrara, the ancient tracks have disappeared, but until the last war blocks were carried down on large carts or sledges for the heaviest blocks, pulled by a variable number of oxen pairs according to the load. It was in this manner that in November 1928 the gigantic monolith was transported,

30 Reconstruction of quarrying in galleries in the tufa of Grotta Oscura (Latium).

31 The descent of marble blocks from the quarry on Pentelikon. (After A.K. Orlandos.)

32m long and weighing, with its sledge, in the region of 600 tonnes, destined to become the obelisk of Mussolini erected in Rome in front of the Olympic Stadium (fig.32).

This transport, by the simplest of means, of such a mass of rock, comparable to the largest stones used in antiquity, helps considerably towards the solution of the problem, which for many has all the attractions of a mystery, of how the heavy blocks were moved. The technical knowledge of the Greek and Roman periods, following trials and experiments made over generations, enabled them to overcome obstacles presented by the

32

32 Mussolini's monolith being transported on a sledge, pulled by a team of sixty oxen, Carrara, 1928. (Photo: Hrand.)

33 *A:* The device of Ctesiphon; *B:* Metagenes' machine. Methods of transporting column drums and architraves for the Temple of Artemis at Ephesus and Temple G at Selinunte.

34 The 'southern stone' still in the quarry at Baalbek, measuring 21.5 x 4.3 x 4.2m, and weighing 970 tonnes.

35 Diagram showing how the lower surface of the megaliths at Baalbek were gradually freed and rollers for transport progressively positioned under the blocks.

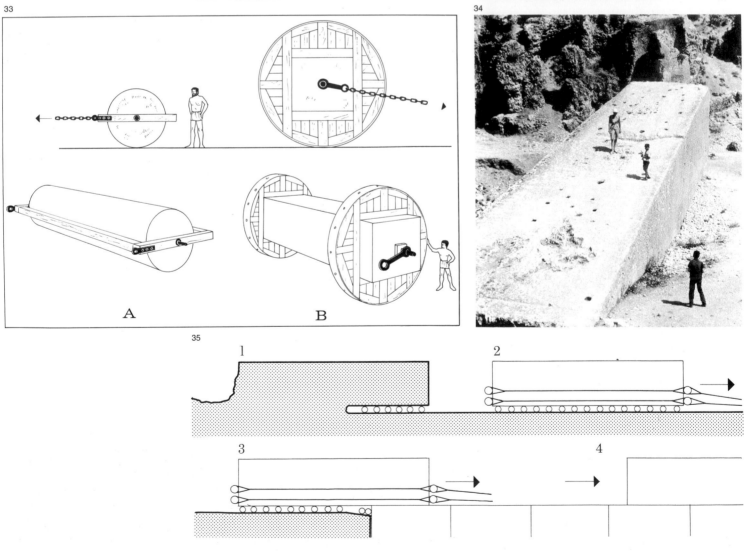

33

A   B

34

35

1   2

3   4

transport from quarry to site of blocks as impressive as those used, in the sixth century BC, the temple G at Selinunte or, later, the podium of the Temple of Jupiter Heliopolitanus at Baalbek.

At Selinunte the methods employed for the transportation of column drums – twins of those left in the quarry at Cusa – and of architraves, can be traced in the stone. They take the form of holes for fixing the means both of attachment: axles inserted at each end for the drums; and of transport: wooden wheels encircling the blocks, both of them then drawn by oxen. Such methods are also mentioned by Vitruvius as having been used for the construction of the Temple of Artemis of the Ephesians (fig.33).[28]

At Baalbek, the builders took on a supreme challenge to human ingenuity by building a podium with decorative facings all of colossal dimensions.[29] The largest are the three trilithons measuring respectively 19.6m, 19.3m and 19.1m long by 4.34m high and 3.65m deep. Their average weight is in the region of 800 tonnes. As the quarry was situated around 800m from the temple and slightly higher up, the megaliths were brought on a track, the path of which was adapted to the bedding level of each course so that there was no raising operation needed. One of the stones left in the quarry shows how they were placed on rollers gradually as the lower face became exposed (figs 34, 35). For the transport itself, capstans attached to pulley blocks placed symmetrically on both sides of the load ensured the slow progress of the enormous block.[30] Sixteen of these machines, each one operated by 32 men (making a total of 512 men) and developing a power of more than 10 tonnes, provided a draught force, multiplied by the pulley systems each with four pulleys (and affected by a large coefficient of friction), of 557 tonnes, or approximately $\frac{2}{3}$ of the load (fig.36).[31]

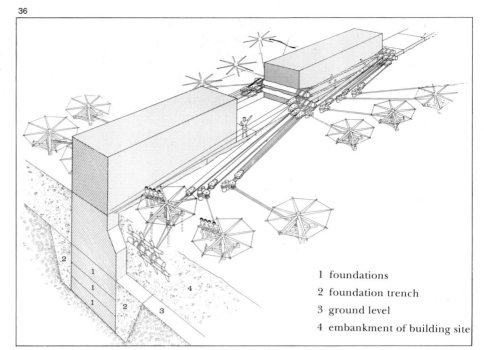

1 foundations
2 foundation trench
3 ground level
4 embankment of building site

Apart from these exceptional situations, transport was by carts pulled by oxen, the use of which is already attested in the Greek period[32] and which Roman iconography portrayed, particularly in the case of the transport of materials in bulk (fig.37).[33]

b Stone-cutting tools

As has already been noted, when blocks of stone were being cut out they were often given a roughed-out form as near as possible to the final size so as to simplify and lighten the burden of transportation; they could also take the

36 Reconstruction of the transport of the trilithon blocks at Baalbek.

37 The Roman method of transport by chariot with solid wheels with projecting rims; the oxen are attached by a neck yoke. (Museo Nazionale; JPA.)

38 A block of tufa with the traces of the sockets for the wedges that were used in cutting it up (Pompeii VIII, 5,30).

39 A line of breakage veering off on a block of lava split with wedges. Terzigno (Campania), 1980.

40 A failed attempt at separating a marble architrave with wedges, later reused in the Later Empire. Trajan's Forum, Rome.

41 A block of marble prepared for separation with wedges, so that it can be reused. Forum of Ostia. The wedges are 18 to 20cm long and 4 to 5cm high.

42 Drawing showing splitting a block using wedges.

form of a rectangular block much larger than the blocks in coursed masonry, but easy to divide into smaller parts. Unshaped blocks removed from the mass along natural fissures were also given some sort of roughing-out after being extracted.

To split the blocks up the same method was used as that for extraction – driving wedges into holes made along the line of the break. To do this the quarryman first drew chalk lines on the best cut face; then sockets for the wedges were made along each of these lines, using a chisel and a mallet, and the wedges were put in place. A series of pick marks was then made between each wedge to indicate and create the line of breakage and, finally, the

38

40

39

41

42

middle wedge was struck a hefty blow with a mallet, achieving the opening of the rock.[34] The efficiency of the technique is such that the break, particularly in hard rocks, results in perfectly cut surfaces sometimes adequate for using in a final form (figs 38, 39, 40, 41, 42, 43).

A saw, more generally associated with woodwork, was quite widely used to cut up large blocks. The accuracy of this method was in fact not much better than that usually obtained using wedges, but it avoided the risk of making a mistake in cutting. It is not rare to find rocks cut using wedges abandoned as a result of a considerable deviation from the break line, caused by an internal cleavage not visible on the surface. An excellent example of an accident of this type is visible in Trajan's Forum in Rome, where an enormous marble architrave was salvaged in a later period and an attempt was made to divide it with wedges; but the break, instead of following a vertical direction, deviated at an angle of 45°. It is understandable that, particularly when cutting up a valuable rock like marble, stonemasons often preferred to use a saw (*serra, serrula*), making the work much longer but less prone to accidents.

When cutting a relatively soft stone, the blade of the saw was serrated, with nothing to distinguish it from a woodsaw; for hard rocks a smooth blade was used with an abrasive (sand).[35] In both cases the line of cut was prepared with a point so that the saw did not deviate and, during the operation, water was poured along the groove to avoid overheating the blade. The saws used were a type of two-handed saw, provided with a pulling handle at each end; the irregular tension of the blade, as well as its path, subject to the steadiness of the movements of the workmen, have left quite typical marks on the stone. However, these are visible only on the back surfaces of blocks or on

43 Splitting blocks of granite in a quarry in Brittany. The principle is the same, but the pneumatic drill replaces the mallet and punch.

44 A sawn block of marble on the building site for the Temple of Venus at Pompeii.

unfinished stones that were abandoned at the work place or building site. In many respects the site of the Temple of Venus at Pompeii, interrupted by the eruption of 24 August 79, offers the best examples of stone cutting using different tools and at different stages of completion, with, among other things, several blocks of marble sawn and stored together awaiting their use in finished form (fig.44). For large blocks the blade of the saw was kept tense by a wooden frame which could be suspended from a portico in the case of the largest saws, as has been suggested in the reconstruction of the quarries of Dokimion.[36]

Once the block had been squared, either at the time of extraction or after

45 The Roman stone-mason's essential tool kit: *1* cutting hammer; *2* scabbling hammer; *3* kivel or stone-mason's hammer; *4* mallet; *5* punch or point; *6* straight chisel; *7* claw chisel; *8* gouge; *9* square.

46 The principal tools of the stone-mason remained the same from the Roman period up to the twentieth century. *Top:* two mallets; (*below, from left to right*): a punch; three chisels; a mallet-headed chisel; a driver; a claw chisel.

47 A scabbled stone block in the process of being squared on the site of the Temple of Venus at Pompeii.

48 Relief of Diogenes Structor, a Pompeian mason, showing a plumb line, a trowel, an apotropaic phallus, levelling square, stone-mason's hammer or kivel, a chisel and two objects difficult to identify, possibly an amphora and a plasterer's tool.

49 Stone-masons preparing stone blocks; their tool seen in profile could be a scabbling hammer (with two points) or a double-bladed stone-hammer. In the basket are the finished products. Relief from a tomb on the Isola Sacra, Ostia (drawn by JPA).

50 Funerary relief of a stone-mason, with the representation of a square, a stone-mason's hammer (or kivel) and a scabbling hammer. (Musée de Berry, Bourges; JPA.)

51 The base of a funerary monument on which are shown, from left to right: a mallet; a levelling square; a plumb line; a square; and a double-bladed stone-hammer. (Museo della Civiltà Romana, room LII; JPA.)

52 Stone-mason's cippus showing: a foot without graduations (29.6cm long); a levelling square; a square; a compass; a maul or a bladed stone-hammer and calipers. (Capitoline Museum; JPA.)

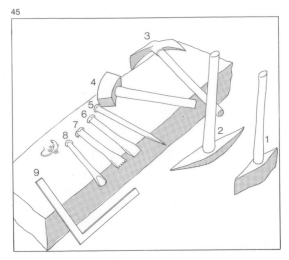

cutting up, the stone-mason gave it its final shape using different tools, the size and form of which vary according to the fineness of the desired appearance. According to a classification established by A. Leroi-Gourhan,[37] two major categories can be distinguished: tools of direct percussion ('percussion lancée') and tools of indirect percussion ('percussion posée'). In the first category the tool is used alone and has a blade with a handle, giving it the shape of an axe or a hammer. The blow against the stone is violent and lacking in precision, thus these tools are used for squaring and for the rough shaping of facings. In the second category the tools are used in pairs, with one placed with its point or blade on the surface and hit with a percussor: the mallet or stone-mason's hammer (figs 45, 46).

The first and the most primitive tool of direct percussion is a pick with two points. This is also used for cutting out but for shaping is generally of smaller size. It is called a scabbling or spalling hammer and its use leaves marks showing the manner in which the stone was worked. For instance when the workman hits the stone vertically, he makes chips fairly close to one another, creating a facing that is pock-marked and rough (fig.47).

Known since the Middle Ages, the stone-hammer,[38] smaller than the pick, appears in two forms. It can either have a head with one end squared with two edges and a point at the other end; or the point is replaced by a blade with the edge parallel to the handle.[39] The stone-hammer in either of these forms cannot be verified in Greek or Roman antiquity – the archaeological record has not yet come up with objects of this type and the sculpted representations, however numerous they may be, are lacking in detail. Nevertheless, three representations can be mentioned that do give some cause for conjecture: the first is the stele of a craftsman found at Pompeii (fig.48) at the House of the

Cock,[40] which shows a view from above of a tool likely to be a stone-hammer (the outline not making it possible to establish whether, at one of the ends, there is a point or a blade); the second is a relief found at Terracina showing a scene at a building site with two work-men working a stone with hammers which are as likely to be mauls as stone-hammers;[41]; thirdly there is a painting from the House of Siricus at Pompeii (VII.1,25)[42] showing the building of a town wall on which two stone-masons are using a stone-hammer.

By contrast, there are numerous examples of hammers with two points which are in fact small scabbling hammers (fig.49) and hammers with two cutting edges (*dolabra*) similar to two-bladed axes.[43] But the reliefs do not make it possible to distinguish, when these tools are seen in profile, whether what is intended is a double-bladed stone-hammer or a maul; it can only be assumed that if it is shown beside a chisel, the tool is in fact a percussor (figs 50, 51, 52). The cutting hammer sometimes has one blade with the same axis as the handle and one which is perpendicular, in which case it is called a kivel or stone-mason's axe. This dual arrangement is a great advantage to the stone-mason who can

49

more easily attack the surfaces to be dressed without having to take up difficult positions. It is the instrument *par excellence* for working soft rock; it is still in standard use in Italy for the cutting of tufa, and excavations have uncovered some excellent examples from antiquity,[44] similar in every way to contemporary models (figs 53, 54, 55, 56). This observation can in fact be extended to the whole range of hand tools, whose forms were established during the Roman epoch and have remained the same into the twentieth century.

50

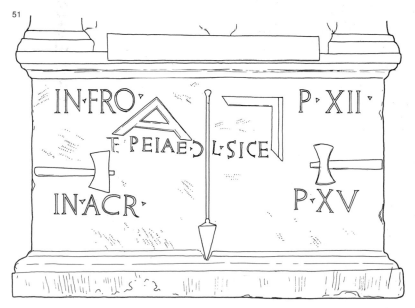

51

IN·FRO
F·PEIAE·L·SICE
IN·ACR·
P·XII·
P·XV

52

X A

0   10   20   30 cm

53 Different treatments of facings dressed with a stone-hammer. Pompeii, House of the Large Fountain (VI,8,22).

54 Marks of a bladed stone-hammer on a facing of lava. On hard rock the tool strikes the surface at an angle of almost 90 degrees, leaving shallow furrows. Herculaneum, *cardo* III.

55 The dressing of the facing of a pier made of tufa using a bladed stone-hammer; the marks carrying on across the joints indicate that the work was done after the blocks were put in position. Note that on this soft stone, the tool strikes obliquely and deeply. Pompeii VIII,5,26.

56 An ancient kivel or stone-mason's hammer and a modern one at Pompeii. The continuity in the form of this tool is remarkable.

57 A stone-mason rough dressing a facing stone with a punch or point.

53

54

55

56

57

In working a hard rock a smooth blade risks having its edge broken or dulled. A better percussion is obtained by using a toothed cutting edge (which can also of course be used on soft rocks), either with flat teeth, the bush-hammer, or with pointed teeth. It is significant that such details are not shown on the sculpted representations and that the cutting edges recovered up to now are not toothed, perhaps because this iron part, being finer and already cut out, has not survived. However, as the typical traces left by toothed tools are numerous and, since no toothed chisels have been found either, the existence of one type and/or the other can be safely assumed.

It is also worth noting that some double blades had their two cutting edges perpendicular to the handle.[45] This form has practically disappeared in France but it can still be found in Greece – with smooth blades for cutting tufa and toothed blades for cutting hard stones.[46]

The second big family of stone-mason's tools are the tools of indirect percussion – tools whose cutting motion is caused by the blow of a percussor, possibly a wooden hammer, the mallet, made out of hard wood – boxwood or olive. This instrument is best used with chisels which also have wooden handles and are designed for soft stone.[47] When the percussor has a metal head its strength is greater and its precision less, and it is used for hard stones with chisels without a handle.

The first tool of indirect percussion, used for preliminary cutting or rustication, is the point or punch. Depending on whether the working was done vertically or obliquely, a punched dressing is obtained with percussion marks joining up, and this cannot be distinguished from dressing with a scabbling hammer; only the workman himself can make the identification, depend-ing on the tool he is using. Alternatively a broached dressing is achieved, with furrows that are parallel, vertical, oblique or concave, following the arc described by the arm movement (an effect that can also be achieved with the scabbling hammer) (figs 57, 58, 59, 60).

With the point or with the scabbling hammer the stone-masons (the *quadratarii* or *lapidarii*) set to work shaping a block, resting it on a wedge of stone or wood, so that it could be fixed at a convenient angle. In this way the block was chiselled to the line which marked out a rectangular face, the workmen checking its outline with a rule (to get a flat surface) and a square (to check right angles).

When the rough dressing has been completed with the scabbling hammer and the punch, the stone mason refines his work with chisels, always starting with peripheral chiselling to define the lines of each face. The chisels either have a smooth edge – the straight chisel (the *scalprum*) – or are toothed – the claw chisel (the *gradine*) (fig.61).

As the work carried out with the chisel is much more precise, analysis of the marks left makes it possible to distinguish whether the tool used was a hammer-blade or a chisel or else a bush-hammer or a *gradine*. Other evidence is provided by the width of the trace left, which is larger in the case of a cutting hammer or bush-hammer than in the case of chisels.

Finally, to the long series of chisels can be added the mallet-headed chisel, which has a cutting edge of greater thickness than its width; the driver, with a cutting edge forming almost a right angle and making it possible to cut the edges; and gouges with a concave cutting edge, used for carving curved mouldings.

58 The stone-mason and sculptor Amabilis, working with a mallet and chisel. Funerary stele. (Musée de Bordeaux; JPA.)

59 A roughed-out block of white limestone, brought from the quarry with scabbled facings, intended for the reconstruction of the Forum at Pompeii after 62. Length: 3.07m; width: 0.73m; height: 1m; weight 5800kg.

60 Dressing on the blocks of a podium from the amphitheatre of Senlis. On the right-hand block the curve of the mason's strokes can be traced, in a regular movement.

61 The carving of the anathyrosis band (with a break at the top), the rebating inside it and the bedding face, with the claw chisel. Site of the Temple of Venus, Pompeii.

62 Rustication in part carried out with a stone-hammer, in part with a claw chisel, with the joints polished or ground. Pompeii, tomb 17, Nucerian Gate.

63 Capital from the Central Baths at Pompeii, in the original state, roughly dressed with a scabbling hammer and a point.

64 At this intermediate stage, the preparation is done with a claw chisel, and the marginal drafts with a straight chisel.

65 The finished and polished capital.

66 Unfinished Corinthian capital, from the sanctuary to the south of the Grand Colonnade at Palmyra. Note the extreme care of the finishing of the worked shapes.

67 A finished capital from the same series, damaged by its fall.

68 Marks of the toothed chisel at the bottom of the fluting left by a continuous scraping with the tool, without the use of a percussor. Temple of Apollo, Pompeii.

69 A block of marble, reused by apprentices for practising dressings. On the right is a sheaf-like dressing, which was scabbled by the workman face-on (*top*), then broached at the end of the movement (*below*), and three exercises with a claw chisel, the one in the middle also having been ground. The rest of the surface is polished. Capital of a pilaster, National Musuem, Rome.

The finishing of the facing of the blocks and the cutting of drafted margins and the anathyrosis rebating and, above all, any carvings, are done with the claw chisels, cutting very precisely. Sometimes the surface is polished, or burnished, by rubbing the stone, sprinkled with water, with a hard, close-grained rock, such as sandstone or volcanic rock (fig.62). A polisher has been recovered on a working site in Pompeii consisting of a semi-spherical cupel of bronze, 6cm in diameter, with a gripping ring and containing a pumice stone.[48]

At cutting sites like quarries, in abandoned deposits such as the one at Ostia, or better still on the building sites at Pompeii, the different stages from the squared block to the finished piece can sometimes be traced with a remarkable continuity, especially when an entire series is found. Thus, in the Central Baths, begun at Pompeii after the earthquake of 62, the workmen were working on the one hand on the masonry of the walls and had got up to the level of the spring of the vaults, and on the other on the cutting of blocks intended for the floor paving and the orders of the portico. A series of four Doric capitals here illustrates perfectly the progress of the cutting: starting with a block of stone which has approximately the shape of a truncated pyramid, the next step is the beginning of a roughed-out form in which the capital is already recognizable, the acanthus leaves appear on a third block while the fourth is complete (figs 63, 64, 65). At each of these stages it can be seen that the stone-mason changed tools, starting with a point and finishing with fine points and narrow chisels, taking care each time to finish the block in a perfectly homogeneous manner, an observation that can be made on the Corinthian capitals of one of the temples of Palmyra, on which the fineness of the dressing of the intermediate stages

equals that of the finished state (figs 66, 67).

It was not rare for blocks to be assembled on the monument without being given their final dressing, with only the marginal drafts and the surfaces of the joints finished. Likewise, the elements of the mouldings were put in place and the decoration carried out at the same time as the final dressing, sometimes long after the end of the construction work. In certain cases this final dressing was only partially realized and the sculptures were unfinished, as can be seen on the gigantic Temple of Apollo at

70 Unfinished column from the Temple of Euromos (Caria). The fluting was prepared by an axial groove indicating the depth to be reached.

71 Trier. The prepared blocks of Porta Nigra.

72 The unfinished tetrapylon of the pyramid of the Circus of Vienne.

Didyma (near Miletus), or at its more modest neighbour, the Temple of Euromus, where the columns are smooth or partially fluted. The Porta Nigra at Trier and the tetrapylon supporting the pyramid of the Circus of Vienne likewise give the general impression of being complete, but the facings are only roughed out with a point or a scabbling hammer and

73

73 Vaulted building at Patara (Lycia) at the west of the port, the blocks of which have retained the protective flanges intended to preserve the edges during transport; final dressing was only carried out on the top course.

74 The sculptor's tools were identical to the stone-mason's, but the tool-kit contained a greater variety of chisels, and sometimes, especially in the Later Empire, a brace and bit to drill the stone, such as the one seen on the stele of a sculptor of sarcophagi of the palaeo-Christian period. (Cemetery of Sant'Elena, via Labicana, Rome; JPA.)

74

the capitals only have the shape of a truncated cone that has just been sketched out (figs 68, 69, 70, 71, 72, 73).

Though turning is mainly associated with woodwork, it is useful to point out its use in the Roman period for shaping, in soft rock, column drums, capitals, Dorics and bases. Unfortunately, although the marks left by this method are clearly visible, no archaeological discovery in the form of either a machine or a representation has been made which would make a reconstruction of the tool possible. It is possible to imagine that the block was first roughed out with the usual tools, then placed in a frame where it was rotated so that it could be worked with a chisel.

To accelerate and simplify the treatment of the mouldings, the sculptor extended the use of the drill, used for small holes, to the preparation of the majority of motifs by stippling. The instrument may be of considerable size and become a rock-drill with a motor-belt, necessitating its operation by two

75

76

75 Marks painted by the quarrymen to distinguish the destination of the stones. Lava quarry of Terzigno. The practice of marking stones to indicate their destination was already standard in ancient quarries.

76 In the Republican period, the stone-masons, following a Greek custom, placed their mark on the blocks. Walls of Bolsena, third century BC. This custom was to reappear occasionally in the Imperial period, notably in North Africa.

77 Graduated rule from the funerary stele of a naval carpenter. Ostia, *Cardo Maximus*.

workmen. A funerary relief from the via Labicana illustrates the working of such a machine (fig.74).

Finally, it is worth noting that symbols on blocks could have been made by quarrymen, generally to indicate the lots by their order, but can also be the work of the stone-masons. This custom of masons' marks was very widespread in Hellenized regions but disappears at the end of the Republican period and makes its reappearance in the imperial era only

sporadically, notably on certain monuments in North Africa (figs 75, 76).

c Measurements and checks

In the course of the different stages of roughing out, preparation and finishing, the stone-cutter periodically used different instruments not actually for working on the material but to ensure its correct form by measurements and checks.

The graduated rule (*regula*) was in constant use as it determined right from the start the outline of the edges of the block, in relation to its height, if it was being incorporated into regular courses, and to its width if it was a bonding stone or parpen.[49] The Roman rule was in fact a graduated foot which could be made of wood with metal ends but was more usually made of bronze. The National Museum of

77

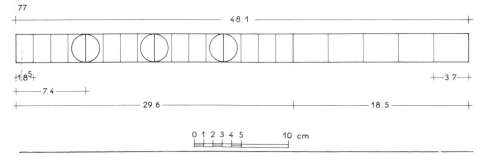

Naples has several examples of these made up of two articulated arms, each of half a foot, maintained in alignment by a locking device. Bone, because of its hardness, could also be used for making rules and one of this type has been found near the Theatre in Ostia with scored division markings (figs 77, 78, 79, 80).[50]

The length of the Roman foot has been the subject of numerous studies,[51] based both on the graduated rules found and on measurement studies carried out on standing structives; the values of the foot and its multiples and multiples of multiples given here were in general use in the Imperial period:

finger – *digitus* .... $\frac{1}{16}$ foot   = 1.848cm
hand – *palmus* .... $\frac{1}{4}$ foot   = 7.392cm
foot – *pes* .... 1 foot   = 29.57cm
palm – foot –
  palmipes .... 1$\frac{1}{4}$ feet   = 36.96cm
cubit – *cubitus* .... 1$\frac{1}{2}$ feet   = 44.355cm
pace – *gradus* .... 2$\frac{1}{2}$ feet   = 73.925cm
double pace –
  passus .... 5 feet   = 1.478m
furrow[52] – *actus* .... 120 feet   = 35.48m
mile – *mille passus*
  .... 5000 feet   = 1478.50m

The standard size of the foot is known from the bronze foot rules as they were made with the greatest precision; but funerary stelae can also be referred to. The Museo della Civiltà Roma in Rome[53] has assembled a series of stelae of arti-

sans on which are depicted graduated rules, some of them almost as long as 29.57cm. Thus of 10 pictorial representations five have rules shown at a size similar to that of the bronze originals – 29cm, 29.6cm, and three at 29.8cm; two are a double foot (58.5cm); and the last three appear to portray an arbitrary length (23cm, 40cm, 50.4cm). On the fine marble stele of a naval carpenter found on the *cardo maximus* at Ostia and still in place, the rule and its graduations are shown with a remarkable accuracy. It is a graduated piece divided unequally by a bold line into two lengths, 29.6cm and 18.5cm respectively, or 1 foot and 10 fingers. The foot is divided into four hands of 7.4cm, each one subdivided into four fingers of 1.85cm; for their part the 10 fingers comprise five divisions of 3.7cm or five double fingers, totalling 48.1cm which, when compared with the equivalent length of 48.05cm measured on bronze feet, gives a perfectly acceptable error of 5mm (approximately $\frac{1}{200}$).

The squares (*normae*) that have survived, like almost all precision instruments, are made of bronze and are of various sizes. Some of them called shouldering squares have a stand along one of their arms allowing them to be left in position. Others with articulated arms, are adjustable squares or bevel-squares allowing any angle to be set, be it dressing voussoirs, polygonal pieces or mouldings (figs 79, 80, 84).

Others again, frequently represented on the reliefs of artisans, had quite a different use: they were used to check

78 Stele of a carter, showing a rule of 2 feet (l.59cm), divided into half-feet, palms ($\frac{1}{4}$ ft) and $\frac{1}{16}$ ft. (Museo della Civiltà Romana, room LII, stele 58; JPA.)

79 Relief of a mason showing a levelling square, a plumb line, an articulated square, a shouldering square and a rule of 1 foot (l.29.8cm). Tomb of a freeman of the *gens Aebutia*. (Capitoline Museum; JPA.)

80 Two bronze squares found in Pompeii. The top one is a shouldering square. (National Museum, Naples.)

80

78

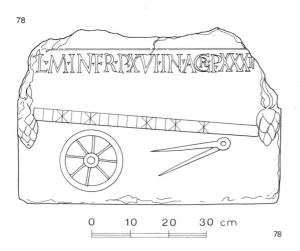

0   10   20   30 cm

78

79

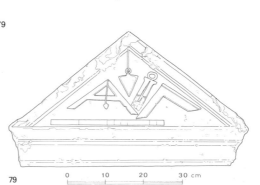

79   0   10   20   30 cm

81

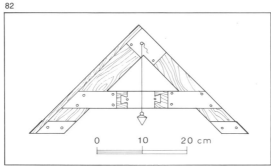

82

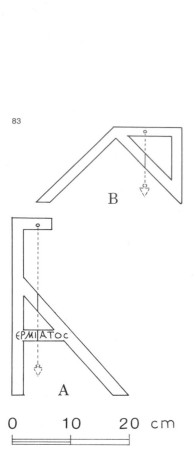

83

B

ЕРМIАТОС

A

0   10   20 cm

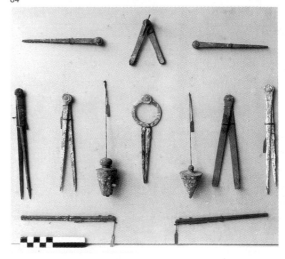

84

the brace; a plumb line suspended from the top of the instrument made it possible to check the verticality of the line and consequently the horizontality of the position. The accuracy of the measurement was obviously related to that of the instrument, that is, the arms being exactly equal and the position of the bracket.

When the two arms were joined at a right angle (which is not always so in the reliefs), the square could verify or

81 Levelling square with wooden arms and bronze attachments. Emblema, from a mosaic in a house in Pompeii (I,V,2). (Museum of Naples; JPA)

82 Reconstruction of a levelling square from the Jardins du Luxembourg; the width of the wood pieces is fixed by the small bronze plates but the length is arbitrary. (JPA after J. Conneau, *Une querre gallo-romaine, Bulletin archéologique du Vexin*, 1, pp.79ff.)

83 *A* Levelling square, used for checking horizontal and vertical planes, found at Tyr (Musée du Louvre); *B* Levelling square used for measuring angles (Musée d'Avignon; JPA.)

84 Instruments found in Rome. (*Top*) Two folded compasses and a compass with a key-pin to fix the arms. (*Middle, from left to right*) Two compasses; a plumb line; a compass; a plumb line; a folding foot-measure; a compass. (*Bottom*) Two folding foot-measures with locking device. (National Museum, Naples.)

the horizontality of the level of a course. This levelling square or plumb level (*libella*), usually made of wood, is composed of two arms held by a brace, giving it the form of a capital A. The three pieces could be held together by bronze plates making the whole thing rigid. A remarkable mosaic with an allegorical meaning, found at Pompeii and preserved in the National Museum in Naples, includes an extremely faithful representation of a levelling square, the wooden parts of which are joined together by bronze elements. In addition, similar pieces were found during excavations carried out in the Jardin du Luxembourg in Paris in 1962 and a model of the instrument can be reconstructed (figs 79, 81, 82, 83).[54]

In order to do their work as instruments of levelling, these squares had a vertical reference point, the zero alignment (*linea*), engraved in the middle of

establish the re-entry angles, and for other related uses different forms were adopted, making it possible in the same way to check projecting angles and even the verticality of the walls.[55]

The plumb line (*perpendiculum*) also holds a prominent position in both the reliefs of artisans and the archaeological record in the form of conical bronze 'bobs' which could be fixed centrally by a line (figs 79, 84).

The compass (*circinus*) is another instrument, like the above, that was used alike by stone-cutter, builder or carpenter. This piece of equipment can be used not only to draw circles and segments of circles, but also to record dimensions with absolute accuracy.

For this purpose, in order to counteract any fluctuation in the spacing of the arms, some examples have a key-pin shaped like a truncated cone to hold them in position, and others have the

85

ends of their arms pointed and slightly bent to facilitate certain measurements. Still others have crossing arms, longer on one side than the other, forming proportional dividers,[56] making it possible to reduce or increase an outline or a design keeping the exact relative dimensions (figs 78, 84).

d Lifting and transportation

Once the stone blocks had been prepared for putting in place, the builders had to move them to the bedding position, then arrange them in order and wedge them together. After the stones had been removed from the vehicle bringing them from the quarry they were transported along the ground either by hauling them on wooden rollers with the help of towing ropes or by heaving them with crowbars (fig.85). Access ramps made it possible to position the foundation and basement courses in this way without lifting operations being required. As soon as the blocks had to be laid on raised courses it was necessary to use machines, the power of which was adapted according to the size of the material involved. Construction with rubble stone and brick could be achieved by carrying material on men's backs, with ladders linking the levels of scaffolding; the load transported was limited to about 15kg but a 'noria' (Persian wheel) of buckets or a chain of workmen throwing each other the material from hand to hand ensured an adequate supply given the time required by the builder for positioning. For very large buildings, however, the majority of workers, often slaves and badly treated, were of no use, given the weight of the pieces to be raised (a stone used in coursed masonry of solid limestone measuring $80 \times 60 \times 50$cm weighs more than 500kg).

If Vitruvius is to be believed (X,2), Roman architects did not need new techniques for hoisting heavy loads since the Greeks had already perfected lifting machines, the *machinae tractores*, adequate for any load. This certainly seems credible when the average size of the stones in Greek temples is considered, whose weight is to be measured in tonnes rather than hundreds of kilos. The Romans, for their part, considered it a point of honour, in the large-scale use of solid masonry, to work with blocks of enormous size simply out of a desire for technical achievement.

The simplest of lifting machines is the pulley (*orbiculus*). This was probably an invention of Greek sailors, as equipment was needed for hoisting the yard-arms carrying the sails. But a load hoisted by a pulley cannot exceed the weight of the workman, though it does use the pulling power very efficiently.

The first reduction ratio appears with the winch (*sucula*). The crank, because the length of its handle or lever is greater than the radius of the roller drum for the rope, reduces the effort of pulling at the cost of an increased distance travelled.

The formula of the winch demonstrates its efficiency: taking P as the load to be raised, L as the length of the turning handle, r as the radius of the drum, F as the force exerted and as the coefficient of friction, in the case of a small winch the result is:

$$P = F \, \frac{L}{r} \, k = 15\text{kg} \, \frac{40\text{cm}}{10\text{cm}} \, 0.8 = 48\text{kg}$$

or a load more than three times greater than the effort exerted.

86

85 Transporting a block on rollers, either as far as a lifting machine on the ground, or on to the bedding course and into the bedding position.

86 Drawing of a well capstan, Naples.

87

88

0 1 2 3 4 5   10   15   20 cm

rately on small sites, could be brought together in a lifting machine that was still in use up until recent times, a type of crane (*rechanum*). Vitruvius describes this clearly: 'Two beams are required for the jib, their thickness depending on the maximum probable load. They are fixed together at the top with an iron bracket, and separated at the base,

87 A representation of two winch cranes operated by levers; the stones are held by grips. Terracotta relief found on the *via Cassia* showing a triumphal scene (with a winged victory and a trophy of weapons) associated with the foundation of a town. (National Museum, Rome; JPA.)

88 Scene of a building site. Painting from the *caldarium* in the villa of San Marco, Stabiae. (Archaeological Museum of Castellmare, no.282; JPA and P. Varène.)

89 Crane (*rechanum*) with winch (*sucula*) and pulley (*orbiculus*) shown on the painting from Stabiae, fig.88.

89

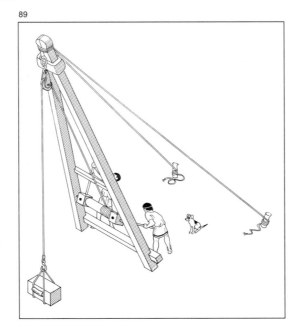

There is, however, an important technical observation to be noted: the turning handle, now a basic piece of equipment, was little used in antiquity;[57] the operation of the winch was carried out with the help of a projecting handspike at one or both ends of the drum. The formula of the winch was no different but the movement was discontinuous (fig.86).

The pulley and the winch, used separately

like an inverted V. Ropes are attached to the head of the jib, and arranged "all around" to keep it steady. A pulley block [*trochlea*] is suspended from the top.'

The Roman pictorial record fortunately completes this description, and that of the most complex machines described later by Vitruvius. Two simple cranes, with winch and pulley, are shown on a terracotta relief found on the via Cassia.[58] On this workmen can be seen operating the winch with the help of levers that are inserted into alternate sockets in the drum (fig.87). Very long levers can be used with this technique, but two workmen are needed to keep the thing turning. It was made safe by the lever being automatically blocked against the legs of the crane or against a cross-bar in the event of a workman letting go.

An identical machine is shown in a painting at Stabiae,[59] in which two men can be seen operating the levers of a winch on a crane anchored to the ground, while a third on the top of the wall is waiting to receive the load, a rectangular block held by a hook, and place it on its designed course (figs 88, 89, 90).

90

As cranes of low or average force were fairly small, they could be installed at different levels in the course of the work. Since they could also be dismantled, they were easily transportable, the only problem with raised positions being the absolute necessity of the legs being firmly anchored as they alone ensured the stability of the mechanism.

To increase the lifting force blocks and tackles were used, adding their power to that of the winch.[60] Another probable naval invention, the block and tackle combines several pulley wheels (*orbiculi*) assembled in pulley blocks (*trochleae*) through which the pulling cable (*ductarius funis*) moves, with a force proportional to the number of pulleys. The formula for the simplest hoist comprising two pulley wheels, one fixed, the other mobile, taking P as the load to be raised and F as the force exerted, is:

$$F = \frac{P}{2}\,k$$

The multiplication of the pulleys (fig. 91) gives:

$$F = \frac{P}{n}\,k$$

Of course, the power of the winch and the block and tackle, and the two combined, was applied not only to lifting operations but also, as seen at Baalbek, to pulling the heaviest loads along the ground.

These remarkable devices, however, did not mark the limits of these machines, which were given still more force by replacing the manual operation of the winch by levers with a large hollow wheel or treadmill (*majus tympanum*). The workmen climbed inside this and their weight caused it to rotate, their number varying according to the size of the load.[61]

Two reliefs once again illustrate the text of Vitruvius and enable an accurate reconstruction of these machines, the power of which was reckoned in tens of tonnes. The first, the relief from the amphitheatre of Capua,[62] shows a primitive representation of a crane, linked to a large wheel from which it is independent; inside the wheel there are two men. The block and tackle is distinctly shown with two pulley blocks and three pulley wheels, while a loop of rope tied to the lower pulley block holds a column, drawing it up and putting it into place (figs 92, 93).

With these machines a certain amount of space had to be allowed for movement, given the weight of the loads which could be manoeuvred and set

90 Scene of a building site on a relief found at Terracina. In the foreground are two workmen cutting blocks, the one on the left possibly with a stone-hammer, the other with a maul. On the wall a man is taking hold of a stone block, held by grips and suspended from a crane. (National Museum, Rome; JPA.)

91 The principles behind the operation and arrangement of the block and tackle.

91

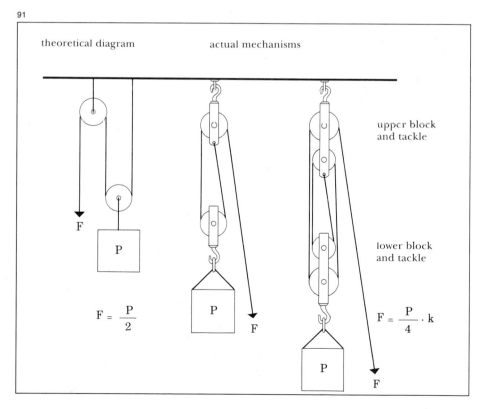

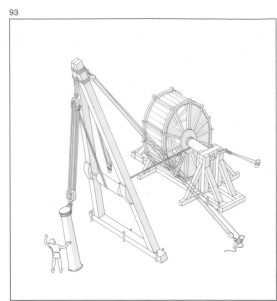

92 A lifting machine shown on a relief found at Capua. The motor wheel, operated by two workmen, is shown as independent from the crane, which is lifting a monolithic column into place using a block and tackle. The workman in the front is carving a capital.

93 Reconstruction of the machine shown in the Capuan relief, fig.92.

94 A lifting machine of great power, with a motor wheel worked by five men, from the funerary relief of the family Haterii, in the reign of Domitian. (Lateran Collections, Vatican Museum.)

95 Reconstruction of the machine shown in the relief of the Haterii, fig.94.

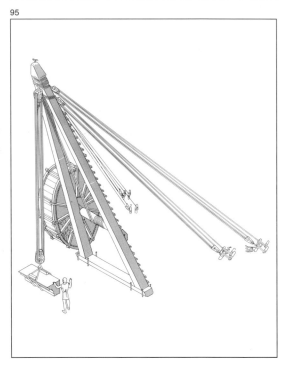

up, such as coursed masonry blocks. Further pulley blocks were therefore used as supporting guys, so that the framework of the crane could be rocked forward or back. This apparatus, not shown on the Capua relief, is

clearly visible on the relief on the tomb of the Haterii[63] where an enormous machine is shown with no fewer than 7 leg supports, 5 at the back, 2 at the front, all with pulley blocks.

This machine, with the hollow drum or treadmill having an estimated diameter of 8m, is moved by five workmen and is located directly over the feet of the crane, the winch thus working in direct transmission. Two men on the ground are there to grab the ropes designed to help hold the drum, whose inertia was considerable. The load, suspended in the vertical plane, is not visible as it is hidden by the monument itself, which is shown completed. To mark this completion two men have climbed to the top of the machine by means of the steps visible on the outline, and attached a garland at the highest point, as they still do in some places to symbolize the end of building work[64] (figs 94, 95, 96, 97).

It should be noted that the power of a block and tackle is limited by the resistance of the parts of the pulleys and particularly the resistance of the cables; a hemp rope 2cm in diameter makes it possible to hoist 500kg without risk, and with one of 4cm diameter 2000kg can be lifted. However, a very thick rope requires very bulky pulleys; and it is therefore preferable to use ropes that are more manageable and double the number of pulley blocks.

Though the cranes were adapted for all kinds of lifting work including for lifting column shafts, it can be imagined that more specialized machines were brought in for this, since what was required was to hold the column in a rigid axis while it was being lifted, which was not the case with the cranes. Works carried out since the Renaissance make it possible for us to suggest a machine pivoting around the horizontal axis, with the

column shaft to be erected on a stretcher placed on the ground, forming one of the arms of a right-angled square; the other arm, firmly attached, is therefore in a vertical position. The latter is attached by cables to hauling capstans that bring it into a horizontal position while the column is raised up and put into place[65] (fig.98).

Handling blocks with lifting machines made use of many techniques, the simplest of which consisted of rope slings with a ring at each end, or straps – ropes with a closed loop that went round the stone and were attached to the hook of the machine. This technique had the advantage of

96

97

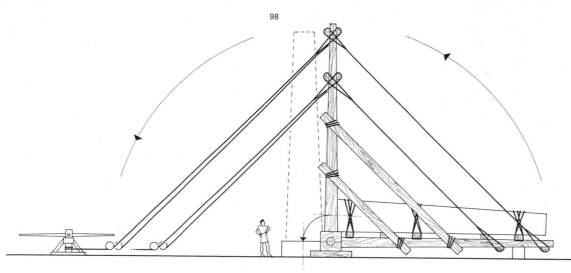

98

96 Medieval lifting machine, powered by a large wheel. (*Histoire Universelle*, thirteenth century; JPA.)

97 'Quarrymen's wheel' at the quarry of Comblanchien (Côte d'Or), from a postcard of the turn of the century (courtesy of A. Olivier).

98 Reconstruction of a machine designed for lifting monolithic shafts.

99

100

99 Lifting bosses, or tenons, on the slabs of stylobates at the portico of the Central Baths, Pompeii; they were being put into position at the time of the eruption of 79.

100 Lifting bosses that have not been trimmed off on the facing blocks of the Porta San Sebastiano (*via Appia*), in Rome, built under Honorius, *c*.400.

101 Side grooves on blocks from the Greek temple in honour of Juno Lacinia at Agrigentum (fifth century BC). The Romans never adopted this system of lifting though it was known in Sicily.

102 Lewis placed in position for lifting (modern).

103 Lewis holes on the outer curve of the archstones of the ambulatory in the arena of Arles.

104 Lewis holes in the floor slabs of the threshold to a public building in Pompeii ('Tollhouse', IV,1,13).

105 Monolithic column from the 'Camp of Diocletian' at Palmyra, with a lewis hole. Height: 4m; diameter: 55cm; lewis hole: 15 x 4cm.

101

requiring no special preparation of the stone, but crowbars were needed to free the ropes after positioning and this put a limit on the weight of the stone block lifted by this method, except for the parts of an architrave with a freely projecting soffit.

To overcome this difficulty Greek builders had perfected four techniques: handling bosses, side grooves, top grooves and lewises or lifting-pins.[66] The Romans took over two of these, the bosses and the lewises, and added another method, the use of grips.

The bosses, or tenons (*ancones*), were projections on the rock, left symmetrically on the front and back faces, providing a convenient attachment for the rope slings. These bosses, when there is only one on each surface, are placed almost at the axis of the block so as to avoid unbalancing during the move, but there are often several on each surface of heavier blocks (figs 99, 100). These projections were removed during the finishing process when the courses were in place or even when the building was completed. Thus interrupted work or unfinished monuments reveal the existence of these tricks of the trade.

Precisely to avoid this extra work, the Greeks resorted to U-shaped grooves (fig.101), made into the end surfaces and consequently invisible when in place and, more rarely, to V-shaped grooves, hollowed into the upper surface, two techniques that the Romans did not follow; they preferred the lewis.

The lewis consisted of metal parts assembled so as to grab hold of the stone; there were three parts together resembling a dovetail in outline, a stirrup-piece allowing attachment to the lifting hook and a metal pin joining these four parts together. In the centre of gravity on the top surface of each block the stone-cutter prepared a cavity with a dovetail outline, the same size as the lewis he was using. Into this were inserted the side parts of the lewis, one after the other, and then the middle part. On some monuments the lewis holes have a lateral slant on one side only. In these cases the lewises used were composed of only two parts, one club-shaped, the other straight, instead of the usual three (figs 102, 103, 104, 105).

While a wide variation of sizes can be recognized, depending on the volume of stone to be lifted, holes measuring in the region of 10cm long by 2cm wide and 10cm deep are often found. Moreover, it was not the metal part that was crucial with the heaviest blocks but rather the resistance of the block of stone to be gripped. Among the largest lewis holes are those made in blocks of travertine used for the construction of the facings, the orders and the arch-stones of the arch of the Colosseum, the holes reaching 22cm long by 6cm wide and 25cm deep.

As the use of lewises had many advantages, both in the speed of preparation and in the ease of handling, it became general throughout the empire. Only when the surface of a stone was intended to remain visible (slabs and stylobates) was it lifted using straps and cut into small pieces to make it lighter and more easily manoeuvrable and to avoid damaging the facing.

Some lewis holes, or what are presumed to be, are found on vertical walls; their position at the axis of the centre of gravity of the blocks means that it is difficult to attribute any other function to them. The use of special pincers, the jaws of which open up in the cavity when the stone is picked up, can therefore be suggested. Such devices, used up to the present day and called self-locking lewises or self-adjusting stone-dogs, most probably existed in the Roman period. In any case, their use is complementary to the holes used in wedging blocks together, and they have the advantage of greater adaptability as they do not

106

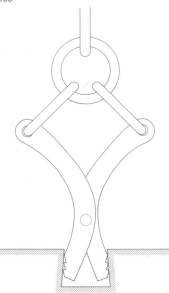

108

109

106 Interior grips or self-adjusting lewises.

107 Grips (modern).

108 Holes for grips carved into a point, at the amphitheatre of El Djem.

109 Square holes for grips, theatre of Bullia Regia.

110 Summary of the different lifting methods in Roman architecture: bosses; grips; lewis.

require an exact size of hole to be cut (fig.106).

With the use of grips or iron forceps (*ferrei forfices*) the preparatory work is even further reduced; all that is necessary is to make sure that the two hooked

points of the self-adjusting pincers grip in small holes made symmetrically in the two vertical surfaces. When the grips are used on the joining surfaces (the pediment monument at Glanum, for instance), the process remains invisible and so is superior to the use of the lewis as it is much quicker. However, when the holes are cut into the front and back faces of a block, the numerous marks are visible on the facing (Porta Maggiore, amphitheatre of El Djem, theatre at Bulla Regia).

The use of grips, even though well

107

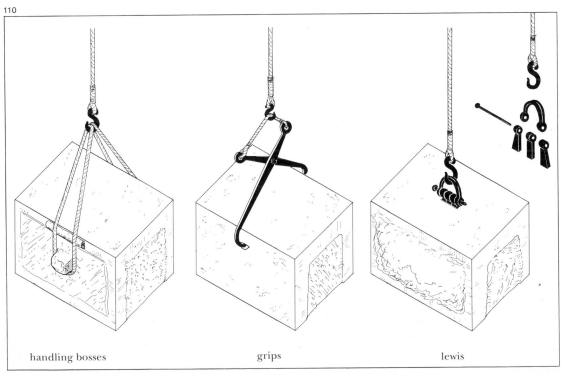
110

handling bosses   grips   lewis

attested in the pictorial record (relief of Terracina, relief of the via Cassia, relief of Pratica di Mare,[67] the painting in the House of Siricus at Pompeii), was limited to the lifting of blocks of modest or average dimensions because of the limitation on how wide the jaws could open and the risk of them slipping (figs 107, 108, 109, 110).

e Wedging, clamping

Large blocks, positioned in their correct course and practically in their final place, still had to undergo one or two more operations to abut them closely to the neighbouring block and, if necessary, to adjust their horizontal and vertical planes. The blocks had already received some preparation when they were cut to establish their orientation, taking account also of transportation and lifting. The front face generally received some special treatment, and could either be given a final dressing or could preserve a more or less marked rustication, whereas the lower surface, or bottom bed, and the upper surface, or top bed, had to be strictly flat in order to guarantee an optimum distribution of pressure. Again to ensure the best resistance to compression the blocks were placed following the lie of the quarry bed, i.e. respecting the horizontal orientation of the natural strata. However, the falling position, with the beds vertical, can sometimes be seen in narrow blocks placed head-on and particularly with monolithic columns of marble, a metamorphic rock that is sufficiently resistant to withstand such a situation.

The side or joining faces did not need any general treatment of their surface since they do not impart any pressure, and for this reason it was enough simply to treat the outer contact frame, the anathyrosis band,[68] with fine chisels, whereas the centre of the face was rebated with a scabbling hammer or a punch. Depending on the

quality of the monument or the position of the stone, the anathyrosis frame could go round all four sides of the joining face, or could be limited to the visible edges only, particularly if the masonry fill was rough. Sometimes, however, with large blocks a partial rebating was carried out to limit the work of fine dressing on the top and bottom beds: this can be found on the blocks of the monumental complex of

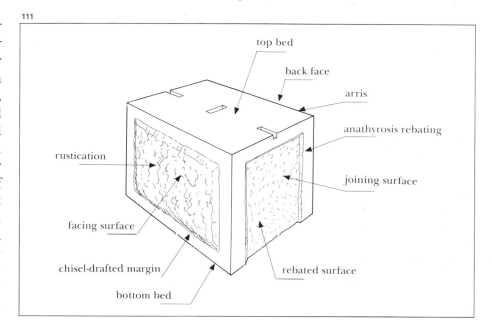

111

113

112

the Temple of Bel at Palmyra (first century).[69] The Greeks already generally applied this technique to their column drums since the narrow supporting parts called for precise joining beds that were more difficult to achieve over large surfaces (figs 111, 112, 113, 114, 115, 116, 117).

114

The order in which the blocks were assembled sometimes necessitated, when the dressing and bedding took place a long way apart, the use of positioning marks, according to a sequence in a work book these marks recorded the specific form of each stone, as dictated by the general design of the monument. The most common example is that of column drums, the diameter of which varies, decreasing

with the height of the bedding position. As the number of drums is itself liable to vary from one column to another, identification has to be doubly accurate. The marks were either drawn in chalk (and have disappeared) or engraved on the top beds of the blocks so as to be visible, and in this way they differ from the marks made by quarrymen and masons found on the facing blocks of walls dating to the archaic period or the Republican era (the Servian Wall in Rome,[70] the walls of Bolsena[71] or of Pompeii) and later on the aqueduct of Carthage.[72] Their significance is linked to accounting: they act as a signature and are in no way an indication of position.[73]

A capital destined for the portico of the Temple of Venus at Pompeii has on its top bed the numbers IIIIV; the order in which the numbers are arranged indicates two successive readings and not a single one. Lacking knowledge of the chronology used by the builders, there are two possible translations: either column four, block five, or block

114 Blocks, reused in the Middle Ages, that came originally from the Temple of Bel at Palmyra. The tops have been made into the facing and are identified by the lewis holes (two series of different lewises), the rebating or linear hollows which reduce the contact surfaces.

115 Diagram showing the central depressions of blocks on both horizontal and vertical faces at the Temple of Bel, Palmyra. (After R. Amy, *Le Temple de Bel*, vol.I, p.111; JPA.)

116 A stone-block facing built by the technique of *emplecton*; the anathyrosis bands are limited to the vertical edges on the facing side. (Nymphaeum of the Letoon, Xanthus).

115

116

118

117

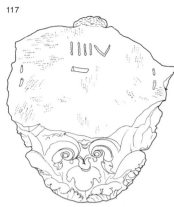

117 A number to indicate the positioning of a capital for the portico of the Temple of Venus, Pompeii.

118 Painting from the House of Siricus showing a scene on a building site. Pompeii, VIII,5,26-57.

four of column five (fig.117).

The exact positioning of a block was done by hand when it was small, but more often with the aid of crowbars. This meant that small cavities – crowbar, or spike, holes – were necessary to provide the tool with a grip for the operation. These holes were cut in the top bed of stones already in place, at the time of manoeuvring, depending on the distance the blocks were to be moved. If they were moved on rollers from the point where they were deposited by the lifting equipment, blocks could not be wedged closely together, since a certain amount of space was needed when pulling the rollers out. Sometimes several successive spike holes are found, indicating separate attempts carried out using several crowbars. These operations are illustrated by the painting in the House of Siricus, in which three workmen can clearly be made out, each using a crowbar or a quarryman's spike to fit the stone blocks closely together (figs 119, 120).

It should be noted that crowbar holes for the lengthways clamping of joints are always found near the joint,

119

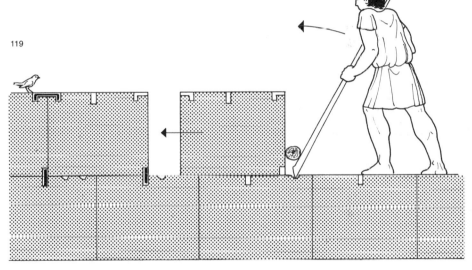

120

119 Wedging together blocks with a crowbar and clamping.

120 The top bed of a block from the foundations of the Roman Temple of Euromos (Caria). Note here, from left to right, the sealing clamp, three sockets for vertical dowels (with channels for the overflow) and two spike holes, thus enabling the block to be clamped to the joint of the upper block.

121 Sideways wedging of the blocks for the facing (*Aqua Claudia*).

122 Side spike hole, hollowed in a projection intended to be removed. Temple of Venus, Pompeii.

123 Spike holes in the side of blocks in a pillar in the aqueduct of *Aqua Claudia*.

the positioning of which may be marked on the lower bedding course by a slight difference of treatment of the surface. This provides a useful clue for the reconstruction of a course that has disappeared (fig 121).

This fitting together of blocks was also carried out sideways from scaffolding levels, with the aid of similar holes but generally set into handling

121

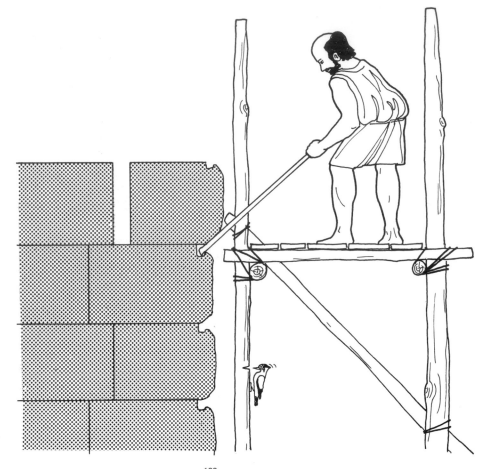

bosses that were intended to disappear on completion of the building work. Where the holes remain, it is on buildings still in course of construction (the Temple of Venus in Pompeii), in facings that have not been given a final dressing (Porta Maggiore in Rome, the theatre of Tusculum), or whose blocks have a strong rustication, the projection of which can accommodate such cavities[74] (the pillars of the Aqua Claudia in Rome) (figs 122, 123, 124).

The aesthetic disadvantage caused by the presence of crowbar holes on the facings disappears when they were cut into the top bed, as they were to aid longitudinal wedging. In such a case two sockets for the spikes were prepared, one in the edge of the block already in place and the other in the

123

124 Four spike holes around the edge intended for the fine positioning of the shaft of a column. Forum of Pompeii.

125 Positioning a block using holes made in the upper part of the edges.

126 Double dovetail clamp at the Temple of Fortuna Augusta, Pompeii.

127 Double-T clamp on a fountain in Pompeii.

128 Pi clamp, the most widely used shape, at the Temple of Venus, Pompeii.

122

joining face of the block to be wedged. This can be observed on the parts of the entablature of the Forum in Pompeii where such an operation may have been attempted (fig.125).

The usual method of construction was the simple fitting together of dry-jointed blocks, but the Romans also borrowed from the Greeks the custom of making the elements of a stone-block construction solid by using wooden or metal clamps and dowels. These were intended to prevent joints

125

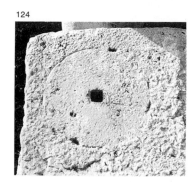

124

126

127

128

and carpentry. In the sixth century BC the Greeks, while still continuing to use wood, also used lead – in the form of tenons and still with the double dovetail – poured in advance into a mould and then inserted into the mortices and hammered in to fix them tightly. These archaic techniques occasionally continued in the Roman period, distinguished from the use of iron clamps by the shape and the enormous size of the mortices (the 'Pagan Wall' of Sainte-Odile, the Fanum of Alesia), but they represent exceptions and, generally speaking, iron was used. Double-dovetail mortices are found but they generally enclose an iron clamp with a pi shape, covered by lead solder filling the rest of the cavity (fig.126)

When a monument and its fastening are well preserved it is sometimes not possible to identify the contents of the mortice as all that is visible is the lead on the surface (for instance, the Temple of Fortuna Augusta in Pompeii). Generally, the dovetail clamp disappeared from the architecture of the peninsula during the first century, even if certain great monuments used it in the Augustan period (the Temple of Mars Ultor in Rome).[76] The double-T clamps, which appeared in Athens at the beginning of the fifth century BC and were much used in Greek architecture up to the Hellenistic period, were less used by Roman builders (fig.127), not because they required a more complicated operation, but because the amount of forging needed for shaping the double-T is much greater than the simple bending of the ends of a bar to give a pi outline. The Greeks, with fewer monumental building programmes and their perfectionism in building, were able to devote more time to the execution of the jointing details, since the entire building work, due to the quality of the stone-cutting, necessarily followed a much slower rhythm than in the Roman world.

widening due to possible movements caused by variations in settlement in the foundations or by seismic shocks. In fact, when the building had proper foundations such precautions were completely superfluous since the pressure was only transmitted through the walls vertically; at the most, clamping counteracted the effect of slipping caused by untrussed roof systems. The metal clamps and dowels were anyway robbed during the Middle Ages without the buildings, losing their stability. Whatever the case may be, the method was already used by the Egyptians who employed thick wooden tenons in the shape of double dovetails to prevent similar damage. It can be found also in Pre-Columbian Andean architecture in the eighth century AD in the form of bronze clamps in a double T; proof, if it were needed, that similar technical problems find identical solutions in totally different times and places.

The earliest shape adopted was that of a double dovetail, for it lent itself to the manufacture of tenons from hard wood – oak, cedar or olive[75] – and besides it was merely a continuation of a shape used for joints in timber-work

129

129

129 Pi clamps, of which only the vertical pieces are sealed with lead. Forum of Bavay.

130 Socket holes of three vertical dowels in a column base. Imperial *triclinium* of Hadrian's Villa, 115 to 125.

130

In the vast majority of cases, pi clamps were therefore used for fastening in Roman stone block construction. Besides the speed of manufacture of the iron piece, the holes cut into the two juxtaposed blocks to hold it did not need to be cut as precisely as they would for double-T mortices. Once the clamp was in place, the remaining space was filled by a solder of lead which could simply seal the two vertical projections or cover the whole thing (figs 128, 129).

With the use of clamps, all the stones of a course were solidly bonded together. Sometimes a vertical bonding was added to the horizontal bonding – more common with the Greeks than with the Romans – consisting of metal

dowels[77] sealed into the top surface of the lower course and inserted into a cavity on the bedding surface of the upper course. Dowelling was essentially used for holding column drums; the dowels were single for columns of small diameter and increased to two, three or four depending on the increase in contact surface. Since inserting lead into the upper cavity was problematic (the Greeks had thought of various solutions using channels on the upper surface, as in the Temple of Apollo at Delphi), the simplest solution consisted of first sealing the dowel of the upper block by turning it over. Then, once the lead and the dowel were in place, molten lead was poured into the lower cavity and the stone adjusted, the dowel settling in the metal that was still liquid. To stop the latter overflowing, a channel was often cut from the hole out to the facing (figs 130, 131).

This two-stage operation was rather complicated and so instead the dowel was simply sealed with lead into the lower block and the upper block was put in place by inserting the dowel dry-jointed into the mortice. In some cases the dowel may also have been placed dry into the lower sockets, as the blocks, especially column shafts that needed delicate adjustment and were impossible to turn over, were placed one upon another and the lead was then poured in by means of a channel leading to the lower mortice. This ensured that when the metal solidified it did not form a projection which could impair the stability.

Sometimes, lacking confidence in the stability of their constructions, the Romans took what may seem the excessive precaution of clamping the voussoirs of arches; thus those in the Cestian Bridge in Rome were fixed in pairs with four dowels.[78] In fact, these metal pieces did give the arch great resistance by counteracting the lateral slippage of the voussoirs of the arch

131 Column drums from the Temple of Bel, Palmyra. The drum on the right (upper face visible as shown by the lewis hole) supported that on the left. The sockets of the dowels are wide to allow for the lead sealing. On the lower surface of the other drum the holes for inserting the dowels dry-jointed are narrower. Note the slight depression of the centre.

caused by the force of water in times of spate.

The use of mortar as a bonding agent in stone-block construction was relatively limited; the quality of the dressing of the adjacent surfaces lent itself better, in preserving the fineness of the joints, to the use of clamps (or to their absence). The use of lime mortar is only ever found in monuments built of a stone with an inferior appearance, sometimes intended to be covered by a decoration. This can be seen in the so-called Temple of Fortuna Virilis, in fact dedicated to the god Portunus, in the Forum Boarium in Rome which was built with blocks of tufa pointed with an almost pure lime mortar, then rendered with stucco imitating blocks of marble (which has almost completely disappeared today). Other monuments that were left bare have been given the same mortared joints, such as the Tabularium,[79] the Emilian Bridge, the Milvian Bridge and the pillars of the Aqua Marcia, all in Rome.[80] This technique is not a Roman invention, since around 300BC the Hellenistic enclosure of Dura-Europos

(Eastern Syria) was built of large blocks of gypsum pointed with plaster.[81]

Though the presence of this thin layer of mortar did not improve the stability of the monument, it had the advantage of guaranteeing an excellent distribution of pressure between each course, even if the top and bedding surfaces were not perfectly finished. The strips of mortar poured into vertical grooves in the joining surfaces of the blocks of aqueduct conduits, basins and fountains, were intended to ensure that these constructions for conveying water were watertight. They can be seen quite clearly on the ruined sections of the Aqua Marcia and between all the paving slabs at the bottom of the public fountains in Pompeii.

When monuments had ashlar facings with a core, the fill of *opus caementicium* consisted of a mass of rubble bonded with lime mortar which also bonded the stone blocks to the supporting masonry of the core. This is the method by which almost all funerary monuments were constructed, some-

132

133

132 Wavy joint in a granite column from the Basilica Ulpia.

133 Vertical sealing clamps with double dovetails. Markets of Trajan, Rome. (Height: 33cm; max.length: 13cm.)

Rome that had granite columns: the Pantheon, the Temple of Venus and Rome and the Basilica Ulpia (fig.132). What can be seen (with the help of binoculars for two columns of the Pantheon) are sinuous joins of remarkable ingenuity, consisting of an undulating ring surrounding a central circular raised part. The complexity of the contact surfaces was such that, when this solution was resorted to, there was no need for dowels for vertical bonding.

Finally another method of clamping should be mentioned. Analogous to that used in the horizontal plane, but applied to the joints between two courses, it consists of clamps with double dovetails, attached to the facing surfaces of the travertine blocks in the Markets of Trajan. These blocks form part of the abutments of a vaulted gallery, and it may have been necessary to reinforce this part of the construction as it was built on quite steeply sloping ground (fig.133).[82]

2 Clay

Clay is the material from which man is made, according to the Book of Genesis, and this image is repeated in numerous mythologies. The idea is justified by the astonishing mechanical qualities of this plastic and malleable material that, soaked in water, maintains the form given to it by the hand and in drying becomes a solid substance.

Though wood, foliage and animal skins were the first constituents of the nascent architecture of temperate countries, clay was and remains the essential building material of the regions of the world where vegetation is scarce, and particularly on most of the shores of the Mediterranean. It is interesting then to find wood and clay combined in a more developed architecture, forming timber-framed struc-

times with headers which stretched from the facing and penetrated deep into the concrete core (the Tomb of Caecilia Metella, Casal Rotondo on the *via Appia*) and the podia of most temples.

The search for technical perfection, as noted above, was held in high esteem by Roman builders, and this ambition can still inspire admiration for the many monuments with monolithic column shafts, sometimes of considerable height. When one of these shafts was accidentally broken in the course of its transportation or use, it was easier, rather than replace it, as the material often came a long distance, to dress the missing piece so as to reconstruct the finished column using blocks intended for repairs.

An accident such as this happened on at least three monuments in

tures that are particularly common when building stone is in short supply, when it is of mediocre quality or, conversely, when it is difficult to work. This combination of materials has such qualities and its cost is so much lower than building with stone that its use is known everywhere, even up to the present (fig.134).

In a number of regions sun-dried clay was considered an adequately efficient material, but it became apparent that clay's vulnerability to water totally disappears when it is baked. This observation, originally accidental, was made by the potter, and it was many centuries before this mundane and waterproof material came to be used for building. Clay was of course baked to form bricks, but since the earliest regions where this transformation had been carried out enjoyed a hot and dry climate – Mesopotamia – baked bricks were for a long time used only for watertight constructions, such as water-troughs or pipes, or for the more vulnerable parts of buildings, such as the frames of openings or the facings of large monuments.[83]

In the western world, both Greek and Roman, the baking of clay occurred much later, and for a long time (often up to the first century BC) then was used only for tiles and roof decorations, intended to provide a waterproof covering and a protection for the ends of the roof timbers. On two widely separated sites are found the first Greek monuments to use baked bricks. One is the Hellenistic palace at Nippur in Mesopotamia,[84] and the other is in the colony of Magna Graecia at Velia in Lucania, where stamped bricks were recovered in large numbers from buildings of the Hellenistic period[85] (fig.135). It is probably this use of baked bricks by Greeks in the south of the peninsula which led to the cities of Campania using the material a long time before Rome.

a Unbaked clay

In its raw state clay is used in several ways today in Mediterranean and Eastern countries: as puddled clay, daub and bricks. Clay, used pure, soaks up a great deal of water and cracks in drying, especially if it is a certain kind of clay, referred to as fat, long or rich. Other clays, which are naturally mixed with sand, are less plastic and less liable to contraction during drying;

134 Timber framing with clay in-filling in the traditional architecture of the region of Bursa (Turkey).

135 Stamped brick of the Hellenistic period at Velia (Lucania), 38 x 23cm, with the seal of the manufacturer and a seal of quality control.

these are known as lean, short or open. Observation of this led to the introduction into the clay of a filler to counteract the effects of shrinking and cracking caused by the loss of water.

Puddled clay and daub are in effect the same material. The initial preparation for making clay walls is also the same whether the material is used in bulk or in the form of unbaked bricks. The clay is placed in a water-filled pit, near a water source, where it is pugged by being trodden by foot with a tempering agent, sometimes vegetable – such as straw, dried grass, cereal chaff – and sometimes ash or mineral in the form of sand or gravel (fig.136).

Only the 'lean' clays can be used after mixing with water. These and ones with sand added have kept the name puddled clay, to distinguish them from the clays 'defattened' with straw, a product recommended by Vitruvius (II,3), which was twisted (*torquere*) to break it up, giving the French name for daub: torchis.[86]

The material obtained, because of its relative fluidity, cannot be used without a support or framework. This determines the width of the wall and is filled

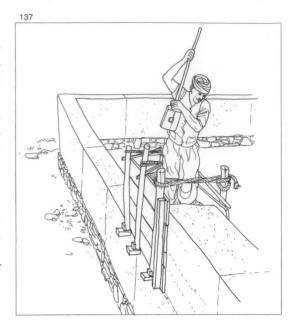

with the clay, after the precaution has been taken of insulating it from the ground, i.e. from rising damp, by a stone base. Construction proceeds in sections of limited length (2 to 3m) and of a height usually not more than 1m, called shuttering (from shutters – the boards of the framework) or formwork. As the material is put in place it is trodden and tamped, and, more specifically, puddled[87] with the aid of a tamper or rammer, a heavy wooden paddle

136 Mixing clay with straw as a defattening agent tempering by treading, in the preparation of puddled clay or unbaked bricks.

137 Tamping of puddled clay inside a formwork. (Moroccan Atlas, twentieth century).

designed for this work. This compression has the dual purpose of compacting the material and ridding it of some of its moisture before it dries (fig.137).

Since this method of working is found in all the countries bordering the Mediterranean and is completely independent of the composition of the mixture, the term 'puddled clay' relates rather to the technique of construction than to the material itself, since this is tempered with vegetable matter (puddled daub) as well as with minerals.

In its first stage, the manufacture of unbaked bricks does not in any way differ from the use of the material in the way described above. The essential difference lies in the creation of rectangular blocks, which are easy to handle and are left to dry in the sun to obtain a solid building material that can be used without a framework, joined together by wet clay. Buildings can in this way reach considerable dimensions and be constructed very quickly. The east was able to create enormous ziggurats and urban enclosures, a method taken up again by the Greeks in their last programmes, still visible at Eleusis and particularly in the fortifications of Gela in Sicily.

Bricks are moulded in a wooden frame without a base and divided into a variable number of boxes of equal size. The workman fills these and then empties them with one throw on to the drying area (figs 138, 139). Although manufacture can be carried out at any season, except times of great rainfall if the drying area is not roofed, Vitruvius recommends autumn or spring for the moulding work, periods when the sun is not too strong so the skin does not dry out too quickly and crack. 'The best thing' he says 'is to keep them for two whole years before using them, for when bricks that have been made recently and are not completely dry are used it can happen that in contracting they can come apart from the covering put on them'. In saying this, Vitruvius

indicates that unbaked bricks were used in construction in the same way as stone and that the walls built in this way were given a covering which allowed a decorative facing to be added. This observation is all the more comprehensible in view of the fact that the author of the *Ten Books*, writing his treatise between 40 and 32BC, makes no mention of baked bricks in the construction of walls.[88] It could be concluded from this silence that Rome and the north of the peninsula were still unaware of the use of baked bricks in the first century BC; however, the surprising thing is that Vitruvius constantly refers to observations made by him in reading or travelling and he speaks at length, three chapters later (III,6, *De pulvere puteolano*), about the region of Vesuvius, where Roman construction using baked bricks had existed at least since the time of Sulla.[89]

The size of the bricks was determined by the frame used and this

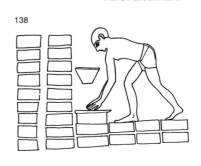

138 Moulding and drying bricks in Egypt. From a painting from the tomb of Rekhmire, Thebes (JPA).

139 Moulding bricks in the drying area, in the region of Kairouan (Tunisia).

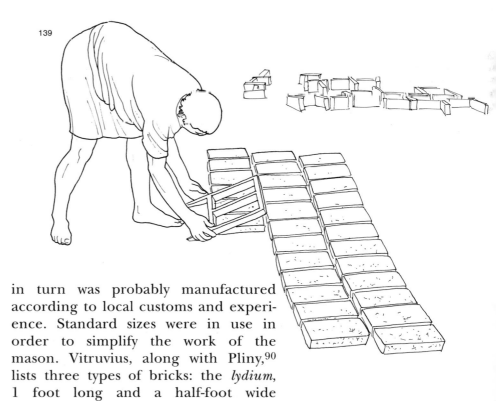

in turn was probably manufactured according to local customs and experience. Standard sizes were in use in order to simplify the work of the mason. Vitruvius, along with Pliny,[90] lists three types of bricks: the *lydium*, 1 foot long and a half-foot wide

140

identical to those used for pottery, except in size, because of the greater volume of material to be fired.

The pottery kiln can be circular or oblong,[91] and is situated partly underground, which conserves heat and makes loading and unloading the material easier. The lower part is made up of the combustion chamber, supplied with fuel by means of an opening that can be partially walled up during the baking to control the ventilation, leaving the space necessary for adding fuel. This consists of highly combustible vegetable matter, such as dried brushwood, grass, various nuts, almond husks or pine-cones; the last

140   A brick kiln.

A   Hearth or combustion chamber.
B   Door for feeding fuel and for ventilation. It is partially blocked up during the firing.
C   Shelf or internal ledge pierced by heat holes or flues.
D   Bricks to be baked piled up in the charge chamber.
E   Loading door completely blocked up during the firing.
F   Fuel supply.
G   Bricks, stones and clay piled up around the side to keep the heat in.

141   Pottery kiln in the region of Deir-ez-Zor (Syria); access to the combustion chamber is on the right in the dip and the opening for loading is on the left.

142   The internal plate or ledge of the same kiln as in fig. 141 and its heat holes or flues.

(29.6 × 14.8cm), the *tetradoron* or four hands, i.e. one square foot (29.6 × 29.6cm) and the *pentadoron* or five-hands (37 × 37cm).

b   Baked clay

As firing clay in a kiln destroys the vegetable tempering agents, mineral agents, principally sand, are used, as in pottery. Kilns for baking bricks are

MATERIALS

three can be retrieved before complete combustion to be reused as charcoal.[92]

The heating chamber is covered by a brick vault (in French called the 'sole', probably from Latin *solea*, sandal) pierced by numerous holes, or flues, allowing heat to escape (figs 140, 141, 142). When the surface area of this base-plate is large, it is supported on pillars; or else the heating chamber can consist of several galleries, each with their own heating vents. In small kilns, specifically intended for firing pottery, the fire is confined to a short gallery, the 'hearth', placed at the entrance to the heating chamber, the heat being thus indirectly communicated to the vault.

The upper space containing the bricks or tiles, the 'charge chamber' or 'pot', is loaded through an access door that is completely blocked up during the firing. In small-sized kilns there is no loading door and a vault is constructed around the products to be fired, which is simply destroyed when firing is complete. The upper part of the charge chamber is always left open so as to provide a draught for the fire. The potter, bearing in mind factors of wind or rain, simply places a variable number of tiles over the bricks and never seals the kiln off completely. For the same reason the bricks are piled up on the internal shelf with sufficient space between them so that the hot air is sucked towards the top hole and the firing is equal throughout the kiln.

The firing time is extremely variable as it depends on the size of the kiln, atmospheric conditions and the fuel used; as a practical indication, a present-day brick kiln in the region of Kairouan (Tunisia), with a charge chamber 3m in diameter and 4m high, heated with brushwood and dried grass in hot dry weather, has a firing time of about three hours. The temperature in the charge chamber can be estimated to be in the region of 800°C near the internal shelf and 450°C near the upper exit. The latter temperature is the minimum threshold below which clay does not solidify and returns to either a dry powdery state or a putty-like condition if water is added. The upper layer of bricks is usually rejected as it is often unsuitable for building work.

Another method of firing, which does not require the construction of a kiln, is firing in a stack. This consists of piling up unbaked bricks, with one or several combustion chambers at the bottom of the pile in which the fire is lit directly. This technique means that large quantities of material can be

143

143 Brick-drying area and baking in a stack (behind) in the region of Mugla (Turkey).

63

144

145

146 A stamp on a Gallo-Roman tile (Musée de Sens).

145 Brick stamp at the Great Baths of Hadrian's Villa, 118 to 125. The crescent shape with a small aperture is very typical of the first half of the second century.

146 Stamps. *1* First century BC (CIL XV,966,7). *2* Flavian period (69 to 96). Note that the manufacturer is a slave: *Domitio(rum) ser(vus) f(ecit)* (CIL XV,1000,a). *3* Period of Nerva (96–98) (CIL XV,1356). *4* Inscription precisely dated by a consular reference, *Apro(niano) et Pae(tino) co(n)s(ulibus)*, 123, reign of Hadrian (CIL XV,801). *5* Period of Vespasian (69–79), decorated with a *sistrum* (CIL XV,1097,f). *6* Reign of Trajan (98–117) (CIL XV,811,d). *7* Inscription dated 150 (reign of Antoninus) by a consular reference: *Gallicano et Vetere Cons(ulibus)*. Decorated with a *bucranium*. (CIL XV,1221,a). *8* Stamp with the monogram of Constantine, fourth century (CIL XV,1563).

The oldest marks, in the style of those from Velia, are rectangular. They then take the form of an open crescent which closes to become a circle. Rectangular stamps reappeared during the later Empire.

146

baked, but at the cost of a considerable surrounding layer that is insufficiently fired. However, it is not certain whether firing in a stack, still practised by the artisans of Greece and particularly in Turkey, was in use in antiquity (fig.143).

Potters marked their products, and so numerous tiles and bricks carry a stamp, such as that of Velia, which gives valuable information of either origin or date.[93] Up to the first century the bricks have only brief inscriptions, simply giving the name of the maker, the equivalent of the mark left by the stone-mason. In the period of Trajan, stamps become more elaborate and at the end of the second century the information provided extends from the name of the land owner where the clay originated to the final monument, e.g. *Castris praetori(s) Aug. n(ostri)*, via the name of the manufacturer, the place of manufacture, the supplier, the depot, the consuls in power, and even declarations, *Valeat qui fecit!*[94] In provinces like Gaul[95] and Africa,[96] stamps giving the names of the legions or cohorts which carried out the construction are often found on the sites of military installations; these provide valuable historical information making it possible to trace troop movements (figs 144, 145, 146).

The builders of southern Italy realized fairly early on the advantages of this material which could be shaped to order. They created the first examples of brick columns made up of sections of discs with the same radius as the shaft to be constructed. The most sophisticated example, and also one of the oldest, is that of the columns of the basilica at Pompeii, erected in the last years of the independence of that city, about 120BC. Here there are bricks with an outline defining the fluting, which was then rendered with white stucco.[97] It should be noted, however, that in many constructions in Pompeii the terracotta elements are not very thick and have traces of cutting on their facings – from which it can be concluded that these were not bricks but tiles trimmed to fit in with the masonry. This secondary use is also confirmed by a good deal of masonry on minor buildings where the edges of the tiles have survived. This reuse was to be standard at Pompeii, particularly after the earthquake of 62, when the city had at its disposal a mass of material resulting from collapsed roofs. Though he speaks only of walls made out of unbaked bricks, Vitruvius also recommends the reuse of tiles as a building material (II,8). However, it is not clear whether he is discussing reusing tiles as bricks or broken fragments of tiling: '... the tiles which cannot withstand a long time on the roofs are not suitable for use in the masonry [*in structura*]. This is why one needs old tiles for terracotta masonry [*testa structi parietes*] which are solid'. As this advice follows on precautions to be taken to protect the tops of walls made of unbaked bricks – *summis parietibus, structura testacea sub tegula subiciatur altitudine circiter sesquipedali*, 'that a masonry of broken tiles be laid at the top of the walls below the tiles, for a height of about a foot and a half' – it is apparently in the form of fragments or powder that the secondary use of tiles should be understood here.

3 Lime and mortar

a The manufacture of lime

The invention of the manufacture of a bonding agent by burning rock appears to be as old as the art of the potter; as early as the town of Çatal Hüyük in the sixth millennium BC, plaster rendering decorated the walls, but it is in Egypt of the third millennium that the idea of bonding stones with the aid of gypsum mortar seems to have first appeared. Generally, the use of cements with a base of gypsum or lime was confined to the east for many centuries and it was not until the Hellenistic period that this technique was introduced, still somewhat intermittently, into Greek architecture. Thus at the Hellenistic site of Dura-Europos on the Euphrates blocks, instead of being joined by cramps, were stuck together with gypsum mortar. The Greek theoretician Philo of Byzantium also recommended its use in fortifications.[98]

However, even if the Greeks were familiar with lime, they used it essentially only for stucco, painted rendering and the lining of cisterns. The important contribution made by the Romans was the widespread use of lime for the manufacture of mortar to bond rubble masonry, replacing clay and thus achieving a permanent 'glue' which enabled the use of concrete masonry in the most enormous constructions. This also notably allowed the development and construction of vaults whose spans still hold the record.

Lime (*calx* in Latin from which is derived the word calcium in English) is obtained by the calcination (a word with the same etymology) of limestone at around 1000°C, during which it releases its carbon dioxide. The chemical equation for the calcination of pure limestone can be expressed as follows:

$$CaCO_3 \longrightarrow CO_2 + CaO$$

calcium carbonate   calcination   calcium oxide

The resulting product, an oxide of calcium, is called quicklime; a stone with a crumbly surface which can be hydrated to obtain a bonding agent. This hydration, or slaking, is achieved by immersion and brings about the decomposition of the blocks, which expand, give off a strong heat and form a putty which is the slaked lime. It is this plastic material that is mixed with aggregates[99] to obtain mortar.

The chemical equation for this second transformation can be expressed as:

$$CaO + H_2O \longrightarrow Ca(OH)_2$$

calcium oxide + water   calcium hydroxide

The presence of other chemically reactive substances can modify the slaking process and vary the nature of the finished product. The most significant of these is clay, but these distinctions will be outlined below, in defining the different qualities of lime. It is useful before coming to that to examine the processes used to achieve the correct calcination of limestone, i.e. the structure of lime kilns.

147

148

149

147 Lime-kiln situated right at the foot of the quarry supplying it at Itri, southern Latium.

148 Lime-kiln on the road to Epidaurus (Peloponnese) in the course of being loaded.

149 Clay being mixed for the repair of the interior surface of the kiln on the road to Epidaurus.

150 Construction and loading of the kiln at Foca (Campania); the combustion chamber is built up with the largest blocks.

150

By looking at the installations used by lime burners in different Mediterranean countries today (Italy, Greece, Tunisia and Syria), where the methods of production have hardly changed since antiquity, it is possible to describe with reasonable certainty the same operation in the Roman period.

Three processes can be distinguished: burning in a kiln with a fire at the bottom; burning in a kiln in stacks; and finally burning in the open air.

The lime kiln, as already mentioned, functions just like a pottery kiln. It is a circular construction resembling a truncated cone in section, varying greatly in size, with the kilns observed ranging from 2 to 7m in both diameter and height,[100] the size generally being related to the length of the process. Wherever possible, the kiln is built into a slope in order to take advantage of an efficient constant temperature and easy access to the lower part for the fire and to the upper part for loading and unloading (figs 147, 148). Clayey ground is sought after as, due to the heat, it hardens and provides a solid surround which is very heat-efficient. The internal walls of the cavity are lined with a facing of coursed fire-proof stones bonded with clay or of any available stones protected by a coating of clay mixed with pottery sherds.[101] In a contemporary kiln examined in the Peloponnese (on the road from Nauplia to Epidaurus), the walls were made of stones of sandstone, the surface of which had vitrified, bonded with clay mixed with pottery; this same clay was used to fill in gaps, wall up the openings and carry out all necessary repairs (fig.149).

Access to the lower part of the kiln was through an opening at ground level large enough (1.5m by 2.5m high) to introduce the material for firing, and partly blocked by the same material. In the centre, the lime burner made a circular area forming the base of the hearth. Around this he stacked the stones, leaving an almost oval space forming a dome, the combustion chamber, linked to the outside by a passage with an opening at the door, thus forming a kiln proper in the middle of limestone. In certain contemporary installations, a supply of fresh air can be provided underneath the hearth (as in forges), linked to the outside by a duct passing beneath the construction. Above the combustion chamber, built up with the largest blocks, the lime burner stacks up more stones, finishing with the smallest fragments, which require a lower firing temperature (figs 150, 151). At the top level of the construction two solutions

151 Completion of the loading of the kiln in fig.149.

152 Exterior cone, or *lamia*, of the kiln at Foca, during the burning. The air-vents, or eyes, open at ground level.

are available, according to climate. The first consists of leaving a more or less horizontal area made up of the last layer of stones, which are then rejected when unloading the kiln as they are not burnt properly – this is possible when the summer climate is completely dry (Peleponnese, Turkey, Tunisia). The second solution consists of building at the top of the kiln a closed cone with walls inclined at 45°, called *lamia*[102] in the region of Naples, pierced by lateral openings, the air-vents or eyes, serving as chimneys, and

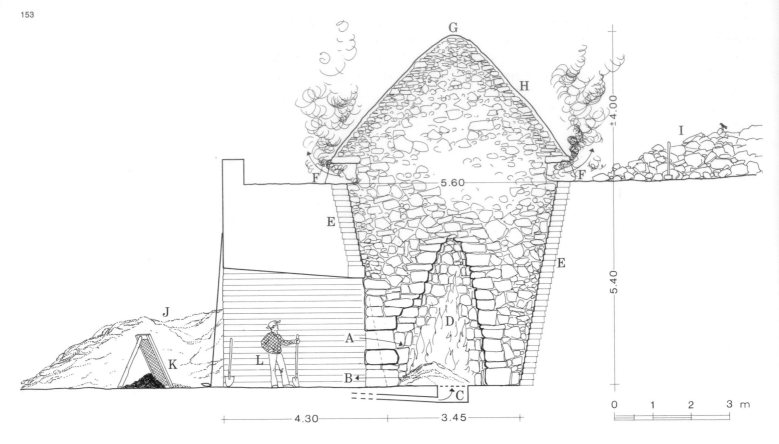

153 Lime-kiln at Foca.
(Campania)

A fuel entrance
B air, removal of the hot ashes
C ventilation
D combustion chamber
E facing of fire-proof bricks
F air-vents (13 in total)
G *lamia*
H lining of fat lime
I supply of stones for burning
J fuel supply
K sieve for hot ashes
L lime burner

covered with a coating of fat lime
(fig.152). This covering has two advantages: in areas where rainfall is relatively abundant (which is the case in
Campania), the water runs off this
steeply sloping wall which has been
hardened by the heat and, in addition,
the waterproofing that it brings to the
interior, even though it reduces the
draught, maintains and even increases
the temperature. Thus the burning
is more even than in kilns open at
the top and it avoids the risk of part
of the load being ruined by a storm,
causing a premature slaking of the upper
layers.

In some kilns in Tunisia (Kairouan,
Nabeul) limestone and bricks are fired
simultaneously. The stones are stacked
up on the internal shelf, with no direct
contact with the flame, and covered
with bricks, protecting the upper half
of the combustion chamber. The
former, requiring more air, thus
occupy the area with the highest
temperature. However, even though

this dual use seems logical, nothing in
documentary sources or in the archaeological record provides evidence to
show whether such a method was practised in antiquity.

When the filling, or in effect the
construction, of the kiln is complete,
the lime burner lights the fire at the
centre of the combustion chamber.
Access for feeding and ventilation is
obtained by one or two openings. The
fuel used has to provide an intense
heat with abundant flame, and must
therefore be fairly small, perfectly dry
and must give off its inflammable gases
quickly, hence the name long-flame
burning. Depending on the season and
the region, pine cones, olive kernels,
cherry stones, plum stones, almond
shells, small bits of wood or even twigs,
brushwood and dried grass can be used
(fig.153).

The fuel is thrown in with a spade or
a fork and sometimes even by hand:
the lime burners of Kairouan throw
handfuls of dried grass almost continu-

ally through an opening made in the middle of the door, which is closed after the fire has taken (fig.154); in Italy, a worm (perpetual screw) replaces the laborious work of feeding by hand. To make sure that the limited space in the combustion chamber does not become obstructed, particularly in kilns without an internal ledge, the fuel is pulled out with a fire-iron (every three hours in the kilns of Campania) before it has completely burnt. It is then sifted to remove the bits of stone that have fallen in the fire and kept as charcoal for domestic use. This is the fuel that was burnt (and still is in rural dwellings) in the braziers found in the private houses in Pompeii, in the kitchen fires and also in the large braziers of the baths of the Samnite period.

The burning continues without interruption for several days, the length of time being related to the size of the kiln, the quality of the fuel and sometimes to the weather conditions. Here, for example, are the times noted for three different workings:

1 Greece
– Kiln on the road from Nauplia to Epidaurus
– situation: set into a slope
– interior lining material: sandstone bonded with clay
– interior diameter at the base: 3.5m
– interior diameter of the upper part: 3m (narrower at the top)
– height: 3.5m
– volume: 29cu.m
– fuel: olive kernels + almond shells
– burning time: 3 full days (72 hours)

2 Tunisia
– Kiln at Kairouan (road to Sbeïtla)
– situation: constructed on flat ground with heating chamber buried and internal ledge
– building material: baked bricks covered on the outside and inside with clay
– interior diameter at the base: 3.6m
– interior diameter of the upper part: 2.2m (narrower at the top)
– height of the combustion chamber: 3.8m
– volume: 25cu.m
– fuel: bushes, dried grass
– burning time: 4 days (96 hours)

3 Italy
– Kiln at Striano (Campania)
– situation: dug into a slope
– interior lining material: fire-proof bricks
– interior diameter at the base: 3.45m

154

154 Mixed kiln in the region of Kairouan, with lime burning in the lower half and brick baking in the upper.

- interior diameter of the upper part 5.6m (wider at the top)
- height: 5.4m + exterior cone 4m
- volume: 120cu.m
- fuel: pine cones or nuts
- burning time: 7 days

It is also worth pointing out that in the case of this last kiln the construction, i.e. charging and setting up the combustion chamber, took 7 days (stopped at night) and the same for taking out the bricks. Thus the complete cycle takes three weeks, which is then interrupted to ensure the supply of limestone and fuel.

Gypsum is burnt in identical kilns but with a much shorter firing time. The temperature needed for the conversion of plaster stone, sulphate of hydrated lime, $CaSo_4(OH)_2$ (which does not react with hydrochloric acid, this being the distinction between plaster and lime), into sulphate of anhydric lime, $CaOSo_3$, is relatively low and generally 48 hours is sufficient time. The stones are then crushed or milled giving a powder which, mixed with water, forms a bonding agent that sets almost instantaneously.

Though Vitruvius is extremely brief on the manufacture of lime (a few lines), another author, Cato, writing some time before – around 160BC, at a time when masonry bonded with lime mortar was becoming widespread –

wrote an agricultural treatise in which he describes in detail the construction of a kiln and the burning of lime:[103]

Make the lime kiln ten feet wide, twenty feet deep, and reduce it to a width of three feet at the top. If you are burning with one stokehole, make a pit inside large enough to hold the ashes, so that it will not be necessary to clear them out. Build the kiln well, and see that a ledge goes round the entire kiln chamber at the bottom. If you burn with two stokeholes, there will be no need for a pit; when it becomes necessary to clear out the ashes, clear through one stokehole while the fire is in the other. Take care not to neglect the fire, but rather keep it going constantly, and be careful not to neglect it at night or at any other time. Charge the kiln with good stone, as white and little mottled as possible. When you build the kiln, let the opening run straight down, and when you have dug deep enough, make a bed for the kiln so as to give it the greatest possible depth and the least exposure to the wind. If you have a spot where you cannot set the kiln deep enough, build up the top with bricks or else with rough stone and clay and daub the top on the outside. If, when you have lit the fire, flame comes out from anywhere except at the round opening at the top, daub it with clay. Ensure that the wind does not approach the stokehole, and be particularly on your guard against the south wind. This shall be the sign when the lime is calcinated: the stones at the top should be burnt, the calcinated stones at the bottom will settle, and a less smoky flame will come out. (Fig. 155)

It will be noticed that the word 'ledge' here most probably refers to the hearth, i.e. the bottom of the kiln and not a perforated plate as in pottery kilns.[104]

The second method of lime burning in a kiln consists of stacking up, above a smaller heating chamber, alternate layers of limestone and slow-burning fuel (charcoal); this is burning with a short flame. This technique means that the temperature of the burning can be raised, and, more importantly, the heat

155

prevailing wind

155 Schematic reconstruction of a lime-kiln according to Cato (XLIV,38).

is distributed better. However, the length of time taken in stacking up and the need to separate and sift through the material after burning have, it seems, made the first method the preferred one for present-day workings. This method, described in the *Encyclopédie,* is not attested to in antiquity.

The third technique, burning in the open air, is a lot more primitive, and is still practised in the Middle East and particularly in the valley of the Euphrates – a region where the use of both lime and plaster goes back to earliest antiquity, due to an abundance of gypsum. On a cleared flat surface, the stones are spread out in a uniform layer, then covered with a thick layer of fuel made up of animal dung. The fire is lit at one end – the side from which the prevailing wind comes – then a slow burning is kept up for several days; after this, the ashes are raked and the calcinated stones are recovered. This method, which only achieves modest temperatures, is only suitable for gypsum, which does not need great heat.

For obvious convenience, lime kilns are best situated near the source of limestone. The transport of the quicklime, i.e. calcinated stones, is easier than that of the quarried rock because of the loss of weight during burning. However, one or more lime-kilns were sometimes erected near important building works, as happened often in the Late Empire in western Europe and in the Byzantine period in the east. The builders of fortifications, basilicas and various buildings fed their kilns directly from the monuments of earlier periods, especially ones which had marble elements.

At Pompeii the extent of the damage caused by the earthquake of the year 62 transformed the city into a building site and, despite the proximity of lime-burners' sites in the area (the Latari Mountains, a limestone chain from Nola to Nuceria), lime was also manufactured on site. This is demonstrated

156

157

156 Temporary lime-kiln situated in a little garden of the House of the Iliac Chapel at Pompeii (I,6,4).(Photo: V. Spinazzola.)

157 Pile of gypsum blocks in the House of the Iliac Chapel.

by the kiln found in the House of the Iliac Chapel (I,6,4), which supplied the needs of different building sites in the area of the via dell'Abbondanza. In this same house, the excavations by Spinazzola[105] also revealed three im-portant stocks of gypsum blocks, intended to be crushed and incorporated in rendering, probably for the manufacture of white stucco (figs 156, 157).

The blocks of limestone are the same size after being taken out of the kiln, but, as already noted, are noticeably lighter;[106] they are then called quick-lime (fig.158). In order to be used as a bonding agent in masonry, these

158　Opening of the kiln at Foca. The mass of quicklime is tackled with a mining iron by the lime burner Giovanni Molisse.

159　Slaking pit of fat lime. Terzigno (Campania).

at least three years. However, given the enormous consumption of material in the Augustan period, such a recommendation may have been overlooked.

The extreme slowness of setting, which is characteristic of pure limestone, was appreciated by the ancient builders as it meant that, due to the plasticity of mortar, there was a slow and progressive settling of the structure as building advanced and an excellent distribution of pressure. The lime burners and builders had noticed that marble fulfilled these characteristics perfectly, as well as white limestone, and so they preferred to use this rock (Vitruvius II,5). In fact they had also noticed that when the stones contained certain impurities which they could not identify, the slaking was less violent, and they thought – wrongly – that this lowered the quality of the lime. Today we know that it is the presence in the limestone of silicate of alumina, i.e. clay, which brings about profound changes affecting the lime both in the slaking and in the crystallizing, or setting.

Depending on the proportion of clay, lime can be divided into two main categories:

1　Non-hydraulic or aerial lime, so-called since the phenomenon of crystallization can take place only in the presence of air (hence the slowness to set and the possibility of storing large quantities of slaked lime). Aerial lime can itself be divided into two qualities:

　a　fat or rich lime,[109] a pure lime, either quicklime or hydrated lime, or containing 0.1 to 1 per cent clay.

　b　lean lime, resulting from calcination and slaking of limestone containing 2 to 8 per cent clay.

2　Hydraulic lime, so-called because it can set in a wet environment: a mortar still fresh, bonded with such lime, can be submerged after moulding and will still harden. This is made with lime-

stones have to be converted by hydration, or slaking. The lime burner generally sells quicklime to the user because of the ease of transport of the stones, and it is the latter who makes a slaking pit on the building site (fig.159). However, as urban building sites do not always have the necessary space, the Roman lime burner could carry out this operation and preserve the fat (or rich) lime – the putty resulting from slaking – in pits covered with earth in which the material kept a long time.[107] Pliny reports[108] that according to an old custom the builders of Rome were advised to use fat lime only after it had been left for

stone containing more than 8 per cent clay.

However, if there is over 20 per cent clay, then limestone is not usable for lime; above 35 per cent the rock becomes extremely soft and brittle and with 50 per cent clay it becomes plastic; it is a limestone marl which can become a clayey marl when the limestone is reduced to less than 30 per cent.

Contemporary analyses[110] indicate that the Roman builders only used non-hydraulic lime. They made their selection by choosing pure rock and testing the burning and slaking to check its quality.

Finally, cement must be considered because of the frequency with which this word occurs in numerous writings on Roman architecture. Etymologically, *caementa* curiously does not refer to the bonding agent, clay, lime or gypsum, but the pebbles that were mixed in at the beginning of making masonry, hence *opus caementicium* defines such a technique; once lime had become the normal bonding agent there must have been first some confusion and then an interchange of terms, cement becoming the mortar, then the bonding agent alone. To keep to the precise terminology defined by modern technology, this word must now be used only to refer to cement which is an artificial mixture of lime with clay and metallic salts (generally iron oxide and oxide of magnesia); such a mixture was clearly unfamiliar to the Romans, so the term cement should not be used at all.

b Mortar

'Fat' lime was only used in its absolutely pure state for the manufacture of lime putty, in fact a white paint, prepared by diluting the basic material with 70 or 80 per cent water and applied to a surface (stone, clay) with a paint brush. Examples can also be found from the Republican period of stone construction bonded with an adhesive (a generic term for bonding agents, plaster or lime and mortar) of pure or almost pure lime (mixed with a small proportion of sand), which is perhaps equivalent to the plaster joints of the Hellenistic period (see, for example, Dura-Europos), this material being also used pure. In fact, the speed with which plaster sets when it is mixed with water causes problems in its preparation, and it is mixed in small quantities at the exact time it is needed.

It is therefore in the form of mortar (from the Latin *mortarium*, initially meaning the builder's mortar-trough, then its contents; the word retains its original meaning when referring to a receptacle for mixing and crushing) that lime was used in masonry, mixed with varying proportions of different substances called aggregates which have the same role as tempering agents in clay. Without these aggregates, lime of any thickness would crack in the process of drying due to shrinkage, losing as a consequence its essential adhesive qualities; moreover, these characteristics would also stop it setting in the core, causing an internal plasticity and leading to a dangerous settling and slipping in the masonry.

The preparation of Roman mortars has always been the object of considerable admiration, often tinged with the reputation of being a secret technique never revealed. In reality, the only buildings with concrete masonry (i.e. bonded with lime mortar) that have survived above ground in a good condition are those that were constructed with great care, using a high-quality lime (of uniform burning) in perfectly measured and mixed mortars and in a stable monument. It is not possible to discuss the innumerable inferior buildings since those remaining in the open air have disappeared due to their vulnerability.

A good idea of the general level of the masonry can be gained by looking at the extreme fragility of many buildings that, when uncovered from their protective burial, immediately pose problems of preservation.[111] The city of Pompeii is informative in this respect: the masonry of the houses, under the high-quality facings, is almost everywhere very inferior, and even in the last phase of construction, the mortar is still earthy and badly prepared.[112]

Standards were, however, laid down, and Vitruvius, who is still the principal source, is quite explicit. The details he gives dismiss the idea of a secret jealously guarded by the Roman builders, and analyses have shown that the recommendations made by the author of the *Ten Books* reflected a practice that was widely carried out.[113]

The mortar recipe he suggests are as follows:

When the lime has been slaked, it is necessary to mix it in the following manner: a part of the lime is put with three parts of quarry sand, or two parts of river or sea sand; this is the correct proportion for this mixture and this will be even better if one adds to the sea sand [that the author considers the most inferior and dangerous to use '. . . because of the salt that dissolves and makes everything crumble . . .' in which he was not mistaken] and the river sand a third part of crushed and broken tiles.

Later on he recommends the use of volcanic sand, pozzolana (*pulvere puteolano*) that he defines:

There is a type of powder to which nature has given an admirable quality; it is found in the country of Baiae [north of the Bay of Naples where the volcanic area of the 'Phlegrean fields' is situated] and in the earth around Mount Vesuvius. This powder mixed with lime and broken stones makes the masonry so hard that it hardens, not only in ordinary buildings but also under water.

This observation is perfectly accurate, though badly explained elsewhere in the text due to the ignorance of this area of chemistry at the time, and underlines the pozzolanic qualities of the aggregate. These qualities, which mean that the mortar is not only water-resistant but can also set in a very damp environment, are due simply to the presence of a large quantity of silicate of alumina. In other words, by adding pozzolana to non-hydraulic lime it is converted to hydraulic lime – the same effect is achieved by mixing crushed pottery with the mortar, a recipe the Romans used for waterproof facings.

The main constituents of ancient mortars can be summed up thus:

bonding agent	aggregate	water
1 part of lime	3 parts of quarry sand (Vitruvius II,V,5)	15 to 20%
1 part of lime	2 parts of river sand (Vitruvius II,V,6)	15 to 20%
1 part of lime	2 parts of river sand 1 part broken tile fragments (Vitruvius II,V,7)	15 to 20%
1 part of lime	2 parts of pozzolana (Vitruvius V,XII,8–9, Maritime Works)	15 to 20%

The proportion of water used in mixing[114] depended both on the climate, i.e. the rate of evaporation, and on use. A mortar intended for use in foundations or infilling is not as wet, because it is less well ventilated, as mortar used for pointing or rendering. Likewise, the amount of sand, and how finely sifted it is, vary according to whether it is mortar for bonding or for the floor, when it is mixed with large grains, or for rendering, when it is made with fine sand.

The quality of mortar depended on the evenness of the burning of the stone, the proportion and nature of the aggregate, and the care taken in mixing (which must be as uniform as possible) the lime with sand and the

160 An amphora with its narrow top intentionally broken, used for carrying lime (Pompeii V,3,4).

161 Pile of lime left in the entrance hall of the House of the Moralist at Pompeii (III,4,2-3).

162 Ancient mixing hoe, found at Pompeii (*rifugio dello scheletro di cavallo*). (Photo: P. Varène.)

163 Preparation of lime mortar or tempering; mixing sand, fat lime and water using a hoe.

broken tile fragments. This operation was carried out close to the building site on an area of beaten earth where the sand was formed into a sort of crater (from 1 to 3m in diameter), into which the pure lime was placed, usually transported from the slaking pit in amphorae which had had their tops broken off,[115] or sometimes in a metal bucket, the imprint of which is still visible in the House of the Iliac Chapel at Pompeii (I,4,4). Here was found, in the middle of the pozzolana, a heap of lime, resembling a rough sand paste, suddenly abandoned, unmixed, at the moment of the eruption of 79. Sometimes, as is also found at Pompeii (the House of the Moralist, the House of Lime, the Villa of the Mysteries), the lime was heaped in a room or a corridor, or any other sheltered place (figs 160, 161).

To make up the mortar, the builder adds water a little at a time and slowly mixes the bonding agent and the aggregates with the aid of a hoe with a long handle (3.5m on average). This is called a *rabot* in French, i.e. a plane,[116] because of the crushing movement carried out with the blade of the tool to get rid of the lumps and to mix in the sand. To assist this function the blade and handle are at an acute angle to each other; the dredge used for stirring the slaking pit

164 Mosaic from the Bardo Museum in Tunis. (*Bottom panel*) A two-wheeled cart, pulled by two mules or horses, is transporting a column. (*Middle panel*) Two masons are preparing mortar. (*Top panel*) An imaginative representation of a workman cutting a column shaft, while the architect, or manager, is watching the operations.

is a hoe with a head at right angles to the long handle. This operation is called mixing or tempering[117] and must be kept up until the mixture has a perfectly uniform appearance and there are no lumps visible (figs 162, 163, 164).

c Methods of construction

Once the mixture is ready, the mortar is carried in a trough to where it is needed. The builder mixes it with stones in the rubble core, thus forming *opus caementicium*, or fills the joints between stones or bricks, or applies it to the wall as a rendering. The slow process of crystallization, or setting, then gets under way, resulting in the concretion of the whole (hence the term concrete masonry) in the form of a crust of calcium carbonate which envelops the grains of sand and broken tile fragments and adheres to the stones or bricks (fig.165).

Separate from the typology of facings, dealt with later, the construc-

tion of a masonry wall[118] can be carried out in various ways, which can be studied by looking at the cross-section of a ruined wall. Whether the walls have the outside appearance of being built of stone or brick, the internal construction is made up of rubble, i.e. stones of all shapes and sizes, debris from stone cutting or fragments of broken tile and bricks, bonded with mortar, contained between the two carefully dressed facings. These facings thus serve as the permanent framework for the material that forms the body of the wall and functions as the supporting element. This is why the elements forming the visible surfaces have so often been removed without affecting the condition of the building. This is what Vitruvius (II,8) calls the *emplecton* (using the Greek term):

'A third way called ἔμπλεκτον, in use among the peasants,[119] is carried out by dressing the facings and filling the middle with mortar and rubble material [*ita uti sunt nata*, just as they are born], putting in here and there bonders [in the form of headers going into the wall]; our builders, who wish to get on quickly, take care with the erection of the facings and strengthen the middle with stone chippings mixed with mortar, thus forming masonry in three layers, two being the facings and one in the middle being the core.' (Fig.166)

This definition of *opus caementicium*, the unshakeable supporting core, should be modified slightly by noting a number of buildings whose walls have the tripartite structure described here, but whose infilling, far from being the essential support, is only made up of an amorphous mixture of rubble roughly bonded with clay (fig.167). This is the case with the majority of buildings at Pompeii where, admittedly, the architecture is mainly of the pre-Imperial period. It is noticeable that well-pointed facings, covered with

165

166

167

168

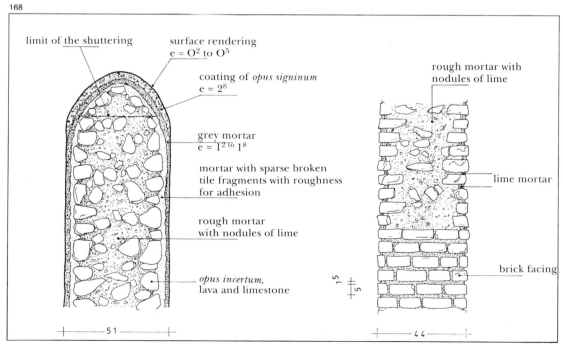

limit of the shuttering

surface rendering
$e = O^2$ to O^5

coating of *opus signinum*
$e = 2^8$

grey mortar
$e = 1^2$ to 1^8

mortar with sparse broken
tile fragments with roughness
for adhesion

rough mortar
with nodules of lime

opus incertum,
lava and limestone

51

rough mortar with
nodules of lime

lime mortar

brick facing

15
5

44

165   A large mausoleum on the *via Appia* which has completely lost its facings and is hollowed out, especially at its base, where rooms of a surrounding medieval construction, since disappeared, were arranged around it. The impressive overhang all the way round the base of the building demonstrates how concrete masonry bonded with lime mortar produced in good-quality buildings a total petrification, that is to say the creation of a monolith capable of defying gravity.

166   Cross-section through masonry of the Later Republican period (walls of Terracina, dating to between 100 and 90 BC) with facings of *opus incertum* and rubble core. Note the horizontal strata of more concentrated lime mortar marking the start and the finish of each shuttering.

167   View of the core of a wall faced with brick, from the last period of Pompeii (site of the Central Baths). Note the scattering of nodules of limestone in the middle of the earthy mortar.

168   Masonry at Pompeii. (*Left*) Via dei Sepolcri, tomb 20 South. (*Right*) Central Baths, *apodyterium*.

the rendering to fall off and letting the wet in (fig.168).

In walls of medium thickness the mixture of mortar with stone is relatively uniform, as the builder could distribute the rubble in the bonding agent easily and by hand (fig.169). When the construction was more important, he systematically alternated one course of mortar and one course of stone, which was then tamped to ensure bonding (fig.170). The regular strata making up these successive layers of material can be seen on the inside of walls; such shuttering lines, marking each stage in the work of putting up the wall, are clearly visible at Pompeii, notably in II,1,2, VI,14,44 and VIII,7,22, where it is also noticeable that the strata tend to be only roughly horizontal.

Occasionally a layer of pure lime, recognizable by the white line it makes, covered each stage of the work. Evidence of this is easy to find in the funerary monuments of the *via Appia* or the *via Latina*, which no longer have their facings (figs 171, 172). In the course of the tamping operations, the builders probably took the precaution of clamping the building within a framework in order to hold up the facings which had not yet totally set. This parallels the use of shuttering in the course of building walls of clay. However, as using such a framework

a triple rendering of excellent quality, provide a rigid and waterproof framework for poor internal masonry. It only collapses when the roof is lost, causing

was both complex and expensive, it seems that the Roman builders limited the system of tamping the rubble infilling to either structures with very thick walls contained by stone facings, or multi-coursed brick facings, as their mass enabled them to resist the impact and pressure of tamping operations.

The resulting concretion, whatever the method of application, had the appearance of concrete (in French *béton*, from Latin *bitumen*[120]) and can be separated into three elements:

1 The bonding agent, in the form of lime, mixed with its aggregate before application and constituting the mortar.
2 Pebbles, stones or broken fragments of pottery introduced into the mortar at the time of construction.
3 Facings made up of finely dressed material, which might in turn receive a surface rendering.

There is, however, a distinction to be made between the concrete of Roman constructions and modern concrete, based on its preparation. The mortar and pebbles of Roman concrete are mixed in the wall, while modern concrete is a mixture of mortar and pebbles prepared in advance that can be put into the framework without then adding any other material.

Certain kinds of Roman material can, however, be compared to modern products, namely the mortars in floorings or in the covering of vaults, which

173

contain quite large fragments of pottery and pebbles pre-mixed with lime. They make an extremely solid rendering, as is proved by the resistance to wear shown by the pavements of this type at Pompeii and by the surfacing of numerous vaults and domes not protected by tile roofs. (fig.173).

d Origins

The date the Romans introduced lime mortar into their architecture has already been mentioned briefly and can be put at the end of the third century BC, though it is understandably difficult to be more precise. The eastern or Hellenistic influences seem to have first affected southern and central Italy, more particularly Campania and Latium, two regions where there is not only limestone suitable for the preparation of lime but also abundant pozzolana for the manufacture of the best mortar. In the documentary sources, Cato, whose description of a lime-kiln has already been quoted, establishes this technique around 160BC,[121] recommending building *ex calce et caementis*, as does Varro[122] after him. These of course were followed by Vitruvius, Pliny and, in the fourth century, Palladius, the author also of a *De re rustica* that was widely distributed in the Middle Ages. Independently of these authors, some inscriptions, admittedly rather few, mention construction bonded with lime mortar, such as the text at Pozzuoli[123] referring to a building as an *opus structile* composed of *calx* mixed with *caementa*, or the inscription on the wall of the Temple of Silvanus at Philippi[124] (the Roman colony of Augusta Iulia Philippi in Macedonia) mentioning the temple built of *opus caementic(ium)*.

Though funerary inscriptions mentioning masons and various builders are numerous, lime burners, more

169 Wall faced with brick from a tomb on the Isola Sacra, Ostia. The rubble core is applied in a mass, mixing stones and broken bits of brick with the mortar.

170 Temple of Palestrina (end of the second century BC), faced with *opus incertum* with engaged stone (travertine) columns. The core alternates layers of mortar and layers of stones, the tamping of which has made an accentuated curve in the line of the masonry.

171 Two tombs on the *via Appia* with facings that have been lost; the core of *opus caementicium* is stratified into successive stages of work, corresponding to the regular quantities of stones and mortar applied between the facings forming the framework. This technique is identical to that of shutterings used in clay construction.

172 Villa dei Sette Bassi on the *via Latina*. Cross-section of a wall faced with *opus mixtum* with a core alternating a bed of mortar and a row of stones. It will be noticed that the horizontal layers of bricks do not go all the way through the wall (middle of the second century AD).

173 Concrete made up of terracotta sherds and broken pieces of pozzolana mixed with mortar. Arch of a tomb on the Isola Sacra in Ostia.

modest artisans comparable to quarrymen or woodmen, are hardly mentioned other than by the edict of Theodosius in the year 438,[125] referring to the guilds of this trade that had already existed for several centuries.

Evidence for the earliest use of masonry is found in Campania and more especially Pompeii. This city preserves an architecture in large part from the Samnite period, the structure of which, despite the destruction and the repairs following the earthquake of the year 62, has survived in its original form. In the oldest houses the side walls and the internal partitions (the façades being decorative stonework made of limestone or tufa) are made of stone masonry or of *opus africanum*, with rubble infilling and bonded with mortar. The mortar has remained earthy but contains nodules of lime, evidence of its use but also of the bad preparation of the material.[126] Examples are: the House of the Surgeon (end of the fourth century BC), the House of Sallust (third century BC), the House of the Menander (third century BC), the House of the Faun II (beginning of the second century BC), the House of the Centenary (middle of the second century BC), to name a few.

The large monuments erected at the end of the independence of the city, such as the Temple of Jupiter built around 150BC, the Stabian Baths rebuilt at the end of the second century BC, and the great basilica of the forum, dating from 120BC, are of masonry bonded with mortar of an excellent quality, notably in the brick columns of the basilica.

Rome, despite the profound upheavals of its townscape, still preserves the traces of masonry architecture of the Republican period.[128] The archaeological remains, confirmed by written sources, support the theory that *opus caementicium*, masonry bonded with lime mortar, was in use there at least by the end of the third century BC; the Temple of Magna Mater on the Palatine,[129] consecrated in 204BC, is the first certain example. Begun a short time later, apparently around 193BC on the initiative of the aediles M. Aemilius Lepidus and M. Aemilius Paulus, the great warehouses of the emporium, the port of Rome, known as the *Porticus Aemilia*, were completed in 174BC by the Censor Q. Fulvius Flaccus and A. Postumus Albinus.[130] The resilience of their masonry faced with *opus incertum* attests to the practical accomplishment of this technique.

It is interesting to note that the method of construction which used not large blocks of dressed stone (though it was still in use for the noble parts of the architecture) but instead a considerable quantity of tiny fragments of roughly dressed stone, developed at the time when Italy, with the victorious campaigns against the Carthaginians (at the end of the second and third Punic Wars), against the Greeks (victories over Philip V in 197BC, over Antiochos III in 190, again over the Macedonians in 146) and against Spain (the victory of Numantia in 133), benefited from the contribution of slave labour in large numbers. This was a labour force that could quickly be detailed to work on the preparation of building materials, especially extracting and dressing stone, tasks that only needed a minimum of training. Likewise, a large number of unskilled labourers could be put to work on a building site under a foreman directing the operation. Under the Romans, with this strict organization of tasks based on the use of prefabricated materials adaptable to all construction whatever their size or purpose (this also goes for the use of brick), architecture, until then reserved essentially for temples and fortifications, became a universal art form. Moreover, completion times were to become remarkably fast. An idea of the time scale sometimes necessary for the erection of large temples

174

175

in dressed stone is given by the construction of the Great Temple of Apollo at Didyma which was started, on the initiative of Alexander, in 332BC. Work was carried on there until the time of Hadrian (around AD130), in other words for four and a half centuries, and the building was abandoned unfinished.[131] These time scales are explained by the fact that on such a monument every stone had its special place and a number of them were very richly decorated. In comparison to this permanent building site, the construction of the second Pantheon and its remarkable dome was carried out between 118 and 125,[132] in other words just seven years; and the sumptuous Baths of Caracalla, occupying a space measuring 330 by 400m, were erected in just five years, from 212 to 217[133] (figs 174, 175).

The standardization of mass-produced building materials is one of the secrets of this incredible speed of operation. However, it is appropriate to mention here also the impressive planning of the building site and the complete docility of the workforce, most certainly broken in to, rather than trained for, the carrying out of defined and simple tasks.

e Scaffolding

One of the many advantages of this type of masonry, and an important

one, lies in the small size of the stones and the bricks used. This simplifies both the transport from the quarry or place of manufacture (by *vecturarii*, land routes, or *lenuncularii*, river routes), and the lifting of the material to the level for laying. For buildings of modest size, the use of lifting machines was unnecessary, as the builders, *structores*, were able to raise the stones on men's backs, in hods or baskets, and the mortar was raised directly in a trough (figs 176, 177). For a building with storeys, a simple pulley was enough to hoist weights of 10 to 30kg without difficulty.

In constructions of large stone blocks workmen could move, work and set down material on the wall itself, with access ladders serving their needs; builders of masonry would have had some difficulty working like this. They therefore erected, parallel to the construction, temporary wooden structures with levels to work from; these are the *machinae scansoriae* or scaffolding. (These were at first called in French *chaufauds*, from the Latin *catafalcum*.[134]) It is worth remembering that in areas where wood was scarce, access to the

174 The Temple of Apollo at Didyma, near Miletus, despite its considerable size (118 x 60m), has an optical correction curve. This perfectionism led to its remaining unfinished after more than four and a half centuries of frequently interrupted construction work (from 332BC to AD 130).

175 The Baths of Caracalla in Rome, under construction for five years, from 212 to 217.

176 Carrying bricks: Egypt, twentieth century.

176

177

178

177 Legionaries building a fortification with unbaked bricks. Trajan's Column.

178 Relief from the Musée de Sens, showing masons and a painter applying a rendering using trestle scaffolding. (Length: 101cm; height: 85cm.)

179 Trestle scaffolding used for low masonry, rendering and painting.

working level was frequently provided by piling up unbaked bricks, which also served as supply ramps, as was the custom in Egypt up until the Roman period.

In the case of both large stone construction and masonry, scaffolding remained a light structure, simply intended to support the workmen,

their tools and small-size material; neither lifting machines nor heavy blocks could be placed on it. The wood used in its construction was therefore fairly small in section: poles, logs and planks. A distinction should be made between scaffolding and props and formwork intended to support the entire weight of the construction and consequently made of wooden beams of considerable size.

The simplest form of scaffolding was mobile trestle scaffolding,[135] used by builders, plasterers and painters, especially for interior work, as illustrated on a stele, unfortunately in very bad state of repair, preserved in the Museum of Sens, with a scene of wall-painting (figs 178, 179). Four figures appear on this relief: at the bottom right a mason is mixing mortar on the ground; behind him is the scaffolding made up of a plank resting on three trestles, accessible via a short ladder and supporting two men, one on the right applying the final layer of mortar with a plaster float, and the other one painting the decoration with a paint brush. On the left of the scene, a seated man, probably the architect, is consulting a document.

As soon as the construction exceeded the height accessible with simple trestles, roughly 3m, scaffolding of several levels was required, which could be built either freestanding or leaning against the building. Freestanding scaffolding had to support itself and of

179

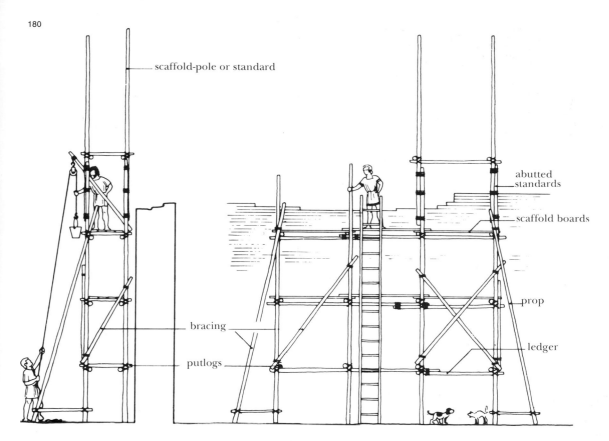

necessity rested on the ground; depending on the thickness of the wall it was put up on one or both sides. From independent scaffolding the work of dressing, moulding and sculpting was carried out, as well as the finishing of stone façades, because of the impossibility of inserting anchoring pieces into this type of wall (fig.180).

The vertical supports were long pieces of wood simply stripped and retaining their natural shape, called standards, fixed to the ground by a socket or a sole-plate made of mortar. When the height of the building demanded it, these pieces were extended by other scaffolding poles fixed together to make the required length and firmly tied. At regular heights, depending on the requirements of the work, horizontal pieces joined two scaffolding poles to one another; the longitudinal pieces (parallel to the wall) are the ledgers; the ones at right angles and supporting the boards, are the putlogs or putlocks. The whole thing was made stable by

the diagonal pieces of bracing, placed obliquely or in a Saint Andrew's cross, and by sloping props resting on the ground.

This type of scaffolding leaves no physical trace, and so the only source of evidence is painted and sculpted

180   Free-standing scaffolding.

181   Scaffolding used in the construction of a brick building. All the mason's operations and materials are shown in this painting: mixing mortar, carrying of materials and construction of the wall. Tomb of Trebius Justus on the *via Latina*.

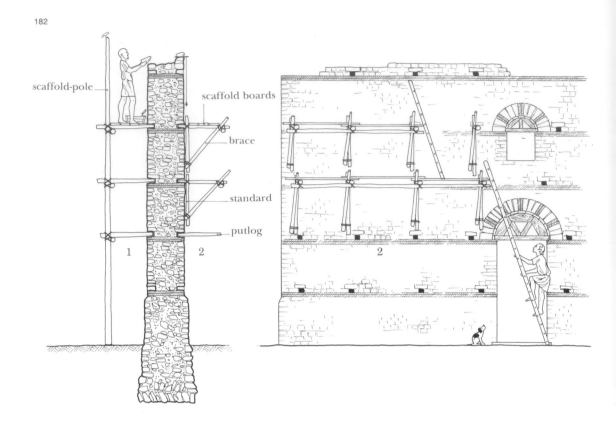

182

scaffold-pole

scaffold boards

brace

standard

putlog

1   2

2

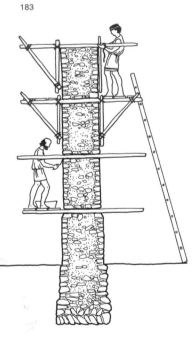

183

184

182   1   Socketed scaffolding with a row of standards.
      2   Socketed cantilever scaffolding.

183   Socketed scaffolding with transverse putlogs.

184   Transverse putlog holes in the aqueduct of the villa dei Sette Bassi (*via Latina*; *c*.140).

representations. The best example is undoubtedly the painting recovered from the tomb of Trebius Justus at the start of the *via Latina* in Rome.[136] This extremely interesting document, occupying the tympanum of a vault, shows five men working on the construction of a brick building (fig.181). On the ground and on the right, as on the Sens relief, a man with a hoe is busy mixing mortar that he is then going to put into a trough placed beside him on a stand. Two workmen are carrying material on their shoulders; the first, on the ground, has bricks in a basket, the second, on a ladder, a trough of mortar. Finally, on the scaffolding, whose standards and ledgers, wind-braces and boards are distinguishable, two masons on either side of the wall (only the scaffolding poles sticking above the building can be seen of the scaffolding on the other side) are laying the bricks and covering them with mortar with their trowels.

To economise on wood, while still guaranteeing complete stability to the arrangement, the Roman builders frequently used socketed scaffolding, which replaced the support of the poles with the masonry itself. As they progressed up the wall, the workmen carefully made a series of holes covered by a small lintel, aligned at the same horizontal level and in which they placed the ends of the putlogs. If there was a row of scaffolding poles to ensure the support of the outer end of the putlogs, they could be put in place straight away, a technique still in use today in traditional Italian masonry; but to do away with the poles completely, a certain height of masonry had to cover the supporting level in order to maintain the embedding of the putlog holes.[137] In this type of scaffolding, called cantilever scaffolding, the putlogs could go straight through the wall and support the floor symmetrically on either side.[138] To increase rigidity and solidity, the putlogs of cantilever scaf-

folding had to be supported on the facing by a vertical scaffolding pole and a diagonal brace (figs 182, 183, 184).

The presence of a little lintel above each putlog hole was designed to prevent the masonry settling over the pieces of wood so they could be pulled out at the end of construction. However, if the putlogs could not be removed they could be sawn flush with

185

186

185 Putlog holes in a wall of *opus incertum*. Pompeii VI,7,22; first century.

186 Putlog holes in a line above a course of bricks, each one with a small lintel over it. Walls of Beauvais, end of the third century.

the masonry and remained stuck there, serving as a cross pier attaching the facings to the infilling.

Whereas in facings of unshaped stones or regular courses, the putlog socket-holes did not present any practical or aesthetic problem (fig.185), masonry of brick or reticulate decoration[139] lent itself less well to these holes. In such cases it was more usual to use independent scaffolding. Nevertheless, traces of putlog holes can sometimes be found; with brick it was

187

188

187 Putlog holes in a brick wall. Pompeii VII,4,24; *c*.70.

188 Wall of reticulate construction, in which can be seen the putlog holes of two levels of scaffolding, each with a small lintel. Pompeii VIII,2,30; *c*.70.

189 Detail of a particularly carefully made putlog hole in a fine reticulate facing. Pompeii VIII,2,14, *c*.70.

190 Construction of a wall – summary of the parts of the building site:
1 foundation trench
2 preparation of mortar
3 socketed scaffolding with standards
4 cantilever scaffolding.

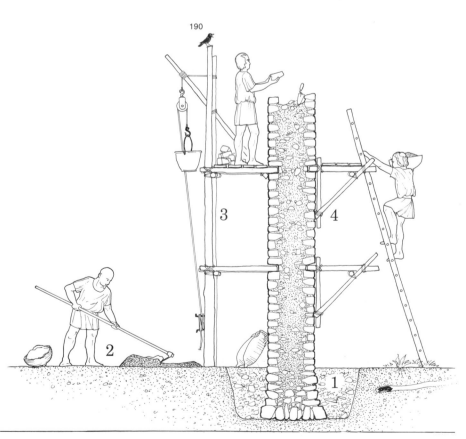

190

189

sufficient to break the material to make holes at the required distances; in reticulated facings, the hole retains the form of a diamond or sometimes an inverted triangle topped by a small relieving arch (figs 186, 187, 188, 189, 190).

4 Wood

a Felling

Wood must be cut between the beginning of autumn and the period before the wind Favonius starts to blow; indeed, in spring the trees bring forth the leaves and the fruit that they produce each year to which they devote all their substance. Thus, the humidity filling them over time makes them porous and weak, as pregnant women are considered not to be in good health, which means that one does not guarantee as healthy those [slaves] sold when they are pregnant.[140]

Thus, using an anthropomorphic metaphor, Vitruvius, to whom this didactic behaviour was natural, specified and justified the most propitious times of year for cutting wood.[141] In theory, it is advisable to cut trees during the winter period, when most of the sap has gone and the fibres have contracted. In practice, necessity often leads to felling at other times of the year, the drying-out process taking place afterwards; for certain purposes, such as in the manufacture of scaffolding, centrings or wooden bridges, no particular preparation is needed.

Vitruvius enumerates the principal species used in architecture (II,9) then found in the peninsula, before it lost its forest cover, and elucidates their relative qualities with explanations that are both colourful and imaginative: '. . . fir [*abies*][142] which contains a lot of air and fire and little water and soil, because of the elements which it is made up of, does not weigh very

much'. This is not the place for an exhaustive list, based on the age-old use of building timber, of the different species and their mechanical qualities; it is sufficient to mention some data established in modern times confirming both the use and the durability of the most common woods. Thus it has been known for centuries that oak is in all respects the wood with the best qualities of strength and longevity, but it is also very slow-growing. This slowness is the reason for its hardness, since the age rings are very thin and close together, producing a fine grain not found in trees of rapid growth such as poplar or coniferous trees.

The optimum age for felling is also related to the speed of growth; whereas a poplar can be cut down after 30 years and a pine at 80, it is necessary to wait for the oak to reach an age of 200 years before it can be cut down. This difference is also noticeable in a comparison of densities:[143]

green oak (*Yeuse*)	1.00
(unsuitable for building because of its small size)	
pedunculate oak (*Quercus* and *Quercus robur*)	0.70–.90
chestnut (*Castanea*)	0.70
ash (*Fraxinus*)	0.65
elm (*Ulmus*)	0.65
beech (*Fagus*)	0.60
fir (*Abies*)	0.50
poplar (*Populus*)	0.45

Depending on where they are used, that is their exposure to air and moisture, woods have a very varied durability:

1 In contact with the ground:

oak, chestnut, elm	10 years
fir, poplar	3-4 years

2 With no contact with the ground, exposed:

oak, chestnut, elm	60-120 years
pine	40-80 years
fir	30-50 years
poplar	less than 30 years

191 Two felling axes for hard wood (dating to the beginning of the twentieth century; France). (*Right*) Total length: 104cm; length of blade: 36.5cm. (*Left*) Total length: 90cm; length of blade: 25.5cm.

192 Felling axe on the Gallo-Roman relief of a tool merchant, found at Saint-Ambroix (Cher).

193 Roman engineers cutting down trees to construct an entrenchment camp; Trajan's Column.

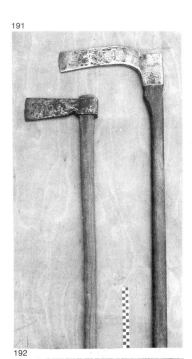

3 With no contact with the ground, covered:

oak, chestnut, elm	200 years or more
pine	150 years
fir	50 years or more
poplar	50 years

4 Timbers in dry, ventilated locations: The majority of species will last 500 years; oak and chestnut last a lot longer.

5 Wood totally immersed in fresh water: Almost unlimited preservation (lake sites)

The tools of the wood-cutter, the *lignarius*, were limited to three types: axes, wedges and saws.

The axe (*ascia, dolabra*) is an essential tool since it can generally be used for the whole job of felling;[144] it is traditionally called the felling axe and has edges that are almost parallel, relatively narrow, thick on the handle side, with a head often forming practically a hammer (when it is called a splitting axe or cleaver).[145] It is used to cut the tree trunk by attacking the grain almost at right angles, that is following the greatest resistance, and

194

194 Cutting down a tree with a
felling axe, two-handed cross-cut
saw and wedges.

195 Splitting axe or cleaver and
wedges, Vosges Mountains,
twentieth century.

196 Ancient wedges; length: 17
and 14cm. (Musée de Sens.)

195

196

this is why it is swung with great force against the wood (figs 191, 192).

Trajan's Column has a number of representations of legionaries cutting down trees for building fortifications, bridges or siege engines; for this they are using a special axe, the *upupa* which has a cutting edge for felling and chopping on one side and on the other a pick-type head for sticking in the ground and for moving logs (fig.193).

The tree trunk is struck on opposite sides, the largest cut determining the direction of fall, chosen in advance. In addition, to prevent the fibres tearing too much when the tree falls, a small circular groove is made to join the two main cuts. This work must, of course, be done as close as possible to the roots, to avoid wasting the wood at the base of the tree where the trunk is thickest. For this reason wood-cutters sometimes dig down into the humus in broad-leaved forests to get to the top of the roots.

When the tree has a uniform diameter the wood-cutter, after beginning with the axe, can, with the aid of an assistant, use a saw[146] with a long free blade and a handle at each end, the two-man cross-cut saw (figs 194 and 201). To prevent the weight of the timber impeding the blade, wedges (*cunei*) are inserted into the split behind it and, when the cut is judged sufficient, they are rammed in, causing the trunk to fall (figs 195, 196).

When the forest is dense falling trees may be caught up by their own

197 Funerary stele of a carpenter. The artisan is leaning on a bill-hook for limbing (taking off branches) and is holding an adze in his right hand. (Musée du Berry at Bourges.)

198 Gallo-Roman billhook for taking off branches; length: 22cm. (Musée de Sens.)

199 Modern billhook. Total length including handle: 1.5m; length of blade: 30cm.

branches and those of neighbouring trees, and so the wood-cutter has to climb along the trunk and clear the branches. To do this he uses a billhook (*sarpa*) (figs 197, 198, 199), a small axe or a small handsaw (fig.202); sometimes it is even necessary to cut off the top of a tree in danger of breaking during its fall.

b Cutting the wood up

Once the tree has been cut down and had its branches lopped off, it is called undressed timber or a log;[147] it is usually in this form that the wood left the forest. It was first dragged along the ground by beasts of burden, mules or oxen, driven by the *muliones* or the *iumentarii*, or simply pulled by men (fig.200) as illustrated in the so-called relief of the 'dendrophores' preserved in the Archaeological Museum at Bordeaux, and then loaded on carts to be taken to the squarer, the *dolabrarius*, working with an axe, or the sawyer. Whenever a river network allowed, the logs were transported by floating. The guild of the *caudicarii* or the *ratiarii* were wood raftsmen, who transported rafts of timber as far as the town where the wood was to be sold. This mode of transport was infinitely quicker and more efficient than land transport and did not require any other motor power than that of the permanently available natural current. In many European countries it was not until the appearance of the railway that this method of transport fell into disuse; in the United States and Canada it still remains common. The branches left after the felling were divided into two: the twigs and smaller branches were chopped for kindling (ideal fuel for the baker), while the larger ones were cut up into smaller logs, sold just as they were or converted into charcoal for cooking, domestic heating or the baths.

200

Wood, even when it is cut in winter and especially when it is green, contains a certain amount of sap which can still affect the timber long after use. To get this sap out of the fibres, the timber is left to season in the open air, so that the rain saturates it, penetrates the material and mixes with the thick sap it contains, making it more fluid. The amount of saturation affects the ensuing evaporation of the mixture, which is made easier if the wood has been well washed. Hard woods can take several years to season, especially oak, which is subject to considerable shrinkage and, also, if it is badly dried, leaks tannin juice that blackens the supporting masonry. Therefore transport by, and even storage in, water greatly helps the removal of the sap.

Depending on its intended use, timber is subjected to a series of preparations, generally involving three trades: the wood-cutter, the squarer or sawyer and the carpenter or joiner; but the user may also buy timber directly and carry out the various preparatory tasks.

The first operation is to cut the log into the lengths required for use. When this job is done with the felling axe, a large amount of wood is lost because a section has to be chopped out first to open an angle of strike

before cutting can proceed. Therefore, a saw is always preferable. If timbers have a small diameter (less than one foot), or if they are branches, a framesaw can be used. This is primarily a carpenter's or joiner's tool, and its use is limited by the obstacle of the frame. Generally the cross-cut saw, used also for felling, is preferable; its blade, 1 to 2m long, is suitable for all cross-sawing. Up to now such saws have not been found complete but there are fragments of blades (Museum of Saint-Germain-en-Laye) and some excellent illustrations. A relief, decorating a little altar probably belonging to a guild, presented to the Capitoline Museum,[148] shows a framesaw together with a cross-

200 Transport of a log using ropes. Relief of the 'Dendrophores' (Archaeological Museum, Bordeaux.)

201 Ancient saw blades from the Musée des Antiquités Nationales at Saint-Germain-en-Laye. (*Top*) Two fragments from a cutting-up saw or a two-handed cross-cut saw (Compiègne). (*Bottom*) Two blades from small single-handled saws (tumulus of Celles and Compiègne).

201

202

202 Small handsaw for limbing or cutting up small pieces of wood (early twentieth century). Compare with the two blades at the bottom of fig.201.

203 Representation of various tools on a small altar: frame saw; two-handed cross-cut saw; two-headed axe; pick-axe; adze. Helmets are also depicted and (*top*) objects belonging to the *sacrificator*. (Capitol Museum.)

204 Stele of the entrepreneur Gaius. The artisan is holding a trowel and a rule; on his right can be seen an adze and a frame-saw. (Musée Rolin at Autun.)

205 Carpenters at work in their workshop; on the wall are suspended a frame-saw and calipers. (Directorate of Antiquities of the City of Rome.)

204

0   30 cm

cut saw and various faithfully reproduced instruments, among them pick-axes and legionaries' helmets; other examples are found on the funerary relief of an artisan preserved at the Museum of Autun and in the representation of a woodworker's workshop preserved at the Directorate of Antiquities in Rome (figs 201, 202, 203, 204, 205).

The undressed timber, whole or cut up into several smaller logs (figs 206, 207), is then stripped of its bark. This debarking is carried out with a squaring axe or, better still, with a barking knife, which consists of a

205

203

narrow metal head attached to the end of a long handle, and whose cutting edge is inclined.[149] The blade is inserted under the bark at one end and, by pushing the tool with short sharp movements, the bark is removed in strips without damaging the wood (figs 208, 209).

In many buildings the whole trunk and the smaller logs can be used in their natural shape. This gives an optimum use of the material, with all the grain taking the strain of bending, if it is a cross-beam, or of compression if it is an upright. For aesthetic and practical reasons, especially in timber framing, it is generally necessary to give the pieces of wood a square or rectangular outline, transforming them into more or less regular long blocks; this is called squaring.

The piece of wood to be squared is placed on two cross-beams off the floor to allow greater freedom of movement and to avoid hitting the floor. The operation is carried out from the side with a squaring axe or broad axe (in French *doloire* from Latin *dolabra*, axe),[150] very different in shape from the felling axe. The action is not

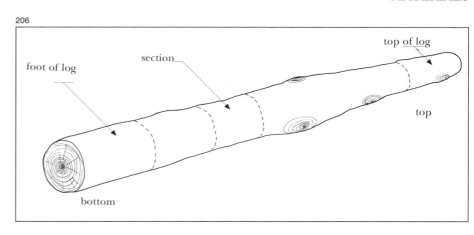

206

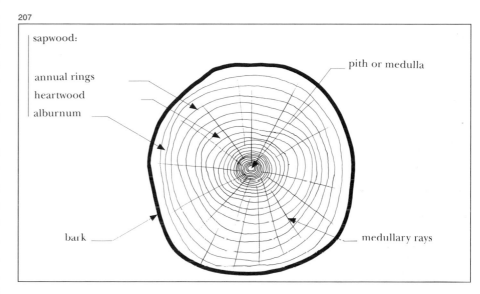

207

208

209

206 A cut log. When the trunk has been cut down, its branches and its top lopped and it has been stripped of its bark, it is called a cropped log; by cutting it up it is divided into small logs.

207 Section through a log.

208 Modern barking knife, Vosges Mountains.

209 Stripping the bark off a log.

210 Two squaring axes (early twentieth century, France). (*Right*) Total length: 97cm; length of blade: 31.5cm. (*Left*) Total length: 64cm; length of blade: 20cm.

211 Four ancient axes. (*Middle left*) a felling axe; (*top and bottom*) two squaring axes; (*middle right*) broad axe with blade off-set to the left. (Musée des Antiquités Nationales at St Germain-en-Laye.)

212 Squaring a piece of wood on site with a broad axe.

213 Modern framed pit-saw, l.2m (Haute-Savoie).

one of cutting across the grain but of virtually separating it by an oblique stroke. The blade must therefore be very fine and wide and does not need to be applied with force. Squaring axes from the Roman period are among the most beautiful tool shapes produced by the hands of blacksmiths and tool-makers (figs 210, 211, 212).

Some squaring axes, designed for finishing a wooden framework and used very close to the wood, have a blade with a cutting edge horizontally off-set, so that the hands holding the tool do not scrape the surface. An example preserved in the Museum of Saint-Germain-en-Laye demonstrates yet again the remarkable continuity of shape in manual tools, in spite of, or perhaps because of, the great number of specialized implements and local traditions passed on by generations of artisans carefully making the most efficient tool.[151]

When not constrained by aesthetic considerations, the carpenter preferred to produce beams and pieces of timber by squaring with an axe rather than the pit-saw. In the former operation the cutting edge naturally follows the direction of the fibres without cutting them, thus it respects the grain of the finished piece; whereas with a straight saw the natural twists and turns are not respected, and it is therefore advisable to use considerably larger sections.

Sawing, however, becomes more effective when dividing a length of timber into several pieces, sometimes with the help of wedges, especially when cutting planks. The framed pit-saw has to divide considerable lengths along a dead straight line and has to have a blade that is at the same time

214

214 Procession of a guild of carpenters carrying effigies of men using a saw and a workman at his bench in a painting from Pompeii.

free but under tension.[152] The result is an enormous rectangular framework, with the blade fixed in the middle and held in place by wedges to prevent it wavering and endangering the regularity of the sawing line (fig.213). The piece of wood is solidly secured on a high bench and one sawyer takes up position there, while another one, or two, as the lower work is more difficult, position themselves underneath, each one holding the respective cross-piece of the framework. Then, following the guideline drawn on the top of the piece of wood, the sawmen slowly proceed, cutting into the wood with a downward movement until the middle of the length is reached. The timber is then turned over to tackle it from its other end, until the sawing lines meet. To simplify the work of turning it over, a lengthy and dangerous job in the case of large pieces of wood, all the lengthways cuts are carried out on the same half (at least four for a beam) before the changeover, which calls for very great skill in the use of the blade.

When the Romans were able to replace men by machines, something which was not possible for example for stone-cutting or brick-making, they showed great ingenuity, as demonstrated by their powerful lifting machines. The question can therefore be asked whether they used hydraulic power for sawing – an extremely laborious and lengthy job – as they did to drive machines for lifting water and millstones for grinding wheat and pressing olives.[153] No Latin text mentions such an application; so perhaps the Romans, though masters of this source of energy, never extended it to wood sawing. The oldest surviving evidence of such an application is a drawing by Villard de Honnecourt (thirteenth century) showing a hydraulic saw, the vertical movement of

216

215

types of saws, has not survived intact and the apparent difference in blades, or fragments of blades, is illusory, except for the small blade handsaws. Once again the pictorial record supplies most information, whether in the form of paintings, such as the scene of a procession of the guild of carpenters at Pompeii, or of funerary reliefs, such as the relief in the Museum of Lorraine discovered at Deneuvre, or the relief of the joiner's

217

218

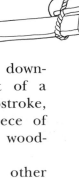

215 Very rustic relief from the Musée Lorrain at Nancy, showing men using a pit-saw.

216 Another scene in a carpenter's workshop placed under the protection of Minerva (*left*); on the wall, a pit-saw and a shoulder square, on the ground a maul.

217 Men using a pit-saw in a workshop (Florence). Drawing from a relief. (Antichi Monumenti, Florence, 1810, pl.XI; JPA.)

218 Pit-sawing a log attached to a support. For long pieces the support is horizontal and rests on two benches.

which is brought about, on the downward stroke, by the camshaft of a waterwheel and, on the upstroke, by the elasticity of a long piece of wood (cf. a cabinet-maker's wood-turning lathe).

The framed pit-saw, as with other

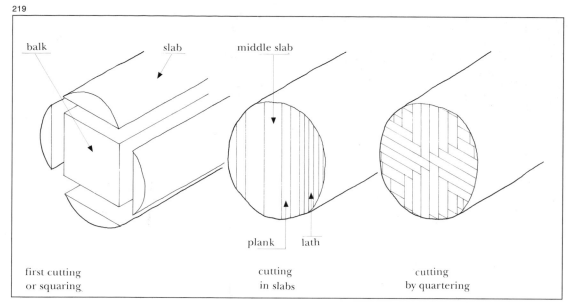

219

balk   slab   middle slab

plank | lath

first cutting
or squaring

cutting
in slabs

cutting
by quartering

219 Different wood cuts.

220 Representation of an adze
on the side face of a funerary
stele. Length: 33.5cm. (Musée de
Sens.)

221 Ancient adze. Length of
blade: 13cm. (Musée de Sens.)

222 Modern adze (Greece).
Total length: 38cm; length of
blade: 13.5cm.

220

221

workshop in Rome[154] (figs 214, 215, 216, 217, 218, 219). This last example also provides useful details about another type of frame saw, though smaller in size, for cutting the wood into small pieces.

To finish off the pieces for use in roof timbering and carpentry and to joint them, a number of more specialized tools are needed, given the accuracy called for. Finishing touches to the surfaces are carried out with the adze (the *ascia* so frequently shown on funerary stones) which, often with a hammer-head, is the all-purpose instrument for carpenters, the *fabri tignarii*,[155] and is always by their side (figs 220, 221, 222, 223). The fine shaping of the most carefully executed surfaces is carried out with the plane,[156] of a form identical to modern-day

examples,[157] as is proved by the plane recovered at Pompeii, or the reliefs of Aquila and Syracuse[158] (fig.224). It can be used for very precise joinery wherever it is necessary to fit together fixed or moving pieces with a delicacy of execution. The same work can be carried out, but in a much less precise manner, using the drawing knife (or

222

225

223

224

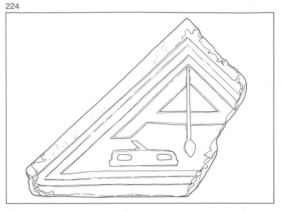

226

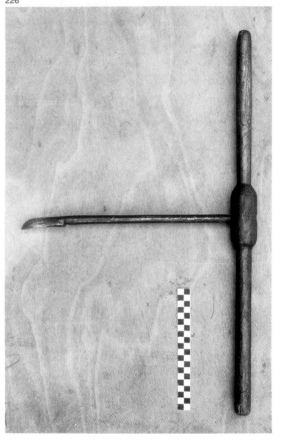

223 Funerary relief of a woodworker, holding in his hands an adze and a ruler. (Archaeological Museum, Bordeaux.)

224 Stele of a carpenter showing a level-square and a plane with a double grip. (Museo della Civiltà Romana, room LII, relief 62.)

225 Gallo-Roman spoon auger (or drill). (Musée de Sens.)

226 Modern spoon auger. Length of blade: 38cm; length of the handles: 64cm.

spokeshave). It has a very sharp blade, like that of the plane, and two handles, and is pulled towards the carpenter, taking off a long shaving from the piece held in place.[159]

When assembling the pieces of wood, the projecting parts, or tenons, can be made with a saw, but the socket holes, or mortices, call for chisels. Wood chisels, in common with stone chisels, have handles and are hit with a percussor which, unlike the metal hammer used for iron chisels, is a mallet of hard wood (*malleus*).

To hold the pieces in position once they have been jointed, the carpenter, to prevent dislodging caused by wind and the weight of snow, as well as by distortions of the wood, takes the precaution of pegging them together. A cylindrical hole is made in the wood with the help of a spoon auger or a drill with three points which removes shavings with a slow circular cutting movement (figs 225, 226). Many examples of this tool have been recovered in excavations. Although the screw had been invented and applied to machines as varied as lifting gear and presses,

spiral drills for augers must have remained very rare. Two examples, one found at Windisch (*Vindonissa*) in Switzerland, the other at Compiègne, show, however, that they did exist.[160] Their use only seems to have become general in the Middle Ages in the form of narrow blades that were twisted while hot.[161]

To make small holes, the joiners, *citrarii*, used a bow drill, still found in countries of the eastern Mediterranean. As with the augers, archaeology has

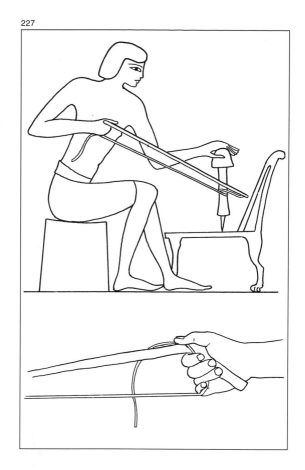

227

228

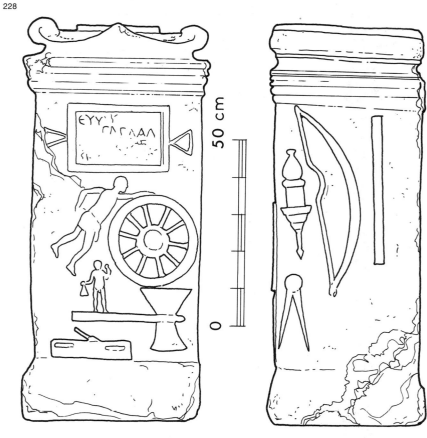

229

only come up with the bits. Two excellent representations, one on a painting from Pompeii,[162] the other on a funerary cippus from Syracuse[163] make it possible to supplement the information (figs 227, 228, 229). In its simplest form the drill has at the top a sort of bearing, a hollowed piece on which the hand presses and in which the actual instrument rotates, then a cylindrical spindle around which is wound the cord of the bow, and finally a sharpened drill-bit which through fast rotation bores through the wood. This instrument is shown in Egyptian paintings. To counteract the braking caused by pressing down on the top, the drill can be improved by extending the drill-bit by a pin rotating in a fixed bobbin held in the workman's hand; the cord of the bow thus acts directly on a groove of the drill. This is the type of tool seen at Pompeii and Syracuse.[164]

Finally, the tools for marking and measuring should be mentioned: the

compasses, squares, plumb lines and rulers, as indispensable to the carpenter and to the joiner as they were to the stone-cutter or the mason.

c Assembly

The wood used in a structure can constitute the entire material, which makes it 'closed and covered', i.e. the walls and the roofing. In this case, the pieces are put together horizontally or

227 Egyptian bow drill. (*Below*) The method of holding the bow to ensure the tension of the string.

228 Stele of a carter showing, on the front face, a wheel, a double-headed axe and a plane on which can be made out the two handles and the blade; and, on the side face, a bow drill, a compass and a rule. (Museum of Syracuse.)

229 Bow drill in use.

230 Timber jointing.
I:
1 splayed scarf-joint (purlins and rafters)
2 splayed joint with part abutments (purlins and rafters)
3 splayed indent scarf (scarf-joint splayed and tabled) or 'Jupiter's shaft' (tie-beam)
4 splayed indent scarf with transverse keys (tie-beam)
5 scarf-joint with tenon
6 halved scarf-joint
7 scarf-joint with slit (slot) mortice
8 splayed scarf-joint
9–10 scarf-joint with indentation ('Jupiter's shaft').

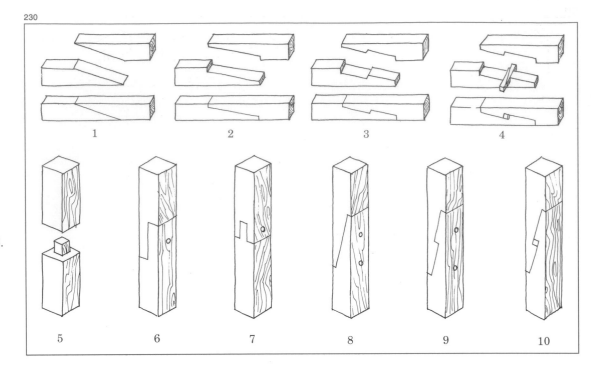

vertically and their assembly is limited to a lap-joint fitting which forms the corners at each end of the wall. This is the way chalets are constructed in mountainous regions where fir trees are plentiful. The trunks are very straight and so suit this type of construction perfectly. None of these perishable buildings survive, but on Trajan's Column are illustrations of palisades (timbers arranged vertically) and houses (laid horizontally). The reliefs also show good examples of jointed timber framing in the form of wooden bridges; the joints were limited to connecting the ends of long pieces, as the structure was not for walls but for a framework.

The elements in timber framing are subjected to various forces: compression, flexion (bending), tension (pulling) and friction. The joints have to remain connected whatever the force, taking into account also the fact that wood is a flexible material liable to considerable warping, caused as much by weight as by climatic conditions.[165]

Compression is the most straightforward case as all that is required is a surface sufficient to support the upper piece. This is called the compressing surface; for instance, an upright on a beam or a beam on an upright.

In the case of flexion (bending), the upper piece has a tenon fixing into a mortice. The tenon and mortice must be such that any warping cannot loosen them; for instance a joist on a beam.

Pieces in tension represent the most difficult situation; the most efficient solution is to cut the two elements to be abutted into a hooked design called a splayed indent scarf (in French called 'trait de Jupiter', Jupiter's shaft, because of its similarity to a stylized lightning bolt). With this joint it is possible to extend the tie-beams of trusses and consequently to increase the span of timber roofing.[166]

Finally, when one piece is resting on another by friction, in a sloping position (for instance a purlin on a principal rafter or a common rafter on a purlin), it is useful to shore it with a socket or a wedge (figs 230, 231, 232, 233).

Bearing in mind the extreme forces ships' hulls have to withstand, as well as

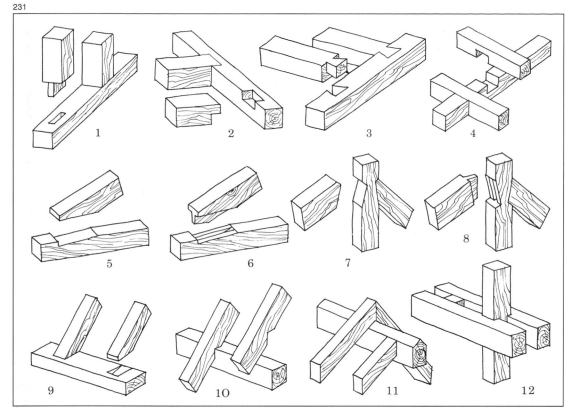

231

232

233

231 Timber jointing.
II:
1 mortice and tenon joint
2 square halved joint
3 dovetail joint
4 halved joint (through-splayed scarf-joint)
5 lap-joint (foot of principal rafter)
6 lap-joint with mortice and tenon (foot of principal rafter)
7 lap-joint with abutments (head of principal rafter)
8 lap-joint with mortice and tenon (head of principal rafter)
9 lap-joint with abutments (foot of common rafter)
10 overhanging base bearer of common rafter
11 heads of common rafters jointed at the roof-ridge
12 braced joint on a double tie-beam holding a vertical piece (king-post).

232 Splayed indent scarf on the keel and stem of a Greek caique. Boatyard on the road from Piraeus to Epidaurus, 1980.

233 Splayed indent scarf in a piece of timber framing. (Restoration at Pompeii, III,4,2.)

the development of naval architecture in the Greek period, it is perhaps justifiable to think that most of the complex wood joints, and notably the splayed indent scarf, were created in shipyards. This latter joint, thanks to the presence of tightening wedges forced between the contact surfaces (see figure), in fact allows alternations of compression, tension and flexion on the elements joined in this way. Although Roman timber work in buildings has disappeared (with the exception of some examples at Herculaneum), examples of naval wood-working and the skill involved in the joints are now known, thanks to finds and recent studies,[167] so that the different types known twenty centuries ago can be identified and appreciated.[168]

3
CONSTRUCTION USING LARGE STONE BLOCKS

234   Walls of the acropolis of Arpino built of large stone blocks of the second type (in the background) and the first type (foreground), fifth century BC.

1   Cyclopean and polygonal stone blocks

Whereas it is quite possible to talk of Greek architecture when referring both to the Temple of Apollo at Corinth and to the Grand Altar of Pergamon – despite the fact that they are separated by four centuries and that, apart from during the short reign of Alexander, they never belonged to the same country – it is more difficult to speak of one Roman architecture when describing the remains of the cities of Latium between the fifth and the third centuries BC.

The name of Rome, though applied to so many territories and to so many centuries, does not figure in the analysis of architecture that might be

234

called pre-Roman, or rather Republican. The Etruscans, along with the Greeks of Sicily and of Magna Graecia, do emerge from this obscurity, along with the Pompeiians. It is, however, with the primitive fortresses on the heights of southern Latium that the typology of large stone block construction begins.

Just like the Mycenaeans, with their huge defensive architecture, the Italic populations[1] surrounded their high towns with large stone walls which, because of their similarity to the defences of Mycenae, Tiryns or Midea,[2] are called Pelasgic. There is, of course, no relation between the walls built between the fifth and third centuries BC and the Mycenaean works that are more than a thousand years older.

What can perhaps be discerned is a common desire to impress forcibly upon any potential aggressor the power of the massive wall with all the psychological impact such an extraordinary physical achievement would have. Such an intention is at the basis of all large stone works designed to be seen by men or by the gods.

The summary dressing of the blocks in Cyclopean walls, or in *opus siliceum*,[3] is a feature of the period when such walls were built, and indicates the rustic nature of the builders, since such techniques were characteristic of mountain settlements. Coastal areas and those under Etruscan and Greek influence were already developing a fine architecture of rectangular blocks of *etrusca disciplina* or *isodomum* (for instance, the walls of Perugia).

Different facings are distinguished by the appearance of the dressed stone – which might, however, be different on the outside and the inside. Sometimes such walls appear very rustic, as at *Circeii*,[4] some sections at Norba (*Norma*) or at Arpino (*Arpinum*) (fig.234), though in some cases this roughness is found only on the interior faces of walls, while the exteriors are carefully dressed, as on the north-west section of *Circeii* or at Ansedonia (*Cosa*).

The most elaborate form of polygonal stone block construction,[5] *opus siliceum*, consists of finely juxtaposed blocks with worked facings, as is found, for instance, at Alatri (the Hernican city of *Aletrium*) (fig.235). Here the remarkable fortifications of the acropolis are completely preserved, with their gates (Porta di Cività and Porta dei Falli), each one surmounted by a gigantic lintel, the whole being just as impressive as Myccnac. Though less elaborately built, the fortifications of Segni (the Volscian *Signum*) form another fine example of polygonal stone construction, also found in most of the walls of Norba, at the acropolis of Terracina,[6] at Alba Fucens, at Cori

235

(figs 236, 237) and at Ferentino. It is noticeable that, for obvious reasons of stability, the polygonal blocks with their random joints are replaced at the corners and for door jambs larger blocks, laid in regular courses, which stop the other courses slipping.

Large, polygonal stone block construction is not only used in defensive

236

235   The southern side of the acropolis of Alatri (*Aletrium*) in southern Latium: polygonal stone block construction of the third type. The Porta Maggiore, one of the two approaches to the Upper Town, is 2.42m wide and 3.75m high; its raised position made it possible to defend the approach with a ramp or a partly wooden staircase. The overlying lintel is 5m long, 1.6m high and 1.65m deep; it weighs in the region of 30 tonnes. The height of the south-east corner is still 15m, the original height being in the region of 17m; *c.*300BC.

236   The Porta Maggiore of the acropolis of Norba (fifth to fourth century BC) with polygonal stone block construction of the third type. The foundation block of the left-hand corner is 3.05m long by 1.15m high and the same width; it weighs in the region of 10 tonnes. The gate opening is 6m wide.

237 The Roman method of transport by chariot with solid wheels with projecting rims; the oxen are attached by a neck yoke.)(Museo Nazionale; JPA.)

238 A block of tufa with the traces of the sockets for the wedges that were used in cutting it up (Pompiii VIII, 5,30).

architecture but can also be found in the facings of temple podia, for instance at Norba and Segni, for supporting walls, the most famous example being at the Temple of Fortuna at Palestrina (fig.238), and for structures supporting roads where the terrain is uneven, as on the *via Appia* (Piazza dei Paladini) and, more spectacularly, along the *via Flacca* (between Sperlonga and Gaeta), where the road is cut into a sea cliff.

Although in general terms it may be sufficient to locate all these achievements within the Republian period, more precise dating is obviously desirable for a period that lasted for four and a half centuries. Unfortunately, intensive occupation of the ground and the monuments from the end of the Republican period has often made it very difficult for archaeologists to record the remains of earlier periods, particularly when they are situated in built-up areas.[7] However, some indications do exist, as much archaeological as documentary, provided by discoveries made from pottery finds and written texts, and these enable an approximate chronology to be built up, with some markers in the story of the growth of Rome.[8] The following suggestions can be made for the principal sites:

Segni, the Volscian city of *Signum:* the foundations of the temple called the 'Capitol' are probably fifth century BC.[9] The fortification is perhaps fifth to second century BC.

Circeii (San Felice Circeo, on the promontory of Mount Circeo): a fortification attributed to the Latin colony of 393BC.[10]

Ferentino, Hernican city of *Ferentinum:* a fortification of the lower town may date from the first half of the fourth century BC; the wall of the acropolis from around 180BC; the reworking of the upper parts and the arch of the

Porta Sanguinara from between 100 and 90BC.[11]

Norma, the Volscian city of *Norba*, in the mountains of Lepini: the core of the small acropolis may date from the beginning of the fifth century BC; the town wall from the fourth century BC. The town was captured and destroyed by Aemilius Lepidus, Sulla's general, in 82BC and the site was abandoned.[12]

Terracina, the old Volscian city of *Anxur*, preserves some fragments of its polygonal stone block wall which date from before 406BC, the date of the Roman occupation, and from the repairs of 320BC. The long wall going up to the temple, made of masonry faced with *opus incertum*, is earlier than, or contemporaneous with, the wars between Marius and Sulla (beginning of the first century BC).[13]

Alba Fucens: a town founded by the Latins in 303BC on territory belonging to the *Aequi* and surrounded by a partly preserved strong wall with four large gates.[14]

Arpino: the Volscian city of *Arpinum*, with a surrounding wall broken by a large corbelled gate, fifth century BC.

Alatri, *Aletrium*, the principal city of the Hernici, has preserved the most complete example of large stone block fortification in Italy, consisting of an acropolis preserved intact, erected around 300BC.[15] The wall of the town is later.

Ansedonia, ancient *Cosa*, dominates the lagoon of Orbetello; material found in the walls and at their foot, makes it possible to attribute them to the Roman colony of 273BC.[16]

Palestrina, *Praeneste:* the town of the famous Sanctuary of Fortuna has preserved several sections of walls which can be attributed to the first half of the fourth century BC.

Spoleto: the wall of the Roman colony dates from 240BC.

Non-military works

Palestrina: the large wall supporting a terrace and ramps leading to the Sanctuary: belongs to a civic phase in the third century BC, much earlier than the Later Republican period.

Via Appia: the support for the Piazza dei Paladini, between Terracina and Formia, dates to the end of the fourth century BC.

Via Flacca: the support for the road in several tortuous sections along the coast between Sperlonga and Gaeta dates to the end of the third century, or the beginning of second century BC.[17]

The walls of the theatre of Pietrabbondante (*Bovianum Vetus*) belong to the end of the first century BC.

The walls of the terraces of Republican villas near Terracina. Monticchio, the so-called "Villa of Galba", Salissano.

This short list highlights the uncertainties there are over the dates and attributions of structures using large stone blocks, but also shows the certain fact that the conquering Romans adopted the architecture and probably the architects of the defeated. Confirmation of this is provided by the fortifications of *Falerii Novi* and of Paestum. The former was built and given magnificent walls after the capture of *Falerii Veteres* in 241BC; this fortification on Etruscan land was built in the Etruscan style in fine, close-fitting courses of regular height. At Paestum, where the Latin colony goes back to 273BC, the fortification was rebuilt, following the same principle of adoption, according to the Greek technique.

This systematic recourse to regional building practices, occurring at least until the end of the third century BC, is indicative of the weak technical and artistic identity of the Romans until their complete conquest of the peninsula and Sicily (with the capture of Syracuse in 212BC). This attitude, lasting for several centuries, makes it possible at least to address the uncertainties outlined above by taking as a point of departure Cyclopean construction or the construction of walls with polygonal stone blocks, sometimes incorporated into Roman practices.

2 Ashlar

Mention of the walls of Paestum and *Falerii Novi* leads naturally to a study of walls of *opus quadratum*, that is those built with rectangular blocks arranged in horizontal courses, or ashlar.

It is no coincidence that the most ancient monuments in Rome that can be placed historically[18] correspond to the Etruscan occupation of the city (from 616 to 509BC). Before the installation of the Tarquin dynasty, the hills of the city centre, if Varro[19] is to be believed on this subject, must have had simple rustic defences in the form of an earthwork, the *murus terreus*, but with no stone structure. The first traces of stone building that have been recovered are the remains of the fortifications from the sixth century BC made of cappellacio (a grey tufa originating in the ground of Rome itself) and a part of the foundations of the Temple of Jupiter on the Capitoline, also belonging to the sixth century, the tufa blocks of which reach a height of 5m.[20]

Both of these works are of *opus quadratum*. The Servian Wall is also built by this method. It is called 'Servian' because it was for a long time attributed to the king Servius Tullius,[21] but it was most certainly built after the taking of Rome by the Gauls in 390BC since they would probably have been incapable of crossing such an obstacle if it had existed.[22]

The temples were to adopt their podia from the Etruscans and their orders from the Greeks, and the latter were to remain the great inspiration for Roman architecture and town planning. Greek architects such as the famous Hermodoros were to move to Rome in the second century BC to erect appropriate monuments to modify the conquerors' building complexes in relation to the monumental art of the Hellenized world. The materials themselves were to come from the Aegean area along with teams of stone-masons and sculptors,[23] as is attested by the round temple of the *Forum Boarium* (called incorrectly 'the Temple of Vesta'), whose capitals, partly of Pentelic marble, were dressed on the site in the last years of the second century BC. This is still a long way, however, from Strabo's visit to Rome or Herodes Atticus' being called to the court of Antoninus Pius to educate his sons after covering Greece with monuments, but the choice of Greece had already been made and Roman architecture, which came of age at the dawn of the Imperial period, took shape in the course of the second century BC following the Hellenistic impetus. The word 'impetus' is preferable to 'model', as, despite, or because of, their teachers' power, the Romans were able to bring about a movement into Rome, and then into the whole peninsula, of workers and also of ideas and forms, which acted as a catalyst and helped consolidate an art of building that because their own.

The first development that earns the designation fine architecture is the use of *opus quadratum*. This is a form which could be adapted successfully to regular buildings, and as well as giving the best stability to the elements of the structure, it was also pleasing visually, with its exclusively horizontal and vertical lines. Curiously, it is this second factor that, with constructions in tufa (the most characteristic Roman material), was to carry more weight: to conceal a stone whose appearance was considered mediocre, a white stucco with a design of rectangular stone blocks traced on it completely covered the facings. The concern to evoke marble, still practically unexploited in second-century Italy, was clear and can be seen both in the 'Greek' tholos of the *Forum Boarium* (whose columns are made of marble) and in its very Roman neighbour, the Temple of Portunus.

a Foundations

The fact that the only remains of the Temple of Jupiter on the Capitoline are its foundations, to a remarkable depth of 5m, demonstrates that there was a considerable concern with good foundations in early Roman architecture, a direct inheritance once again from Etrusco-Greek practices.[24]

The search for good ground was thus to become the first concern of the architect:

The foundations [fundamenta] *of the towers and walls are to be carried out as follows: one must dig as far as the solid ground, if it can be reached, and into the solid ground as far as seems necessary according to the size of the building, over an area wider than that of the walls to be erected . . . (Vitruvius I, 9).*

Solid ground (*solidum*), that is good ground which is sufficiently compact to take the weight of a construction uniformly without it sinking, is ideally the bedrock. This is what the Greek builders looked for and after them the Romans, to raise their buildings on. The Greeks had also noticed that in the Aegean area, which is prone to frequent earthquakes, rocky ground was more resistant to the effects of tremors and that fissures, cracks and landslides, due to rising underground water in alluvial plains, did not occur there. Sometimes, therefore, they dug to a considerable depth, removing enormous quantities of soil or earth[25] to cut levels into the solid rock to take the first courses of the foundations.

The depth reached at the Athenaion at Syracuse and at the Temple of Athena Polias at Priene is 4.5m, and it is 3m at the small temple of Aphaia on Aegina. The Temple on the Capitol therefore clearly followed the same rule and it is astonishing to consider that the amount of stone used for the foundations was often greater than for the visible part of the monument.

Vitruvius' recommendation to provide a width of foundations greater than the width of the wall has a necessary mechanical logic: the lower courses take all the weight of the building and they must both ensure its stability and also prevent it sinking into the ground by distributing the weight over a bigger area (a precaution that is particularly worthwhile when the ground is not rocky). This is what is called the footing of the foundations, and is encountered also in the form of plinths for wooden posts and under masonry walls, and also nowadays in reinforced concrete foundations.

In certain situations the Romans prepared the ground artificially where it was unstable to too great a depth. On the banks of the Tiber, the Temple of Portunus rests on a layer of crushed and broken tufa, completely occupying the base of the excavation to a depth of more than 3m and also filling the foundation trenches (fig.239).

When concrete masonry became widespread, the Romans gave up building

239 Foundations of the Temple of Portunus in Rome consisting of a course of tufa (the dark layer) resting on a thick compacted layer of crushed and tamped tufa intended to compress ground rich in mud clay; *c.*100BC.

240

241

242

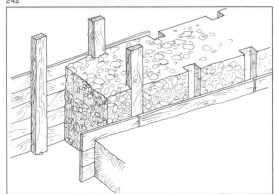

240 The extension of a structure of stone blocks by a large body of brickwork under supporting elements (here columns on a podium) can perhaps be considered as constituting foundations. Temple of Hadrian in Rome, finished in AD 145.

241 Foundations made out of coursed brickwork bearing traces of formwork, under the Arch of Titus; built by Domitian after AD 81.

242 Foundations with formwork from the area of Rome.

stone block foundations, particularly when they took up a considerable space, and went over to *opus caementicium*, whatever the nature of the planned building (figs 240, 241).[26]

In the area around Rome, where the soil of compact volcanic sand allows for sound trenches, the builders were able to frame their foundations with planks, or shutters, placed against the walls of the excavation and held on the inside by vertical posts; the mortar and rubble stones were then thrown into this formwork and solidly tamped (fig.242). Traces left by the posts and sometimes by the shutters can be seen on the walls of foundations that are now exposed, often at a considerable depth, as under the Temple of Venus and Rome, on the boundary of the Domus Aurea, or on the Palatine. Conversely, the many masonry fortifications that were to be erected in Gaul in the Later Empire had foundations made of large stone blocks looted and reused from monuments.

Finally the special foundations adapted to marshy land should be mentioned. These consisted of wooden piles driven in with a pile-driver, which Vitruvius also discusses (V,12): '. . . if on the contrary the ground is soft, one digs in piles made of alder or olive that have been slightly burnt [to harden them].' The author, though eloquent on the subject of lifting machines, does not explain the mechanism of the pile-drivers, but they may well have consisted of a vertical wooden construction along which the ram could slide and fall with some force and come up again, a weight serving as a percussor. The piles, driven home like this, were then sawn off to the same horizontal level, and would have held (or not) beams on which the construction rested (fig.243).[27]

b   The elevation

The appearance of facings made of rectangular stone blocks can differ

quite markedly, depending on a number of factors, the main ones being the arrangement of the stones in the wall, determining the pattern of the joints, and the treatment of the visible surfaces forming the skin (fig.244).

The stones which occupy the entire width of the wall, and therefore have two visible facings, are the bonding blocks or parpens. If the bonding block is positioned with its length, that is its greatest dimension, perpendicular to the axis of the wall, it is a header, i.e. seen head on. If, however, its axis is the same as that of the wall, it is a stretcher, resting either 'on edge', i.e. on its narrowest long side, or on its widest long side.

When the wall is thicker, it is necessary to alternate head-on bonding blocks with two parallel stretchers, or else to have no bonding blocks at all, only stretchers and headers. The use of concrete masonry simplified these structures as stone block construction was limited to the facings, which were

bonded to the body of the building by headers projecting tail-on into the masonry (figs 245, 246, 247).

The oldest surviving Roman construction with rectangular stone blocks is the so-called Servian Wall, mentioned above, built at the beginning of the fourth century BC. Its facing now has a rather untidy appearance, but this is due in part to the heavy erosion of the tufa blocks of which it is made (fig.248). In fact its stones and joints are not as neat or close-fitting as later examples, but it is noticeable that in a number of places an attempt was made to alternate between courses of stretchers and courses of headers, which went right through the entire thickness of the wall (approximately 4m at the base).

At *Falerii Novi*, the wall is more carefully built than the Servian Wall, but is also a century and a half later. It has the same method of construction through its entire thickness and here too an alternation of stretchers and headers can be observed, though

243 Operation of the pulley pile-driver, in use from antiquity until the nineteenth century for driving in piles.

244 Walls of Pompeii. Second phase. Note the curvilinear joints from the cut of a saw.

245 The names of the different positions of stones in walls of block construction.

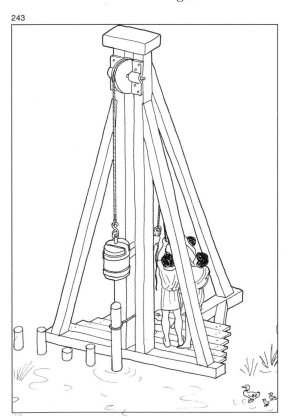

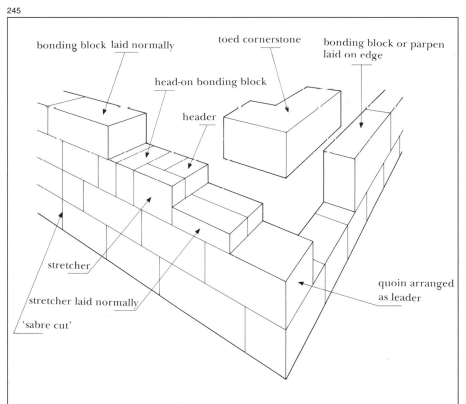

bonding block laid normally

toed cornerstone

bonding block or parpen laid on edge

head-on bonding block

header

stretcher

stretcher laid normally

'sabre cut'

quoin arranged as leader

without forming a regular pattern (fig.249). Another detail of this wall is that the dressing of the exterior facing is very carefully finished off, while the interior is left practically untouched. This is perhaps one of the latest examples of a feature already noted in connection with the 'Pelasgic' walls, and is understandable when it is remembered that ancient ramparts were covered on the inside by a bank of loose earth, the *agger*,[28] that can still be seen in place at Pompeii but does not seem to have existed at *Falerii*.

The arrangement of alternate courses of stretchers and headers, already seen on the Servian Wall, was to persist in the Imperial period and was favoured by many builders because of its systematic nature, perfectly in keeping with Roman ideas of planning, efficiency and speed of execution.

246

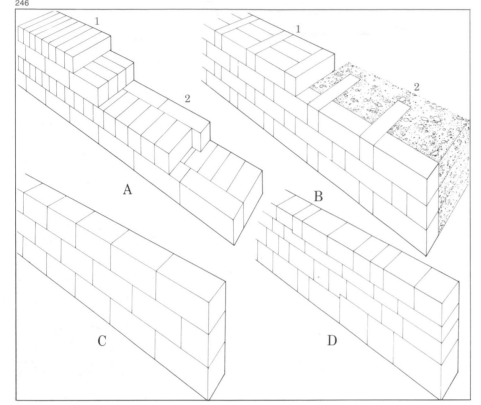

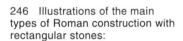

248

247

249

246 Illustrations of the main types of Roman construction with rectangular stones:

A
Alternation of courses of stretchers and headers:
1 with courses of heading bonding blocks and courses of stretchers;
2 with mixed courses of stretchers and headers juxtaposed through the wall.

B
Courses alternating stretchers and headers:
1 wall with two facings without rubble backing;
2 facing of a large wall of rubble masonry.

C
Wall of bonding blocks of regular height.

D
Wall of pseudo-regular height with irregularities.

Around Rome this system is found in all the major building works from the Republican period to the second half of the first century: in the viaduct of the valley of Ariccia on the *via Appia*; in the ramp of the *via Flaminia* (fig.250); in the bridge of Nona; on the *via Praenestina* built around 100BC; in the foundations of the *Tabularium*, constructed in 78BC; on the facings of the Later Republican mausoleum on the *via Appia* called the 'Tomb of the Horatii and Curiatii'; on the great rear wall of the Forum of Augustus inaugurated in 2BC (fig.251); in the bridge of Augustus at Narni; in the pillars of the *aqua Claudia*, the construction of which took fourteen years from 38 to 52; and in those on the aqueduct of Nero joined to the preceding at the Porta Maggiore (fig.252).

The technique of constantly alternating stretchers and headers in the same course, though it appears in a very systematic way in the Greek walls of Selinunte, seems to have made only a casual appearance in Republican architecture, corresponding rather to an alternation of joints according to the size of the blocks. Nor was the Imperial period to make frequent use of the technique – it was mainly headers bonding with the masonry (fig.253) in the large constructions of *opus caementicium*, that were alternated regularly in each course. Two good examples are the podium of the Temple of Augustus and Livia at Vienne (fig.254) and the tomb of Cartilius Publicola at Ostia.

The most methodical applications are in fact quite late and again for fortifications, as at the Porta San Sebastiano in Rome (the ancient *Porta Appia*) rebuilt under Honorius (395 to 423) or, far from there, Justinian's walls at Palmyra (figs 255, 256). By contrast, the graphic pattern inspired by this arrangement of stones was freely and very quickly adopted by painters in the artificial recreation of

250

251

247   Wall made up exclusively of bonding blocks: peribolos of the Temple of Bel at Palmyra; first century.

248   So-called 'Servian' Wall of Rome on the Viminal. Note the alternation of courses of stretchers and courses of headers; early fourth century BC.

249   Facing of a tower on the walls of *Falerii Novi*, built after 241BC with alternate courses of stretchers and courses of headers.

252

250   Ramp of the *via Flaminia* near the Civita Castellana. The courses of rectangular blocks of tufa follow the slope of the road with alternate rows of stretchers and rows of headers. Work began in 220BC.

251   Detail of the wall of the Forum of Augustus showing the alternation of courses of stretchers and courses of headers.

252   Regularly alternating courses of stretchers and headers on the *aqua Claudia* (38 to 52). The angled rustications (joints chamfered across their width) are coarsely scored. The whole takes on a great monumental force that the Florentine Renaissance was to exploit again.

253

253

253 Headers penetrating a large mass of brickwork (the facing has disappeared at this level) from the Tomb of Caecilia Metella; Augustan Period.

254 Podium of the Temple of Augustus and Livia at Vienne (Isère) with three courses of regular alternating stretchers and headers.

254

facings of stone block construction (the Villa of the Mysteries, the House of Trebius Valens at Pompeii, the Villa of Varano at Stabiae).

Finally, the most regular construction type, or isodomic construction, was most frequently used when the pattern of joints was desired to contribute to the decoration of the facing. Without ever reaching the perfection in stone working of the Greek masterpieces, among which the Parthenon and the Hephaisteion stand as true exemplars, nor daring to transfer to their temples those subtle curvilinear tensions designed to deceive and please the eye, the Roman architects and their stone-masons nevertheless knew how to build with delicacy and play with light and shade in the regular division of facings and the concealment of joints.

At Pompeii there is scarcely any

255

257

simulate different kinds of marble. This was taken up by the Later Republican architecture of Rome, in the use of stucco on the walls of the two well-preserved temples in the *Forum Boarium*, imitating regular courses with joints highlighted by chiselling.

The Augustan period was to produce some excellent examples of stone

256

architecture from the fourth and third centuries BC except limestone walls of primitive appearance, but after they turned to volcanic tufa as a construction material,[29] the stone-masons became complete masters of their art and gave this Campanian city its greatest architecture, in its 'second Samnite period', which flowered until the conquests of Sulla. The buildings using stone blocks, for the most part straightforward individual houses, adopted the regular fashion of courses and joints highlighted by a finely chiselled, very shallow framing band cut into this fine grained stone, with delicate lines marked at right angles with an awl (fig.257). At the same time, the painted renderings of the first Pompeiian style, while concealing the masonry, reproduced the same regular facing with sunken joints; and each imitation stone was embellished with colours designed to

block facings treated in this way, in quite different building projects; for instance the Temple of Mars Ultor, the Maison Carrée at Nîmes, the Temple of Augustus and Livia at Vienne (walls of the cella), the Temple of Rome and Augustus at Ankara, the Trophy of Augustus at La Turbie and the tomb of Caecilia Metella. This last monument deserves attention for a particular detail, visible because of displacement and gaps in the arrangement of the blocks: it is noticeable that the joints, highlighted by chiselled depressions, are not all real and are in reality only a surface pattern intended to create the illusion of perfectly regular stone block construction (fig.258). The real vertical joints correspond to longer blocks, generally consisting of two or three imitation blocks, with the breaks sometimes appearing in the middle of the facing, a technique that can be seen even

255 Facings of the Porta San Sebastiano (Porta Appia) in Rome, with stretchers and headers of reused blocks. Period of Honorius 395 to 423.

256 A systematic alternation of stretchers and headers is visible in the facing of Justinian's Wall at Palmyra; sixth century.

257 Wall of regular construction, the House of the Large Fountain at Pompeii (second century BC). On a lower course of smooth orthostats, the normal courses have a perfect rhythm of carved framing bands, highlighting the joints.

258

259

258 Facing of travertine on the tomb of Caecilia Metella. Because of the deterioration of the upper courses it is noticeable that the actual lengths of the blocks do not correspond to the regularly incised joints.

259 Actual and imitation joints in a regular facing of a funerary monument at Pompeii; necropolis of the Nucerian Gate.

260 Fine regular marble construction, with drafted margins, resting on a row of orthostats; Library of Hadrian in Athens, c.130.

261 Podium of the Temple of Portunus (c.100BC) made up of a single row of orthostats.

262 Pseudo-regular stone block construction with irregularities, from the 'Theatre of the Mysteries' at Vienne.

260

262

261

more clearly on a tomb in the necropolis of the Nucerian Gate at Pompeii (tomb 17, South-West) (fig.259).

Later, very fine examples of isodomic masonry with chiselled joints can be found, for instance the marble monuments erected by Hadrian (117 to 138) in Athens, particularly the library (fig.260) built in 130 and the arch given to that city and, later still, the delicate small round temple of Vesta on the Roman Forum, in its reconstruction of the Severan period. In imitation of Greek examples, some walls of isodomic stone block construction have a higher first course made up of orthostats, probably as a memory of the masonry foundation walls of clay structures. Although the Romans referred to this arrangement, they used it less frequently than their predecessors, except in renderings of the first Pompeian style, a direct inheritance from Hellenistic models. A well-known example is the wall of the cella of the Maison Carrée, which has a row of orthostats separated from the coursed masonry by a cornice acting as a second, panelled podium,[30] while at the House of the Large Fountain at Pompeii (second century BC) the row of orthostats, more in keeping with the Greek model, is not separated from the rest of the wall.

It is generally temple podia whose entire height is made up of a single course of blocks arranged so that they are taller than they are wide that can be considered as an isolated row of orthostats (fig.261). Apart from the search for more plastic forms, which manifested itself in a particular treatment of the joints and facings in various forms of rustication, the vast majority of Roman buildings constructed of stone blocks were made simply of blocks of different lengths placed in courses of uniform height, sometimes interrupted by recesses (fig.262). The courses usually noticeably decrease in height the higher up they are, as this simplifies the tasks of lifting and bedding by putting the lighter blocks in the upper parts of the construction (fig.263). This technique, when the stone has a fine tight grain, creates, even on large plain surfaces, a great architectural beauty in which the skill of the stone-mason can be appreciated without resorting to mouldings or sculpted decorations (which can be deceptive). The enormous peribolos of the Temple of Bel at Palmyra and the exterior surface of the Theatre at Orange are works where the wall is worth admiring for its own sake, independently of the form and the function of the monument.

263

263 Pseudo-regular stone block construction on the peribolos of the Temple of Bel at Palmyra; note the decreasing height of the courses higher up the wall. The plainness of the wall and the sober moulding set one another off in perfect harmony (first century). Note also the systematic pillaging of the cramps carried out in the Middle Ages.

3 Columns and pillars made of stone blocks

Freestanding vertical supports, both circular and square – columns and pillars[31] – are the most significant translation into stone of wooden architecture. The base on which they rest and the capital which separates them from the architrave are simply reminders of the stone base separating the wooden post from the ground and of the corbelled cap reducing the span of the lintel and reinforcing the head of the wooden piece (fig.264).[32]

The fluting may well be only a memory of the grain of the wood or the long marks left by the squaring axe. The use of stone, apart from the advantage of durability, offered the benefit of protection against fire and the possibility to produce in theory an almost unlimited freestanding vertical support by superimposing elements on top of one another – the drums. By a curious paradox, however, it is precisely the tallest columns of Roman

264

265

267

266

264 Technical perfection and the genesis of the capital in a rustic building in the Peloponnese.

265 Columns of monolithic shafts of granite from Aswan at the Pantheon (118–125). Total height: 14.2m; height of shaft: 11.6m; diameter at the base: 1.51m; diameter at the top: 1.31m; weight: approx. 50 tonnes.

266 Temple of Antoninus and Faustina in the Roman Forum, built in AD 141. Prostyle monument whose columns, 14m high in total, have monolithic shafts in 'cipolino' marble from the island of Euboea.

267 Villa of the Mysteries at Pompeii, colonnade made of Sarno limestone, initially belonging to the Samnite period.

268 Peristyle colonnade of volcanic tufa; Doric order without a base, Pompeii, House of Obelius Firmus, Samnite period.

269 Portico with upper storey, from the Forum of Pompeii (Julio-Claudian period), made of white limestone. The heavy proportions of the Doric order must originally have been in relation to the other parts of the original portico made of volcanic tufa (*right*).

architecture that are monolithic shafts; and some extremely modest porticoes in small urban or rural houses are provided with little columns made up of drums.[33] But, as already noted in the discussion about the extraction, cutting and transport of stone, this paradox sometimes appeared quite logical and in addition fitted in well with the pursuit of technical achievement so dear to the hearts of architects in the Imperial period. The Pantheon, the Basilica Ulpia or the Temple of Antoninus and Faustina, already mentioned, are examples of buildings with porticoes made up of colossi of granite or marble (figs 265, 266). These two materials are the most frequently used for monolithic shafts because the qualities of the stone allowed the extraction, transport and dressing of long and relatively slender elements. Other materials, notably the volcanic tufa so widely used in the peninsula and most limestone, saturated with quarry sap and therefore very brittle at the time of extraction, would not take even the force of their own weight under flexion.

When materials were not imported, the columns followed same treatment as the walls of stone construction. At Pompeii it is clear that the oldest colonnades are made of limestone from the Sarno; next they are made of tufa; and finally, in the Imperial period, of white limestone and, very rarely, of marble (figs 267, 268, 269).

Drums with a large diameter were joined together, as already noted, with the aid of vertical clamps. The effec-

116

tiveness of this method in the event of an earthquake should not be disparaged because of the rapid loss of stability of the individual superimposed elements. The record for displacement of drums without total ruin seems to be held by the Athenaion of Syracuse,[34] victim in 1693 of a serious earthquake that dislodged in particular the north colonnade, with a shift in axis between the drums up to 0.7m for a diameter, fortunately uniform, of 1.9m. Conversely, at the Temple of Bacchus at Baalbek, a column, despite being knocked over against the wall of the cella, kept its drums connected thanks to the presence of the vertical metal clamps still connecting them.

Applied or engaged columns and pillars (when they are called pilasters) constitute different structures, since by losing the particular characteristic of being freestanding supports, they in fact become simple projections of the wall of which they are a solid part, and often relate more to the decoration than to the support. Examples can be found in the oldest (pseudo-peripteral) temples in which the engaged columns or pilasters around the walls of the cella suggest a complete peristyle.[35] This typically Roman form,[36] perfectly illustrated by the Temple of Fortuna Virilis (fig.270), can perhaps be

268

269

270

explained in the case of these cult buildings by the situation of the cella, which is placed on a podium and not accessible to the public, as it was in Greek temples whose porticoes could then form a sheltered meeting place.

The monumental portico with arcades, from its authoritative definition in the *tabularium*, was to bring harmony to façades with engaged orders that could be superimposed as

270 Engaged columns from the Temple of Portunus in Rome (*c.*100BC). In the 'pseudo-peripteros' arrangement, they no longer act as supports and remain only as the suggestion of a peristyle. The columns are incorporated into the wall of which they are merely aspects of the relief. The building is made of local volcanic tufa; with foundations, bases, corner columns and detached columns of travertine, a hard rock from Tivoli; it was entirely covered with white stucco.

271 Column shaft of artificial polychrome marble. Fragments of different types were added to the column, placed in the cavities and fixed with the help of an iron cramp sealed with lead. Found in the marble depot of the port of Ostia.

272 Marble pillars of rectangular section, in the portico of the House of Julia Felix at Pompeii (II,4) c.65.

273 Rectangular marble pillars in the 'Hall of Doric Pillars' at Hadrian's Villa, 118 to 125. Only the corner pillar, with the square section, is of massive proportions.

required, and became the ideal form for the exteriors of theatres and amphitheatres.

When the engaged colonnade is located inside a monument, as can be seen at the Greek Temple of Bassae, and as the Basilica at Pompeii demonstrates fairly well, it is a fair conclusion that each column supported the end of a beam of the ceiling or the roof timbers, acting thus as a vertical support and a buttress.

Square pillars, which might easily be imagined to be very large elements, often appear on the contrary as remarkably slender marble monoliths,[37] as is witnessed by the portico of the House of Julia Felix at Pompeii, one of the porticoes of Hadrian's Villa, that of the *domus* of *Fortuna annoraria* at Ostia, or, also at Ostia, one of the apses of the Forum Baths (figs 272, 273).

4
STRUCTURES OF MIXED CONSTRUCTION

Apart from walls of large stone blocks or rubble masonry, there are two other types of technique, used particularly in the early period, and a third, universal, practice, which each call for very different materials according to their size and their function within a wall. These are: 'chequer-work'; *opus africanum*; and timber-framing.[1]

1 'Chequer-work construction'

This arrangement of materials consisted of alternating large stone blocks with rubble infilling. The large blocks always rested on one another, in a lattice, and acted as the supporting elements. The rubble infilling could therefore be removed without affecting the stability of the structure. Since the smaller stones only occupied a relatively limited area, they could be dry-jointed (as at Velia) or jointed with a simple earth mortar (as at Bolsena) (figs 274, 275).

This technique seems to have been little used,[2] but it had the advantage of being economical with materials in a period when architecture of any importance called for construction with stone blocks only. Only the visible faces of the large blocks making up the supporting structure were carefully dressed; their joining faces could be fairly roughly dressed, and the off-cuts from the dressing at the quarry could be turned into the rubble for the infilling. The two examples of this type at Velia (first half of the third century BC) and at Bolsena (beginning

274

275

274 'Chequer-work' construction at Velia, with coursed rubble infilling. (Third century BC.)

275 Bolsena, wall of 'chequer-work' construction at the 'domus with atrium' (beginning of the second century BC). The dimensions of the infilled sections are relatively small because of the inferiority of the local tufa.

276

277

of the second century BC)[3] show slight differences which are perhaps due to the nature of the materials used. At Velia the space occupied by the rubble is much larger, and the pieces have been dressed quite carefully allowing them to be positioned with complete stability, while at Bolsena the volcanic tufa is more brittle and so had a more restricted use.

It seems that the appearance of lime mortar in the second century BC led to the disappearance of this interesting technique, the origin and ancient name of which are still unknown.[4]

Geographically and historically the distribution of 'chequer-work' construction seems very odd; while it is found at Velia, in Lucania in the Hellenistic period, it is present in Etruria in the fourth century (at Tarquinia), in the third century at la Canicella at Orvieto[5] and at the beginning of the second century at Bolsena, where it is encountered for the last time.[6]

2   Opus africanum

The name of this construction technique plainly indicates the region where its use was most widespread. Though in origin, as will be seen below, it seems definitely North African, it was transported by the Carthaginians and found in several places in Sicily and even southern Italy.

Technically, *opus africanum* is made up of vertical chains of large stone blocks in which upright blocks alternate with horizontal ones. These stacks form the supporting elements of the wall and are bound to the infilling of rubble by the projection of the horizontal pieces.

This is in effect a technique called 'framework and fill', comparable in every respect with building using a

timber framework. This is why Italian archaeologists call it *opera a telaio*, that is 'frame work'. It was in fact the scarcity of wood that gave rise to the idea in Carthaginian architecture of supporting the buildings with stone pillars connected by sections of rubble stones, which, depending on the way they were dressed, could be put in place with dry jointing or bonded with clay mortar.

Unfortunately there are only a few examples of monuments using this technique in the country of its origin, and it is western Sicily, on the island of Mozia (ancient Motiae) and on the acropolis of Selinunte, that has preserved the remains of walls of *opus africanum*, dating to the end of the fourth century BC.

Curiously, the oldest walls *a telaio* at Pompeii date from the same period; the intermediary link, either chronological or geographical, has not been established between these two regions.[7] The first walls of this type in Pompeii are filled with small pieces of limestone, sometimes carefully dressed and assembled, bonded with clay mortar. The technique was to persist over the centuries, the filling stones being modified and simplified due to the use of lime mortar, which permitted a facing of *opus incertum* of different types, including lava, which would be very laborious to cut into regular pieces (figs 276, 277).

The Romans, always ready to adopt local techniques when these fitted in with their construction schemes,[8] made use of *opus africanum* in North Africa throughout the period of their occupation and under them it became an exclusive and standard technique in this part of the world (figs 278, 279). There are very few variations in the method and the fill always consists of roughly squared blocks. It is worth noting, however, that the original structure of a building at *Bulla Regia*,[9] perhaps a basilica, situated near the large baths, had fill begun on foundations of stone blocks and continued with facings of reticulate above (fig.280).

276 Wall of '*opera a telaio*', *opus africanum*, at Pompeii, in a house of the first Samnite period, made of Sarno limestone (VII,3,16).

277 Wall of *opus africanum* with vertical chains of limestone blocks and infill of lava rubble. Pompeii I,12,1.

278 Wall of *opus africanum* from the House of the Trifolium at Thugga (Dougga, Tunisia), from the third century AD. The stone blocks of the vertical chains are of extremely variable length, as is often the case (width of the vertical pieces: 20 to 40cm, height: 70 to 120cm). On some monuments the horizontal pieces are totally absent and the chains are simply pillars socketed together. An element of Punic architecture, *opus africanum* was to remain a permanent feature of African construction during the Roman period. (Photo: A. Olivier.)

279 Thugga (Dougga), the Capitol (Antoninus Pius). A wall with niches, made of *opus africanum* with infill of coursed rubble bonded with mortar.

280

remains because of the perishable nature of the supporting elements. It is once again Pompeii and, above all, Herculaneum that provide the only Roman examples that have survived. It is important to remember, therefore, that these represent urban architecture, as the rural models are lost, still perhaps buried in the ashes of Vesuvius. For this latter category, the archaeological remains consist of bases of masonry, ending with a horizontal course on which stood the perishable structure of timber-framing, or simply clay, the distinction being sometimes impossible to establish due to the lack of sufficient standing remains.

The examples of this technique visible at Herculaneum and Pompeii occupy two different positions in the buildings: on the external faces timber work is used for the upper floor (or floors), the ground floor being made of various sorts of masonry; while inside the houses numerous timber partitions, on all levels, separate the rooms and rest directly on the floor.

3   Timber-framing

Timber-framing, or *opus craticium*, is the most widely used mixed construction method, not only in Roman architecture but in most ancient and traditional forms of architecture. However, of all the Roman techniques it is the one that has left the least number of

The reasons for this are related to three factors. The first is the vulnerability at ground level of the wood and clay infill, both to rain and rising damp, and to the wear and tear of urban life, particularly on busy commercial streets. The second reason relates to the ease with which a wall made of clay and wood can be broken into by thieves, though it is true that the surviving examples are all filled in with rubble masonry. The third reason is purely functional, relating to the extreme lightness of the walls using this technique – the wood itself is comparatively light while at the same time rigid, so that partitions may be less than 20cm thick, as against 40 to 50cm for the majority of walls made of masonry or dressed stone.

280   Building at *Bulla Regia* (Tunisia) with reticulated facings between vertical chains.

281   Elements of ancient timber-framing.

281

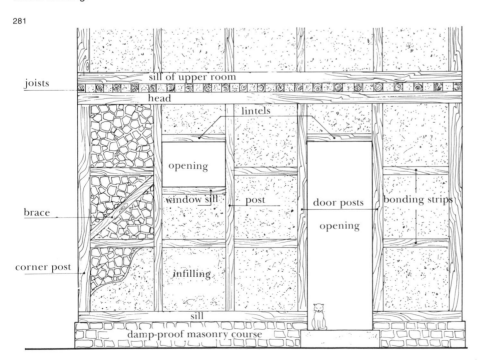

In the absence of the ancient vocabulary it is convenient to define the composition of timber-framing by the terms used for vernacular architecture

on the basis of Campanian examples. If the wall is external and encloses a ground floor it rests on a damp-proof course of masonry intended to protect the wood (and clay if present) from moisture; the internal partitions, posts and infill rest directly on the ground. The supporting elements are, of course, vertical. The posts[10] are thus door posts when they frame an opening, or corner posts when they are placed at the corners of the construction, in which case they are generally thicker as they are subject to the stresses of the two walls meeting at a right angle. In vernacular architecture the posts often do not rest directly on the masonry base, but on a horizontal piece of wood that acts as an intermediary and is called a sill;[11] no examples of this have been found below known ground-floor partitions in Herculaneum and Pompeii (fig.281).

In the upper part of the wall all the posts are connected by a horizontal beam, sometimes called the head, which supports the ceiling or roof timbers. To stop the supporting elements bending sideways and to hold the infill in place, horizontal pieces, the bonding strips, are placed parallel with one another, generally dividing the partition into sections that are almost square; these same bonding strips are also found in the openings where they form lintels and under the windows as window sills (figs 282, 283).

Modern timber-framing has a number of pieces that act at the same time as bonding strips and as trusses – these are the braces placed diagonally in the sections of infill; such pieces seem to have been rarely used in Campania. Only one example has been found, in an upper room at the Villa of Diomedes, which is quite clearly ancient, as shown by the rendering still partially covering the cavities where the wood used to be (fig.284).[12]

The beams of the ceiling, which also form those of the floor when there is

282

283

282 Herculaneum: timber-frame partition, *opus craticium*, built between 62 and 79 at the College of the Augustales. The infill is *opus incertum* and the whole was rendered. Thickness with rendering: 18cm. Section of the pieces of wood: 9 x 9cm.

283 Partition of *opus craticium* at the House of the Moralist in Pompeii (restored).

an upper storey, rest on two opposite sides, on the head; above this level a new sill takes the roof timbers or, as the case may be, a new vertical wall.

Another advantage of the use of these light structures was that by projecting the ground-floor ceiling beams, the habitable area on the upper floor could be increased using corbelling. Numerous houses, particularly in the main streets of Herculaneum and Pompeii, thus had a storey of timber-framing overhanging the pavement,

284

sometimes even supported by posts because of the large amount of projection (figs 285, 286).

At Pompeii and Herculaneum the infill, which was put in place when all the timber work was finished, is made up of masonry of *opus incertum* bonded with mortar, but it seems certain that the majority of materials found in the timber-framing in the Middle Ages were used on the basis of local availability.

285

284 Timber-framing with diagonal pieces or braces at the Villa of Diomedes, Pompeii.

285 Timber-framed shutterings of a corbelled upper storey on the via dell'Abbondanza at Pompeii, III,5,2.

286 Timber-framed houses with corbelling, probably identical to ancient examples, in the region of Bursa, Turkey.

286

5
MASONRY CONSTRUCTION

1 The foundations

The procedures followed in laying the foundations for ashlar construction remained the same whatever the nature of the structure being erected, and the manner in which the foundations of masonry structures were built also remained unchanged. As already noted, many stone block monuments rested on massive masonry, and when this is all that survives it is no longer possible to work out what form the building above took.

In northern Italy and particularly in Gaul, the layer of cultivable soil is often deep and so builders, especially of modest structures, did not attempt to reach rock but simply went down to a level at which the foundations would be resting on ground not affected by freezing and thawing, that is a depth of 50 to 70cm, depending on the harshness of the climate (fig.287).

Footing the base of the foundations is often a course of flat rubble stones, arranged on end in rows to ensure the drainage of water seepage and continuing in decreasing thickness up to street level (figs 288, 289, 290, 291).

The use of rubble masonry bonded with lime mortar, beginning in the second century BC, was to lead the Romans to an astonishing diversity in the application of construction materials. Not only were all types of rock or artificial materials made use of, but the methods of dressing, jointing and presentation were open to many possibilities. It is, however, possible to draw up a typological series of the different

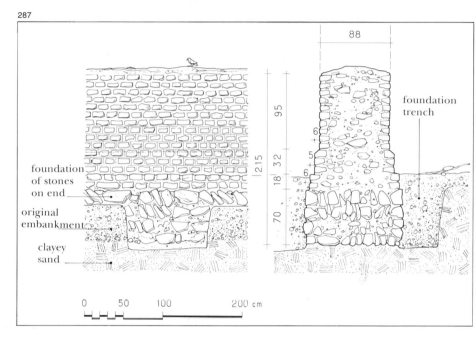

types of facing in stone and brick, though it must be remembered that each category can, even in the same wall, be combined with one or more of the others.[1]

287 Diagram of the foundations of a masonry wall, the facing of which has vertical joints deeply marked with a round iron and the lines of the courses highlighted with a flat tool (a trowel?). Theatre of Argentomagus. (St-Marcel, Indre.)

288 Foundations of a masonry wall from the Theatre of Argentomagus (St-Marcel, Indre).

MASONRY CONSTRUCTION

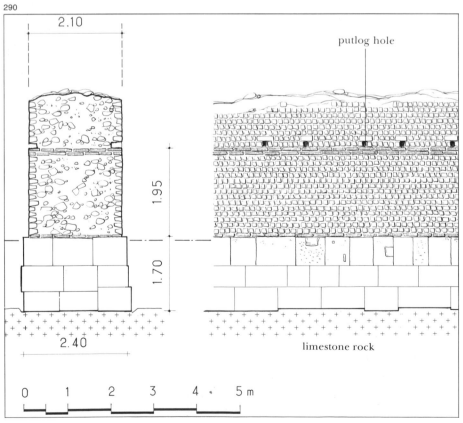

289 Foundations of the Casa dei Dipinti at Ostia, showing the imprints of the uprights of the framework (third century) used for buildings with walls of masonry or for ashlar construction.

290 Walls of Beauvais (end of the third century). This construction of reused stone blocks supported on levelled limestone bedrock demonstrates how stone block foundations are found underneath masonry structures.

291 Bourges (*Avaricum*). Cross-section through a wall where it crosses a levelled dip, necessitating an enormous mass of foundations with a wide footing to guarantee the stability of the construction.

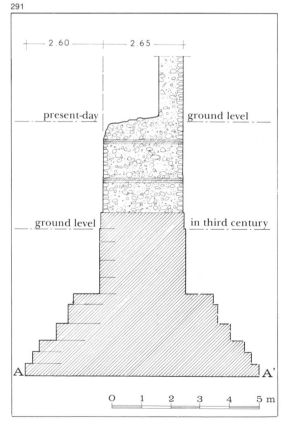

putlog hole

limestone rock

present-day
ground level

ground level

in third century

A   A'

292

294

293

295

2 *Opus incertum*

This type of facing, consisting of irregular small stones sometimes dressed on the exterior face, is actually the outer skin of *opus caementicium*, that is the supporting masonry bonded with mortar (figs 292, 293).

It should be remembered that the core of the masonry, as centuries progressed and the facing varied, remained an all-purpose fill unrelated to its outer appearance (except for *opus incertum*). In some cases it was not even the same material as the facing. Even brick walls were not on the whole totally homogeneous.

Opus incertum[2] appears alongside *a telaio* construction at Pompeii, both forms with roughly rectangular blocks (figs 294, 295), in the third century BC, and is found at the end of the same century at the Temple of Magna Mater on the Palatine[3] (in 204), and in a supporting wall of the Capitol[4] erected in 189BC,[5] then at the Porticus Aemilia and on the viaduct of the Roman Forum built in 174BC.[6] It is still found at the end of the second century BC at the Basilica in Pompeii, at the temple in Palestrina (fig.296) and at the Temple of Largo Argentina[7], and, above all, in numerous fortifications erected or completed between 100 and

292 *Opus caementicium* rendered with white stucco (surviving on the right) on the podium of the Temple of Jupiter at Pompeii. Second half of the second century BC.

293 *Opus incertum* at Pompeii, from the Samnite period (third-second century BC) at the House of Obellius Firmus (IX,14,4).

294 Rough rubble in walls of *opus incertum* at Pompeii lends itself particularly well to the attachment of different materials or foreign bodies, such as mortar, plaster and other things (VIII,3,17).

295 Masonry of *opus incertum*, liberally pointed ('buttered joints') (IX,6,5).

296

297

296   Temple of Fortuna at Palestrina (end of the second century BC). A facing of *opus incertum* with horizontal courses made of tufa rubble.

297   Walls of Terracina (between 90 and 82BC). A wall of *opus caementicium*, faced with *opus incertum*, showing the lines where the shuttering stopped.

298   Supporting terrace from the Temple of Jupiter Anxur at Terracina (c.90BC) with a facing of *opus incertum* with regular quoins.

91, the years preceding (and fore-shadowing) the Social War followed by the Civil War. Examples of structures faced with *opus incertum* on a support of *opus caementicium* include: the acropolis of Ardea,[8] the walls of Cori,[9] the walls of Formia[10] and, most spectacular of all, the walls of Terracina[11] (partly restored), not forgetting the Temple of Jupiter Anxur at the top[12] (figs 297, 298).

It is precisely during the bloody years straddling the second and the first centuries that this style of walling saw

its greatest development, its most carefully finished appearance, heralding its gradual disappearance at the end of the Republican period. It is somewhat surprising that it is found again in the nymphaeum of the 'domus with *atrium*' at Bolsena, dating from 40-30BC,[13] or at the funerary monument at Capua, known as 'La Conocchia' (the distaff), thought to be from the first century AD (fig.299).[14]

In general, however, with the exception of rural and rustic constructions that always call for the use of all-purpose stones, *opus incertum* declined in the Sullan period. It was replaced by reticulate construction that had already existed for a generation. This decline was due to the socio-economic evolution affecting the whole peninsula, bringing with it a systematization of the work of stone-cutters and masons and leading to massive production of prefabricated elements that could be used anywhere. If quasi-reticulate and then reticulate masonry brought about the demise of *opus incertum*, it is to a great extent due to the 'standardization' of stones;[15] with polygonal stones of random shape, the mason had to do a certain amount of selection and cutting to ensure that the facing fitted together. With reticulate masonry, as well as the later use of bricks, the job of the *structores* became simply one of assembly, the craft being in the preparation of the mortar and laying the stones.

There is one exception to this evolving sequence – reconstruction. The best example of this is the reconstruction of Pompeii (and Herculaneum) after the earthquake of 62 (fig.300). The systematic reuse of materials salvaged from ruins and employed without further preparation led to a considerable use of *opus incertum* in the buildings restored after that date, most frequently in association with the piers and the brick courses of *opus mixtum*.[16]

298

299

300

3 *Opus quasi reticulatum* and *opus reticulatum*

The transition from *opus incertum* to reticulate facings, in their initial rough form called *quasi reticulatum*,[17] took place, as far as can be judged from the discoveries made to date, in the last quarter of the second century BC. The original facing of the basin of the *Lacus Iuturnae*, or Fountain of the Nymph Iuturna in the Roman Forum (fig.301), is of quasi-reticulate, using small pieces of stone, and dates to 116BC,[18] and a similar treatment is found in phase II of the walls of the Temple of Magna Mater and at the Horrea Galbana.[19] The House of the Griffins on the Palatine and the cella of Temple B in Largo Argentina date to 100BC.[20] At Ostia, the façade of the podium of the four Republican temples is of quasi-reticulate construction,[21] as well as two of the three temples of the Temple of Hercules, all buildings dating from the first quarter of the first century BC.

The years that followed the founding of a Roman colony at Pompeii, around

299 La Conocchia (the Distaff), the funerary monument erected on the *via Appia* near Santa Maria Capua Vetere. A late example of masonry faced with *opus incertum*, erected at the end of the first century or the beginning of the second. Notice the use of brick for most of the piers, for the lintels and the mouldings.

300 An example of composite masonry from the last phase at Pompeii (62 to 79) which escapes definitive typing since there is *opus incertum* with courses of *opus mixtum* and piers, one of brick, the other of *opus mixtum* (VIII,4,53).

301

303

302

301 The Fountain of the Nymph Iuturna, or Lacus Iuturnae, in the Roman Forum, is one of the most ancient buildings with a reticulate facing: the lower part of the walls in fact goes back to 116BC; the upper part is a restoration from the Imperial period.

302 A facing of uncertain definition, with *opus incertum* alongside particularly hesitant *opus quasi reticulatum*, on the great cistern of the Forum Baths at Pompeii, built around 80BC. The facing stones are approximately 12 by 16cm.

80BC, were to provide this town with civic schemes intended as much conciliation as a display of power.

Among the new buildings, the Forum Baths, the amphitheatre and the Odeon (figs 302, 303. 304), all have, to varying degrees, facings of *opus quasi reticulatum*. On the great cistern supplying the Forum Baths the *quasi reticulatum* is not continuous and it even ends higher up the wall in random *opus incertum*. The same observation can be made at the baths themselves and at the amphitheatre, where the work of assembly is far from regularly executed; only the Odeon seems to have received more coherent facings.

The use of this new arrangement of small square stones laid diagonally posed a problem for the buttressing of projecting angles because of the absence of horizontal courses; this problem was resolved at first by the adoption of quoins of bricks which were cut out to form serrations and thus fitted better into the reticulate design. This technique, however, adopted at Pompeii for the Odeon and some houses, remained rare and it is hardly found except at the Theatre of Cassino (fig.305) built around 40BC;[22] elsewhere rubble stones or bricks in horizontal courses and cut like quoins made of stone blocks were employed.

The transformation from quasi-reticulate to reticulate took place in a very irregular fashion depending on the locality or the building scheme. The walls of Sepino (*Saepinum*), built between 2BC and AD3,[23] have a mixture of quasi-reticulate and very fine regular courses. The theatre of Gubbio has an extremely rustic facing put up in the first century BC, while its equivalent in Cassino already displays considerable

305

304

regularity. The same precision can also be found on the Republican warehouses at Ostia[24] and, better still, at the temple with three cellae at Terracina (the 'Capitol') erected in the middle of the first century BC with a beautiful facing of reticulate construction, in which horizontal rows of white limestone alternate with dark tufa.[25]

The choice of an arrangement of small stones at 45 degrees might at first appear odd, but it is in fact in line with the economic and social evolution of the Roman world, an evolution which led to the creation and expansion of new techniques. It has already been noted that the use of an abundant supply of servile labour from the end of the third century BC had encouraged the aediles to go in for the rapid manufacture of construction materials that could easily be worked after a brief period of specialized training. This was to lead to an even more precise standardization, bringing about a simplification of the mason's job as mentioned before. If the small stones were laid in oblique courses a problem arose, because of their square outline and the variations in the thickness of the joins, of how to ensure a regular intersection and so avoid

vertical alignments or 'sabre cuts'; it was easier instead to lay the stones in the right-angled cavities provided by the course in place. This is why, later, *opus vittatum* was to use blocks that were more generally rectangular. However, the masons noticed that the cementation brought about by good mortar made the arrangement of the stones irrelevant, which is perhaps the reason why the stones in Gallo-Roman coursed rubble masonry often had an approximately square facing surface.

In very general terms, regular reticulate construction was adopted in central and central-southern Italy at the end of the Republican period, and the Theatre of Pompey at Rome, completed in 55BC[26] confirms its well-established use in the construction of great public buildings.

Vitruvius describes it as the ideal masonry of his period: *Structurarum genera, sunt haec: reticulatum, quo nunc omnes utuntur; et antiquum, quod incertum*

303 The Amphitheatre of Pompeii, like the Odeon or the Forum Baths, forms a part of the public monuments erected by the Roman colony from 80BC; it is a relatively unified construction in the form of quasi-reticulate facing, clearly showing how far behind Campania was in relation to Rome and the still approximate nature of this newly imported technique.

304 *Opus quasi reticulatum* from the Odeon at Pompeii (c.80BC) made of lava rubble with serrated brick piers. This distinctive arrangement, of which there are a number of examples at Pompeii, can also be found at the Theatre of Cassino, dating from the Augustan period.

305 The amphitheatre of Cassino (*Casinum*) (late first century BC), with a facing of *opus quasi-reticulatum* with quoins of ashlar construction.

306

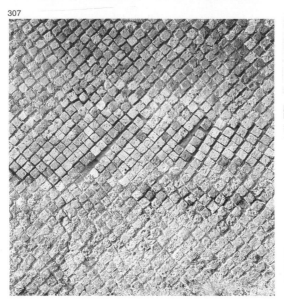

307

308

306 Pompeii, Julian-Claudian period. A reticulate façade which is randomly polychrome due to the use of different local rocks. The quoin is made of tufa blocks (VI,6,18).

307 Reticulate construction at Pompeii (VI,3,25) showing a curious misfit between two sections of work (first century). Dimensions of the reticulate tesserae: 7 x 7 to 8 x 8cm.

308 Very fine *opus reticulatum* from the last phase at Pompeii (62- 79) with tight joints and quoins made of brick (door) and of small blocks (window). Notice the putlog-holes, one of them relieved by a small arch. Dimension of the reticulate tesserae: 8 x 8cm (VIII,2,14).

309 Aqueduct of Minturno (*Minturnae*). Masonry bonded with lime mortar with reticulate facings, the quoins and arch crowns made of small blocks. Augustan period.

310 Certain types of mortar have proved to be much more resistant than the rubble that they were used to bond, notably in volcanic areas where mortar made of pozzolana has excellent qualities of resistance. On the other hand, the tufa of these areas used for building is often very soft and susceptible to the effects of erosion, as for example this Phlegrean tufa ('tufo giallo' from Cuma) which here has become particularly pitted. This is caused by the variation in ageing in a reticulate facing, a rigid network that becomes the skeleton of the wall. The so-called Temple of Jupiter on the Acropolis of Cuma, Julian-Claudian period. Dimensions of the reticulate tesserae: 9 x 9cm.

dicitur: 'There are two kinds of masonry: the reticulate which everyone uses today and the old one which is called uncertain' (II,8).

At Herculaneum there is a proliferation of *opus reticulatum* for facing both public and private monuments, such as the Theatre, built around 30BC, or the Suburban Baths, and also on numerous buildings of Pompeii, where the finest reticulate work is seen on the *macellum*, in the south wall (figs 306, 307, 308).

It seems that the area of the use of reticulate masonry remained essentially central and central-southern Italy, where it developed in the course of the first century BC and the first century AD in very numerous structures (figs 309, 310). Curiously, however, this success was not to extend over the whole peninsula, and the southern provinces of Campania have so far only provided rare examples, among them a tomb at Scolacium, the temenos of the Temple of Hera at Croton and the Theatre of Grumentum.[27] But no reticulate wall has yet appeared in the cities, however important, such as Paestum, Velia, Locri or Heraclea. Again, in the north of Italy, towards Emilia, Venetia, Liguria, reticulate construction disappears; its presence in the aqueduct of the Gier supplying Lyon, perhaps built in the middle of the first century, is all the more unusual since, apart from this monument there is hardly any reticulate construction in Gaul other than the *horrea* of Narbonne, from the Later Republican period, and, some sections of the walls and the aqueduct at Fréjus. Outside the peninsula to the south, Sardinia has preserved only one example,[28] Sicily almost none,[29] and proconsular Africa offers the curious and surprising building at Bulla Regia made of *opus africanum* with reticulate sections;[30] as for the Eastern Mediterranean there are only two examples of its use of any importance.[31]

In the area where it developed,

central Italy and Campania, *opus reticulatum* remained in frequent use throughout the first century and the first half of the second, with perhaps its final use in the Phlegrean Baths and in the complex of Hadrian's Villa; and it was most probably the growing use of brick, another standardized and mass-produced material, that was to lead to its decrease and then disappearance in the first half of the second century. In fact it is found right up until the time of Antoninus Pius; thus it is present in the amphitheatre of Lecce dated by an inscription of Trajan,[32] and apparently had a final revival in the reign of Hadrian. It is visible in the buildings of Ostia (Small Market, the House of the Triclinia) (fig.311), on the additions to the baths at Baia ('Temple of Venus') and particularly in the sumptuous residence at Tivoli[33] built between 118 and 133 (fig.312).

The use of brick for corners, whatever the nature of the construction, produced a multi-coloured effect which could enhance the appearance of the facings, and the simple mixture of rocks of different types allowed variations which masons, particularly at Pompeii, could exploit very attractively. The great range of stones from around Vesuvius already created mixtures in *opus incertum*, admittedly random, that reticulate construction was to accentuate considerably. It was natural that the masons sometimes carried out a selection when stones were delivered and in the walls they amused themselves making lines and more complex figures, even letters. Though in Rome the remains are scarce, at Ostia polychrome compositions can be found mixing tufa, lava and bricks (figs 313, 314, 315, 316, 317).

In studying these polychrome masonry walls, however, one surprising thing is noticeable: the majority have the remains of rendering on them which would once have masked them completely. Indeed it is curious

309

to think that, whatever trouble the masons took, it was doomed to be hidden by the application of a covering decoration for which more rough and ready masonry would have been sufficient. It is more satisfying to believe that these renderings were applied later to fit in with architectural fashion or the whims of successive owners.

310

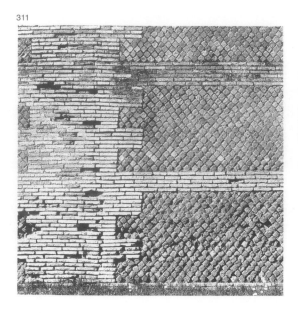

311   Reticulate façade of tufa with vertical and horizontal brick pier and string-course, in the Piccolo Mercato at Ostia. First half of the first century AD.

312   Reticulate facing with a pier of small blocks and coursing consisting of three rows of bricks at Hadrian's Villa, 118 to 133.

313   Polychrome reticulate facing, with a course of bricks, on the bridge of Beaunant on the aqueduct of the Gier, one of the four installations supplying Lyon. Middle of the first century (?). (Photo: A. Olivier.)

314   Reticulate construction from a tomb at Ostia, near the Porta Romana, made of tufa, lava and brick (middle of the second century). The composition of the colouring of this wall is very similar to the aqueduct of the Gier.

315   Facing of polychrome *opus reticulatum* with a quoin of *opus mixtum* at Pompeii (VI,3,3). The richness in the coloration of such a wall, very typical of Pompeii, is an indication that it was intended to remain visible.

316   Herculaneum, façade of *Insula* VI, the lower part *opus incertum*, the upper part *opus reticulatum* made of tufa with the inclusion of the letters V and A made of lava; it was completely covered with rendering.

4 *Opus vittatum*

This use of blocks which seems the most logical and the most conventional consists simply of arranging stones with a rectangular outline and of equal height in horizontal courses; it is in effect isodomic or pseudo-isodomic construction on a small scale.

Despite this apparent simplicity, *opus vittatum*[34] hardly appears before the Augustan period. However, at Pompeii, regular courses of small limestone blocks are found filling sections of the *a telaio* constructions as early as the third century BC. During the first century BC, with the systematic use of volcanic tufa, these rectangular blocks (called locally tufelli) were used above all for quoins. The first large works to survive that made use of rectangular stones are not homogeneous buildings but restorations, admittedly of some importance, carried out on the Sullan walls of Segni and Cori, in the second half of the first century BC. In the Augustan period it is likewise fortification projects that first profited from a systematic use of *opus vittatum* as is attested on the walls of Fano,[35] of Nîmes and especially of Spello (fig.318).[36]

At Pompeii it is the towers built to break the pressure of the water supply, erected in the Augustan period, that represent the first projects entirely using tufelli and, subsequently, apart from some isolated walls (fig.319), there is only the enormous building of Eumachia, the wool market on the forum, built in the reign of Tiberius, that made exclusive use of it.[37]

In Rome and its immediate environs, construction using small stones in regular courses was practically unknown before the middle of the second century AD, and even during this period it was still found associated with brick. Its use there declined in the Antonine period and is only found again in the reign of Maxentius (307 to

317

312) when it became more general due to the ease of reusing materials of earlier periods.

The situation was different in other regions, particularly Gaul, where, in the Augustan period, *opus vittatum* became the standard form of architecture bonded with mortar, in parallel with ashlar construction, and was to remain so right up until the end of the Roman period and even beyond, in the regions where the art of building had not been lost. In other provinces, such as Spain, Asia Minor or North Africa,[38] rectangular pieces were used in rubble masonry, but without ever affecting the architecture as they did in Gaul. In the Hellenized world ashlar construction retained, until the division of the Empire, a considerable predominance, and the Roman masonry additions (such as the Baths of Epidaurus or the Serapeum of Pergamon), having lost

317 Reticulate construction from the last phase at Pompeii (62-79) with brick courses and quoins made of *opus mixtum* decorated with geometric motifs devised by the mason according to the nature and colour of his materials (VIII,2,30).

318

320

318 Augustan walls of Spello, *Colonia Iulia Hispellum*, faced with perfectly dressed and coursed rectangular blocks of limestone. Average height of the courses: 22 to 29cm; joints of grey, very hard mortar, width: 0.2 to 0.8cm.

319 Pompeii (VIII,2,30), wall of *opus vittatum* with 'buttered joints'. Facings of small coursed blocks on their own are not very common in this city; they are only rarely found in the pillars of secondary water towers and in the great building of Eumachia (the wool market) built in the Julio-Claudian period.

320 A tower in the walls of Fréjus faced with *opus vittatum* in which the putlog-holes are visible. Beginning of the first century AD.

their renderings, still have an incongruous appearance.

It is at Forum Julii (Fréjus), which became *Octavianorum colonia* with the installation of the colony of the veterans of the VIII legion by Octavius after his victory at Actium (31BC), that the first truly Roman town was built in Gaul. Fortunately a number of the

319

ancient buildings of this city have survived, including the walls and the theatre, belonging to the Augustan building scheme and built entirely of *opus vittatum*; the aqueduct and the amphitheatre that followed used the same technique (figs 320, 321).[39]

No other type of masonry was found in Gaul until the beginning of the second century and, even after the introduction of brick courses, the use of small squared stones remained largely predominant for the body and the surface of the walls. It is sufficient to mention here, apart from the constructions of Fréjus, some other notable building works from the period from Augustus to Trajan, in which solely *opus vittatum* was used:[40] the Tour Magne at Nîmes; the 'Basilica' of Vaison; the amphitheatre at Saintes; the amphitheatre at Senlis (figs 322, 323); the amphitheatre at Lutèce (original state); the amphitheatre at Grand; the Temple at Puy de Dôme; the aqueduct at Metz; the Theatre of Vienne; the Great Theatre of Lyon; and the Theatre of Autun.

The typology of regular 'petit appareil' block construction encompasses a great variety of appearances, from the most

321

322   323

321 Amphitheatre of Fréjus (first century) built of 'petit appareil' in masonry with regular courses.

322 Facing of 'petit appareil' of the amphitheatre of Senlis (first century). The coarseness of the masonry of the facing is visible in the irregular size of the rubble and their approximate alignment.

323 Amphitheatre of Senlis (first century). Facing of *opus vittatum*, with quoins of ashlar.

basic to the most carefully assembled. The finest achievement is surely the facing of the aqueduct at Metz, still visible along a section of the Moselle at Jouy-aux-Arches, where the masons actually fashioned small rectangular blocks into a regular construction of equal courses and of regularly alternating joints (fig.324). This perfectionism was extremely rare and in the vast majority of cases the illusion of regularity was created by the way the

stones were fitted together. The joints between the stones were, as a general rule, much finer during the first half of the Empire (1 to 2cm), although this

rule is far from exact. However, the space was always sufficient to allow a mark to be made in the fresh mortar separating each stone from the next, using any instrument to hand (the blade of a trowel, a small stick or a piece of metal), so as to highlight the vertical joints and the lines of the horizontal courses (figs 325, 326). One of the best examples of the application of this technique is found in the facings of the amphitheatre of Grand, which is also made up of regular 'petit appareil' laid very exactly. This structure has another peculiarity worth mentioning: exceptionally, the core behind the facings was coursed all the way through the wall instead of being made of a mass of *opus caementicium*.

It is probable that this marking of the joints allowed the stone-masons to simplify their task, and in many cases the disappearance of the pointing or repointing mortar (depending on whether it was applied between the stones during construction or added after from the outside) reveals a considerable mediocrity in the dressing of the facing stones.

This method of construction could be adapted to any form and any building scheme thanks to its reduced dimensions (the height of courses are very generally on average 10 to 12cm for small blocks from 10 to 20cm long) and the masons always laid the stones in horizontal courses. The ends of the walls were buttressed by piers which alternated larger stretchers and headers; in the largest buildings, the quoins of the walls and the jambs of the openings might be made of stone blocks, while in Italy it was almost always brick that provided the corner support. The courses which, instead of remaining horizontal, follow the slope of the ground, must therefore be considered as exceptional, as can be seen in the vomitoria of the Theatre of St-Marcel (Argentomagus), near Argenton-sur-Creuse or, even more scenically, in numerous sections of Hadrian's Wall where the construction follows the undulations of the ground (figs 327, 328, 329).

5 *Opus mixtum*

Under this heading can be included a number of types of masonry, the majority of which have already been referred to; it is generally in facings that rubble and brick are found together. As noted above, in the first applications of quasi-reticulate construction, brick was used to construct quoins with serrated edges like those visible at the Odeon of Pompeii. In this southern region terracotta was used in construction long before it was in Rome, always mixed with rubble masonry and often in the form of trimmed *tegulae*, a use that continued even after the more systematic manufacture of bricks.

The great gate at the north-west corner of Pompeii, known as the Herculaneum Gate and identified by its Oscan name as the *veru sarinu*, poses an interesting problem of chronology in relation to *opus mixtum* (fig.330). Here the bases are made up of alternate courses of small rectangular blocks and bricks, a technique that was used all the way up the quoins; then, above the side arches, there is a facing of *opus incertum* of lava rubble typical of the masonry of the second and the beginning of the first century BC, found, among other places, in the towers of the first phase of the walls put up before 90. Finally, the whole building was rendered with white stucco imitating a work of ashlar construction, identical itself to the wall decoration of the towers. However, it is not possible to establish a link between a defensive system, by definition continuous, and this gate, the most substantial of the city with its enormous central passage for vehicles and its two side passages for pedestrians. Besides this, there is also a noticeable change of orientation in relation to the alignment of the curtain wall in this section built with stone blocks, as well as an absence of towers or of a flanking

324 Aqueduct of Metz at Jouy-aux-Arches (end of the first century) with very fine, regular 'petit appareil' facing with crossed joints. Notice the maize-corn outline of the rubble stones going into the infill.

325 Wall of 'petit appareil' at the Theatre of Argentomagus (St-Marcel). The stones of the quoins have been made larger so as to have a greater contact surface with the masonry and so give more cohesion to this section.

326 Facing of *opus vittatum* made up of almost square blocks, the joints of which have been carefully alternated. Notice the marks left by the cutting and the lines of the courses highlighted by a trowel imprint in the pointing mortar. Walls of Beauvais, end of the third century.

327 Internal wall of a vomitorium in the Gallo-Roman Theatre of Argentomagus, the courses of which follow the slope. First century.

328 Section of Hadrian's Wall on a steep slope where the facing blocks are arranged in horizontal courses (c.128).

329 Section of Hadrian's Wall where the courses of the facing blocks follow the variations in the land surface (c.128).

330

331

330 The Herculaneum Gate at Pompeii built between 80BC and the Augustan period. The masonry is faced with *opus incertum* made of lava, with wide quoins of *opus mixtum* made of tufa block and brick, perhaps the oldest of this type at Pompeii. The central arch collapsed during the earthquake of AD 62 and was not rebuilt. Plaster imitating ashlar construction covered the walls.

331 Complex *opus mixtum*, with a reticulate facing on a foundation of limestone blocks and quoins of block and brick. Pompeii VI,3,17.

bastion and, in addition, a perceptible widening of the thoroughfare. It therefore seems certain that this was a structure whose monumental appearance and arrangement testify to a concern for both architectural display at the entrance to the city and ease of access. The use of *opus incertum* of lava and the similarity of the stucco to that on the towers and the basilica (erected *c.*120BC) associated with the founding of the Sullan colony and with the change in use of the fortifications, combine to place the gate's construction in the period of the civic building projects after the year 80. Without being able to be more precise, it is tempting to suggest the period between the year 80 and the reign of Augustus for the construction of this building.[41] The presence of *opus mixtum* would not contradict this suggestion, since brick and rubble are associated with the Odeon (built shortly after 80) and numerous houses from the first century BC. Finally, there is some archaeological evidence that can be used to establish a lower limit for the construction of the Herculaneum Gate: the presence of a tomb from the first century against the monument on its external face and built after it.[42]

From that time, *opus mixtum* remained in use in the city, alongside or juxtaposed with *opus reticulatum* (fig.331), until the eruption of the year 79. There are innumerable examples of walls, quoins, brick courses and masonry columns using this arrangement of materials, the last including the shops bordering the Central Baths along the via Stabiana.

It seems that the use of *opus mixtum* in the north of Campania must be almost contemporary since it is found, in an admittedly rustic form, at the villa of the Centroni on the *via Latina*, built in the first half of the first century BC where there is a mixture of bricks and *opus incertum*;[43] however, examples remain rare before the Flavian period.[44]

Among the great public monuments erected before the end of the first century AD worth mentioning are: the amphitheatre of Carsulae[45] near Terni, from the Julio-Claudian period, and the theatre and the amphitheatre of Scolacium, in Magna Graecia,[46] built by Nerva (96–8), while the amphitheatre of Tibur (Tivoli) once thought to date to the first century, seems most likely to have been finished, to judge from a donor's inscription,[47] in the Hadrianic period.

During the early second century *opus mixtum* coexisted with *opus reticulatum*, which was already very restricted, and then gave way to the intensive use of brick. However, unlike reticulate construction, it did not disappear completely since, on the contrary, its use was to become general in Gaul and it was always present in the peninsula.

The width of the courses of brick

332

that punctuate the rubble facings in the different versions of *opus mixtum* varies considerably. In the case of the *opus incertum* in the reconstructions at Pompeii (fig.332) and in reticulate construction, the distance apart remained quite substantial (1m or more) while, in the case of *opus vittatum mixtum*, the gap could either be large or considerably reduced until it reached an alternation of one or two courses of bricks to one course of blocks (figs 333, 334, 335). It should be remembered, however, that this last arrangement can in no way serve as an indication of chronology, since it is found at Pompeii in the Herculaneum Gate up to the restorations after the year 62; at Hadrian's Villa in the last additions of

332 *Opus mixtum* from the last phase at Pompeii (62-79) made up of *opus incertum* with courses and quoins of brick (VI,10,15).

333 *Opus mixtum* at the Villa dei Sette Bassi on the *via Latina* (c.140-50). In the gaps it is noticeable that the bricks are only present in the facing, and that the core, instead of being a single mass, is coursed. Note also that the previous example from Pompeii, with courses of six rows of bricks but some eighty years older, proves the durability of certain fashions and techniques making it difficult to date them if these criteria are the only ones taken into account.

333

334

336

137-8; at the aqueduct of Sette Bassi on the *via Latina* in the third quarter of the second century;[48] at the large nympheum of the Quintilii (fig.336); on the *via Appia* in the period of Commodus (after 181);[49] at the Curia of Paestum in the Severan period;[50] at Ostia in numerous constructions from the second and third centuries

including a number of tombs, the foundations of the Round Temple (*c.*230), the southern part of the *Schola* of Trajan (end of the third century),[51] the House of Amor and Psyche (*c.*300) (fig.337); and particularly in the monumental works of Maxentius, between 306 and 312, not only his building complex on the *via Appia*[52] where his Palace, the tomb of Romulus and the circus were erected, but also the extension work to the Aurelian Wall.[53]

In Roman Gaul, for which the history of architectural techniques is much more basic, only two types of masonry were known: simple *opus vittatum* and *opus vittatum mixtum*. This second type, as already indicated, seems to have made its apearance during the reign of Trajan (98 to 117) and to have spread during the reign of Hadrian, becoming the only method of masonry construction until the end of the Empire.

Here again the date of the introduction of brick into architecture, as a contributory element, is not and never will be fixed with any accuracy.[54] What is certain is that the two largest temples of indigenous type that have survived: the so-called 'Temple of Janus' at Autun and the 'Tower of Vésone' at Périgueux (fig.338), the erection of which can be placed between the

335

334 The alternation of block and brick courses can vary within the same building, as on this tomb from the Eastern Necropolis at Ostia.

335 Variety of *opus mixtum* from the last phase at Pompeii (62-79), in a shop at the Central Baths (IX,4,4). The regular alternation of one course of block and two brick courses cannot be used as a clue to the chronology as it is found again at the Circus of Maxentius.

336 *Opus mixtum*, from the great nympheum of the Villa of the Quintilii on the *via Appia*, with a regular alternation of brick courses and courses of tufa blocks. This type of facing is not seen in the vaults where the *opus caementicium* was laid directly on the centring, and in the arches crowning the niches which are of radially laid bricks. Third century.

338

337

reigns of Trajan and Hadrian, represent definite stages in the use of brick in Gaul, in the form of the frames of openings and horizontal strings. However, the presence of brick courses in the monumental complex of the 'Incarnate Word' at Lyon, based on the oldest dedication of the temple dating from the period of Tiberius – if this date can be extended to all the buildings – could provide a new chronological point of reference for the introduction of this material north of the Rhône valley.[55]

Whereas in the *opus mixtum* constructions in Italy the brick courses are only elements of the facings, perhaps used to check the level, the Gallo-Roman builders used this material to great benefit in making true horizontal bonds connecting the two faces of the walls. Thus the three separate parts, consisting of facings and core, were united at intervals, for instance the walls of a building fixed by the floor levels. In many cases, these brick courses corresponded to one shuttering in height or one day's work and their intervals followed the gaps between successive levels of scaffolding, as is evident from the positions of the putlog-holes (figs 339, 340).

The observations made about *opus vittatum* apply also to mixed facings:

the joints can be emphasized by a groove, while the small facing blocks, the shape of which was approximately that of a truncated pyramid, display on their visible surfaces the various marks of the blade used in dressing.

In the last quarter of the third century, Gaul had to initiate a construction programme of urban fortifications, unprecedented in history, in order to protect its open cities. These considerable works were all constructed in exactly the same way – with foundations of reused stone blocks and *opus caementicium* faced with 'petit appareil' using brick courses.

The remarks made above about polychrome masonry in Italy covered with rendering also apply to Gallo-Roman

337 Ostia, House of Amor and Psyche, c.AD 300. *Opus mixtum*, alternating one course of blocks and two courses of bricks.

338 The 'Tour de Vésone' at Périgueux, a large *fanum* with circular cella, erected at the earliest in the reign of Trajan, is one of the first Gallo-Roman monuments to use brick.

339 Brick courses appeared in Gallo-Roman architecture at the beginning of the second century, and were to remain in constant use but with varying thickness until the end of the Empire. Frequently, as here in the walls of Beauvais (end of the third century), the brick courses were made use of to align the putlog-holes.

339

340

341

340 Wall of 'petit appareil' with brick courses joining the two facings, at the Forum of Bavay. Second century.

341 Rubble in reticulate arrangement in the walls of Bavay. End of the third century.

342 Walled up doorway with rough masonry of *opus spicatum*, at the House of the Antes at Glanum.

constructions, since, with the exception of defensive walls, the majority of walls retain on the inside and sometimes on the outside, the remains of a coating of mortar which masks walls that frequently have, as at the forum of Bavay, real decorative value.

6 *Opus spicatum*

This type of facing owes its name, meaning 'ear of wheat' (also called 'herring-bone' or 'fern-leaf' construc-

tion) to the arrangement of the small stones of which it consists. Instead of being arranged in horizontal courses, placed on their largest side, these are laid at an angle of about 45 degrees, one on top of another, each course alternating its direction of incline. The technique arose in the areas where there are stones which split naturally into small flattened blocks, or flatstones in river valleys rich in this material. Such shapes were much easier to arrange in this way, simply bonded with clay mortar, and there are still many examples in the Rhône valley of these attractive facings.

This technique was used particularly for the footing and the bulk of foundations or under floors and roadways; laid like this, the stones of the lowest level do not impede the passage of water that has penetrated the construction. The technique is sometimes found also in the core of defensive walls, a technique visible in the walls of Bavay in places where the facing has disappeared (fig.341). This is also sometimes how gaps were filled and openings blocked up, using unworked material, as shown by a blocked-up door in the house of the Antes at Glanum or a repair job at the theatre of Argentomagus (fig.342).

The only monument of any size

342

where *opus spicatum* appears on the facing is the large undated building called the 'Mansio' in Thésée,[56] erected at the entrance to this commune (Loir et Cher; fig.343). The visible masonry is not entirely of herring-bone formation but alternates with horizontal courses and courses of brick which, exceptionally for Gaul, do not go all the way through the wall. However, it is noticeable that the masons, when pointing, carefully scored with a metal tool both the oblique and the right-angled joints without attempting to unify the facing.

7 Brick, *opus testaceum*

The strongest visual memory left in the minds of those who have visited Rome and its vicinity is one of a monumental body of brick from which there emerge, now and then, some isolated remains of travertine or marble. In fact it is remarkable that the most impressive achievements of Imperial architecture in Rome, especially from the time of Nero onwards, owe most of their architecture to brick. The following are some of the milestones in this development: perhaps the first great brick construction, the *Castra praetoria*, or camp of the Praetorian Guard, built by

Tiberius between 21 and 23; then the Domus Aurea, built after the fire of 64; the internal masonry of the Colosseum, begun under Vespasian; the complex on the Palatine built by Domitian from 81 to 92; the Ludus Magnus of the same emperor; the major buildings of Trajan – the Forum and the Markets, from 107 to 113; the Baths of 109; and the whole townscape of Ostia in the second century, beginning with the works carried out by Trajan; the Baths of Agrippa restored by Hadrian; the Pantheon constructed between 118 and 125; the Tomb of Hadrian (Castel Sant'Angelo) finished in 139; the Amphitheatre Castrense erected at the beginning of the third century; the Baths of Caracalla built between 212 and 216; the Aurelian Wall begun in 271; the great building works of Diocletian – the Baths of 298 to 306; the reconstruction of the Curia and of the Basilica Julia on the Forum; and finally the Basilica of Maxentius begun in 306 (figs 344, 345, 346).

This long list, although incomplete and relating to the city of Rome only,

343 Facing of 'petit appareil' mixing regular courses with *opus spicatum*, at the 'Mansio' of Thésée.

344 Street in the *Insula* of Diana at Ostia. The expansion of the city at the beginning of the second century saw the triumph of brick in the majority of façades. In the foreground the 'Casa dei Dipinti'.

345

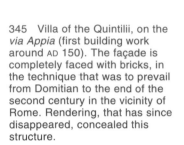

345 Villa of the Quintilii, on the *via Appia* (first building work around AD 150). The façade is completely faced with bricks, in the technique that was to prevail from Domitian to the end of the second century in the vicinity of Rome. Rendering, that has since disappeared, concealed this structure.

346 The Amphitheatre Castrense, built of brick in the Severan period (beginning of the third century). Of the three levels only the first has survived, and its Corinthian order with brick capitals.

346

is sufficient to show the dominant position occupied by brick in Roman architecture. It is also testimony to the remarkable economic planning estab-

lished in the Imperial period, on the basis of the mass-production of building materials, abandoning the extraction and dressing of blocks of stone, despite the fact that this was already highly standardized, in favour of the industrial manufacture of bricks – which could be produced more quickly and were easier to use due to their absolute regularity and greater surface area for support.

North of Rome, if the proposed dating is accurate, the oldest large building work in brick is the majestic Porta Palatini in Turin, with its internal court and side towers, the façade of which, pierced by four passage openings and topped by two levels of arches, is perfectly faced with brick.[57] The construction of this monument is attributed to Augustus because of the purity of its composition and the simplicity of its mouldings. Its structural distinctiveness, however, makes some scholars think that the date should be moved to the Flavian period. But whatever its age, this monument remains a spectacular example of architectural achievement, whose balanced design is independent of the nature of the building materials and proves that the Romans were able to overcome all technical problems.

The impression of visitors to Rome referred to above is, admittedly, only an impression of the skeletal remains, since just as with the buildings made of rubble masonry, the brick monuments were in many cases covered with a rendering of mortar or a layer of marble. It is perhaps paradoxical that this architecture, well-planned, cost-effective, time-saving and deceptive to the eye, maintains an extraordinarily varied compositon often made of an core of *opus caementicium*, facings of brick (or small stone), and a veneer of marble or three layers of plaster finished with a relief or a painted decoration.

As noted above, up until the Augustan period, the unbaked bricks described by Vitruvius,[58] referred to as *opus latericium,* were in current use, but their remains have by now disappeared, while the oldest structures of baked brick, the *opus testaceum* of the monuments of Campania at the end of the period of independence (the columns of the Basilica in Pompeii) have fortunately survived.

The typology of brick facings is fairly straightforward and the variations through the centuries relate only to the dimensions and form of the material, the quality of its manufacture and the care taken over its use. These different factors, referred to in the chapter on the manufacture of ceramic materials – though they have no chronological weight especially in the absence of stamp marks – must be taken into consideration with regards to the relative chronology of a monumental complex, and certainly allow a value judgement regarding the production process and its applications. It seems in any case that, from the time ceramic materials were first used, at least in Italy, they were deliberately broken up. Evidence for this is found in the innumerable examples of cut up tiles incorporated in the masonry of Pompeii.

The basic elements are large square bricks, the manufacture of which was standardized in the first century AD. The main formats and their names were: *bessales,* $\frac{2}{3}$ foot long or 19.7cm; *sesquipedales,* $1\frac{1}{2}$ foot long or 44.4cm; *bipedales,* 2 feet long or 59.2cm.

These different bricks could be used in their original sizes or broken up into regular pieces, in particular triangles. The advantage of this was that they could then be adapted to building needs and also, because of the roughness of the break, made with a cutting tool[59] or a saw, they adhered very well to the mortar of the infilling. The usual divisions were:

bessales: 2 triangular bricks 19.7 × 19.7 × 28cm, or 4 triangular bricks 19.7 × 14 × 14cm

sesquipedales: 8 triangular bricks 22.2 × 22.2 × 31.4cm

bipedales: 18 triangular bricks 19.7 × 19.7 × 27.8cm (fig.347).

These bricks and their subdivisions are found at absolutely every level of the buildings as well as in walls, frames, arches and lintels, vaults, floors or heating installations (figs 348, 349, 350, 351). However, the figures given here do not constitute a rule and local customs as well as those of the manufacturers and builders lead to considerable variations in the types of bricks, whether square, rectangular, triangular or circular (for the small pillars in hypocausts).[60] Also, although the bricks used whole maintain a certain uniformity of size, it is evident that they can, especially the broken tiles, end up irregular. So in the Baths of Cluny in Paris (end of the second, beginning of the third century) are found at least three rectangular brick sizes in the brick courses, with the foot as a common

347 The division of square bricks into standard sizes.

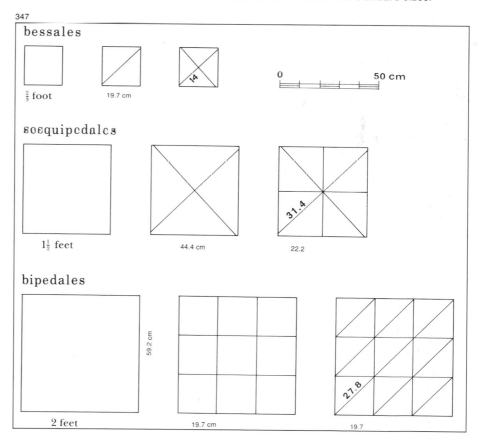

348

349

348 Masonry wall faced with triangular bricks. Ostia, beginning of the second century.

349 Quoin of finely constructed brick in a reticulate wall, with a less carefully executed horizontal course. Ostia, tomb on the Isola Sacra, Flavian period.

350 Ostia, tomb of the second century on the Isola Sacra with an unusual facing of bricks arranged in *opus spicatum* in the manner of a floor-covering.

351 Polychrome rosette at the corner of two streets in Pompeii, made of lava, tufa and terracotta (VIII,4,53). Dating to the last building phase. This is not polychromy using bricks carried out over a large area with another material, but a restrained decoration similar to the *lararia* of Ostia (but very slightly earlier).

factor: 30 × 38cm, 29.5 × 42cm and 29.5 × 44.5cm; some of them have two bosses projecting very slightly to facilitate bonding with the mortar. Their thickness also varies, ranging from 3 to 4.2cm. Such bricks, when they were used to bond the two facings, as was generally the case in Gaul, were not broken but used in their original size. However, trimming was carried out to assist in positioning and to line up the corners.

Just as the different qualities of stone had encouraged the masons to create polychrome facings, the various colorations of the bricks, which resulted from different clays and firing temperatures, led to the creation of façades in which the colours were combined with moulding in the same material, so dispensing with the need for stucco or stone.

The first major construction which took advantage of brick walls, left bare and juxtaposed with a different material, is perhaps the complex of the Markets of Trajan. Here the openings are framed with travertine contrasting sharply with the broad red surfaces, emphasizing the harmony and the balance of this remarkable composition (fig.352). In the course of the second century the examples of decoration carried out using brick alone multiply, above all in the region of Rome and

350

351

Ostia. In this second city, buildings like the House of the Lararium, or the *Horrea Epagathiana* erected in the middle of the second century, and the multitude of contemporary tombs on the Isola Sacra, are witness to a certain taste in this period for such compositions (fig.353).

If there are no examples in Rome, the *via Appia*, by contrast, still displays several tombs from the second century combining different tones of brick and a harmonious moulding. It is not by chance that these monuments, unlike other tombs, have survived better, for it is precisely because they do not have any rendering or veneers of travertine or marble, materials that were the first to be reused, that they were better respected than their more sumptuous counterparts (fig.354).

Of these numerous examples, one monument stands out clearly, as much for its state of preservation, due in part to its isolated situation in the valley of the Caffarella, between the *via Appia* and the *via Latina,* as for its remarkable artistic quality. Once known as the 'Temple of Rediculus'[61] (fig.355), this seventeenth-century name was succeeded by that of the 'Tomb of Annia Regilla', the wife of Herodes Atticus, who died in 150, because of the proximity of his villa. This second designation seems arguable now, but it

352

353

nevertheless correctly dates the building, which was indeed built around this time.

This fairly large funerary monument is in the form of a pseudo-peripteros temple, measuring 8 × 11.5m, on a podium fronted by a portico of four columns that has today disappeared, though the cella has remained intact. The architect chose sandy yellow bricks to carry out the base panels of the walls and used two other darker tones for the pilasters, the elements of the order of the base and the entablature and the window frames. These juxtapositions of colours, enriched by a great delicacy in the cutting of the relief decoration, form a monumental cameo and the most remarkable example of this architectural style that has survived from the second century.[62]

These forms, however, were not found outside the peninsula, and the only example that can be cited in Gaul of a monument faced in brick with added polychrome decoration, is the funerary edifice of Cinq Mars erected on the banks of the Loire, whose presence in this province is entirely

352 The exedra of the Markets of Trajan: a systematic use of brick facings with frames, bases and capitals of travertine; presumably this dual coloration was intended to remain visible.

353 Necropolis of the Isola Sacra at Ostia, tombs with brick façades of the second century. Tombs 77-78 and 79 South.

355

354

354 *Via Appia*, tomb with a facing of polychrome bricks. Antonine period.

355 The pseudo – 'Temple of Rediculus', in reality a great funerary monument from the middle of the second century, between the *via Appia* and the *via Latina*. Only the tetrastyle porch of the main façade (against the modern house) has not survived.

356 The 'Basilica' of Trier, in fact a large hall of the Palace of Constantine, built at the beginning of the fourth century. Its façades are entirely faced in brick. This is now a church.

exceptional. The archaeological information relating to this isolated monument is unfortunately insufficient to determine whether it is the tomb of a person originating in Rome who had himself buried there in the course of the second century. Apart from this

356

monument, brick facings were hardly ever used in Gaul except in the region of Toulouse – to be more precise in Toulouse itself, where important remains of the amphitheatre of Toulouse-Purpan (second half of first century?) faced in this way have been discovered. To find brick used as a complete facing it is necessary to go as far as Trier, *Augusta Trevirorum*, where the Imperial basilica erected by Constantine at the beginning of the fourth century displays such an outer skin (fig.356).

8 Restorations and reconstructions

Monuments that remained in use for a long time generally underwent modifications or repairs that provide evidence for a relative chronology; this can sometimes be converted into an absolute chronology, albeit an approximate one. Walls built for defence, and so bound to receive damage, show such reconstruction works most clearly. At Pompeii the powerful stone block wall, despite being judged to be unsuitable and deprived of its towers, was considerably reinforced at the time of the Civil War by additions of *opus incertum* masonry. Curiously for such a project, the towers were rendered with stucco in ashlar decoration. Later, the walls of Rome had, from the time of Maxentius, been reinforced and raised with additions of *opus mixtum*, standing out against the original brick masonry; many others were to follow.

These large-scale undertakings, as with the reconstruction of large ruined monuments (often following fires), such as the Roman Forum, the Curia or the Basilica Julia, in fact follow the original construction techniques. It is, rather, the more modest repairs that display new or different styles, often imposed by shortage of time or lack of money. As noted above, a repair to a breach in a precinct wall of inferior construction at the Theatre of Argentomagus was carried out in a rough and ready way with flat rubble stones arranged in *opus spicatum*.

Once again, however, it is Pompeii that provides the most varied and original solutions to restoration. The earthquake that badly damaged that city and the neighbourhood of Vesuvius in 62, only seventeen years before the eruption of 24 August 79, has already been mentioned.[63] This first drama was sufficiently impressive for Seneca[64] and Tacitus[65] to report the event.[66] The first, more sensitive to the

357

catastrophe (he was 66 years of age, Tacitus was only 17), starts his narrative

Pompeii, the famous city of Campania, before which, on one side the shore of Stabiae and Sorrento, on the other that of Herculaneum join up to form a charming gulf facing the open sea, has just been overturned by an earthquake that has affected all the surrounding area . . .

Another written testimony, found on site, describing the event is the dedication of the Temple of Isis (fig.357):

Numerus Popidius Celsinus has raised from these foundations the Temple of Isis overturned by the earthquake; the Council of the Decurions in recognition of his liberality accepted him at the age of six without fees into their order.[67]

Finally, two remarkable marble bas-reliefs, given as a votive offering by a surviving Pompeian, show the Forum and Vesuvius Gate at the very moment of their destruction[68] (fig. 358).

Independently of these accounts, the city of Pompeii, like Herculaneum, displays both visible scars and the

357 The Temple of Isis, entirely rebuilt at the expense of a citizen of Pompeii after 62, was the first monument in Pompeii to be identified after its discovery in June 1765. Adapting to new techniques, the masonry was entirely faced in brick, but rendered with a stucco of rich mouldings.

358   A moving record: the marble relief socketed into the *lararium* belonging to the House of L. Caecilius Iucundus (V,1,26) showing the destruction of the Temple of Jupiter and the triumphal arch beside it, during the earthquake of the year 62. On the right, the expiatory sacrifice offered after the catastrophe (Antiquarium of Pompeii).

359   Reinforcement of the galleries in the amphitheatre of Pompeii using buttresses and rib arches: the great northern *vomitorium*.

ruins, still not restored by 79, of its toppled monuments. Thus the visitors who now enter the forum think they are seeing a complex destroyed by Vesuvius, while in fact it was still a building site where the buildings had simply been cleared (Basilica, Temple of Jupiter, porticoes, Temple of Apollo) but not reconstructed, and others were in the process of being completed (structures on the eastern side, buildings of the Curia). The most important building under construction was the enormous Central Baths, laid out on a cleared *insula* and, faced like the new buildings of the forum, almost exclusively with brick.

This is an excellent example of the adaptation in a monumental way of a restoration project on a large scale, comparable to the reconstructions mentioned above: a systematic programme in which there is no resort to technical tricks and original solutions. Brick can be found all over the city in consolidating elements which, depending on the extent of the damage and its suitability for the monument, could provide different forms of support: isolated buttresses as well as jambs reinforcing leaning walls and openings (numerous individual houses); buttresses and rib arches supporting the threatened vaulted passages (at the amphitheatre) (fig.359); buttress walls repairing the walls that were leaning too much (in VI,13,11 and in VI,2,1) (fig.360).

Walls that had been opened up by large breaches or cracks were almost always repaired using materials re-

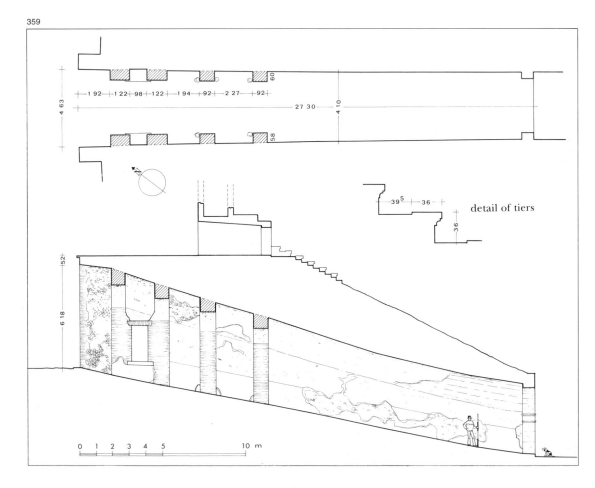

detail of tiers

360

362

361

covered from the ruins (figs 361, 362). Such reuse was standard and was confirmed by the discovery of a deposit of material deriving from the clearing of the city in a dump set up by the municipality north of the city walls.[69] All that was found there were small fragments of mortar, painted rendering, stucco or terracotta, i.e. only the remains unsuitable for reuse.

Rubble of all types was reintroduced into the masonry (hence the abundance, already mentioned, of *opus incertum* in the last civic phase), alternating with architectural ceramics, bricks (fig.363) or tiles, that could be used. Fragments of amphorae and vases of all sizes are found, both in the core and in the facings; there are even walls that are almost totally made up of them (IX,6,3) (figs 364, 365). Use was even made of the mortar and *opus signinum* from ruined floors to obtain in effect 'concrete blocks' (fig.366) which were used to re-erect walls or pillars, as

360 Pompeii, buttress-wall of brick and rubble stones, applied to a damaged building (Pompeii, VI,2,4).

361 Pompeii, reconstruction after the earthquake of 62. A crack filled in with terracotta material and rubble (VI,7,5).

362 Pompeii, reconstruction after the earthquake of 62. A wall made of limestone blocks from the first Samnite period (fourth-third century BC) rebuilt with rubble and brick (VI,9,8).

363 Restoration of the corner of a wall at Herculaneum (*Insula* II) following the earthquake of 62.

364 Masonry at Herculaneum (III,14) built after the earthquake of 62 with reused material, including a number of smashed amphorae.

365 Pompeii, reconstruction after the earthquake of 62. Wall made up of varied terracotta material: bricks, tiles, fragments of amphorae (IX,6,3).

366 Pompeii, restoration of a wall after the earthquake of 62. Among the reused material are pieces of *opus signinum* paving (VI,7,2).

367 A masonry column of the Great *Palaestra*, Pompeii, fixed into place with a layer of lead (visible at the level of the *scotia*) after the earthquake of 62.

is done nowadays with these artificial materials (for instance VI,7,2 and particularly the lower portico of the villa of Diomedes).

At the Large *Palaestra*, bordering the amphitheatre, a particularly original solution was found to put back in place accurately the columns that had been shaken by the quake. These were set upright, probably using cranes, then once in position a hole was dug at their foot, into which lead was poured. This set much faster than mortar, permanently wedging them into place (fig.367).

The ruin of the houses, as well as the departure of the owners, brought about a change in use of certain houses that were renovated, divided between several new occupants (such as the House of the *Cryptoporticus*) and sometimes turned into workshops or business premises (fig.368). In well-organized reconstructions, both public and private, great use was made of brick, a standardized material quick to produce and use that could, if necessary, be combined with the recovered rubble (fig.369).[70]

368 Pompeii, façade of a *domus* turned into a bakery after the earthquake of 62. The high door framed with cubic capitals was hidden by the addition of a first floor; the oven, visible at the back, was constructed in the *atrium* (VIII,4,26).

369 Adapting to new techniques and to the modern fashion, the House of Caius Vibius (VII,2,18) was totally rebuilt of new brick masonry and salvaged *opus incertum*.

370

372

+ — 52 — +

+10$\frac{5}{}$+

+7+

371

9 Masonry columns

If it seemed natural to include a section on columns in the chapter devoted to stone block construction, it might appear less so to do the same in this one. Nevertheless, in the peninsula this is how thousands of columns of all sizes were built.

The first known example of a complex of masonry columns is that already mentioned of the basilica at Pompeii, erected around 120BC (fig.370).[71] The fluted shafts of the central colonnade, 11m high and 1.06m wide at the base, are made up of a regular assemblage of brick sections, 4.5 to 5cm thick. The whole is in the shape of a flower, composed of a circular core surrounded by 10 'petals' and completed by 10 lozenge-shaped segments, so as to form an outline, seen from above, of 20 flutings.

In each course the arrangement is alternated so as to overlap the joints, except of course for the central core which forms an internal column; once the columns were up they were covered with a white stucco, delicately defining the flutings and creating the illusion of marble.

This achievement may well have seemed unique in the great age of its construction, but the principle was carried on and innumerable colonnades made use of bricks (figs 371, 372), such as the great complex of colonnades in the portico of the Guilds at Ostia. The method, except for the small hypocaust pillars that are piles of small discs or squares, remains the same everywhere: sections of terracotta are assembled to form a succession of circular levels, either by themselves, or around a cylindrical core of masonry.

373

374

375

Rubble masonry, particularly at Pompeii after the earthquake of 62, was used to create columns of modest size in the peristyles of houses. These were sometimes organized in a homogeneous or mixed pattern, sometimes rough and ready, with a finish of a thick coat of rendering, giving a regular tapering appearance to the shafts constructed in this way (figs 373, 374).

Still on this inexhaustible site can be admired, for they are a real tour de force, the columns faced with *opus reticulatum mixtum* of remarkable regularity: at the southern portico of the House of the Mysteries, at the gladiators' camp (V,5,3) and, above all, the finest example, a large isolated column, formerly holding a *gnomon*, erected behind the Forum Baths (fig.375).

370 Brick column from the Basilica of Pompeii. Around a central cylinder are arranged the 'petals' forming the fluting; a stucco rendering covered the facing.

371 Column shaft made of bricks in irregular quarters; diameter without the rendering: 45cm. House of Terentius Proculus at Pompeii.

372 Brick column from the second peristyle in the House of the Faun at Pompeii. Restoration from 62.

373 Masonry columns from a peristyle at Pompeii (VI,13,9): two are made of bricks, the third of *opus mixtum*; the capitals are dressed tufa. Fluted stucco decorated the outside.

374 Masonry column made of rendered rubble stones of lava. The block of the capital is tufa. Pompeii, VIII,3,27.

375 Masonry column alternating a tufa and lava reticulate and rings of bricks. Standing behind the Forum Baths at Pompeii, it carried a sun dial.

157

6
ARCHES AND VAULTS

1 Origins of the voussoir arch

The voussoir (or true) arch is rightly considered to be one of the fundamental elements in the conquest of space, a contribution made by the Romans in their monumental architecture. An image traditionally accepted for generations was that the Etruscans were the inventors of this technique and responsible for its transmission into Roman architecture.[1] It is to the Tarquins in the sixth century BC that we traditionally attribute the construction of drains, gates in city walls and vaulted tombs, providing the early models that were to inspire their successors. In fact, the reality is a lot less certain (fig.376).[2]

For a long time the *Cloaca Maxima*, the long underground vaulted channel draining water from the low-lying Forum Romanum into the Tiber, was considered to be originally the work of the Etruscans (fig.377). However, although in the period of the Tarquins a small natural water course leading into the river had in fact been channelled and made into a main drain, archaeological excavations have shown that the *Cloaca Maxima*, at first open to the sky, had been repaired and reconstructed several times, the last time by Agrippa, in the reign of Augustus. Two levels of evidence have served to confirm this on the Forum,[3] as it has been possible to establish that the extrados of the vault was at a higher level than the flooring of the Republican period. The fine outflow with three rows of concentric voussoirs that can be admired today in the bank of the Tiber at the level of the Ponte Palatino can there-

376 The invention of the voussoir arch took place in the third millennium in regions with little wood and using unbaked brick, in Mesopotamia and the Nile valley. This is a true arch made of unbaked bricks at Ur (Iraq). (Photo: Hrand.)

377 The outflow of the *Cloaca Maxima* into the Tiber, at the level of the *Forum Boarium*. The crown of the arch is made up of three rows of short voussoirs. The date of its construction is estimated to be the beginning of the first century BC.

377

376

fore be dated to the beginning of the first century BC at the earliest.

The walls of the Etruscan towns of Volterra (*Velathri*), Perugia (*Aperusia*) and *Falerii Novi* have monumental gates closed above by a voussoir arch which, just like the drain in Rome, have been considered to be the oldest models. The study of these ramparts has led to a more accurate assessment, and at both Volterra and Perugia,[4] it has proved possible to identify the Etruscan walls and their gates that were rebuilt after the Roman conquest (fig.378). At *Falerii Novi* the situation is much more interesting since this town is in fact a new city, built by the Romans, perhaps using Etruscan engineers, to rehouse the inhabitants of *Falerii Veteres*, besieged and taken by Rome in 241BC.[5] It is possible here to be certain that shortly after this date, which forms the only definite marker in the early history of the voussoir arch, Etruscans and Romans knew the art of the true arch (fig.379).

As for the vaulted Etruscan tombs, it must be remembered that all the funerary halls from the seventh to the second century BC are either hypogea cut into the rock imitating the interiors of wooden houses (necropolises of Cerveteri, Orvieto and Tarquinia), or long spaces covered by corbelling of slabs or circular chambers, correctly given the name tholoi (tomb of Casal Marittimo or of Montagnola).[6] The fine tombs covered with true vaults in a full arc at Perugia (tomb of San Manno) and Bettona (20km south-east of Perugia), formerly held to be Etruscan models because of their location in that territory, are in fact Roman tombs of the second century BC (fig.380).

The fact that, as has already been mentioned, the Romans often adopted monumental techniques from the people they conquered, may have led to the attribution of the arch to the Etruscans. In any case, neither in Rome nor its vicinity is there evidence of the

378 Perugia, gate in the Etruscan wall called the Augustan Gate. The arch was built at the end of the second century BC.

379 A true arch from the Gate of Jupiter at *Falerii Novi* dating after 241BC. The long and narrow voussoirs have an archivolt added; it also has a very carefully made extrados. Width: 3.3m.

159

380

381

380 An Etruscan cinerary urn showing a temple with a gate with a voussoir arch, dating from the end of the third/beginning of the second century BC. (Museum of Florence).

381 The Gate of the Siren, in the eastern face of the walls of Paestum. It could belong to the work carried out by the Latin colony after 273BC. Width: 3.6m.

smallest arch at such an early period and nothing points to there having been any before the second century BC.

Curiously, the Romans themselves did not consider the Etruscans their masters in this field though they attributed to them such important inventions as surveying; instead, according to the writings of Seneca, they considered the Greeks to be the inventors of the voussoir arch.[7] This author reports that Democritus of Abdera, the philosopher of optimism, was its brilliant creator. His text, though it may be misleading, could, however, be the approximate truth in so far as the

Greeks were ahead of the Romans in the technique of vaulting; it is therefore in the colonies of Magna Graecia and Sicily that possible models should be sought. Sicily has up to now revealed nothing in this context that could provide the slightest clue, but two Lucanian cities, Paestum and Velia, both offer an excellent example.

The town of Poseidonia, which became a Lucanian city after 326BC, already had a strong wall, attributable to the Greeks, when the Romans established a colony there in 273BC[8] and gave it the name of Paestum. The large east gate of the town, called the Gate of the Siren, covered by a voussoir arch, forms part of the latest repairs to the walls and the work is attributed to the Latin colony. If exact stratigraphic excavations, still to be carried out, confirmed this origin it could be Roman work, or Lucano-Roman, predating by about thirty years the building of *Falerii Novi* (fig.381).

A little to the south, the Phocaean colony of Elea, Latinized to Velia, had built a wall which, in its original state, dated to about 340BC; it enclosed two parallel valleys open to the sea, separated by a ridge on which was the acropolis. It was discovered in 1964 that the height of the acropolis was in fact made up of two hills connected by a strong wall, forming a *diateichisma* between the two halves of the town, a wall interrupted at its base by a gate, the Porta Rosa, topped by a voussoir arch 2.68m wide, itself having a relieving arch (fig.382).[9] The problem of dating this gate can in fact be solved as the opening in the wall is datable, by means of stratigraphy, to the second half of the fourth century BC, but the arch over the top of it could well be the result of a later repair, as was the case at Volterra and Perugia.

In addition there is considerable recessing of the facing exactly at the spring of the arch, and, in the upper courses, a difference in the treatment of the stones. However, these remarks in no way constitute chronological proof and possible explanations can be found: the recess is justified by the decreased support demanded from the wall in its upper part and the difference of treatment indicates that a team of specialist stone-masons carried out this delicate part of the work. These arguments also have their weak points but, whatever the case may be, the construction remains and can be cited as an early possible indication of the origin of the arch.

Crossing the Adriatic, and also the Aegean, in the Greek world there are a number of examples from the third century BC providing evidence for the use of voussoir arches, which became fairly common by the Hellenistic period. Examples can be found in the posterns and gates of defensive walls (Oiniadai, Palairos, Heraclea on Mount Latmos, Assos[10]) or in arches over Macedonian tombs (Langhada, Leucadia, Paltitsa,[11] Vergina) (figs 383, 384).

In conclusion, it can be established that the technique of the true arch

382

385

383

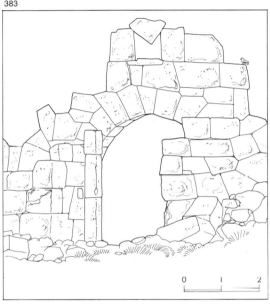

384

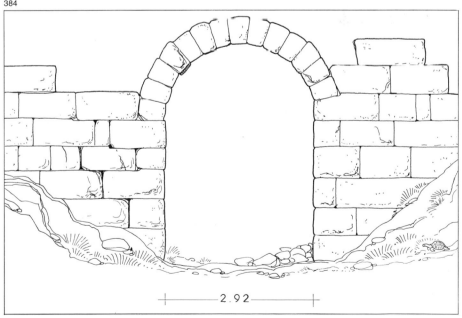

2.92

382 The Porta Rosa at Velia (Lucania) opened in a wall built c.340BC. Width: 2.68m. Note the difference in the treatment of the blocks in the covering arch and in the relieving arch.

383 The Gate of the Port, in the Hellenistic fortification of Oiniadai (Acarnania) built by Philip V after his capture of the town in 219BC. Width: 3.15m. The extrados of the voussoirs is incorporated into the polygonal construction of the wall.

384 A keyed gateway at Heraclea (Caria), in the south-east of the city, third century BC. Width: 2.92m. Here the voussoirs have a regular extrados.

385 The Nolan Gate in the north-eastern section of the wall of Pompeii, made of blocks of tufa with dry jointing (the masonry is a later restoration). The surviving keystone is decorated with the head of Minerva. Width: 4.2m; c.200BC.

386

arrived in the Italian peninsula gradually and that the Greeks and the Etruscans, more advanced in the art of stone-work, worked out the first models known to the Romans. The latter adopted the technique and improved upon it, achieving an almost complete mastery, as much in the forms and the materials as in the calculation of thrusts and span, and making the most accomplished use of it in architecture.

To recapitulate on the development of voussoir arches (and vaults) in the peninsula, here is a brief table of some structures erected between established dates, i.e. *Falerii Novi* (which clearly owes a lot to earlier examples) and the *Tabularium*, evidence of a technique that was to become of great importance:

386 An opening for an artillery piece built into the Servian Wall, Rome around 90BC.

after	241	Gates of *Falerii Novi* and the fortifications built by Roman and/or Etruscan engineers (fig.379)
after	241	Bridge on the *via Amerina*, leading from *Falerii Novi* towards Rome
around	200	The Nolan Gate at Pompeii (fig.385)
around	200	Porta dell'Arco at Volterra
around	200	Arch of the *Cloaca Maxima* under the *Basilica Aemilia*
	179	Supporting arch under the *Clivus Capitolinus* in Rome
	142	Arches of the Aemilian Bridge (the pillars had been built between 181 and 179)
second half of second century –		
		Viaduct of Valle Ariccia on the *Via Appia* (2 arches)
		First bridge of Nona (single arch) on the *via Praenestina*
		Porta Sanguinara at Ferentino
	120	Triumphal arch of the Consul Quintus Fabius (no longer in existence)
between	120 and 100 –	
		Gate called the 'Arch of Augustus' at Perugia (fig.378)
	109	The Milvian Bridge at Rome, two arches with a span of 17.5m
around	100	New bridge of Nona with seven arches
around	100	High arch of the *Tullanium* (Mamertine prison)
around	90	Arch opening for artillery piece, in the Servian Wall on the Aventine (fig.386)
around	80	Amphitheatre at Pompeii (fig.387)
around	80	Arch of the *Cloaca Maxima* at its outflow (fig.377)
around	80	Porta Maggiore or Santa Maria at Ferentino (fig.388)
	78	*Tabularium*, built by the architect Lucius Cornelius

To conclude this quick check list – with still uncertain dates that should be supplemented by a study of the archi-

tecture of Etruria and *Latium* – it is possible to state that, in the course of the second half of the second century BC, the art of crossing spaces with voussoir arches was introduced into all areas of architecture and public works, from drains to the biggest viaducts, not to mention the parallel development of the brick arch that was to be integrated into and placed alongside ashlar construction. This mastery and this familiarity are such that, in 62BC Lucius Fabricius built a bridge over the Tiber, connecting the left bank to the island in the river, made with stone blocks of tufa and travertine,[12] of an extraordinary delicacy, the two arches of which, 24.5m in span, were rarely surpassed and still arouse admiration.[13]

387 The entrance arch to the northern vomitorium of the amphitheatre of Pompeii with a span of 3.45m. The voussoirs are here incorporated into the rectangular shape of the passage; date around 80BC.

388 The Porta Maggiore at Ferentino (*Ferentinum*). The two arches of an opening 4.2m wide with a double row of short voussoirs are to be compared with the outflow of the *Cloaca Maxima*; date around 80BC.

2 The mechanics of corbelling and the true arch[14]

Mention has already been made, in connection with the structures of *Latium* and Etruscan tombs, of buildings, doors, corridors and rooms covered by corbelling. This is the most basic and simplest method of covering a space, and is in fact a development of the principle of the lintel. In the absence of a material capable of spanning, without breaking, a great length, the span of a single lintel is reduced by means of a series of supports overlapping one another, forming an overhang.[15]

Corbelling consists basically of a supporting part and a projecting part, the first having to be sufficiently heavy to prevent it toppling over. The only difficult operation for the builders, therefore, consists in the loading of the pendant part, whose non-projecting length must be greater than the projection. It is also useful to estimate empirically the limits of the material's resistance and to counteract this by an adequate thickness to prevent its breaking under the effect of flexion.

Artificial corbelling, constructed to enable an opening to be made in a wall or a space to be covered, is in reality a natural shape which can be created spontaneously, for example as a result of the collapse of a vault in a cave; in this case a stable cavity is formed, almost conical, called 'bell-shaped subsidence', which is in fact a corbelling of the ground, that has recovered a balanced shape, the curve of which is called a 'natural arch'. The same accident can occur in any drystone masonry, and this is what happens over openings when a lintel begins to break.

Roman stone block architecture hardly ever used this technique, whereas the Etruscans made great use of it, and the only examples that can be cited belong to the Cyclopean architecture of primitive fortifications, such as the gates of the acropolises of Signia, Arpino, Sezze or Palestrina, all from the fifth to the third centuries BC (fig.389). By contrast, simple corbelling, consisting merely of reducing the span of a lintel (in fact the projection of the capitals supporting the architrave) was in quite universal use.

In the construction of masonry, particularly brick, vaults corbelling is sometimes achieved by piling up the elements more steeply, sometimes up to the height of the haunches, sometimes higher; but in this method, in which the construction was turned into a monolith, corbelling did not play any particular mechanical role, the essential thing being the cohesion that was ensured by the use of good mortar (fig.390).

389 The great corbelled gate in the megalithic wall of Arpino (southern Latium) of polygonal stone, the so-called second type. Width: 1.9m; height of the opening: 4.2m. Fifth century BC.

389

Whereas in the mechanics of corbelling the main aim is to avoid the elements toppling over, it is the opposite for the true arch.[16] This makes use of the force of gravity, i.e. the weight, to secure the pieces of the arch, called archstones or voussoirs. In order to harness this downward force, each element is supported by its neighbours, its wedge-shaped outline preventing its fall. The wedge-shaped outline is thus repeated from the spring to the keystone.

The first practitioners realized that the support of each voussoir at its widest end tended to drive its neighbours apart and this had the result of producing lateral pressures capable of causing the areas acting as support, the abutments, to be driven apart. However, for a long time, master, in the form of calculation or estimation of the abutments did not exist; this is why until the second century BC, both among the Greeks and the Romans, all the true arches (and vaults) were openings in walls, where the lateral mass was considerable, or underground structures (Macedonian tombs), or rested on the ground (bridges). The honour goes to the architects of the later Republican period for daring to transform the arch which was simply a hole in a mass to a structure to enclose open space.

The question remains, why, in spite of this difficulty, which the Gothic architects in their turn were to overcome, was it the true arch that took off and conferred on architecture a total victory over space, and not corbelling, which is so simple and subject only to vertical pressures?

One explanation lies in the saving of space and the economy of material which result from the use of a semicircular arch rather than a corbelled one to cover the same distance. In fact, the closer corbelling is to the vertical, the more stable it is. Corbelling over a large span thus reaches a great

390

390 A gallery covered with *tegulae* arranged in gable-roof form; in this way a permanent coffering was achieved for corbelled masonry. Baths of Venus at Baia. Width of the passage: 90cm.

height.[17] In addition, the necessity of weighting the pendant elements leads to the formation of still larger abutments than those required to withstand the pressure of a voussoir arch of the same span (figs 391, 392, 393).

Finally, combinations of intersections between voussoir arches enabled an enormous increase in the solutions to the problem of connecting masses and openings for passage and light, by distributing pressures, whatever their origin or their direction, on to precise points.

The processes of estimation – calculation is not the correct term – which made it possible for the Roman architects to work out the size of arches are unknown. Simply put, at the level of its supports a voussoir arch brings about an oblique thrust, which is the result, R_1, of the thrusts of each voussoir.[18] In order to reabsorb this thrust, the builder thus has to create a mass, the vertical weight of which, P, is greater than the sum of the thrusts. In reality a simple balance of forces is not enough, for it is necessary to take into account external constraints such as settling

391 The stability of a corbelled arch. The centre of gravity of the supporting polygon must be at the balance of the support; if G1 does not meet this requirement the arch will collapse on the inside. This can be corrected by moving G outwards and downwards, by narrowing the outline in the upper part and widening it at the bottom. The dot-dash line gives the outline of a perfect arch of the same span.

392 A break in the form of a 'natural arch' above a bent lintel, determining the weight actually supported by it. It can clearly be seen that it is at its maximum in the middle, the point where the horizontal lintel bends the most. (Pompeii IX,6e.)

393 Stone lintel (travertine) relieved by the opening of an impost, itself overlaid by a lintel of smaller span. The principle is that of shifting the corbel upwards. The entrance to a shop in the Markets of Trajan, c.110.

394 A diagram of the mechanics of a voussoir arch. The forces acting on the arch are at the springing level made up of:
P = total of the load supported and of the weight of the arch;
Q = lateral force;
R = result of the combination of P and Q.
Each voussoir tends to fall vertically under the effect of the weight P, but is held by its keyed outline that is wider at the top than at the bottom; the force q is transmitted laterally to the neighbouring voussoirs.
A The construction is balanced so that R is contained in the central of the abutment, at its base.
B If the abutment is insufficient, R moves outside the central and there is a risk of collapse.

395 The effects of excess of weight on a true arch, showing the position of the breaking points brought about by the dislocation of the arch; these demonstrate that not too much weight should be placed at the crown; rather the weight should be on the haunches to draw together the voussoirs.

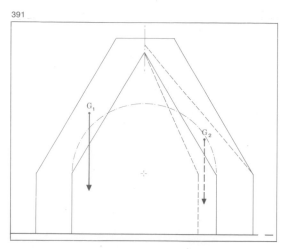

391

392

393

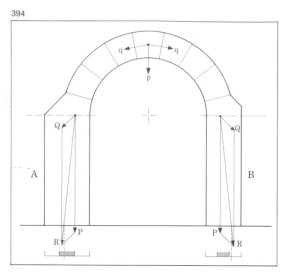

394

of the foundations, wind pressure and various forces acting upon the building. On the other hand, since construction materials are not completely uniform, either in their structure or in their use, the mass, P, of the abutment always has to be slightly larger than the force R_1, which can be expressed graphically, by a third force R_2, resulting from the intersection of the other two and, to maintain equilibrium, meeting ground level in the central third of the thickness of the abutment. Thus the more an arch is raised, the thicker the abutment has to be at the base (figs 394, 395, 396, 397, 398).

A graphic procedure, known since the Renaissance, permits a very satisfactory estimation of the size of the abutments of voussoir arches;[19] it cannot be ruled out that this is a case of a practice that has been handed down in the most commonplace way by traditional and professional teaching since the Roman period (fig.399).[20]

Although, both in principle and in the vast majority of its applications, a voussoir arch implies one of a semicircular outline, called a true arch, in fact all shapes capable of closing a curve, even if they are not put into practice, can be made in the same way. When an arch maintains a curved shape it can be called a stilted arch if its height is

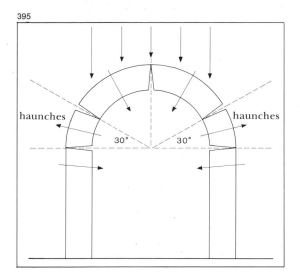

396 A large funerary monument at Patara (Lycia) with a perfect arch made of stone blocks and infilling of masonry. Despite the disappearance of the roof, directly supported by the extrados, the original outline of the load of the arch is clearly visible: it reaches its maximum thickness at the haunches.

397 The dome of the 'Tomb of the Gordians' on the via Praenestina, showing in section the outline of the arch loaded progressively from the haunches. Internal width: 13.2m; c. 320.

398 An abutted buttress built into the wall mass and following the actual direction of the forces. Villa of the Quintilii; c.150.

399 The method of estimating abutment masses:
1 perfect arch
2 segmental arch.
In the two cases the arch is segmented by using three equal cords extended beyond the springing line. Points C and F thus obtained are on the outside of the abutments. The method used by the Romans to guarantee the stability of their arches is not known, but it can be assumed that they were aware of similar methods to these, known to the architects of the Renaissance. It is clear that, with an equal span, the more the arch is lowered, the thicker the abutments must be. However, an element of empiricism remains, since this method does not take account of the height of the springing level.

402

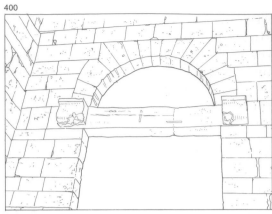

400

401

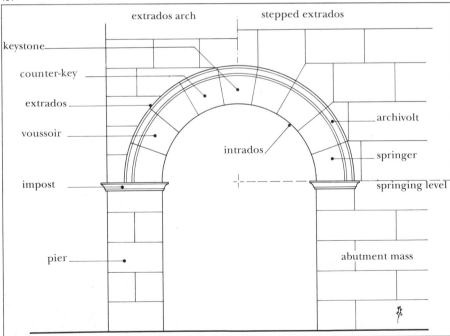

keystone

counter-key

extrados

voussoir

impost

pier

extrados arch

stepped extrados

archivolt

intrados

springer

springing level

abutment mass

400 A stone lintel relieved by an arch creating an impost opening. Capitol of Sufetula (Sbeïtla), middle of the first century.

401 The perfect arch made of stone blocks.

a horseshoe arch (where the circle is closed below the horizontal diameter), or a multifoil arch if it results from the intersection of several circular arcs. But these last shapes are more relevant to more recent periods (in oriental and medieval architecture); the Romans hardly used anything but perfect, segmental and flat arches, these last being in reality lintels made of voussoirs.

The voussoir arch has the advantage of distributing sideways the loads carried (they 'slide' on to the extrados), and it can therefore have more applications than the simple crossing of an opening. It can act as a 'discharge' above straight lintels (fig.400) and it can be used in networks of stiffeners in large masses of masonry which distribute the thrusts on to strong points arranged one above another vertically, as can be seen in the large brick façades of the Palatine, the Pantheon and the Capitol at Ostia.

Artistically and practically, the integration of a circular shape into a wall created some problems for the stonemasons who were confronted with cutting blocks with angled outlines before fitting them on to the extrados of the voussoirs (figs 401, 402). This method of fitting is, however, the most functional, as in this way the arch remains an independent structure from the wall that it is supporting and the weight can in fact settle on the haunches, compressing the voussoirs

greater than its width (vertical ellipse) or a segmental arch if its width is greater than its height (horizontal ellipse). It can be a triangular arch, broken into two semi-arcs, or it can be

without threatening to break them (figs 403, 404). It is both for this reason and also to give the arches more resistance, that certain architects of the Later Republican period provided them with several concentric rows of voussoirs, as, for instance, the *Cloaca Maxima* or the Porta Santa Maria at Ferentino.

However, it is not possible to say whether the mechanical aspect was the deciding factor, since it was for aesthetic reasons that the Romans very soon attempted to connect the voussoirs in such a way as to fit them in the construction lines of the wall (figs 405, 406). The solution adopted at the great *vomitoria* of the amphitheatre at Pompeii (around 80BC) consisted of extending the joints of the voussoirs as far as a shared horizontal extrados, dominated by one construction course. This is quite a simple method that was quickly taken up everywhere and in all periods, as it can be found, for example, around 230 in the Arch of Alexander Severus at Thugga (Dougga) (fig.407).

A second method consists of giving the ends of the voussoirs a right-angled profile so that they fit into their respective courses (fig.408). A final method, more sophisticated and

reserved for hard stones that stand up to carving well, is to extend the ends of the voussoirs by means of horizontal returns, termed crossettes, creating toed voussoirs, fitting into each course. This arrangement can be seen in the Theatre at Orange or in the 'Baths' at Sens (there is a reconstruction in the Museum).

When considering the upper part of arches of which the voussoirs are lined up on a construction course of the wall (see figs 406, 407, 408), it is easy to see how the lengths of the radiating joints made it possible also to align them horizontally following the intrados;

402 Porta Urbica at Spello. This arch, of stone blocks faced with rubble, has like that at *Falerii*, an archivolt with an extrados. The monumental opening stands flanked by pilasters and crowned by a pediment. Augustan period.

403 An axonometric projection of a voussoir in a perfect arch, starting with a rectangular shape.

404 An axonometric projection of the voussoir of a hemispherical dome. All the edges of all the voussoirs converge towards a single centre, O.

405 An triple arch with a rough extrados of *opus quadratum*. The irregular extrados is visually corrected by a sharply projecting archivolt springing from the band of the impost. Monumental gateway of Patara, second century, Lycia.

403

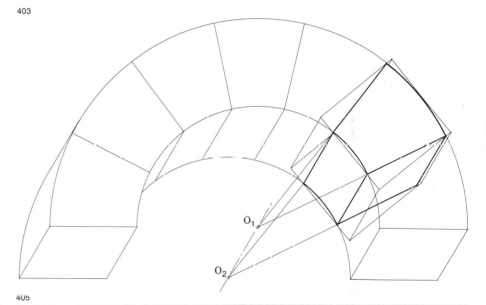

404

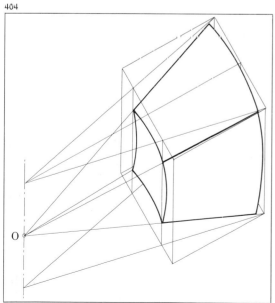

405

406   The Gate of Antoninus at Sbeïtla (Sufetula). The internal facing shows the random incorporation of the voussoirs in the construction of the wall.

407   The Arch of Alexander Severus at Thugga (Dougga), *c.*230. The extrados lines of the archstones form right angles aligned on the pilasters of the framework and a crowning band.

408 One of the accesses to the Forum of Augustus, the arco dei Pantani, with travertine voussoirs that have springing points on the extrados; to avoid lengthening them excessively, those at the top, seven in all, are aligned on the same course.

409 A lintel constructed of three elements, the Temple of Bacchus at Baalbek. Second century AD.

410 Peribolos of the Capitol at Sbeïtla (Sufetula). A lintel arch made of stone blocks. Note the gripping holes designed for the lifting grips. When compared with the upper part of the arch of the Forum of Augustus, it can be seen that the latter in fact ended in a lintel arch.

411

thus forming a bonded lintel arch. The Roman builders made frequent use of this technique of stone block construction to create straight openings when the span made the use of a true lintel impossible, both in doorways and architraves. Further, in masonry, lintel arches, particularly those made of brick, made it possible to replace wooden or stone lintels, including for apsidal openings (figs 409 to 416).

411 A wooden lintel surviving at Herculaneum, relieved by an impost opening and a relieving arch. Eastern *insula* II. In this context the recommendation by Vitruvius, VI,10 should be noted.

412 Openings at the Central Baths at Pompeii (62-79) overlaid by a lintel of tufa and relieved by a discharging arch.

412

415

413

414

413   A bonded flat lintel without engaged voussoirs in the supports, with relieving arch. Public *lararium* of Pompeii, c.60.

414   Openings in a portico of masonry pillars and lintel of mixed construction which are not relieved. Pompeii, Villa of Diomedes, after 62.

415   A window in an exedra of the Villa of the Mysteries. The flat arch serves as a lintel, and the relieving arch of bricks follows the circular shape of the wall.

173

416

416   A sloping lintel of brick masonry under a stairway at Ostia. Total length: 4m. The supporting pillar is 1.3m from the base.

417   Centrings for arches and vaults with a small span.

3   Construction and centring

Whereas the stone-cutter and the mason simply assemble the building materials from the scaffolding, to build an arch – a structure crossing an open space in stages – it is necessary to provide a robust support with the exact outline of the curve to be built; this support is the centring.

The centring is made up of at least two arcs of a circle made of wood and solidly braced, joined by a semi-cylindrical base called the formwork which is a moulding of the arch. The whole had to be supported, either directly on the ground using posts, or at the level of the spring of the arch to save on wood (figs 417, 418). This second solution was very frequently chosen by the Romans who built projecting pieces, which could also have a decorative value as cornices, at the level of the last horizontal course on which it was easy to set up centrings (fig.419).

In order to plan the work and to save on materials, the builders devised the

417

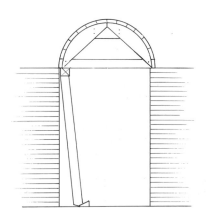

418

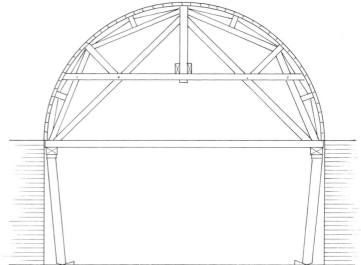

method of putting up certain arches (for instance at the Pont du Gard, at Nîmes in the passageway of the 'Temple of Diana') in parallel sections next to each other without cross-bonding the joints, so that each was built separately. The same centring was then moved along to put up the next section (figs 420, 421). Similarly, the architect who built the arch of the 'Temple of Diana' at Nîmes, devised a method of separating each section by an equal gap; the arches already in place then acted as a centring and slabs were positioned in the gaps to finish the structure (fig.422).

As there is so far no representation in the Roman pictorial record of the building of an arch with a centring, no model can be put forward as a precise picture'. The only justifiable assumption is that the technique is in every respect comparable to that shown in medieval pictures – one which remained essentially the same until the use of steel tubing.

It should not, however, be seen as a simple problem with straightforward solutions; what was a mechanical problem in the construction of small buildings turned into a formidable problem in the construction of very large monuments such as baths, basilicas or large domes. The technical

solution to the problem of bridging an open space by the mastery of the arch was itself a remarkable achievement, but it was still necessary to resolve the practical problems of carrying it out. For the construction of a dome such as that of the Pantheon, 43.3m wide, with a spring 22m above the ground it was necessary to devise a wooden cage capable of moulding such a colossus.[21]

419

418 Models of centrings with a large span.

419 The arches of the aqueduct of Metz (*Divodurum*) at Jouy-aux-Arches, display a double row of voussoirs. The centrings for building were supported on the projection of the cornices made of stone blocks.

420

420 The middle series of arches in the Pont du Gard, showing the projections for supporting the centrings and the three parallel rows of voussoirs; *c.*AD 15.

421 A suggested reconstruction of the centring in the construction of the Pont du Gard.

421

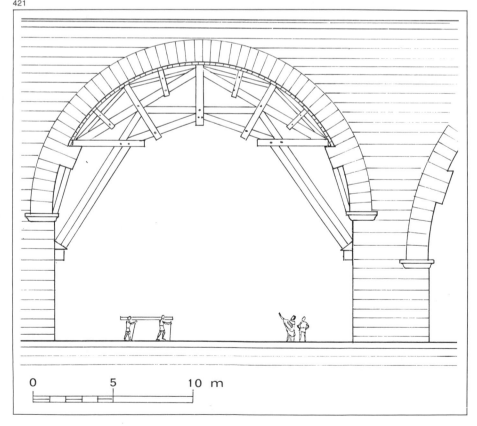

0   5   10 m

The solution probably lay in the construction of arched interlace ribs, supported on the cornice and connected by formwork, as E. Viollet-le-Duc suggested, which has provided the most plausible reconstruction.[22]

In North Africa, where the wood needed for making coffering was lacking, the builders came up with the use of permanently erected centrings made of terracotta cylinders (vaulting tubes). These cylinders, open at both ends and pinched at one extremity, were fitted together to form arcs that were put up very quickly with a minimum of supports (fig.423). The work was greatly facilitated by the use, not of lime mortar, but of pure plaster, which sets extremely quickly. These ceramic frames, just like wooden coffering, lent themselves to all kinds of spatial arrangements, making possible barrel vaults as well as all types of insertions.

By way of an experiment, the architect Albéric Olivier[23] in 1980 entirely reconstructed on the site of *Bulla Regia* (near Jendouba in Tunisia) the arch of a small square room, reusing ceramic cylinders recovered from the site and without any wooden support.

On to this ceramic shell, which, depending on the span, could be several rows thick, the mason then applied the masonry, as he did on the extrados of the wooden centring. This method was to remain for a long time unique to North Africa and it only appears in Sicily at the end of the third century in the arch of a villa near Marsala;[24] it is found again, in the Byzantine period, in Rome, Milan and particularly Ravenna in the construction of the Basilica San Vitale (521-47).

4   The concrete vault

It is appropriate to treat separately vaults built of masonry bonded with mortar because of the static nature that they adopt when, once the setting is complete, the centring has been taken away. The result is in effect a monolith (assuming best-quality mortar) in which a space has been carved out. The effects of the lateral pressures remain, but are considerably absorbed by the cohesive power of the bonding agent,

preventing the elements from moving. As already noted, this is the reason why Roman masons often assembled brick arches with horizontal courses up to a high level. The method was not without risk, however, for it relied on the use of perfect mortar and a calculated distribution of weights and abutments. So much so that, when there was a break in the concrete, there was a risk of a large piece of masonry falling until a natural arch formed. By contrast, if the mason had been careful in dividing the elements radially, at least on the intrados, the fissure went in a radial direction and simply formed a new joint counteracting the fall (fig.424).

422   The 'Temple of Diana' at Nîmes. A stone block arch, whose rib arches with lateral supporting projections were constructed on a centring. The slabs of the infilling were then simply put in position by lifting gear. (P. Varène.)

423   An arch on permanent coffering made up of a double row of ceramic cylinders. Baths at Sbeïtla (Sufetula).

424   A section of the niche arches of a terrace at the temple of Fortune at Praeneste. The masonry mass was applied to a row of radiating rubble stones arranged on the centring; *c.*110BC.

425

426

425 The arrangement of bricks resting on centring at the intersection of vaults, at the Baths of Caracalla. (A. Choisy.)

426 Marks of bricks placed straight on to the centring (which has collapsed) and ends of the radiating bricks visible in the intrados of the arch in the *frigidarium* of the Great Baths of Hadrian's Villa. Between 118 and 125.

This solution, combining care in dividing the material into wedges with speed in applying the masonry mass on to the centring, was chosen by most Roman masons (particularly in *Latium*) from the Flavian period. The method, visible in numerous monuments in Ostia and the region of Rome, consisted of laying on the centring a first layer of square bricks, which in fact formed a second centring, this time a permanent one, to form a thin shell. On this, at regular intervals, starting at the crown of the facing, more arches of brick were put up, connected by lines of bricks placed edgeways, i.e. radiating out. Thus a series of coffers was established and then filled with masonry.[25]

Once it had set, the result was a flexible and resistant cellular structure, the efficiency of which is amply demonstrated by the strength of the structures and their extraordinary longevity, despite the deliberate destruction of a

427

ture and giving the barrel vault a regular outline on which a decoration, either painted or in relief, could be added.

If this method, which had a certain technical sophistication, was not used, the concrete arch was simply and directly applied in a mass on to the centring, and the imprint of the shutterings has

427 The intrados of an arch showing the arrangement of the bricks placed directly on to the centring. Villa dei Quintilii; *c*.150.

428

large number of the supports and numerous earthquakes.

In more modest constructions the mason simply placed, above the brick shell, a quarter or half brick to the right of each joint intersection, intended to contain the flow of bonding mortar; then he applied his masonry core up to the coursing of the upper level (figs 425 to 431).

After removing the centring, the masons completed the intrados by applying a rendering masking the struc-

429

430

428 An arch in masonry faced in brick, the crown of which has partially disappeared. The voussoir arrangement here is only a decorative element of the functional aspect, and the core of the arch is made up of elements (brick and rubble) that are simply coursed and bonded with mortar. Villa dei Quintilii; *c*.150.

429 The arch here appears in its most rudimentary form: a row of flat bricks placed on a rough centring for construction serves as a permanent centring in the masonry. An access corridor to the furnaces of the Baths of the Six Columns at Ostia, second century.

430 Arches of the *aqua Alexandriana*, one of the aqueducts of Rome. The upper arches, bearing the weight, are faced at the crown with two rows of bricks; the lower braces have only one; *c*.226.

431

431 Niche arches at the Harbour Baths at Ephesus, made up of triple rows of bricks, built in the second century and restored under Constantine II in the fourth century.

432 An imprint of centring made of wide planks (25 to 30cm) in the arch of a staircase in the Villa of the Mysteries.

432

434

433 The traces of the planks or shutters of the centring in the intrados of an arch in the terrace at Terracina. Beginning of the first century BC.

434 The traces of reed formwork covering the centring, used in the construction of a masonry vault. Pompeii, I,3,31.

435 An angular vault of concrete masonry moulded on a centring in which the outline of the coffers had been prepared. Temple of Fortune at Praeneste. End of the second century BC.

435

survived faithfully set in those arches that have lost their rendering (figs 432, 433, 434). This aspect of a moulded form was quickly exploited by Roman builders, who, using appropriate formwork, provided their arches in advance with elements of decoration in the form of coffers. This is found in the temple at Palestrina, with a white stucco rendering imitating Greek marble soffits (fig.435). The intrados of the enormous dome of the Pantheon remains the most spectacular example of the application of moulded decoration.

433

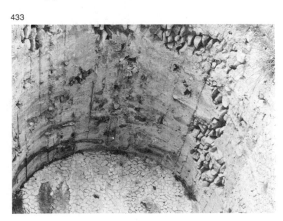

436

It was noted above that the Roman builders were capable of adapting arches to any architectural volume and this observation can be extended to situations very different from those required by the crossing of a space. Thus great use was made of vaults on a vertical axis, acting as a support in buildings that had to retain or contain large amounts of earth (fig.436). A reversed position is found in a series of arches forming an integral part of the long enclosure wall of a dwelling in Pompeii (VII,II,14), where these masonry stiffeners take on a secondary role with a visual effect that was surely intentional (fig.437).

In the building of domes, the principle of using ribs integrated into the masonry made it possible to create a skeleton forming a rigid cage concealed by sections of infill. This method is found at the temple of

436 Fréjus: a retaining wall reinforced by apses acting as vaults with vertical axes following the technique known as 'dam-vaulting' (first century). This unusual and rational use of arches is also found in the stone masses of the *cavea* in theatres and amphitheatres, the type of buildings above all others where there are masses of earth to be retained (Augst, Autun, les Bouchauds, Drevant, Lutèce, Trier, Vieux).

437 Not only is this use of voussoir arches unusual, it is perhaps also unique: inverted arches in a boundary wall at Pompeii (VIII,2,14). Notice a putlog-hole at the spring of the arches. Though they do go all the way along the masonry, these arches play only a minor role as stiffeners in this long wall and it is not clear whether they had any function other than decorative.

437

Minerva Medica[26] in Rome (fig.438). Sometimes these ribs are accentuated by a projection which created a shell effect on the inside – this is still visible in the baths at Baia and in the remains of one of the bath rooms in the villa of the *Gordians* on the *via Praenestina*[27] (around 240) (figs 439, 440). In this last building there also survives another octagonal room, the dome of which was lightened by the inclusion of amphorae buried in the masonry (fig.441). The same device is visible in the Tomb of Saint Helena (Tor Pignattara) on the *via Labicana*, perhaps intended for Constantine, and where his mother was buried,[28] covered by a vast dome with a span of 20.2m, built between 326 and 330.

The same lightening method already used at the Central Baths in Pompeii (fig.442) was employed in the dome of the Pantheon,[29] probably datable to 118 to 125 from the stamps on the bricks. In this building there are a total of six circular horizontal layers of

438

439
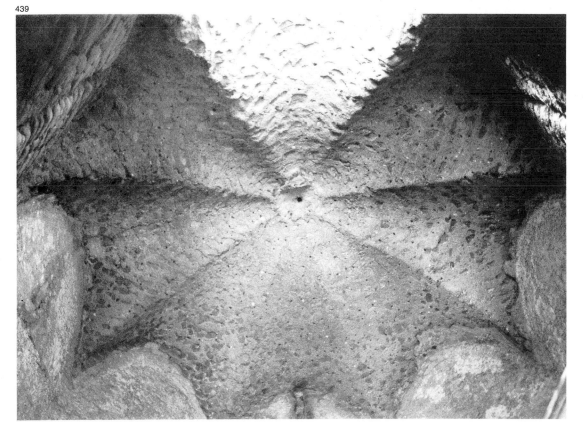

438 The interior of the dome of the 'Temple of Minerva Medica' in Rome. The transition from a ten-sided to a circular shape is carried out by means of a progressive and undetectable tapering of the masonry. The structure is that of coffers and ribbing, defined by brick frameworks containing a fill of rubble. Notice that the strong ribs radiating out distribute the pressures on to the piers, allowing large openings to be made in the drum. Beginning of the fourth century.

439 An octagonal dome ribbed in an 'umbrella' shape over a room in the Baths at Baia, width, 5.4m. The masonry of *opus caementicium* in the vault was, like the walls, covered by a wall mosaic. Hadrianic period.

440

441

442

material, including the foundations (fig.443):

1 a foundation mass made up of a layer of *opus caementicium* 4.5m thick, with rubble of travertine;
2 a vertical section up to the top of the order made up of *opus caementicium* with tufa and travertine rubble;
3 a second vertical section up to the spring of the arch made of *opus caementicium* mixing tufa and bricks;
4 a first ring of the dome with a fill of only brick fragments;
5 a second ring alternating brick and tufa rubble;
6 the final capping, mixing tufa rubble and aerated lava.

The heaviest materials are used in the concrete fill of the lower part of the structure and further up travertine gives way to tufa, brick and finally volcanic rocks that have a low density but a resistant granite skeleton.

Externally, the whole of this composite masonry was given a facing of

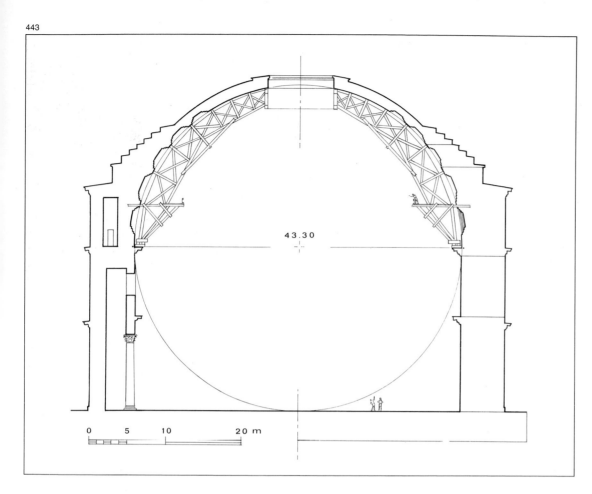

443

43.30

0   5   10   20 m

440   The apse of a large room in the Villa dei Gordiani, crudely covered by a semi-dome in an umbrella shape with very pronounced ribbing. Third century.

441   The capping of a dome made of tufa masonry, in which amphorae were sunk to lighten it. Large octagonal hall in the Baths of the Villa dei Gordiani, on the *via Praenestina*. Third century.

442   A dome with niches in the *laconicum* of the Central Baths at Pompeii. Notice here three successive layers of material: bricks for the drum, *opus caementicium*, tufa rubble for the haunches and thin honeycomb lava for the capping. Between 62 and 79.

443   Cross-section of the Pantheon showing the strongest and the weakest sections of the structure, the layers of building materials and a reconstruction of the centring of the dome.

444   The Pantheon (118-25), a network of stiffening arches reinforcing the masonry of the drum.

brick in which can be seen the heads of arches forming a discharge network of relieving arches, stiffening the construction and creating zones displacing pressure vertically, promoting a clever distribution of all the stresses (fig.444).

By contrast, a honeycomb partition using the same play of arches in the masonry of the dome itself is by no means certain and is based only on a single statement by Piranesi, who claimed to have discovered them.[30] The only bricks that have been found at this level are those belonging to the rings of the oculus, 9m in diameter, serving as a light well (fig.445).

In more than one respect the dome of the Pantheon remains the masterpiece of Roman architecture; to sum up the qualities of this building it can be said that it combines in perfect harmony the majestic size of its volume, whose geometric simplicity accentuates its aesthetic quality, with

the most functional and ingenious technology. In fact, unlike a number of domes that were built in imitation of it, the Pantheon displays, in the twentieth century, no sign of weakness

444

in its structure[31] despite deliberate mutilations and repeated earth tremors.

It is instructive to look beyond the ancient background and place the Pantheon in the history of monumental domes to show that this model was in fact a true archetype, never to be equalled:

certain bath-houses, notably the hot rooms, already by the first century had modest hemispherical roofing, it was only in the Flavian period that sizeable constructions suddenly appeared.

The first sizeable building which may have had a vast dome is the great bath-house of Agrippa,[32] the oldest public baths in Rome, built between 25 and

period	monument	internal diameter
Julio-Claudian	Bath house called the 'Temple of Mercury' at Baia (figs 446, 447)	21.5m
c.65 AD	Octagonal hall of the Domus Aurea (fig.448)	13m
81-96	Nympheum of the *Albanum* of Domitian at Alba	16.1m
109	Rotundas of the Baths of Trajan	20m
118-25	Pantheon (figs 443, 444, 445)	43.3m
Hadrian	Bath house at Baia called the 'Temple of Venus' (fig.449)	26.3m
Hadrian	Half-dome of the Serapeum of Hadrian's Villa	16.75m
Second century	The 'Temple of Apollo' at Lake Averno (fig.451)	35.5m
Second half of the second century	Bath house at Baia called the 'Temple of Diana' (fig.450)	29.5m
Alexander Severus	Round Temple at Ostia	18m
309	Mausoleum of Romulus, son of Maxentius	24.5m
c.320	Mausoleum of the Villa of the Gordianii (Tor of Schiavi)	13.2m
Beginning of the fourth century	Pseudo 'Temple of Minerva Medica' (figs 438, 452)	24.5m
326-30	Mausoleum of Saint Helena (Tor Pignattara)	20.2m
532-7	Santa Sophia in Constantinople	32.6m
1420-1434	Cathedral of Florence	42.2m
1551-8	Suleymaniye Mosque, Istanbul	26m
Completion 1564	Saint Peter's in Rome	42m
1570-5	Selimiye Mosque at Edirne	30m
1636-59	Gol Gambaz, tomb of Mahmud at Bijapur (India)	38m
1680-1691	Les Invalides in Paris	27.6m
1675-1710	St Paul's Cathedral in London	30.8m
1755-92	The Panthéon in Paris	21m
1817-26	St Francesco de Paulo in Naples	34m

It was not until the second half of the twentieth century, with the introduction of reinforced concrete, that the record held by the Pantheon was broken by the dome of the CNIT at the Roundabout of la Défense in Paris.

The most extraordinary thing is the speed with which Roman architects worked out the basic technology and construction of domes, for though

19BC. However, this rotunda, divided in two by the via Arco della Ciambella (between the Largo Argentina and the Pantheon), the base of which is still visible, has been dated by the brick stamps as being a construction or a reconstruction from the Severan period (beginning of the third century). Only excavations carried out at a depth under the roadway would ascertain whether this dome is only the reconstruction, on earlier foundations, of an identical dome of the Augustan period. In the present state of knowledge it could not be used as a definite starting point, but the supposition remains interesting.

The date of the dome, measuring 21.5m in diameter, covering the central hall of the 'Baths of Mercury' at Baia, north of Naples, is more certain. The archaeologist who made a study of it, A. Maiuri,[33] places its construction in the Augustan period, owing to the use of packed tufa rubble and not of bricks or a masonry mass, for the construction of the dome (figs 446, 447). Whatever the case may be, this building certainly has characteristics of the early Imperial period and could not have been built after the first half of the first century AD.

Next, with total certainty as to date, is the great octagonal hall of the Domus Aurea (fig.448), erected by Nero after 64, the dome of which spans a little more than 13m.[34] But it is in the reign of Domitian that large vaults become popular and domes become

445

standard in architecture. Of the latter, the only one preserved intact is the 'rotunda' of Albano (today the church of Santa Maria della Rotunda), probably the nymphaeum of the Alban villa of Domitian, with a diameter of 16.1m.

446

445 The unique dome of the Pantheon and its five concentric rows of coffers, lit by an oculus opening 9m across. The ancient decoration of the drum has been reconstructed in the lighter section. Diameter: 43.3m.

446 A dome in the Baths of Baia, the so-called 'Temple of Mercury', seen from the terraces. This building has sunk into the ground as a result of slow tectonic movements, called bradyseisms, that have affected the Phlegrean region. For the same reason part of the monumental complex of Baia is now under the sea.

447

447 The interior of the dome of the 'Temple of Mercury'. Ground water now rises nearly up to the spring of the arch, making it impossible to excavate it, thus the height of the hall cannot be established. The construction of this dome, 21.55m in diameter and made of tufa rubble bonded with mortar, dates back to the Augustan period; it is the oldest one known.

448 An octagonal room with interior dome from the Domus Aurea of Nero. Span: 13m; c.65. Axonometric section (after Giovannoni).

449 The 'Temple of Venus', the second great dome at the Baths of Baia, is of brick and reticulate construction; its interior diameter is 26.3m. Middle of the second century. In the break the coursed arrangement of the materials can be seen, and in the corner buttresses the water run-offs built into the masonry are visible.

In the palace of this emperor on the Palatine,[35] there remain the foundations of an apse, the half dome of which had an opening of 11m. The large neighbouring *aula* remains a great mystery to archaeology. It is a vast hall, 38m long and 30.5m wide, with side walls 3m thick. The preserved height of the remaining masonry does not allow the identification of the type of covering over this enormous volume, and so the question of a choice between a barrel vault and timber roofing is open to debate. The estimated span, 30.5m, would suggest a vault, the creation of which, though indeed ambitious, was perfectly within the capability of the period. Unfortunately, calculation shows that the abutment masses necessary to stabilize such a construction,

449

448

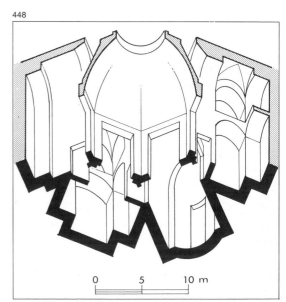

0   5   10 m

giving it a height of 30m at the crown (width = height, as at the Pantheon), would have to be 4.2 to 4.5m thick; the existing walls, however, do not exceed 3m. If a vault actually existed over this *aula*, it would represent a masterpiece of skill and daring, exceeding the bounds of safety.

If instead a covering in the form of timber roofing is favoured, the thickness of the walls is perfectly satisfactory, but that presumes a knowledge of triangulated trusses applied precociously to a span never reached before or after. Either way, it remains a feat.

In the reign of Trajan, and in all probability on the initiative of Apollodorus of Damascus, apses and exedras with half-domes and domes become standard components of architecture, illustrated by the baths partially erected on the Domus Aurea and finished in 109 (20m diameter for the two rotundas) and found again in the 'Markets' along the north-east of the forum (with apses of 13 and 18m).

If not inevitable, it was at least natural that Hadrian should continue the architecture of his illustrious predecessor and the Apollodorian fashion of monument building (although the latter met with disgrace and death). This endowed the architectural story of the capital with the Pantheon, the Temple of Venus and Rome,[36] the Mausoleum of Hadrian and the enormous residence at Tivoli, where apses and domes freely multiply.[37]

In the course of the second century Campania also, if not more so than *Latium*, witnessed the building of domes that remain among the most considerable in the Roman world. This fact is even more surprising as these structures are concentrated in the Phlegrean area in the immediate vicinity of Naples. The explanation perhaps lies in the intense volcanic activity in the locality. This means that numerous springs rise there and particularly large baths complexes were built

around these, most of them grouped together in the area between Pozzuoli and Cuma (where volcanic gases and hot springs abound).[38] If this made the choice obvious, the centuries that followed have clearly shown that it was a particularly dangerous one due to the seismic activity.

In the bath complex at Baia, already the possessor of the oldest surviving dome, there rises near the present seashore the great hall known as the 'Temple of Venus'. This is octagonal outside and circular inside and faced in *opus reticulatum* with brick piers. Its partially collapsed dome spanned 26.3m (fig.449). The monument, sunk into the ground to a depth of about 3m, is still of an impressive size, though smaller than the third dome of this bath complex, that known as the 'Baths of Diana' (fig.450) laid out at the north of the site.[39] This dome, like the preceding one, consisted of a vast octagon of *opus mixtum*, erected in the middle of the second century, enclosing a circular hall 29.5m (100 feet) in diameter covered by a dome of ogival profile, mainly composed of courses of bricks and capped with a thin vault of tufa rubble. Due to seismic activity caused by the slow movement of the earth's crust which affects the whole Phlegrean area, this

450 The building called the 'Temple of Diana' at Baia, in fact connected to the bath complex for which it could have been a nymphaeum. With a span of 29.5m, this dome is third in order of size; it has an ogival shape unique among these large buildings. The walls of the drum are faced with *opus mixtum* and the dome is constructed of bricks in horizontal courses, the capping ending with light tufa. It is thus, paradoxically, by using a corbelling technique, transformed into a concrete and monolithic structure by lime mortar, that the Roman architects created some of their finest vaults. Second half of the second century.

450

451 The remains (that have collapsed and been buried in the ground due to seismic activity) of the vast dome, the so-called 'Temple of Apollo', built in the second century on the shore of Lake Averno near Baia. More than 36m in diameter (the lack of precise detail is due to the state of the monument), it is, in order of size, the second biggest surviving from the Roman world.

452 The dome, decagonal in plan, of the great monument of the *Horti Liciniani* in Rome, known as the 'Temple of Minerva Medica', in an engraving of 1825. At this time, the dome was still closed in. Built in the fourth century it has an internal diameter of 24.5m.

monument, together with the previous ones, partially subsided into the ground and lost its southern half, making a vertical section visible.[40]

The fourth great dome of Campania, which is also second in order of size of surviving Roman examples, was also built in the second century, on the shore of Lake Averno. This was perhaps part of another baths complex and is known as the 'Temple of Apollo' (fig.451). More damaged than the others by seismic activity, it still majestically dominates the remains that surround it and the dark waters of the lake in which it is reflected. With an internal diameter of some 36m, it still leaves a strong impression on the rare visitors who approach it.[41]

5 Intersections

Among the innumerable possibilities afforded by the concrete arch is the ideal solution to the dreaded problem of the intersection of two arched volumes. Although the Greeks created multiple arches in stone blocks and knew how to cover a number of chambers with barrel vaults (the tombs of Macedonia) and tunnels (stadium of Nemea, Didymeion, theatre of Letoon), only Pergamon, with its second century architecture (after Attalus I) has preserved two examples of intersecting arches. One of these is the Gymnasium, where a flight of stairs meets a perpendicular landing, and the other is in a tomb.[42]

It might be thought that the Romans, who were familiar with arches and keyed vaults in stone block construction, would have overcome this difficult problem by the cross-vault, but this was not the case. On the contrary, whenever the risk of intersection arose, they shifted the keystone so that the spring of one arch was higher than the key of the other, so that the lower arch opened in a vertical wall while the barrel vault of the higher one continued without interruption (fig.453). The only monument in the Italian peninsula with a cross-vault, a building which is in all respects a masterpiece of stone cutting, is the Tomb of Theodoric, in Ravenna, built in 530 (fig.454). The astonishing quality of the cutting and laying of the blocks here has such striking parallels with the Early Christian architecture of Syria that it is almost certain that the architect must have come from that country, where the art of the vault had reached a remarkable level of development. In fact, the theatre at Philippopolis (the village of Chahba in the Djebel Druse), built in the middle of the third century AD, has preserved a number of rising vaults and intersections. Among these is a cross-vault, one of two originally situated at the intersection of the ambulacrum and the corridors of the *postcaenium* (fig.455).[43] One surprising aspect of the Ravenna tomb is that, despite the perfect mastery of the most complex keying, as shown by the cross-vault in the crypt and the toed arches, the builder crowned the building with a monstrous monolithic dome, 10.7m in diameter and weighing 470 tonnes.

The reason behind the Roman side-stepping of the question of intersections is in fact very simple. The development early on of concrete masonry and the ease with which any shape could be created by using wooden centring, without all the problems of dressing or precise arrangement, enabled the builders to make intersections of arches at all levels and in all directions. Indeed, as complex and varied as the profiles and the volumes are, intersections of arches can be reduced to two situations:

1 Intersection – when two barrel vaults meet at different levels;

2 Cross-vault – when the two barrel vaults spring at the same level with the same level of key (fig.456).

453

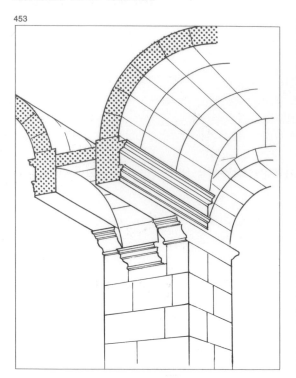

454

455

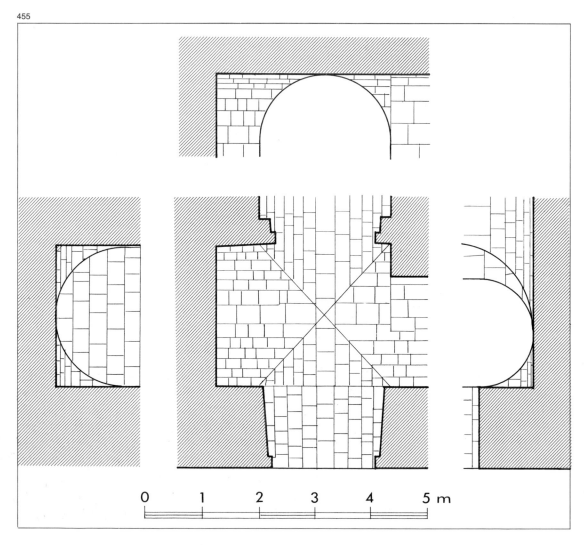

453 The solution adopted in the amphitheatre at Nîmes to circumvent the intersection of two vaults in this stone block construction: two lintels separate the radiating arches from the tunnel vault whose crown is, in addition, below the level of the springing of the former. Augustan period. (After J. Durm.)

454 A groined vault in the Tomb of Theodoric at Ravenna (530).

455 A groined vault at the intersection of two tunnels at the Theatre of Philippopolis in Syria; c.250. (After the survey by P. Coupel.)

0   1   2   3   4   5 m

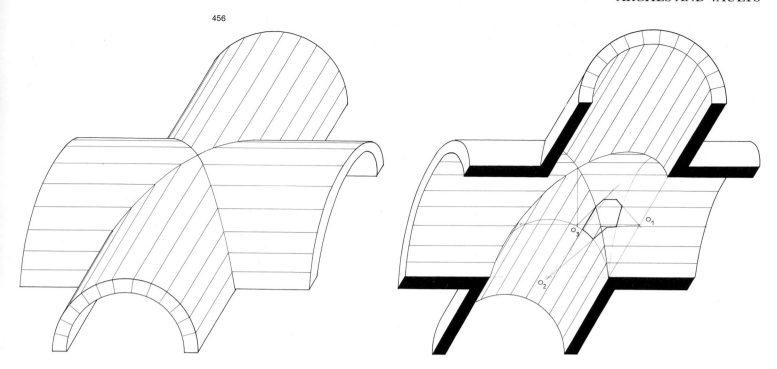

456

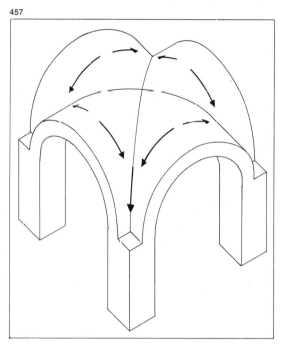

457

Both of these methods have the considerable advantage of making possible openings for passage and lighting, without weakening the vault, due to the distribution of pressure on to the strong points of the spring of the groins (figs. 457 to 462).

It is noticeable that many halls covered by domes are actually polygonal in plan, and are not strictly circular. The solution to the problem of roofing is then to divide the curve of the dome into facets, or flat surfaces. Sometimes, however, the dome appears as a hemispherical capping. In that case the connection between the polygon and the circle is achieved by means of masonry shapes called pendentives, which can be easily made in concrete. The true 'pendentive dome' involving the placing of a circular-shaped volume on a square shape, was rarely built by the Romans, but was to become a fairly standard element in Byzantine architecture, in response to the demand of the cruciform shape centred by a dome on a drum. The technique for this was, however, known

in the middle of the second century, since its application can be found in two funerary monuments in the *via Nomentana*, the 'Sedia del Diavolo' and the 'Torracio della Cecchina', built of brick masonry with two vaulted levels, the upper hall being covered by a pendentive dome.[44]

456 Axonometric projections of a groined vault and plan of a hip voussoir or groin.

457 The mechanism of the groined vault. In this system, the forces are distributed by the groins and transmitted to the piers. Walls acting as abutment masses disappear and all four sides can be opened up.

458   Rows of groined vaults made of masonry constructed on a permanent centring of square bricks. Ostia, House of Serapis.

459   Portico with groined vaults opening on to column arches. Such a solution, the best as regards lightness and lighting, would have been impossible with a barrel vault. Licinian Baths at Dougga (Thugga), third century.

460   Ribbed groined vaults on the Palatine. (A. Choisy.)

461   A line of groined vaults (in a ring) in the ambulatories of the Colosseum. The remains of the centring are still visible wherever the rendering of the intrados has disappeared. Flavian period.

462   Halabiye (Zenobia), Syria: three successive vaulted levels of the 'Praetorium' of Justinian, with arches built of stone blocks and groined vaults made of brick.

7
CARPENTRY

1 Floors and ceilings

Timber-framing, dealt with above under mixed structures, could just as well have figured here, since with this type of construction as with timber work in general, wood forms the main supporting element. This hesitancy as regards classification in fact highlights the great richness of an architecture that used all the building techniques in all their combinations.

Whereas in Roman Gaul, Germany and Britain wooden floors have sometimes been found in the lower level of houses, Italy and other parts of the empire had ground floors consisting of stone or simply beaten earth in the case of more humble dwellings.

Wooden floors were thus more common in northern regions, being less refined and more generous with this material, which was easier to replace and, paradoxically, more comfortable than a paved or mosaic floor. The remains of floors found in houses at Bavay simply consisted, in so far as it has been possible to analyse them, of wide planks arranged on a floor of beaten earth.[1] This sort of arrangement must have existed in many wooded regions, and is probably what forms the numerous black layers, called 'burnt layers', which could also just as well have been caused by the slow carbonization of a decomposing wood level.

In Britain, the grain store, *horrea*, of the fort of Housesteads (*Borovicus*), at the half-way point of Hadrian's Wall, has a ground floor which matches up to the standards of high-quality architecture and, in addition, has retained clear traces of the installation. To keep the floor ventilated and insulated from damp, the builders created a 'sanitary void', a method that is still carried out in the same way today. Sockets in the walls, 50cm from the ground, took the ends of joists supporting the floor; these joists also rested on small intermediate pillars of stone, and openings around the edge provided ventilation for this insulated space (fig.463).

The floors of upper storeys are known from houses of Ostia, Pompeii and especially Herculaneum. In the first two sites this is due to the height of preserved walls, and in the third because the elements themselves have remained *in situ*.

Pompeii and its immediate region, however, was not an area that was very well forested; in fact, the land was so rich that it was completely given over

463   Hadrian's Wall: *horrea* of the garrison of *Borovicus* (Housesteads). Sockets and small supporting columns for the floor joists.

463

to agriculture. By constrast, the foothills of the Lattari Mountains, which dominate Stabiae, were very steep and unsuitable for cultivation and so were covered with woods; the area is still a great producer of chestnut wood which is used by local industry. In the east and south-east, the chain of the Appenines offered a great variety of species and was sufficiently rich and close at hand to provide the coastal cities with an adequate supply of wood for use in architecture and ship-building.

The principle of flooring an upper level consists of covering a space so that it remains clear, as it forms both a ceiling and the level for walking on above. The solution adopted in the smallest dwellings, not exceeding 5m, was to rest a row of joists[2] on a projection from the wall (fig.464) or in sockets in the masonry. These joists had very variable sections, depending on their span or the quality of the wood. The following are some dimensions recorded at Pompeii:

width	height	interval between	site
14cm	34cm	28cm	VI,1,8
15.5cm	29cm	29.5cm	portico of west forum
17cm	25cm	28cm	IX,6,1
14 to 18cm	(round timbers)	25cm	IX,6,1

The supporting sockets were often carefully made, with ceramic frames insulating the wood from the masonry and making it possible, if necessary, to replace it easily (fig.465). Some joists retained their natural circular section, which allowed the use of pieces with a small diameter; in this case their ends were bonded with the masonry of the wall (fig.466).

On these joists, and at right-angles to them, was placed or nailed a floor or floor-boarding.[3] This did not form the

464

465

466

464 Corbels of travertine socketed into the brick walls to take the beams parallel to the wall and forming a support for the joists of the floor. Ostia, House of the *Lararium*.

465 Housings for beams supporting a floor, framed with bricks. Pompeii, VI,14,31.

466 Housings for joists used in their natural circular shape and enclosed in the masonry. Pompeii, IX,6,e.

actual level for walking on (except probably in rustic dwellings, though there is no surviving evidence for this),

467

467 Cross-section of the Doric portico made of tufa at the Forum of Pompeii. Doubting the resilience of this material, the builders made the entablature and joists of the upper floor rest on wooden beams.

468 Remains of a floor and the beams supporting it in a house in Herculaneum.

469 Ceiling of a ruined farm at Pompeii, showing the same structure as ancient ceilings: the beams support a parquet on which a layer of mortar is placed.

0   1 m

but a level of support. A layer of mortar was applied to this floor, 15 to 30cm thick, which then had a covering of *opus signinum* (mortar with broken fragments of stone and terracotta) or mosaic (fig.467). The mason thus recreated on the upper floors a floor covering identical to that on the ground floor. The dimensions of the upper flooring of house No.20 of the *Decumanus Maximus* at Herculaneum can serve as illustration. The joists measured 17.5 by 13cm and covered a span of 5m; the floor was 2.8cm thick; and the capping with broken ceramic concretion was 28.5 thick (fig.470). This technique is verifiable only at Herculaneum and Pompeii but must have been standard since Vitruvius gives a description of it (VII,1) which conforms in all respects to these surviving examples (figs 468, 469). In addition, Vitruvius also gives recommendations that cannot be corroborated but were probably in common use. One such is spreading on the floor-boards a bed of ferns or straw before the layer of mortar was poured on, so that the wood would not come into direct contact with the lime.

This technique resulted in floors that were extremely heavy, explaining the thickness of the joists found throughout Pompeii; the advantage, however,

468

469

lay in the excellent insulation provided and in the fact that this network of heavily-laden joints tied the walls together.

When the span to be covered was greater than 5m, the need to increase the diameter of the joists would mean an excessive consumption of wood and so the thickness of the joists remained the same but they were provided with a series of supports limiting their span. This series of supports, depending on the size of the room, was made up of one or several beams[4] of considerable thickness. They stretched from one wall to another, depending on the width, and supported the joists (fig.471).

It was usual in rooms of houses to conceal the joists or beams by means of a ceiling that could be decorated. Thin pieces of wood were nailed to the underside of the joists which could be lined with reeds and then rendered. This also could have one or two additional layers applied, in which a relief decoration, of greater or lesser definition, could be created.

Visitors to the cities around Vesuvius notice that a large number of rooms are covered by vaults, sometimes composite, generally low and often

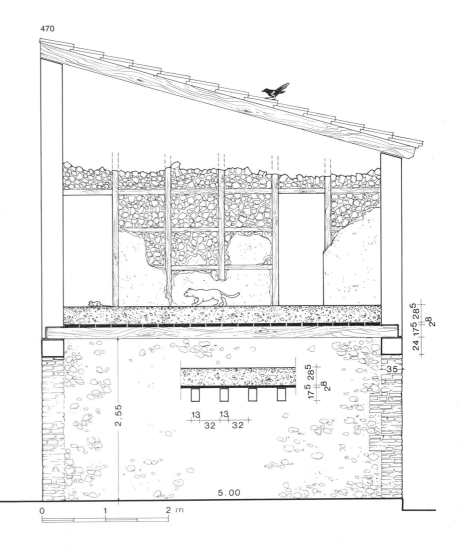

470

471

470 Cross-section of an urban house with a shop on the ground floor. The upper floor is *opus signinum* spread on the floor, a wooden partition separates the two rooms on the storey and the restored roof timbers are simply a row of rafters supporting the tiles. Herculaneum, *Insula* V, no.20.

471 Cerveteri, the so-called Tomb of the Capitals, Etruscan. The space consists of a room, roofed by a ceiling resting on joists supported by two main beams, themselves on pillars; *c.*500BC.

472

473

2   Wooden staircases

472   Example of an unusual arch suspended on joists in a *cubiculum* at Pompeii. House of Fabius Rufus.

473   Remains of the sockets of the beams supporting a hanging vault, covering a room at Pompeii, IX,5,21.

mysteriously lacking supports. In fact these are not vaults, they are simply vaulted ceilings, *camararum* as Vitruvius calls them in his chapter devoted to ceilings (VII,3).

The curved shape of the soffit[5] was obtained by making the sockets for the joists in a curved line, creating in fact a permanent centring below which the ceiling was suspended. As the joists reached from one wall to the other it was possible to make any sort of curve and even to create a central recess bordered by horizontal surfaces, giving the illusion of hanging vaults.

Sometimes the centred soffit was limited to the alcove situated above a bed; in that case it was sufficient to rest the joists on a cross beam or to suspend them from it by using pieces of iron, the rest of the ceiling being at a different level (figs 472, 473).

In the absence of sufficient preserved height, one indicator, though not a sure one, of the existence of at least one upper storey, is a more substantial wall; but it is the presence of the masonry base of a staircase that makes it certain. At Ostia, despite the fact that the buildings have been exposed to the open air, the widespread choice of staircases made of masonry makes identification simple. However Herculaneum and Pompeii demonstrate that even quite luxurious houses had only wooden staircases, which have survived by chance (at Herculaneum), or have left clear traces of their supports.

Most staircases begin with a small pedestal of masonry with one to three steps, supporting the rising pieces of wood called strings which in turn support the steps. The incline of the strings, and therefore of the staircase, which is always quite steep,[6] is easy to reconstruct from the support groove visible in the wall, generally corresponding to a simple break in the rendering along the staircase. This clue can be traced as far as the level of the upper floor, where it is sometimes possible even to measure the width of the passage opening.

Two types of wooden staircase are still recognizable at Herculaneum: the staircase of solid steps[7] and the open-tread staircase.[8] The remains of supports left in the masonry at Pompeii show that it was the same there. The best preserved example of a staircase with solid steps is in a shop in region IV at no.20.[9] In the original layout of the site the staircase had no connection to the shop since, leading straight from the pavement, it led directly to one or several upper dwellings.[10] The shop itself had its own staircase that to begin with is made of masonry, partially surviving in the south-west corner, and connected with the trader's dwellings, consisting of a bedroom on the first floor looking out to the back of the house (fig.474). The wooden section of the staircase was formerly separated from the premises by a wooden partition or a light wooden framework whose support, 10cm wide, is still visible on the last step of the masonry which held the strings.

From this point, corresponding to the fourth step up from the ground level of the pavement, the construction is made entirely of wood as far as the upper landing, situated 3.8m above the ground level of the shop, a height indicated by the upper limit of a socket trench made in the reticulate wall (figs 475, 476). The beams of the upper storey were supported either on two beam bearings resting on corbels, or in socket holes that have now disappeared with the collapse of the upper part of the wall. There is also a horizontal groove, subsequently hidden by rubble fill, 3m above the ground, which marks the position of a loggia attached to the shop in its original state and probably used as a store.

Some strings survive from the wooden staircase. Made of straight pieces 16cm high, they supported solid steps, of which four remain. These are very regular,

22cm high, 25cm deep, 1.23m wide (the masonry staircase of the shop is 0.88m wide); its incline is in the region of 40 degrees. The rising cut, because of its small width (5 to 6cm), must have held wooden pegs or metal pieces fixed in to the string to stop it bending.

Using this as a model, since it is particularly clear, it is possible to identify another staircase whose wooden steps have completely disappeared leaving only the initial pedestal made of masonry and, a valuable piece of evidence, part of the outline incised in the rendering covering the side wall. It is a staircase belonging to the House of the Faun at Pompeii (VI,12,2)[11] and built in a corridor leading from the secondary atrium to the second peristyle bordering the baths and the kitchen (fig.477). There can be seen, on a pedestal 1.5m long and 0.86 m wide, three steps made of hard lava and a fourth of masonry; then the drawn design, which must have served as a guideline for the carpenter, with one string 19cm thick supporting three

474 Plan of a shop at Herculaneum, *Insula* IV, no.20. The wooden staircase did not belong to this shop.

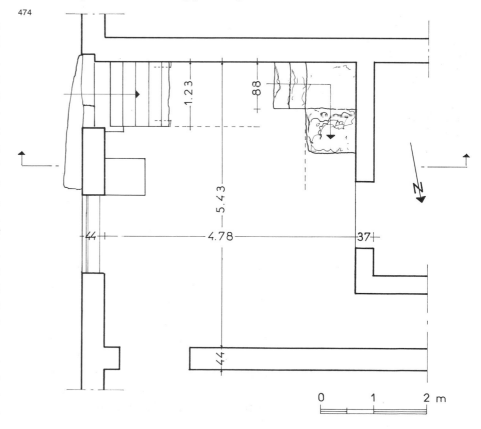

475　Detail of the wooden staircase in fig. 474, which had solid steps.

476　Longitudinal cross-section showing the position of the wooden staircase passing above the internal staircase of the shop.

476

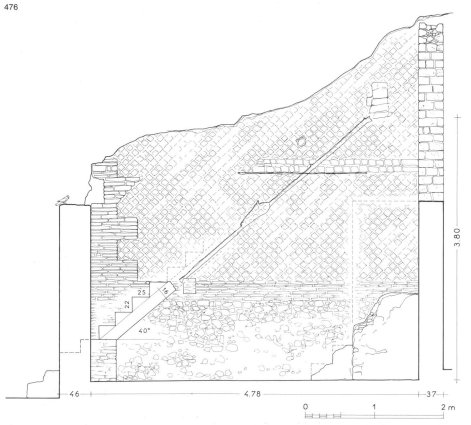

steps 26cm high and 32cm deep, plus the start of two others, with an incline in the region of 38 degrees. This sketch points to the existence of a staircase with solid steps identical in structure to the one at Herculaneum but slightly different in its dimensions since, though its incline is gentler, the height of the steps would have made them difficult to climb (figs 478, 479). The upper level is still marked by the support holes of the landing beams which occupied the total width of the corridor, 1.63m. Due to the collapse of the walls, the layout of the upper rooms is unknown.

Another staircase in the House of the Faun, although no clue survives as to its upper wooden structure, has preserved six lower steps, made of lava and limestone tuff, a more comfortable 19 to 21cm high (the limestone is more worn down) and 29cm deep, equivalent to an incline of 35 degrees.

The second category of staircases that can be identified is that of open-tread stairs; this sort, to judge by the numerous traces of supports in the facings of masonry, was much more typical than staircases with solid steps. Two reasons for this are that this type takes up less space than the preceding one, thanks to the steep incline made possible by the openwork steps, and that it uses far fewer materials.

Herculaneum again provides a perfect illustration, in a shop situated in the Eastern *insula* IIA at No.9 (the area dominating the Great *Palaestra*), which is also one of the best preserved in the city.[12] Still visible (protected by glass plates admittedly only moderately efficient due to the greenhouse effect that they produce) are the shelf arrangements designed for holding amphorae, the floor of a mezzanine and the upper part of a flight of open-tread stairs (fig.480).

The two lengths of string boards are pieces of wood 15cm wide and 4.5cm thick which still hold up four steps, 3cm thick and 19.5cm apart, giving a height to clear of 22.5cm. The absence of risers in this type of staircase makes it possible to create a steep incline – here it reaches 65 degrees (fig.481). In addition, the floor is held up by joists measuring 9.5 × 8cm, supported on a beam 19 × 10cm. Finally, two doors, one above the other, each gave access to a back room, the one on the ground floor still containing the wooden uprights of a bed.

In the houses and shops of Pompeii there are numerous traces left by open-tread stairs. In the vast majority of cases they are located in the corner of a room, where a block of masonry supports a few steps, ending with a small landing from which rose, at a steep angle, the wooden flight of steps.

The string, supported by the wall, leaves a rising mark, often accompanied, when the wall was rendered, by a painted band of the same colour as the

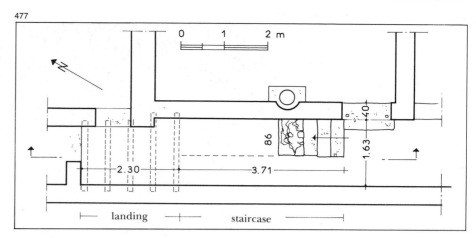

477   Position of the staircase built in a corridor of the House of the Faun at Pompeii, VI,12,2.

478   Preparatory marking, incised in the mortar, for a flight of wooden steps.

479   Cross-section lengthways along a corridor in the House of the Faun, showing the solid base of the staircase, the location and marking of the flight of wooden steps and the support level of the landing.

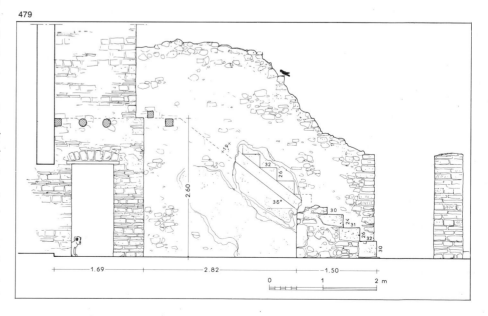

basement, indicating the incline of the string (fig.482).

One of the staircases, in VI,5,8, has left a collection of support marks that is particularly complete, making it possible to reconstruct not only the access to the upper storey, but also the landing and the floor. It began on the right of a partition wall which it pierces by a door 1.98m high (established by the socket of the lintel), and then rose on an incline of 46 degrees to the upstairs floor, 3.1m above. The mark of the string in the masonry is from 30 to 35cm wide and ends with a short landing measuring only 48cm, while the passage opening, clearly visible in the interruption in the support between the floor and the landing, had an opening of 1.73m; its width, like that of the staircase, which goes directly from the ground without a masonry pedestal, remains unknown (fig.483).

The structure of the ceiling and the floor of the adjoining room is perfectly clear: firstly there is a thin socket trench for the ceiling laths that are

480

482

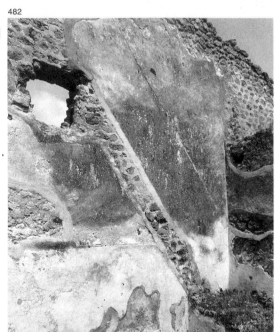

481

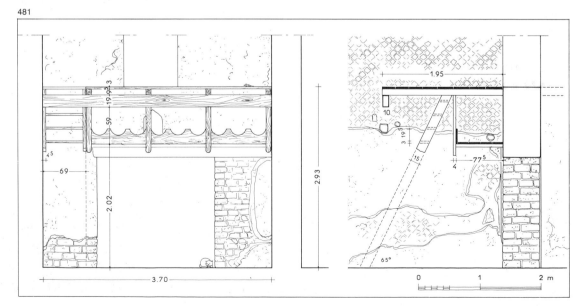

480   Overall view of the shop at Herculaneum situated in the Eastern *Insula* IIA, no.9, with (at the back) a bedroom in which the steps up to a bed have survived.

481   Cross-section and lengthways section showing the surviving wooden structures and their arrangement.

482   The remains of a wooden staircase support with a masonry base. The decoration of the rendering followed the incline as far as the upper landing. Pompeii, IX,1,4.

nailed under the joists, then the support holes for the joists, 22cm high, 12cm wide and spaced only 15 to 17cm apart. This density can be explained by the considerable weight of the upper floor, made up first of all of a flooring, then a bed of mortar holding the surface for walking on – in total it here reached 18 to 19cm.

Finally, it is worth noting that the lower face of these walking surfaces could be given a sloping lath ceiling identical to the horizontal ceilings, to which it was possible to apply a painted rendering, as can be found at the House of the Iliac Chapel (I,6,4) on the via dell'Abbondanza.[13]

3   Roof timbering

As with all other wooden structures, the remains of roof timbering are unfortunately few. Even at Herculaneum and Pompeii there are scarcely any, except for traces of supports and sockets usually from roofs of modest dimensions where the solutions to the problem of roofing were fairly rudimentary (fig.484). Of the methods used to cover the great monuments there remains absolutely nothing;[14] the last ancient building which preserved its roof timbers throughout its history was the basilica of St-Paul's-outside-the-Walls, built between 384 and 403. Unfortunately, these roof timbers were totally destroyed by a fire in 1823. It is thus useful to turn to the literary and iconographic sources, which are equally few in number, and to the remains of the supports left in the monuments.

Though Vitruvius tells us at length about the different species of wood used in roof timbering (II,9), he is hardly loquacious on their method of arrangement and treats us only to a very brief passage (IV,2). In a few lines, he outlines carpentry of a wide span, *de majora spatia*, in which can be identi-

fied the truss (see below), and of more modest spans, *commoda*, simply resting on the upright pieces.

In the face of such reticence it would be useful to be able to turn to the texts of estimates describing an official order for a monument or other architectural work. However, these documents, common

483

483   The remains of a support for a wooden staircase, its passage opening and the upper floor, at Pompeii (VI,5,8 and 20).

484   Excavation of the peristyle of the House of Cuspius Pansa (I,6,1), revealing the roof that collapsed on to the lapilli. (Photo: V. Spinazzola.)

484

among the Greeks who simply carved them in marble, are totally lacking for the Romans who wrote them on parchment, though there is, admittedly, the detailed estimate concerning the erection of a modest porch in front of the Temple of Serapis at Pozzuoli.[15]

The Roman pictorial record, as already seen, is rich in scenes of building sites and representations of machines and tools, but it fails to show the construction of roof timbers. One of the only sources of illustration of a large-scale wooden structure is Trajan's Column,

485

which shows the bridge built on the Danube by Apollodoros of Damascus.

By contrast, models of roof timbering on a large scale appear very often inside Etruscan hypogea, cut into the rock. The rooms of these funerary monuments invariably represented the house of the living, and the choice of carving these spaces into the tufa made it possible to reproduce the details of the interior of buildings with remarkable accuracy. A visit to the Banditaccia necropolis, near Cerveteri (*Caere*), is of great interest in this regard, as it provides several stages in the evolution of roofing techniques (fig.485).

One of the oldest forms of roofing is a simple support of posts on a roof-ridge, itself resting on the top of the wall of each façade. This hut form exists in the tombs of the seventh century called 'hut tombs', resembling on the inside a tent space, produced by the two slopes of the roof (sometimes called a 'gable roof').

Up to the third century BC roofs can be found with this same profile, but very much lowered, often even consisting of just a ceiling and joists.[16] A steeply pitched roof reappears occasionally, as

485 Etruscan tomb at Cerveteri showing the ridge beam supporting the two slopes of the roof and, on the tympanum, the jointing of the pieces forming timber framing on the façade; *c.*500 BC.

486 A reconstruction in section of the Naval Arsenal, built by Philo in the fourth century BC in the port of Piraeus. The appearance of this building is recorded in a descriptive estimate, defining the position and the dimensions of the walls, pillars and especially the timbers, the vast size of which is apparent.

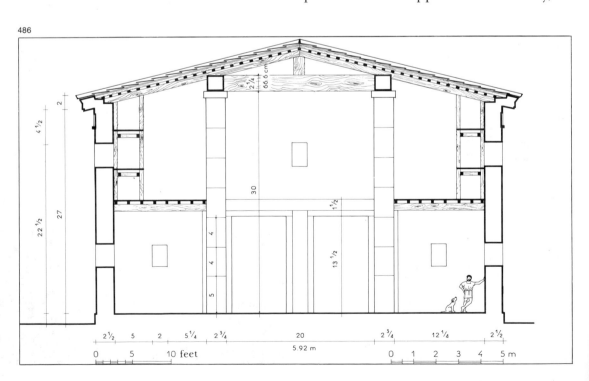

486

487

487 Socket holes for rafters supporting the pent roof of a peristyle gallery. The first row of tiles and junction-covers has remained partially fixed in the masonry, Pompeii, IX,6,5. The housings for the joists (circular section, i.e. non-squared pieces) are not aligned according to the distances between the tiles and, in addition, are separated from the latter by a height of about 8cm, proving that between the joists and the tiles were laths which supported the roofing material.

488 Façade of the House of the Black Salon at Herculaneum. The vast canopy has been restored thanks to the remarkable survival of the wooden pieces, notably of two imposing sculpted beams acting as corbels for the pent roof.

at the tomb of the Volumnii (second century BC) near Perugia and even the opening of the *compluvium* can be found (Tomb of Mercareggia, 'Tombe dei due ingressi' at Vulci). Of particular interest is the fact that in some hypogea the sculptor has shown the triangular outline of the roof timbers in a transverse section, thus giving details of all the constituent pieces.

Other useful clues for identification and research are the remains of the timber supports left in the top part of walls. With these few data and some written sources it has been possible to reconstruct Greek roof timbers (fig.486), thanks to the abundance of sockets visible in the stone construction blocks. In Roman masonry architecture this evidence is often lacking, being situated at levels that are too vulnerable, and it can only be studied in monuments of dressed stone.

The simplest form of roof, as shown by examples from the cities of Vesuvius, is the lean-to or pent roof,[17] that is a roof with only one slope, stretching from one wall to another or from one wall to a colonnade. The porticoes of the houses at Pompeii (the portico being a type of pent roof) were simply made up of rafters[18] holding a level of boarding or laths, at right angles to the former and designed to hold the tiles (fig.487).[19] The rafters were supported by the entablature of the colonnade.

The canopies that are so common above the doors at Pompeii are simply pent roofs whose lower support is replaced by one horizontal piece resting on two putlogs socketed in the wall and acting as corbels (fig.488).

488

489 Reconstructed roof timbering of the *atrium* of the 'Tuscan' type according to Vitruvius (VI,3,1-6), in a *domus* at Herculaneum. Two main beams support the rising pieces, called the 'valley rafters', from each corner. The tiles are laid directly on the two cross-members of the *compluvium* and the rafters in this reconstruction. House of the Wooden Partition.

490 Remains of the roof support of an arched room in the Villa dei Sette Bassi. There were no timbers here – the tiles were placed on a sloping bed of mortar.

At Pompeii, most timber roofing for houses, with one or two sides, follows a fairly simple pattern. The horizontal pieces, the purlins (*cathenae*), go from one gable wall to another; these pieces hold the rafters, which form a projection at the front of the wall (*cantherii prominentes ad extremam suggrundationem*, Vitruvius IV,2), and hold the laths (*templa*). On these are placed, either the tiles directly, or, following the recommendation of Vitruvius, a layer of small pieces, *asseres*, which are turned at 90 degrees with each application, then followed by the tiles laid lengthways.

Such rudimentary roof timbers were suitable for the vast majority of dwelling houses (figs 489, 490) which had rooms of modest size. The roofing might be divided by internal walls which would help to support the purlins. The Greeks did the same and must have often used very strong pieces to cover quite modest spans as they were unaware of the arrangement that was to timber what the arch is to stone: the truss.[20]

In fact, the question of origin asked in connection with the voussoir arch can be repeated for the invention of the truss, but in this case with complete uncertainty. Indeed it appears that, from the Hellenistic period, the Greek world built monuments covering an enormous area in which there are no supports close to one another, such as the Bouleuterion of Priene, with pillars 14m apart, and the Olympieion at Athens – 14.8m apart in the *pronaos* and the *opisthodomos*. Unless the Greeks used beams of a very large size (80cm thick or more), which would have been difficult to find in such lengths (though several beams could be joined in a bundle), it seems certain that they had devised a means of working wood in such a way that it could cover large spaces with optimum economy. Classical Greek roof timbers, such as are known, used only horizontal and sloping beams, supported both directly on the walls or on posts, and working by compression, transmitting the weight of the roof to the side walls, with an effect similar to the forces acting on a voussoir arch.

The great discovery, perhaps originating with a ship's hull, consisted of interconnecting the separate elements of roof timbers so as to create a self-supporting structure that would not lose its shape, called a triangulated truss[21] or more simply a truss, since triangulation is vital to it. The elements making up the basic truss are defined by Vitruvius for timbers for a roof of large span: two rising pieces, following the pitch of the roof – these are the principal rafters (*capreoli*) – connected at the top; and, holding the foot of these principal rafters, a horizontal piece, the tie-beam (*transtrum*). In such an arrangement the two principal

rafters take the weight of the roof (purlins, rafters and tiles) and consequently they bend. This bending is cancelled out at the point where the two pieces meet at the roof-ridge and is transmitted to the lower part in the form of a pulling apart at the joints with the tie-beam. The latter thus becomes a piece under tension, subject to traction, and functions exactly like the string of a bow under tension, giving an extreme rigidity to the structure. In addition to the great solidity it gives to the arrangement, this clever distribution of forces also makes it possible to reduce considerably the size of the components and to bridge spaces that only the masonry vault has been able to exceed (figs 491, 492).

Although there are no surviving examples of these first triangulated timber roofs, there are in a number of great churches in Sicily (Syracuse,

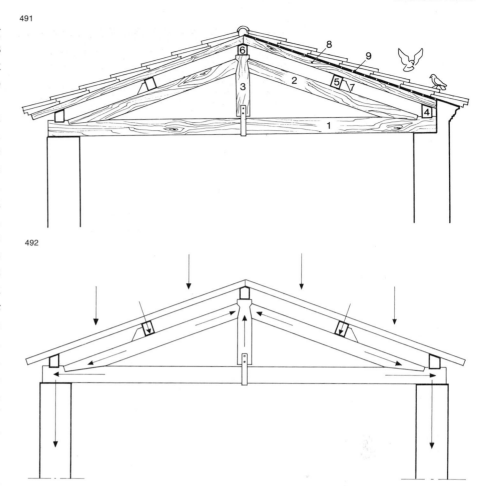

491 The triangulated truss. On the left, the tiles rest directly on the rafters, imposing regular distances between axes; on the right, they are on a base of laths, making it possible to place the rafters at random (cf. fig.497).
1 tie-beam (in tension);
2 principal rafter (in compression);
3 king post (in tension) pulled upwards by the principal rafters and relieving the bending of the tie-beam by a stirrup;
4 wall-plate (purlin);
5 purlin;
6 ridge purlin;
7 cleat;
8 common rafter;
9 boarding (laths).

492 The mechanism of the triangulated truss. The rafters and the principal rafters work in flexion by transmitting the oblique forces to the tie-beam, which naturally has a tendency to bend, and to the king post, both of them placed under tension. The various forces are integrated and the timbers only transmit vertical pressures to the walls.

493

493 Roof timbers in a basic triangulated truss (one tie-beam, two principal rafters) supporting purlins and then boarding holding the tiles. The pieces of wood are not cut with a long saw but squared with an axe respecting the natural pattern of the grain. Roof of the Byzantine basilica of Aegosthenes (Porto Germeno, Attica). Span: 3.40m.

494 Roof timbers in the Cathedral of Syracuse, forming a series of basic triangulated trusses made up of one tie-beam and two principal rafters, as in the preceding more rustic example. Despite their modest span of 9.8m, the pieces are of considerable size; the tie-beam is 60 x 35cm and the principal rafters are 35 x 35cm. The original timbers date back to the Byzantine period.

494

Cefalù, Monreale) some basic trusses which correspond exactly to those described by Vitruvius and which have not been modified since their erection in the Middle Ages (figs 493, 494).

Nevertheless, however great the advantages of this basic truss, it still had limited possibilities. Despite the silence of Vitruvius, Roman carpenters must have extended the principle of triangulation on the basis of this model so as to bridge greater and greater spans without excessively increasing the size of the pieces. Though the mechanism of this development is known through medieval evidence, from Roman times there is only a single painting with a representation of what the roof timbering of the great monuments of Rome was like. This document, preserved in the Palace of the Canons in the Vatican, shows in section (fig.495), the first basilica of St Peter's, built around 330, before its demolition. The building was some

65m wide and consisted of a central nave with a span of approximately 24m,[22] bordered on each side by two aisles following a layout that is identical to that of St Paul's-outside-the-Walls (fig.496).

Each truss of the timber roofing of the nave consisted of two principal rafters, held by a lower tie-beam, of 24m, and a higher tie-beam called a straining beam, and a piece linking the tie-beams vertically to the top of the principal rafters, called the king post or crown post. It is very probable that all these very long pieces were made from elements joined together using scarf joints, splayed and tabled. The arrangement of these joints would have enabled the whole to function with pieces subject to bending as well as under tension. Elsewhere, both upper and lower tie-beams, were made up of two pieces spliced together,[23] a method allowing the useful section to be doubled and the use of thin pieces.

The king post (a piece not mentioned by Vitruvius) functions in a very subtle manner: it receives the upward pressure of the tops of the principal rafters, and this vertical pull, against gravity, is made use of to relieve the natural bending of the tie-beam, to which it is firmly attached by a stirrup or strong pegs.

The aisle roofing in the basilica of St Peter's was provided by pent-roof timbers that are in fact half-trusses, in which the straining beam is replaced by a slanting piece called a strut.

Thus, in this timber roofing of a fourth-century basilica can be found all the elements that comprise trusses. This was not improved upon, apart from slight changes of shape and arrangement, until the invention in the twentieth century of lattice-girders and timbers of glued-laminated wood.[24]

The remarkable span of the timbers in the basilicas of St Peter's and St Paul's-outside-the-Walls (in both cases 24m) is not, however, the record for

Roman carpenters. At the Imperial basilica in Trier the span reached 28m and, if the version of this structure at the Palace of Domitian is allowed, a space of 30m was already crossed at the end of the first century, which supposes an equal mastery of triangulation at this period. In the Augustan period, Vitruvius, having roofed in timber the basilica of Fano, the central nave of which measured 120 feet long by 60 wide (34.8m × 17.8m) (V,1), no doubt possessed a similar knowledge.

A written document, unfortunately not from the Roman period but from the early Middle Ages, provides very interesting statistics, showing the progress made with the triangulated truss. It refers to the replacement in the ninth century of a truss that had deteriorated in the basilica of St Paul's-outside-the-Walls[25] and the dimensions given are as follows:

495

495 Fresco showing the first basilica of St Peter's in Rome, in section, painted during its demolition. The particularly precise and detailed drawing of the timbers is the best surviving representation of ancient timbering on a large scale. (Vatican, Palace of the Canons.)

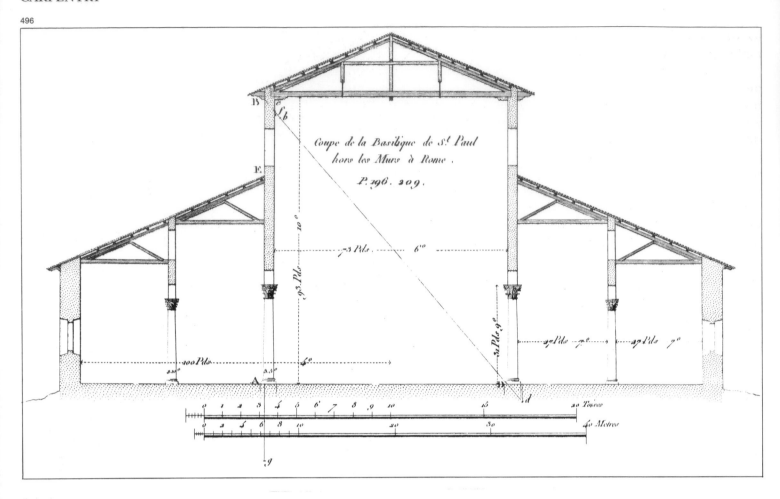

Coupe de la Basilique de St Paul
hors les Murs à Rome.
P. 196. 209.

496 Cross-section of the basilica of St Paul's-outside-the-Walls, showing the roof timbers such as they were before destruction in the fire of 1823. (J. Rondelet, *Traité théorique et pratique de l'Art de bâtir*, Paris, 1814, vol.III, pl.LXXVI.)

Tie-beam:
span = 24.25m; height = 0.495m; width = 0.385m

Principal rafters:
height = 0.415m; width = 0.385m

King post:
section of 0.33m × 0.275m

The wood mentioned is fir and the trusses were 3.33m apart.

These data, which presumably reflect the dimensions of the original truss since it is only a matter of a repair, can be usefully compared with those provided by the estimate from the Arsenal of Piraeus (fourth century BC), describing non-triangulated timbers[26]:

Supporting tie-beam:
span = 6.16m; height = 0.69m; width = 0.77m

Roof-ridge:
height = 0.42m; width = 0.54m

Purlins:
height = 0.69m; width = 0.77m

Apart from the large sections, note also that the pieces were placed along their greatest width, which gave them a low resistance to bending.

The arithmetical ratios between the surface areas of the sections of the tie-beams and the span speak for themselves:

11.59 for the Arsenal of Piraeus;
127.29 for St. Paul, or a profile eleven times more efficient.

Finally, mention should be made of the use of metal in Roman roofing, since the porch of the Pantheon, at least, preserved pieces of bronze for a long time. Still in place after fifteen centuries and despite frequent robbing,[27] these metal pieces were unfortunately removed by Urban VIII to be melted down, it is believed, to make the Bernini baldaquin.

The accounts that have come down describe sheets of bronze made in the form of a U, which suggests that they were not supporting elements but decorative facings with a minimal technical role. It is not, however, totally out of the question that they had a supporting role, either as reinforcements for the wooden pieces or, a more daring theory, as moulded metal beams. Palladio, who made a complete record of the Pantheon, includes a cross-section of the porch.[28] In his version, the timber frame appears to be made of pieces of wood pegged together; but above the central bay he shows an arch made of a single piece (fig.497); did this support a framework concealing the roofing? In that case, only the pieces of this arch would have been of bronze or faced with bronze. In his commentary the architect simply indicates: *Le travi del portico sono fatte di tavole di bronzo*, or: 'The beams of the portico are all made of plates of bronze'. This statement seems in fact to include all the timber roofing in his observation, but the solution to the problem is not precisely given.

4 Roofing materials

a Ceramic

Directly inherited from Greek roofing, Roman tiled roofs are all arranged in the same way: flat ceramic roof tiles, *tegulae*, were laid lengthways, overlapping one another following the pitch of the roof, and *imbrices*, water-tight tiles covered the junction between two tiles (figs 498, 499).

The overall shape of the *tegulae* varied little – they have a rectangular or trapezoidal form – but their dimensions were not very standardized and each region made its own types:

497

Dimensions recorded in Ostia (in cm): 48 × 72; 45 × 60; 41 × 57; 40.5 × 53.

Dimensions recorded in Rome: 49 × 66; 39 × 46.

Dimensions recorded in Pompeii: 69 × 47.5; 52.5 × 66; 47.5 × 64; 50 × 59; 48 × 59.

The largest ceramic tiles ever found are the ones on the roof of the *sacellum* at Paestum which measure 75 × 110.5cm.

497 Cross-section of the porch of the Pantheon by A. Palladio.

The junction-covers can have one of two outlines: the so-called Corinthian outline, a dihedron, or the so-called Laconian outline that is semicircular, more rustic and more widespread.[29] At the end of the Roman period, Gaul abandoned the manufacture of *tegulae*, which needed complex moulding for fitting together, in favour of the *imbrex* which is cone-shaped in section.

At the edge of the roof, along the gutter, each line of *imbrices* usually ended with an antefix (*antefixus*), an *imbrex* with a lower section closed off by a plate decorated with a palmette or the head of Mercury.[30] The edges of the four pent roofs surrounding the *compluvium* were the object of more ambitious ornamentation and the houses of Pompeii show a great variety of antefixes with water spouts in the shape of plants and fantastic animals.

Finally, the roof-ridge was made waterproof by a line of junction-covers, either of the usual type with a filling of mortar to ensure the bonding, or of special types shaped to provide sockets at the junctions.

The sides of the roof were provided with tiles of a particular shape allowing openings to be made for light and ventilation. A number of skylight tiles have been recovered from Pompeii, with circular or rectangular openings and flanges letting the water flow off, some even with a protective hood.[31] Above kitchens without proper chimneys, one or two ventilation tiles were placed with a hooded opening to allow smoke and cooking odours to escape (figs 500, 501).

b Stone

Greek funerary architecture, with its concept of eternity, made use of imperishable materials: stone replaced all the materials which were part of the construction of a building designed for the living. The massive size of funerary monuments and the narrowness of their rooms made it easy to manage without timbers; they were replaced, for instance, with 'stone trusses', as in the 'Nereid monument' at Xanthos[32]; or a roof was laid of marble tiles, in shape an exact copy of ceramic ones. Roman tombs followed this tradition, but restricted it to modest shrines; the great tombs and

498 A canopy on a house façade in the via dell'Abbondanza, IX,7,7 in excavations by V. Spinazzola.

499 An ancient roof with flat flanged tiles (*tegulae*) and junction-covers (*imbrices*) reconstructed at Vaison-la-Romaine.

500 Tiles from the roof of the House of the Moralist at Pompeii (III,4,2–3). One of them has an oculus, 26cm in diameter.

501 A tile with a hood, intended for lighting or the escape of cooking fumes. Pompeii, House of the Centenary (IX,8,6).

502 Roof covering of sawn limestone tiles at the *fanum* of Mâlain. (After the study and reconstruction by A. Olivier, *Revue Archéologique de l'Est*, XXVI, 3–4, pp.235ff, fig.6.)

503 Roof covering of limestone tiles on a rural building in the Peloponnese.

498

499

funerary piles were generally given stone roofs, on which scales were sculpted in shallow relief.

These stone scales were not just a fanciful decorative invention but reflected the appearance of actual thin hexagonal tiles which were used for roofing; many examples have been found in Mâlain (Côte d'Or) (fig.502), at Alesia, at Glanum,[33] in Belgium and in Germany.[34] Overlooked for a long time because when they split they leave only sparse remains, these flat stone tiles were probably in quite common use in Gaul, in the regions where limestone and schists can be split into relatively thin sheets.

It is quite likely, even if it is not proved, that, given this use of stone in an elaborate form, there was an equally widespread use of more rustic pieces as roofing material, still traditional in many mountainous regions (fig.503).

c Vegetable matter

Vegetable matter is another rustic material, of which obviously no traces survive. Cereal or reed thatch, tied up in bundles, was in all likelihood used to roof a large number of rural buildings. The use of such materials can be assumed when there is a total absence of broken tiles in and around a building, particularly if its architecture shows other signs of

being fairly rustic (for instance, clay walls).

d Metal

Already mentioned for the presence of metal in its timbers, the Pantheon also had the privilege of being roofed with bronze tiles, later removed by Constantine II. Even if such a use of this material remains totally exceptional, it is nonetheless a further example of the inexhaustible imagination of the Roman builders, who, it seems, were capable of overcoming all technical difficulties.

500

501

502
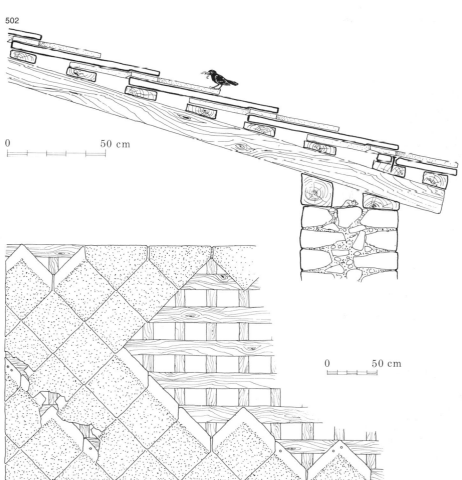

503

215

8
WALL COVERING

1 Rendering

a The structure

504 Remains of white stucco on the Temple of the Dioscuri at Agrigentum, one of the Greek temples of the city. Fifth century BC.

505 Column base, roughly dressed, intended to be stuccoed to give it its final outline. The so-called Temple of Jupiter at Cumae, Julio-Claudian period. This is a long way from the previous Greek formula which, in effect, simply applied consistent white paint to a surface judged too rough and too dark. For the Romans, the supporting element remained nothing but a framework, the real moulding being provided by stucco (see, in fig.524, the treatment of the cornice of the Temple of Portunus).

506 Stucco imitating construction with marble blocks at the Basilica of Pompeii. It is in fact carried out on a monumental scale, a characteristic of the First Style; c.120BC.

The intensive use of masonry and lime mortar could only lead the Romans to combine these techniques, resulting in the standard use of both protective and decorative wall renderings.

The first renderings, judging by the many Greek models from Magna Graecia and Sicily, consisted of white-wash – mixtures of lime and powdered limestone – intended to give a noble, marble-like appearance to monuments constructed with blocks of tufa (fig.504). Transferred to masonry or roughly dressed stone, these render-ings became thicker, to mask the irregularity of the surface (fig.505) and, when the purpose was decorative, it was incised to make it look like ashlar (fig.506). This ornamental appearance, however, will not be dealt with in this book, which deals only with techniques.

Thick rendering made up of several

504

layers of mortar certainly existed in Campania in the third century BC, and in this period its quality is attested by

505

506

the existence of a number of examples at Pompeii which survived changes of fashions and owners. The methods of application seem to have evolved very little and, at least at Pompeii, there is a consistent, highly uniform technique consisting of only four or five variations, based on the same search for a good adhesion.

If the recommendations of Vitruvius are believed (VII,3), seven successive layers of three different qualities made a good rendering: a first rough layer; three layers of mortar made with sand; then three layers of mortar made with powdered marble. Pliny, more modest-ly, recommends only five layers: three of mortar made with sand and two made with limestone and marble. It has to be admitted that such luxury, recommended by the authors for the preparation of a wall to be painted, is only rarely encountered in the Roman monuments studied,[1] and usually the *tectoria*, the external and internal wall coverings, are made up of three successive layers (figs 507, 508, 509).[2]

The first layer, applied directly on to the backing, presented no difficulty as

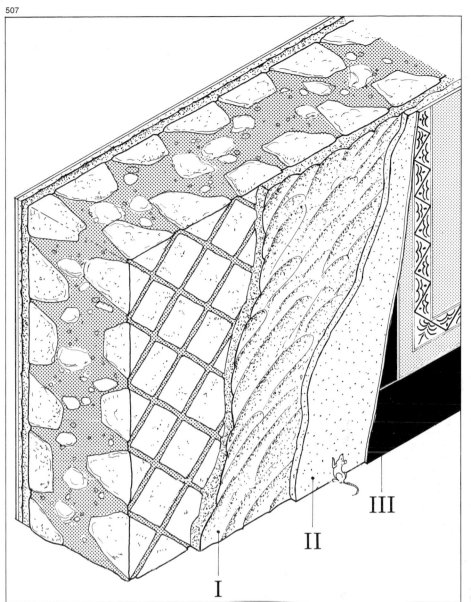

507

508

509

507 Rendered reticulate masonry. I: First layer of rendering covering the masonry and roughened with a trowel. II: Second layer, finer, applied with a float in order to provide a supporting surface. III: Third layer, the finest, to which painted decoration is applied.

508 Rendering in three layers of decreasing thickness on a wall at Pompeii (V,3,10). Note that the outside layer, the finest, made of almost pure lime and carefully smoothed, is much more clearly visible.

509 Triple layer of rendering on a brick column. The first two layers have uneven surfaces for adhesion: the first is furrowed and the second contains broken fragments. Pompeii, VI,13,9.

510

regards adhesion to masonry walls; the roughness of the rubble and the bricks and the relief of the joints were good artificial aids. When buildings were made of clay, it was useful to prepare the surface by scoring the fresh material with the fingers or a point, making scratches in the shape of an arc or a V which can still be found either on the wall, if it has been preserved, or in the impression left on the back of the layer of rendering (fig.510).

The first rendering was made up of lime and unsifted sand, to maintain a certain roughness; its thickness, which varied considerably according to the nature and irregularity of the surface to be covered, was always considerable (approx. 3 to 5cm).[3] As the skin of this first layer was sometimes considered too smooth, the masons who specialized in rendering, the *tectorii*, worked it with their trowels to create a relief of random or ordered lines to promote maximum adhesion of the following layer (figs 511, 512, 513).

A different method consisted of mixing fragments of terracotta, or sometimes marble, in this preparatory layer (fig.514). This method, still used by the masons of Naples, is apparently intended to reinforce this thick rendering, keeping it solid in the

511

512

513

510   Different masonry structures which could be rendered:
A Clay wall with an armature of branches.
B Puddled clay wall on a masonry pedestal.
C Masonry wall with facings of rubble stones and brick.

511   Underlayer of rendering, with furrows made with a trowel to give a good surface for adhesion. Pompeii, Temple of Vespasian.

512   Adhesion marks, made with a trowel, in the first layer of rendering in the access tunnel to the upper town of *Avaricum* (Bourges).

513   Preparation layer of rendering given a herring-bone relief made with a trowel, to facilitate the adhesion of the next layer. Pompeii, I,4,22.

course of setting, and to prevent cracking of the thickly layered mortar, as well as improving the adhesion of the second layer.

The second coating, of a similar thickness or less (2 to 4cm), was done with a finer mortar made with sifted sand. Its surface was not treated to give it a relief but was smoothed with a float – this made it possible to apply a very fine finishing coat.

The last layer, which could be as fine as one or two millimetres thick, was often made of pure lime that had been carefully thinned. When it was in the form of mortar the sand was finely sifted, or could be replaced (according to ancient recommendations) by limestone, gypsum or powdered marble. Depending on the quality or the location of the wall, this surface might remain bare, in which case it preserved its original colour, or was given a coloured pigment, or pigments, as decoration.

The House of the Faun at Pompeii offers a remarkable example of the preparation of walls before the application of a painted rendering. The walls of the rooms surrounding the western *atrium*, dating to the second century BC, were covered with sheets of lead nailed into the masonry. The builders thought that this would keep dampness away from the rendering, decorated in the First Style. Such an extravagant method, which was probably not very effective due to the vast number of nails perforating the plates, cannot have been employed very often and can be considered as a one-off attempt.

In a room opening on to the second peristyle of the same house, under a rendering in the Second Style, there was a wall covering made up of large plates of terracotta, measuring 62 x 49cm, which in fact are tiles with the edges turned in. These plates, applied with the same intention of protecting against damp, were attached by a layer of mortar reinforced by nails (fig.515). Another example of this original

514 Ceramic fragments intended to reinforce a wall rendering, first peristyle of the House of the Faun at Pompeii.

515 House of the Faun at Pompeii. Insulating wall covering made of *tegulae*. Size of the tiles: 64 x 48cm.

516 Wall covering of *tegulae* in the bathing establishment of Villards d'Heria (Jura).

219

arrangement has been found in the walls of the portico of the temple at Villards d'Heria in the Jura, also for insulation. Here *tegulae* had been applied to the walls, held in place by T-cramps (fig.516).

b The technique of painted decoration

Walls intended to have painted decoration were not rendered in the same way as those given a simple external protection. They were prepared more carefully and in stages, with the same sequence maintained of starting at the top of the wall.[4] But before analysing the composition of the painter's work it is useful to attempt to define what Roman mural painting was, as there remains some uncertainty.

This type of painting is usually defined by the word *fresco*,[5] in accordance with one of the most used methods of ensuring that wall paintings had a long life. The principle of this technique, effectively in use in antiquity, consists of trapping pigments in the lime mortar before it sets. The colour is then sealed in the crystallized surface film, rather than itself forming an added layer. It is therefore necessary for the painter to work on a layer of rendering that is still wet, and for the application of the design to be done quickly, to ensure that the decoration takes properly; as Vitruvius clearly states: *colores autem, udo tectorio cum diligenter sunt inducti ideo non remittunt sed sunt perpetuo permanentes*, 'as for the colours, carefully applied on the wet rendering, they do not come off and are fixed for ever' (VII,3).

So the artist prepared, or had prepared by an assistant, a limited surface of rendering, corresponding to the area that he would be able to cover with painted decoration, starting work at the top of the wall and working downwards so as not to spoil the surfaces once covered. The final rendering and its decoration thus descended in horizontal sections which represent the corresponding number of working days. An example of this method is clearly visible in a house at Pompeii, the House of the Iliac Chapel (I,6,4). This was in the process of being decorated in 79 and the application of painting was at different stages in different rooms. In one of them, only the top horizontal section had been applied and decorated and – a feature which is a measure of the remarkable overall view of the artist and of his sense of composition – not only had the background colour been applied but also the fine details of the complex architecture of the Fourth Style adorning it (fig 517).

The periodic interruption in applying the rendering necessitated a high degree of skill to ensure that the joins were invisible; however, despite the care taken, the individual phenomena of setting and contraction sometimes caused slight cracks. Aware of the appearance of such faults, the painters tried, wherever possible, to

517 House of the Iliac Chapel at Pompeii (I,6,4). In this *domus*, in the process of being rebuilt in 79, one wall of a room had only been given its painted decoration in the upper zone. Note that the decoration was completely finished before the painters started on another section.

517

Garden wall of the House of the Ceii at Pompeii (I,6,15), final Third Style, in which can be clearly seen the division of the work into horizontal bands which correspond to the changes of colour.

make their finishing point at the end of the day coincide with a horizontal band separating two areas of the decoration. The great panel of wild animals in the House of the Ceii at Pompeii (I,6,15) provides a typical illustration of this (fig.518). In the same way, the paintings on wood or canvas that were incorporated into the wall after the completion of the background decoration, almost always stand out due to the slight cracks around their frames.

Part of the decoration was often added afterwards and forms a light relief against the background. Since it was not applied on the wet plaster it could not blend in with it and was fixed by an adhesive mixed with the pigment. This adhesive, either vegetable (gum-arabic) or animal (egg white), diluted in water with the pigment, constituted a distemper (*tempera*) and forms the other method of affixing paintings to the walls. Sometimes white details were simply painted with pure lime on the coloured background; in this way a colour mixed with lime could also be put on as a new layer of rendering.

If, in the majority of cases, the artist was skilful enough to carry out the design 'at a single stroke', he nevertheless made it easier by using preparatory outlines made with a cord or a rule, at least for positioning the axes and the divisions of the walls. The cord and the compass were also used for the circular and the symmetrical motifs found particularly on painted ceilings. Finally, some characters and animals were sketched out with a sharp point or rough brush strokes before being carefully painted (figs 519, 520).

The quality of the Roman paintings, the liveliness of their colours and the extraordinary polish of the surfaces, have led to as many theories about the formula of the materials used as there have been about mortar. Mention has been made, for example, of the use of encaustic, of wax and of various other organic materials. Vitruvius does

519

519   Preparatory incisions for decoration, consisting of straight lines and angles, using a cord or a rule and a stiletto.

520   Incised sketch of a griffin, appearing under the faded painting in a room of the House of the Small Fountain (Pompeii, VI,8,23).

520

indeed recommend, after the application of vermilion (VII,9), rendering the wall with wax and oil, then after its impregnation, rubbing it with a cloth soaked in candle-grease. This treatment, intended to enliven the colour and protect it, is perfectly reasonable and other methods could be used to the same end; what has never been proved is the introduction of wax and soap in the preparation of these colours, as these products would probably have been incompatible with the technique of wet painting.

The pigments themselves were normally of mineral origin, and could both survive without alteration and be mixed with lime; Vitruvius speaks at length of their origin (VII,7) and their characteristics and enumerates seven native colours each extracted directly from a crushed mineral and nine composite colours obtained by an often complex process of preparation. In this list there are, however, two colours of organic origin: the black obtained by calcination of resin or calcination of the lees of wine and the famous purple extracted from murex. This last one appears rather to be a dye, even though it was used in the preparation of distemper.

In fact, analysis more or less confirms Vitruvius' list[6] and reveals subtle mixtures of crushed glass and metallic pigments, following the technique of roasting, mentioned by the author of the *Ten Books* in reference to the preparation of azure. As for the blacks, they are in fact obtained from calcinated organic bodies, usually bones (animal black) or from fats.[7]

The work of the painter on site,[8] although it is visible thanks at least to the unfinished panels at Pompeii, was not portrayed or not very often. Even at Pompeii only one artist is illustrated in position on a scaffold, occupied in smoothing the surface of a wall with a wooden or marble polisher.[9] Some distance away, in the villa of San Marco overlooking Stabiae, a scene of a building site (already referred to several times) shows a workman applying a rendering with a float. These two comparable examples in fact show the painter's assistants and not the artist himself. It is necessary to go to Gaul to find, on a relief preserved at the Musée de Sens (also quoted in connection with scaffolding), a complete team at work comprising two masons, one mixing the mortar, the other applying the

521

522

521 The different stages of preparation and execution of fresco wall painting.

522 Reconstruction from the Sens relief.

rendering to the wall, and the painter holding his palette in his left hand and painting with his right (figs 521, 522).[10]

Depending on their task or their speciality, the painters were given a different name: the *dealbator* white-washed the surfaces of the walls, either to clean them or to apply a base; this was a simple labouring job prior to the decoration. The *pictor*, the painter-decorator, could be a *parietarius*, in which case he did the background colours, the panels or decoration 'by the metre' with a repeated motif, a job that could range from the most cursory to the most refined artistic work depending on the ability of the workman in question. Finally, the true master was the *imaginarius*, who was entrusted with the task of doing the pictorial scenes, the tableaux or the faces.

It is strange and regrettable to note that, despite the place occupied by the painted surfaces at Pompeii, many of which deserve to be called master-pieces, only one example out of thousands has provided us with the name of the painter: it is a decoration framing a small fountain that closes off the summer *biclinium* (outside dining-room) in the House of Octavius Quartio (II,2,2). The signature, *Lucius pinxit*, has been modestly added by the artist in a corner of the right-hand couch, a discreet place to put it, as it was formerly hidden by the mattress covering this masonry pedestal.[11]

Faced with this general anonymity, specialists in the painting of Pompeii can only attempt to establish connections between different works to define the existence of anonymous schools and 'masters' each one distinguished by its own peculiar style.[12]

c The styles at Pompeii

Research into schools or trends in painting at Pompeii is only one of the many areas of precise study aimed at establishing a chronological typology for Roman painting, based on the only city that has provided us with an uninterrupted history several centuries long. All Roman paintings, up to 79, can be placed within the divisions of styles at Pompeii and remain dominated by Pompeii as regards their variety and quality, just as though destiny had specifically picked out the city of Campania as a paragon to be handed on intact to posterity.

Nature, in the shape of Vesuvius, made a good choice as far as archaeology is concerned. Not only was Pompeii wealthy. The geographical position of the city, the richness of its soil, the meeting of cultures and the abundance of their inheritance, are likewise inevitably favourable to a flowering of art. Art was supported by everyone there according to their means and their rank, in both private and collective ways.

It was A. Mau, working at the end of the last century, who made the initial classification into four styles of painting at Pompeii.[13] This masterly work of classification remains, even today, the basis of all studies, both typological and chronological, leading to finer distinctions within the four styles, such as have been established by H.-G. Beyen,[14] M. Borda[15] and K. Schefold.[16] Within the four subdivisions the work of differentiation is carried out based on an increasingly precise and detailed study of the motifs; trying to trace the evolution of forms, the success of fashions or the transmission of themes.[17]

But this is not the place for an analysis of decoration, so the reader is referred to the bibliography.

d Stucco

The name stucco (from the Italian) is used to refer to all decorations in relief executed in mortar; this is why the term can just as well be applied to the fine renderings covering the fluted columns as to the imitations of stone block construction in the First Style, or to the various iconographies decorating walls or arches. Distinctions therefore do not arise from a difference of composition in the renderings but from a difference in form (figs 523, 524, 525).[18]

White stucco, intended to remain

523

523   Painted stucco from decoration of the First Style in the peristyle of the House of the Faun at Pompeii. The false pilasters correspond to columns situated opposite. Second century BC.

524   Detail from the cornice on the Temple of Portunus in Rome, showing the final moulding (*left*) in stucco (Lesbian cymatium, dentils, cyma) applied to a surface cut into the supporting tufa; *c.*100BC.

525   A wall covering intended to create a rock effect, the garden of Julia Felix at Pompeii (II,4). The materials used are fragments of limestone from the Sarno with fossil concretions. This peculiar covering is neither a painted rendering nor stucco, but combines facings of both rubble stones and stucco to achieve the desired effect.

524

525

526

527

528

bare, was in fact the most 'noble', since the desired effect was that of marble; its composition was simply a mixture of limestone and powdered marble or powder from various sorts of white limestone (at Pompeii calcite from Vesuvius). It was originally used to embellish architecture built of tufa. This role continued later, after the appearance of painted decoration, for the creation of cornices (Vitruvius, VII,3), the whiteness of which contrasted with the vivid colours of the panels, particularly in compositions of the Second Style (Villa of the Mysteries, Oplontis). These reliefs had to be fairly shallow to be moulded only in a mixture of limestone and powdered marble; when the depth of the motif was considerable, the main part of the body consisted of mortar made of sand and broken tile fragments and only the final surface was carried out with the finest mixture (fig.526).

In view of the weight and depth of some motifs, especially the decoration of the entrance *fauces* at the House of the Faun, the stucco often needed a support bracket to fix it to the wall. This bracket, visible under detached cornices, consisted – depending on the importance of the relief – of nails of different lengths or wooden pegs of variable thickness, inserted deep into the masonry and around which the plasterer fixed the mortar in the approximate form.

The execution of the final moulding was carried out using templates, making it possible to extend the outline, or moulds that were pressed on to the fresh mortar for complex reliefs (fig.527). The most intricate decoration was cut or sculpted in the same way as the sculptor worked with clay, starting with an outline sketched on to the background (portico of the Stabian Baths) (figs 528, 529).

In the First Style the stucco makes up the whole of the decoration while in the Second Style it is limited to the cornices. The Third and Fourth styles witness the beginning of whole panels of stucco using themes from the two periods. The preferred surfaces for this treatment were above rooms in the baths, where the vaults and the walls provided enormous areas where the artists carried out their finest compositions (the Forum Baths, Pompeii [fig.530], Sarno Baths, Stabian Baths).

2 Veneer

Veneer is also used for the same job of economically embellishing structures with a noble or decorative material. This time it is arranged in panels, sheets or various fragments and fixed to the wall by different means.

In fact, the idea of reserving the finest materials for the surface already contains within it the idea of veneer, and monuments like the tomb of Caecilia Metella or the Tower at La Turbie are none other than enormous masses of masonry with facings of large stone blocks. In such buildings, the size of the facing blocks means that the outer layer is in fact self-supporting, even if precautions have been taken to bond it to the masonry. Such thickness was not always necessary and the intensified use of marble from the Augustan period made it possible to cut thin panels with a saw (frequently under 1cm), allowing for the most refined decoration and its adaptation to all shapes and sizes.

The solidity of the fixing was proportionate to the weight and the balance of the panel to be held in place. Thick slabs called for the use of metal cramps which were to become more plunder for the pillagers of the Middle Ages, who removed the means of attachment and left nothing but a lot of holes.

526 Stucco moulding from the decoration of a bedroom. Note the housings for the beams of the hanging vault. Pompeii, VII,2,51.

527 Decoration stuccoed with bucrania and garlands, at the entrance to the Baths of the Seven Sages at Ostia.

528 Three methods of creating stucco, from left to right: regular moulding using a template; repeated motif done with a mould; and decoration sculpted with a spatula.

529 Damaged stucco from the *palaestra* of the Stabian Baths at Pompeii. Under the design modelled in relief can be seen the incisions sketched by the artist for positioning the figures: Daedalus and Icarus trying their wings.

530 Polychrome stucco with coffers and candelabra and foliated scroll, on the vault of the *tepidarium* of the Forum Baths at Pompeii. Restored in 62.

529

530

531 Wall covering of large veneer panels of marble with polychrome frames in the House of Amor and Psyche, Ostia, *c*.300.

532 Marble veneer in front of *tubuli*, in the *caldarium* of the Forum Baths at Ostia.

533 Broken fragments from the marble facings of large monuments were reused for more modest coverings, such as this tavern counter at Pompeii (VII,2,33).

531

532

533

Thin panels did not need cramps and were fixed to the wall by the simple application of a layer of mortar; the skill of the mason consisted in achieving a uniformly level juxtaposition to avoid discontinuities between the components. Frequently the mason used fragments and chippings of marble to form a reference level as part of the preparation for positioning. He glued them into the surface of the penultimate layer and levelled them off using a large rule; the inside surfaces of the panels of the facing were then applied against them.

The systematic plundering of materials has not left many sites with their veneered decoration, and mostly only the bases of pedestals and other lower surfaces of the walls remain. Some of the buildings at Ostia, notably the rooms of the baths and some individual houses, such as that named after Amor and Psyche, represent rare examples that are sufficiently complete to be singled out (figs 531, 532).

For once Pompeii does not stand as a reference for a series of veneer decorations (fig.533), due both to the small use of marble in that city and also to the reuse of material after 62 from the ruined or damaged monuments of the Forum. By contrast, Herculaneum has preserved, in a house of the Eastern *insula* I, the House of the Relief of Telephus,[19] on a terrace on the edge of the city, a wall still entirely decorated with marble in *opus sectile* of very high quality (fig.534).

3 Wall mosaics

Polychrome compositions using small fragments, *tessellae* (hence the name *opus tessellatum*), were mainly found in flooring but were also popular as an element of wall decoration, especially around fountains, where they are often mixed with a baroque decoration of rocks and shells. The cities around Vesuvius, where these small construc-

534

tions often adorn summer *triclinia*, provide some intact examples (Pompeii: House of the Small Fountain, VI,8,23; House of Marcus Lucretius, IX,3,5; Herculaneum: House of Neptune and Amphitrite) (fig.535).

However, the Romans only occasionally used wall mosaic as a method of decorating large surfaces and the Byzantines have the honour of making a major art form out of it, as a corollary to their sacred monumental art. There are, however, examples among the great Roman buildings decorated in this way, notably the decoration of the *cryptoporticus* of Hadrian's Villa, part of the Baths

535

536

of Baia, where the mosaics occupy a large area of the vault but are difficult to see, and better pre-served but on a more limited scale, the surviving mosaics on the rotunda of the Baths of the Seven Sages at Ostia (fig.536).

534 Wall decorated with polychrome marble panels and pilasters, in the House of the Relief of Telephus at Herculaneum, Augustan period, restored after 62.

535 Wall mosaic made of various stones and glass paste, decorating a *triclinium* with a fountain at the House of Neptune and Amphitrite at Herculaneum.

536 Wall mosaic, decorating the vaults of the Baths of the Seven Sages at Ostia, reign of Hadrian.

9
FLOORS

1 Tiling

The simplest way to guarantee the stability of the ground for walking on and for traffic is to cover it with stone tiles placed directly on the surface, or, better still, laid in a preparatory layer of sand and gravel.

This is the solution adopted for the paving of thoroughfares and public areas in Roman towns. A distinction was made, however, when there was a difference in the kind of traffic. Certain public spaces were reserved exclusively for pedestrians – such as the *palaestrae* or the sacred areas surrounding temples within the *peribolos*;

but also the forum in a number of cities such as Pompeii was kept free of vehicles by markers and walkways. For this reason the paving there was made of slabs of thin stone laid on a prepared ground that had been carefully levelled (the work was unfinished in 79) and consisted of a layer of crushed limestone tuff (fig.537).[1]

By contrast, in the streets of Pompeii, as elsewhere, where carts threatened to break up the ground, the covered surface was made up of very thick hard stone slabs (30 to 50cm), firmly set in a foundation of one or two layers of stones, gravel and sand (figs 538, 539).

537

537 Thin limestone tiles in a regular rectangular pattern in an area reserved for pedestrians: the forum at Pompeii.

Since the entrances to public monuments, the rooms within them and rooms in private houses were worn down by feet only, they could be covered with thin marble slabs fixed in a bed of mortar. There are various arrangements of marble slabs, from a simple division into square or rectangular tiles to the most impressive *opus sectile*, a fashion that reappeared in Italy in the Renaissance (Ostia: House of Amor and Psyche; Pompeii: House of Ephebe, I,7,11) (fig.540).

Stone slabs, at least in pedestrian areas, were sometimes replaced by ceramic tiles. This custom seems in particular to have been characteristic of Sicily, where brick flooring has been found at Helesa, Agrigentum and particularly at Solunto.[2] In that city a large traffic-free thoroughfare, identified as the *Decumanus,* was skilfully tiled with bricks laid flat, the square ones measuring 33cm each side and the rectangular ones 33 × 38cm, both being 5 to 6cm thick.

In order to prevent this material wearing out, as it was more brittle than stone, the bricks were usually laid in a

538

herring-bone pattern, to ensure good fitting (there are several examples at Ostia, at Hadrian's Villa and the House of the Vestal Virgins) (fig.541).

539

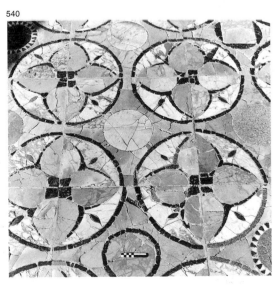

540

538 The paving of a commercial street in Pompeii, the via della Fortuna, of large slabs of lava, about 30cm thick.

539 Laying a road surface of lava flagstones at Scafati (near Pompeii) on a bed of sand. October 1981.

540 Surface of *opus sectile*, marquetry made with different types of marble, granite and porphyry. Ostia, House of Amor and Psyche, *c.*300.

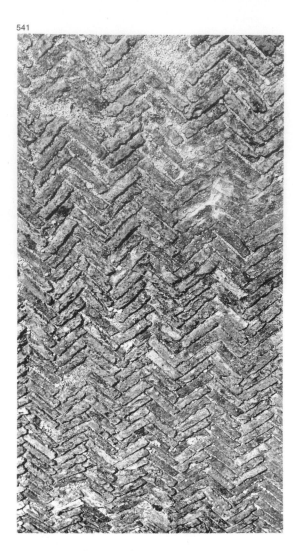

541

541 A flooring of bricks arranged in herring-bone pattern of *opus spicatum*. Hadrian's Villa, Great Baths.

542 Pavement surface at Pompeii made of concrete with large ceramic fragments, dotted with white *tessellae* on the surface forming *opus signinum* (the Italian 'coccio pesto'). Via di Porta Marina.

542

2   Mortar and cement floors

Thin tiles and bricks were laid on a bed of mortar which varied in thickness, and which could also itself form a flooring without a surface of another material.

In fact, in good-quality construction the masonry floor was made in the same way, whether or not there was a surface of slabs or mosaic. Vitruvius devotes the whole of chapter 1 of his Book VII to this, and the advice found there can be verified in the majority of good-quality floors.

First the *statumen* is put in place, a bed of pebble stones laid dry-jointed and if possible placed on-end to allow water to run off. This is followed by a layer of lime and sand with gravel or pebbles, forming a thick concretion, the *rudus*.

Finally, there is a layer of mortar made with broken fragments of tiles, the *nucleus*, which is covered by whatever the surface is for walking on. The most common, since it is the most economical, type of *nucleus* is mixed with large bits of broken terracotta or fragments of marble, *crustae*, scattered at random or arranged more or less geometrically. Such a flooring is called *opus signinum* (fig.542).[3]

3   Mosaics

Although Vitruvius speaks at length about painting, both in relation to style and technique, on the subject of mosaics he only mentions the cubes, *tesserae*,[4] as one of the materials that can be embedded in the *nucleus* (VII,1), taking great care to keep them level. The art of the mosaic maker in fact depended to a large extent on the quality of the surface level, but all the other factors should not be forgotten –

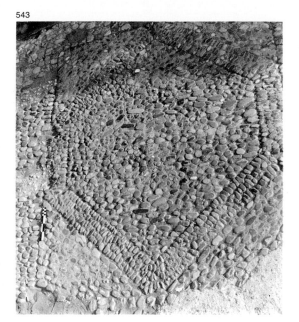

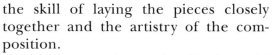

543 A flooring of pebble-work on a pavement in Pompeii, via di Porta Marina.

544 Geometric decoration in a mosaic in Ostia framed by a braid; cubes of 1 to 1.5cm each side.

545 A mosaic decorated with a foliated scroll in the *vestibulum* of a house in the Insula Occidentalis of Pompeii; beyond the black band, the floor is a simple mosaic with *tesserae* of polychrome marble made from scraps of stone; cubes 0.3 to 1cm.

the skill of laying the pieces closely together and the artistry of the composition.

The first mosaics in the Greek world were probably inspired by contacts with the East. However, the possibility of the spontaneous creation of floors with coloured pebbles, which became increasingly organized, should not be ruled out, such as are found in Asia Minor in the eighth and seventh centuries BC. The primitive mosaics found in Greece, as in the Roman world, are simple pebble-work (fig.543), formed of small pebbles arranged in a geometric pattern or outlines. These were made by the Greeks up to the period of Alexander, at which point their use was at its highest, as can be seen by the surviving examples at Olynthus and Pella (Macedonia).

The makers of mosaics noticed that by splitting the pebbles they achieved a flat surface, better suited to making a floor and, at the end of the fourth century BC, as cutting became more precise, the half pebble became the cube and it was probably in Sicily (Gela) and in Magna Graecia that *opus tessellatum* was adopted definitively for quality mosaics (figs 544, 545).[5]

The use of a material cut into tiny fragments allowed the mosaicist to compete with the painter in the pursuit of more and more subtle forms of expression. In the second century BC, central-southern Italy was to achieve perfect mastery of the polychrome mosaic, as is brilliantly demonstrated in

233

546

546 Portrait of a woman made of *opus vermiculatum*, originally the *emblema* of a mosaic from Pompeii (Museum of Naples). Cubes 0.2 to 0.8cm.

the decoration of the House of the Faun, from which comes the justly famous mosaic of Alexander and Darius.

Opus musivum,[6] 'work inspired by the Muses', the origin of the word mosaic, perhaps owes its name to its use in decorating fountains (see also wall mosaics) recalling the fountain of Hippocrene[7] around which the Muses assembled to sing and dance. This type of decoration was subject to as many trends and styles as painting, with two traditions developing in parallel, one purely geometric, the other figurative; the two could be combined in cloisonné mosaics. However, the criteria for the chronological development of the two were never as clear as for the painting styles at Pompeii.[8]

The most realistic and most subtle achievements, called *opus vermiculatum*, were carried out with cubes of very small size, cut from different types of marble and embellished with tesserae of coloured glass. These works, painstaking and expensive, usually covered only a limited area (the mosaic of Alexander being a remarkable exception[9]) or were confined to a central panel, the *emblema*, inserted in the middle of the composition and containing the most meticulous decoration. As with the central panel of a wall painting, carried out in part when the background was finished, the *emblema* could be put together in the studio on a ceramic plate and arranged in the mosaic when it had been finished (fig.546).[10]

10
CIVIL ENGINEERING

1 Water

a Collection and catchment

The supply of water, always a major concern and one which has often determined the choice of site for sedentary groups, would be certain to play a large part in Roman technology. The stages in the development of the provision of running water are clearly and precisely illustrated (as usual) by the history of the water supply at Pompeii. The original Oscan town was built on a rocky spur, in fact a lava flow, projecting towards the sea and surrounded by a small river, the Sarno. This watercourse was for a long time exploited to supply the water needed by the first citizens of Pompeii.

Then, from the sixth century BC, the houses were provided with cisterns storing rainwater from the roofs. For this purpose the roof opening, the *compluvium*, in the middle of the *atrium* was introduced, perhaps at the start of the third century BC. The water was then drawn through a hole, the rim of which became a decorative element.

Public buildings were provided with cisterns for public use. The most capacious was that for the Forum Baths, built in 80BC and measuring 15m wide and 9m high; a raising device transferred water from it to the pools of the men's and the women's sections.

The need for inexhaustible reserves of water (for dry seasons or sieges) prompted the citizens of Pompeii in the second half of the sixth century BC to search for underground water by sinking wells. However, because of the thick layer of lava that had to be dug through, these wells, 25 to 39m deep depending on the location, remained few in number. There were five for public use in streets and squares, and two for use in the baths.[1] Three of them, each with a capacious collection trough, were provided with a bucket-chain hoist, driven by human or animal power (Stabian Baths, Forum Baths, House of the Queen of England), the others had a simple hand-operated pulley system.

In the Augustan period domestic crafts and agricultural needs called for considerable quantities of water and the city was supplied by the building of an aqueduct. This captured a plentiful source from the foothills of the Apennines, near Serino, and carried it to Naples, with a branch line to Pompeii. Here there was a water distribution centre where the water was filtered before being fed by underground channels to the different parts of the city.

The different methods observable at Pompeii existed in all Roman cities of any size; when there was no aqueduct, the wells and cisterns remained the main supply.[2] It is worth noting, however, that the cistern is, above all, a storage device typical of Mediterranean countries, while wells proliferate in northern regions, such as Gaul, with each house often having its own. Their construction seems always to have been rustic, with walls made of blocks, often roughly squared, dry jointed and usually laid in a circular shape which was more secure than a square shape because of the wedging together of the elements of the facing.

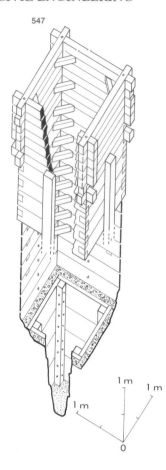

547

1 m

1 m

1 m

0

Stone was not the only material used: in Belgium,[3] Germany[4] and England[5] wells have been discovered that are square in shape and faced with planks, jointed with half-joints; they are surprisingly well preserved due to the extreme dampness of the subsoil into which they were sunk (fig.547).

Though cisterns for rainwater were numerous, they have rarely left any traces of the system of supply. Fortunately, the systems at Pompeii provide answers to every question. The architects always made the roofs incline towards the interior of the houses; this is the principle of the *compluvium*. The water flowing off the edge of the roof, either along its length or via water-spouts, was collected on the ground in the trough of the *atrium*, the *impluvium* or, in peristyles, gardens and *palaestrae*, in a gutter made of stone or masonry. Apart from having a decorative function, the *impluvium* served to settle the water, depositing any particles collected on the roof. A

hole, preferably slightly above the bottom, then led to the cistern (*cisterna*) beneath the *atrium*. In peristyles the gutter was inclined and conducted the water to a basin or trough which served as a decanting tank and in which, always above the bottom, the conduit of the cistern opened (fig.548).

Water was drawn through an opening into the *atrium*, sometimes into the peristyle, more rarely into the kitchen, depending on the position of the cisterns. The edge of the hole, the *puteal*, was a marble or ceramic cylinder that was often decorated (fig.549).

As an exceptionally rainy season was capable of causing the cistern to flood, an overflow pipe opened at a level lower than that of the supply. At Pompeii, which did not have a town sewer, the excess water was conducted into the street, passing underneath the pavement (figs 550, 551).

The dimensions of the cisterns were extremely variable, depending on their

547 A wooden well from the Roman period discovered at Skeldergate, York. The horizontal pieces are half-jointed and reinforced against earth pressure by corner braces. (After D. Raines, *The Archaeology of York*, York, 1975, p.9, fig.5.)

548 Arrangements for collecting rainwater in the second peristyle at the House of the Faun, Pompeii:

A gutter along the foot of each portico
B settling basin
C conduit leading to the cistern
D well of the cistern
E drawing hole.

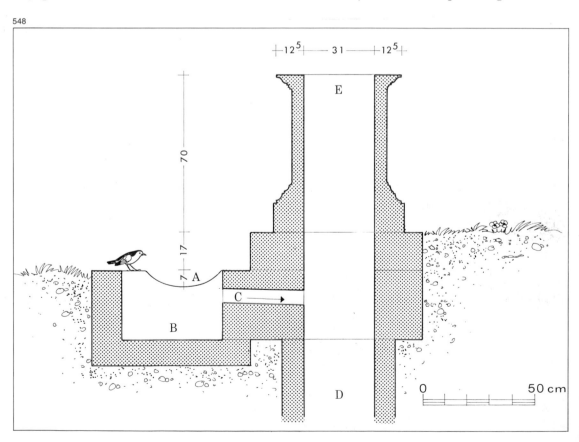

548

location. In private houses they were carefully lined, usually with mortar mixed with tile fragments, and could be as small as 2m³, while a bath-house called for tens of thousands of litres of water.

Once the water-supply system had been installed at Pompeii, many cisterns were linked to the town network, maintaining their role as reservoirs. Conversely, after the earthquake of 62, when the mains supply of Pompeii had been destroyed, those cisterns which had been kept in order once more took on the job of collecting rainwater.

The ideal supply, as regards both quality and quantity, remained a permanent spring, whether it had been improved upon or not.

These springs, particularly if they rose into a hollow, were usually accorded in addition a ritual role, associated with Nymphs, hence the name 'nymphaeum' given to ornamental fountains. The Muses, the river gods,

549 The well of a cistern made of terracotta in the peristyle of the House of the Lovers (I,10,11). Note in the gutter the hole for collecting rainwater.

550 Outflow pipe of a cistern overflow in a *domus* at Pompeii.IX, 3, 5.

551 Relieving arch in a wall at Pompeii over the course of a drain outflow. With this arrangement if repairs were needed the rubble masonry under the arch could be opened up without risking damaging the wall.

552

552 The Great Nymphaeum at Corinth, called the Fountain of Priere. with its first-century monumental development. The arcades mask the Greek façade (which can just be seen in the shadows behind), itself forming the entrance to the catchment grottoes. The final stage of the work was carried out by Herodes Atticus in about 150.

553 Catchment basin of the spring at Glanum (St-Rémy-de-Provence).

553

Narcissus and Pan were also to be found in these places.

Springs were sometimes developed to increase the rate of flow by joining together several natural outlets to create a pool, making it easier to draw water. The Romans could find inspiration in installations laid out by the Greeks, such as the Pirene fountain at Corinth, the largest ancient 'nymphaeum' still surviving. Its supply was ensured by the capture of two springs, of which the underground conduits had been cut for a distance of 150m and 600m respectively (fig.552). The Romans reconditioned the fountain, giving it a monumental façade overlooking a vast basin.[6] At Glanum[7] in Gaul a water catchment installation dating to the Hellenistic period of the city consists of an enormous rectangular well reaching down to the rock. This collected water from a spring and had stairs going down to it for drawing water (fig.553).[8]

All the methods above, despite their relative efficiency, had the disadvantage of only providing water that had to be drawn. This had then to be carried, manually or with raising devices, to the place of use, or diverted into raised reservoirs in order to be then distributed under pressure. The creation of aqueducts fed by permanent springs made it possible to resolve all the problems of water catchment, transport, reliability of supply and distribution to all parts of a city or to a system of agricultural irrigation.

Considerable effort went into the catchment of a spring and well-sinkers not only joined together different sources but also followed underground courses to check that no breakage in

554

the rock was threatening a loss of supply. The water first ran into a reservoir where initial filtering and settling took place; the aqueduct was connected to this reservoir. In arid areas, or when the source of supply was intermittent, a retaining dam was built to form a regulating reservoir which maintained a volume of water sufficient for the dry season. One such installation has been discovered at the foot of the Alpilles, collecting spring and surface water behind a dam to which the aqueduct of Glanum[9] was connected. The construction of dams was particularly necessary in harsher climates, in Spain, North Africa and the Middle East.

The construction techniques of these works are surprising in their modernity and their variety. Spain had at least three earth dams: two fed the aqueducts of Merida and the third, 550m long, supplied Toledo. In the areas of Tripolitania that were formerly under cultivation, particularly around Leptis Magna, there are also earth dams, which were quite low but very long, ensuring the retention of water for irrigation systems.

Dams with masonry cores and stone block facing were the largest and have left impressive remains, such as the dam at Kasserine in Tunisia, 7m wide at the base and surviving to a height of 10m, or the dam of Harbaka in Syria, still 20m at its highest and damming a valley developed over 365m.[10]

In the Italian peninsula itself dams seem to have been quite rare. One, of modest size, has been discovered in the hollow of a river valley in the neighbourhood of a coastal villa near Sperlonga, the villa of Pian della Salse; this dam supplied the cisterns and the neighbouring gardens (fig.554). More impressive were the dams constructed to supply water to Nero's villa near Subiaco. A series of three lakes was created artificially, the *Simbruina stagna*,[11] each retained by a dam. The largest of these dams, all of which are now destroyed, reached the remarkable height of 130 feet (39m).

b Aqueducts

The planning and construction of aqueducts formed the most skilful and the most considerable undertaking as regards accuracy of surveying and distances covered.

Historically, the Greeks are generally regarded as having built aqueducts well before the Roman engineers, such as the aqueduct dug into the rock to supply Samos in the sixth century BC; but the first Greek aqueduct with watertight channels was that at Pergamon, with its remarkable siphon, 190m at its highest point, built in the reign of Eumenes II (197 to 159BC).

At the end of this sovereign's reign, two aqueducts, admittedly without a siphon, had already supplied the city of Rome for a long time: *Aqua Appia* built in 312BC by the Consul Appius Claudius and the *Anio Vetus* built in 272BC by the Censor Manius Curius Dentatus.[12] However, these two constructions did not have the characteristic outline of long lines of arches that can be seen today in the Roman

554 Remains of a Later Republican villa near Sperlonga on the *via Flacca*. Below the vegetation can be seen the masonry of the terraces supporting the buildings and containing enormous cisterns supplied by a dam built at the foot of the slopes (beyond the windmill and to its left).

555

555 The impressive arcaded section of the raised stretch of the *Aqua Claudia* in the Roman campagna. Built from 38 to 52, this aqueduct runs for 68km, 15 of them raised. Its daily capacity was 184,280m³. Later the *Anio Novus* was connected to this aqueduct; its channel was superimposed on the earlier one and is distinguishable by its masonry construction.

556 Ashlar construction was not the only method of building raised aqueducts and the following examples show that quite impressive structures could be achieved using masonry. For example, the aqueduct of *Minturnae* (Minturno) in southern Latium, with reticulate, facing, can be followed for practically the whole 11km from the water catchment at Capo d'Acqua. Augustan period.

557 The arcaded section of the aqueduct at Metz (*Divodurum*) crossing the Moselle at Jouy-aux-Arches. First century.

558 The *Aqua Alexandriana* crossing a small valley about 19km outside Rome. The last aqueduct for the capital, it was built in 226 and its raised sections were entirely faced with brick. Its total length was 22km and it supplied 21,160m³ daily.

556

countryside. Only with the construction in 144BC of the *Aqua Marcia*, on the initiative of the Praetor Marcius Rex, was an aqueduct supported on arches for its raised sections.

The construction dates of the eleven aqueducts supplying the city of Rome are as follows:

1 The *Aqua Appia*, 312BC, restored twice.
2 The *Anio Vetus*, 272BC, restored three times.
3 The *Aqua Marcia*, 144BC.
4 The *Aqua Tepula*, 125BC.
5 The *Aqua Iulia*, 33BC.
6 The *Aqua Virgo*, 19BC.
7 The *Aqua Alsietina*, 2BC, unfit for consumption, according to Frontinus.
8 The *Aqua Claudia*, AD38 to 52.
9 The *Anio Novus*, 38 to 52.
10 The *Aqua Traiana*, 109.
11 The *Aqua Alexandriana*, 206.

The distances covered, which gave added difficulties as much to the surveyors as to the builders, depended on how far removed the springs were, but the Romans seem to have met the challenge, and the scale of the successful undertakings was inevitably linked with the prestige of such achievements.[13] Discussion of constructions such as the Pont du Gard or the aqueduct at Jouy-aux-Arches must not overlook the consideration that they are only a very small fraction of the total length of an aqueduct, forming the solution, certainly spectacular, to an unevenness in its course. The best impression of the raised sections of such constructions is undoubtedly provided by the view, over some kilometres, of the *Aqua Claudia* and the *Anio Novus* (built in the reigns of Caligula and Claudius) which extend along the *via Appia* and the *via Latina* (figs 555 to 563).

The following are the distances covered by some aqueducts:

Antioch .... 6km[14]
Saintes .... 7.5km[15]
Toulouse .... 9.5km[16]
Minturno (fig.556) .... 11km[17]
Maktar (fig.562) 15km
Lutèce .... 16km[18]
Rome, *Aqua Appia* .... 16km[19]
Sens .... 17km[20]
Aqua Iulia .... 21.6km[21]
Metz (fig.557) .... 22km[22]
Rome, *Aqua Alexandriana*
(fig.558) .... 22km[23]
Bougie .... 25km[24]
Lyon-Craponne .... 25km[25]
Lyon-Mont d'Or .... 28km[26]
Tarragona .... 35km[27]
Cherchel (second lay-out) ... 35km[28]
Fréjus (fig.559) .... 40 km[29]
Cherchel (initial lay-out) .... 45km[30]
Nîmes (fig.560) .... 50km[31]
Rome, *Anio Vetus* .... 64km[32]
Lyon-Brévenne .... 66km[33]
Rome, *Aqua Claudia* .... 69km[34]
Lyon-Gier (fig.563) .... 75km[35]
Cologne .... 78km[36]
Rome, *Anio Novus* .... 87km[37]
Rome, *Aqua Marcia*
(fig.567) .... 91km[38]
Misenum (aqueduct of
Campania) .... 96km[39]
Carthage .... 132km[40]

The great length of some aqueducts was due not only to the distance from the water catchment, but also to the lie of the land. Obstacles had to be crossed or bypassed without imposing too many constraints on the average

557

558

559

incline to be maintained. In fact it was preferable to avoid level stretches which caused the water to stagnate, but equally too strong an incline brought about the rapid erosion of the watertight lining of the canal. To break the speed of a strong current of water on a long incline, the engineers were sometimes forced to create short falls (for instance, the aqueduct over the Brévenne, aqueduct of Cherchel, and the *Aqua Marcia*) between two reservoirs, making it possible then to resume a slight and regular incline, following the method of regulating torrents of water by means of levels.

Whatever the recommendations may have been, the average inclines of the aqueducts appear to be extremely variable; the following are some figures for Roman Gaul:

Nîmes .... 0.34m per km
Metz .... 1m per km
Lyon-Gier .... 1.46m per km

560

559   The pillars of the aqueduct of Fréjus, made of petit appareil, were supported by buttresses. First century.

560   The Pont du Gard. The facings are made of large stone blocks up to the arches of the third level; the walls of the channel are of rubble masonry. Augustan period. Length: 275m; height: 48.77m.

561

Lutèce	1.65m per km
Lyon-Mont d'Or	3.21m per km
Lyon Brévenne	5.3m per km
Lyon-Craponne	16.8m per km

These average inclines could, of course, vary frequently in the course of the long distances between sharp drops and a level stretch.[41] It was precisely to

562

561 The most beautiful Roman aqueduct is undoubtedly that at Ephesus; its façades are more reminiscent of a triumphal arch or amphitheatre than a simple water channel. (Built between 4 and 14.)

562 The massive arcaded section made of rusticated stone blocks of the aqueduct of *Mactaris* (Maktar) in Tunisia. Here a projecting cornice was used to support the centring.

563

prevent these variations that the most substantial construction works were carried out, including tunnels dug through mountains, raised aqueducts and siphons. An example of a tunnel is the aqueduct of Saldae, others are the tunnels of the *emissarium* of Lake Fucino (5679m), Lake Albano (1425m) and Lake Nemi (1650m)[42] (figs 564, 565). These last are aqueducts of a particular type, since instead of supplying the water requirements of a city, they regulated the overflow from lakes that had a variable level;[43] these drainage works were called *cuniculi*. As for the raised aqueducts, they are suffi-

563   The aqueducts of Lyon, after crossing a depression almost parallel to the Rhône, using siphons, were for a short distance raised on sections of massive construction. The decrease in height meant that a system of arches was no longer needed. The occasional arches through the aqueduct of Gier were made to allow passage through it.

564   A cross-section of the *emissarium* of Lake Nemi. Designed to control the level of this crater lake, the tunnel, which flows into the Ariccia valley, is 1653m long with a difference in level of 12.63m.

aqueduct	maximum height	length*
Fréjus, arches over the Gargalon	14m	130m
Aspendos, siphon-bridge	15m	1000m
Lyon-Gier, arches of Chaponost	15m	
Lutèce, aqueduct of Arcueil	16m	330m(?)
Lyon-Gier, siphon-bridge over the Garon	21m	208m
Tarragona	30m	217m
Segovia	31m	818m
Rome, *Aqua Claudia*	32m	11km
Rome, *Aqua Novus*	32m	11km
Metz, Jouy-aux-Arches (estimate)	32m	1100m(?)
Cherchel, bridge over the Chebet Ilelouine	33m	136m
Carthage, oued Miliane	38m	
Nîmes, Pont du Gard	48.77m	275m

*Valley crossings

564

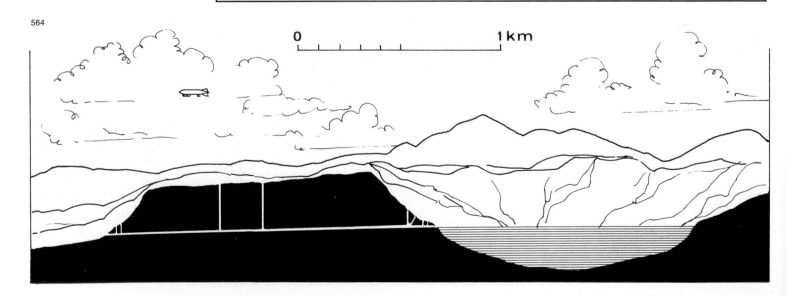

0   1 km

ciently fixed in everyone's visual memory to be recalled simply by reference to a few dimensions (see table).

Another factor to be included in the statistics relating to the size of an aqueduct is its daily capacity. To the usual domestic needs can be added, in the case of Roman cities, consumption by artisans (such as fullers and tanners), bath-houses, monumental fountains and large private dwellings. Such an increase in demand led, on the part of the aediles and the engineers, to the creation of water systems approaching and sometimes overtaking the standards laid down today for consumption within towns – at present approximately 500 litres of water per day per inhabitant.[44]

It has been possible to estimate the daily output of the majority of the great aqueducts, based on the sections of the pipes and the average incline:

Lutèce	$2400m^3$
Pompeii	$6460m^3$
Lyon-Mont d'Or	$10,000m^3$
Lyon-Craponne	$13,000m^3$
Carthage	$17,280m^3$
Lyon-Gier	$25,000m^3$
Lyon-Brévenne	$28,000m^3$
Cherchel	$34,000m^3$
Sens	$40,760m^3$
Rome, *Aqua Appia*	$73,000m^3$
Nîmes	$124,000m^3$
Rome, *Anio Vetus*	$175,920m^3$
Rome, *Aqua Claudia*	$184,220m^3$
Rome, *Aqua Marcia*	$187,600m^3$
Rome, *Anio Novus*	$189,520m^3$

If the maximum population of Pompeii is estimated to be 12,000 inhabitants, each used 540 litres of water per day; and, if Rome had a million inhabitants, its 11 aqueducts, adding up to $1,127,280m^3$, guaranteed more than 1100 litres per day per head.

These flows, however, are assuming new water pipes, but, depending on the nature of the subsoil, the water would contain various minerals, particularly lime in suspension which reacts with the open air and forms a deposit along the walls of the pipes. The size of this deposit varies from zero (for water off granite or sandstone rock) to sufficient to bring about a considerable reduction of the flow. A. Triou, in his study of the aqueduct of Saintes, estimated that the supply of the new catchment installation from the spring of le Doubret was in the order of $10,850m^3$ per day – a figure reduced by limescale to $2200m^3$, or practically one fifth of the initial figure. A demonstration of this is given by the remaining fragments of lead piping preserved in the Museo Nazionale delle Terme in Rome.[45] Their initial diameter is in the region of 29cm (probably measured as 1 foot), but this is reduced by concretions to 15cm, i.e. the initial section of $600.18 cm^2$ has become $176.62cm^2$.

The third method for overcoming obstacles, in this case depressions, is the siphon. The aqueduct of Pergamon mentioned above was the first to make use of the principle of communicating vessels of watertight piping, i.e. a siphon, probably made of lead (fig. 566).[46]

When the Romans provided towns with a water supply under pressure

565

565 Relief discovered in the *emissarium* of Lake Fucino, showing two machines with two drums, one above the other, driven by capstans. The arrangement was designed to remove the waste material from boring the tunnel, via vertical shafts. The double roll of cables indicates that one bucket went up while the other came down. At the bottom, a galley is seen sailing on the lake. (Museo della Civiltà Romana.)

they rarely made use of the siphon in the construction of their aqueducts. When faced by a deep depression they preferred to cross it or avoid it altogether, even at the price of a wide detour. This was not an admission of an insurmountable difficulty, as a number of siphons were built, but rather showed an awareness of the weaknesses of the technique of the siphon in comparison with the efficient simplicity of a channel with a constant incline.

Three towns at least had siphon aqueducts: Aspendos, Saintes and Lyon, the last having one such installation on each of its four water supply systems. These few examples represent a modest proportion of the total number of known aqueducts, though it is likely that many siphons have escaped detection as a result of their destruction and the systematic recovery of the precious lead piping of which they were made. Vitruvius describes the siphon as one of the convenient ways of crossing a depression (VIII,6). He recommends the construction, at the bottom of the valley, in the centre of the siphon, of a straight aqueduct which would reduce the height of the drop and moderate the force of the current, and connecting it up to the two inclines by gentle variations of level to prevent 'water-hammering'.

Technically then, the problem was well known and it was even known how to bind together the pipe junctions by enclosing them in blocks of stone each time there was a sharp bend. However, the enormous quantity of lead required,[47] its high cost, the need for a highly specialized workforce, the uncertainty of the soldered joints, the difficulties and the cost of maintenance, caused the Romans to moderate their use of this technique, easily explaining their preference for either extending an aqueduct over a longer route or constructing a raised aqueduct.

The builders of the Lyon aqueducts, faced with the problem of crossing a valley about 100m deep and 2.5 km wide, were forced to make use of siphons and these installations (at least the aqueduct of Gier) have partially survived. Of the eight siphons in total, only one, however, has preserved the main part of its layout: this is the siphon of Soucieu-en-Jarrest. It functions as follows: upstream, the canal of the aqueduct, the *specus*, made of a masonry conduit carefully lined with mortar mixed with broken tiles, flows into a tank, the header, situated at the start of the incline (the header at Soucieu measures 1.54m × 4.6m internally). From this vaulted basin, lead pipes descend (9 lead tubes, 27cm in diameter at Soucieu)[48], the height of fall being reduced by a venter crossing the deepest part of the depression. After this the tubes rise and flow into

566 Diagram showing the principle of the siphons at Lyon. From A to B the water is channelled through watertight lead pipes. F = maximum rise (reduced by the height of the siphon bridge) and H = loss of level or force between A and B.

566

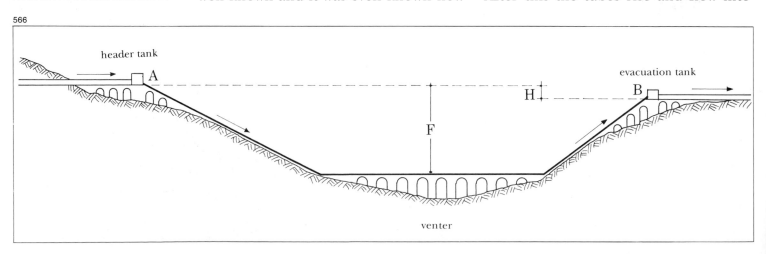

header tank

evacuation tank

A

H

B

F

venter

an escape tank, the position of which must be calculated carefully (too high and the water would not reach it, too low and there would be a geyser effect), after which the *specus* returns to its course.

Whatever the form of its support, the supply channel had a fairly standard structure and shape: a tunnel, dug into the ground or rock, or raised in the air, big enough for the passage of a man, the bottom of which consisted of a conduit made watertight by a thick mortar containing broken tiles. It was generally roofed by a vault, which might be replaced, in raised sections, by flat tiles. It was also periodically provided with inspection chambers, *putei*, often quite deep when the aqueduct was buried underground, to ensure maintenance[49] (figs 566 to 570).

568

567 Section of the *Aqua Marcia* showing the gallery of the channel. Internal height: 1.46m; width of the stone: 74cm; width of the lining: 61cm. Notice the thickness of the lining at the bottom (18cm) and the grooves made vertically in the surface of the joints of the side blocks, into which a string-course of mortar was poured to waterproof it.

568 Channel of the *Aqua Claudia* on an arcaded section. Height: 1.7m; width across the stone: 1.17m; width of the channel: 1.03m.

569 Underground section of the aqueduct of Traslay supplying water to *Avaricum* (Bourges). The channel or *specus* is lined with two prominent kerbs made of rendered masonry. There is a coating of limestone concretion which, even though it restricted the volume of circulation, added to the waterproofing of the walls.

567

569

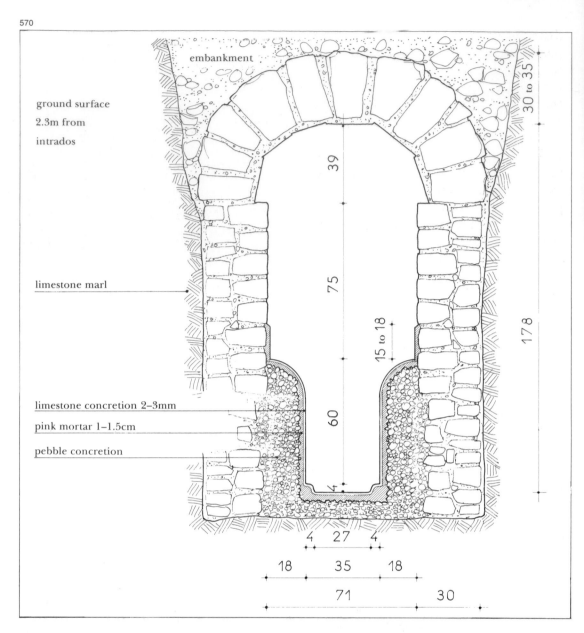

570

embankment

ground surface
2.3m from
intrados

30 to 35

39

limestone marl

75

15 to 18

178

limestone concretion 2–3mm

pink mortar 1–1.5cm

pebble concretion

60

4

4 27 4

18 35 18

71 30

570 Cross-section of the
aqueduct at Traslay.

c Urban water supply

Water channelled to the high point of a town had to begin a new course from storage to user, passing through a distribution network that was often very complex. The techniques of such systems, as well as the politics of their management, are known to us through a treatise on the aqueducts of Rome, the *De aquis urbis Romae*, written by Frontinus (Sextus Iulius Frontinus), who was *curator aquarum* under Nerva, in 97.[50] The information provided by this work answers almost all the questions that might be asked about the distribution of water in Rome. It gives the name and the construction date of all aqueducts then supplying the city, the cost of some (for instance, the *Aqua Marcia*: 180 million sesterces, I,7), the nature of the maintenance work on the aqueducts, fountains and drains, the administrative organization of the Water Board (700 people, including the architect) and an inventory of the fountains in Rome (640).

Unfortunately, even though Frontinus' treatise has survived and the aqueducts can be traced as far as their entry into Rome, the urban storage and distribution network is known only very partially through isolated installations, such as the Great Baths or the reservoirs of the great nymphaea, such as that on the Esquiline supplied by the *Aqua Julia*.

Despite the careful choice of spring, the water was always liable to carry impurities which it was advisable to extract before they reached the narrow piping of the town main. Filters, in the form of grilles and settling troughs, were therefore laid out at the place where the aqueduct entered the city, or even along its course. These were the *piscinae limariae*, basins which could themselves be cut off and emptied for cleaning (fig.571).

Depending on the climate and in case of drought, it was wise to provide for water storage in large cisterns (which have survived in great numbers in North Africa and Syria). These were often old rainwater cisterns maintained in use and were also where the aqueduct came to an end. While the domestic cisterns were all spaces dug into the rock or enclosed by a vault, the great aqueduct reservoirs sometimes called for different techniques. In fact three types of construction can be distinguished:

1 Chambers with pillars or columns, such as the reservoir called the 'Piscina Mirabile' at Misenum.[51] It is the final water supply point served by the Augustan aqueduct (probably built by Agrippa) that went from Serino, supplying in passing Pompeii and Naples (figs 572, 573, 574), to Misenum.

At this point on the coast, Agrippa had had a port constructed, which was to become the first naval base in the south of the peninsula, and the great cistern was intended to provide a supply of drinking water for the base and its ships. The hall of the reservoir measures 25.45 by 66m and is 11.4m high. Its vaults are supported by 48 cruci-form pillars and its capacity is

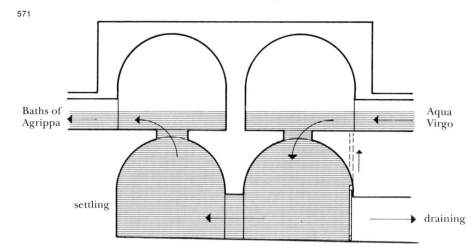

571

Baths of Agrippa

Aqua Virgo

settling

draining

estimated as 12,600m³. This construction, still remarkable today, is very rarely visited, unlike the famous 'Yerebatan Sarayi' in Istanbul. Built under Constantine, this great reservoir, linked to the aqueducts of Hadrian and Valens, measures 70 by 140m, and its cover of brick vaults is supported by 336 Corinthian columns.[52]

2 Barrel-vaulted chambers – by far the most numerous. Their shape is conditioned by this choice of construction technique and is that of a simple gallery with a semi-circular arch. Among the largest constructions of this

571 *Piscinae limariae* or settling chambers where the *Aqua Virgo* enters the Pincio in Rome. (After L. Canina, *Gli edifizi di Roma Antica*, vol.IV, pl.CCXXXI, fig.6.)

572 The 'Piscina Mirabilis' at *Misenum* (present-day Bacoli), a gigantic cistern dating from the Augustan period, built of masonry with reticulate facings and quoins of rubble stones; its capacity is 12,600m³. All the horizontal and vertical re-entrants have watertight rims. The rendering survives almost intact on the floor as well as on the pillars and the walls. The roofing consists of 13 barrel vaults, whose springing walls are punctuated by 60 arches supported by 48 cruciform pillars.

572

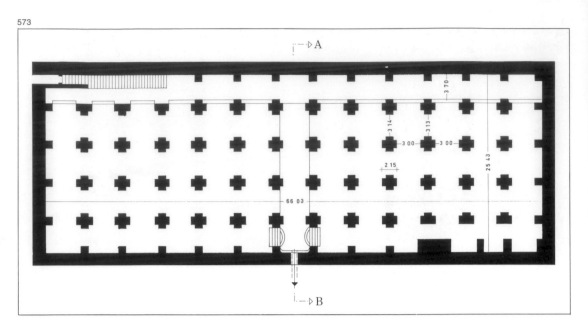

573

573 Plan of the 'Piscina Mirabile'. This underground reservoir is 66m long, 25.45m wide and 11.4m high. It is entered by two staircases, diagonally opposite one another. The middle transverse bay has a settling basin with a draining hole out of it. The aqueduct enters at the north corner.

574 Transverse cross-section of the 'Piscina Mirabile'.

574

type is the great cistern of Domitian's villa at Albano, supplied by a special aqueduct. It is an enormous vaulted structure, 11m wide and 123m long, divided by two partitions into three interconnecting compartments – a fairly considerable reservoir, to which was added another more modest one, which supplied not only the Imperial residence with drinking water, but also a number of fountains and nymphaea adorning the gardens, after which the water was distributed to an irrigation network.[53] Also in this category, the compartments of the 'Cento Camarelle' of Misenum, partially explored, form a cruciform network of vaulted galleries (fig.575).

3 Parallel chambers, which are a variation or development of barrel-vaulted ones, consisting of a series of parallel and interconnecting vaulted galleries, an arrangement that can be seen in the five chambers of the cisterns of Albano (10,000m³) still in service (fig.576), in the cisterns of the Villa Jovis on Capri, and in the towns of North Africa (cisterns of *Bulla Regia* or Thugga). This is also the arrangement adopted in the cistern for the Baths of Trajan on the Esquiline, known as the 'Sette sale'.[54] In reality there are nine parallel galleries included in a construction measuring 42 by 56m, interconnected by staggered openings to increase the action of settling. This arrangement could also make settling more efficient by ensuring the progress of water through successive chambers by a passage cut through at a certain height, as at the cisterns of Dar-Saniat at Carthage, or at Thugga.

The relatively modest water installations at Pompeii (see the table of daily supply) have the great advantage of being visible from the entry of the aqueduct into the city right up to the different points of use. The water-distribution building, the *castellum aquae*, was built to the north of the city

575

576

near the 'Vesuvius Gate', at the highest point of the city, i.e. 34m above the lowest point at the south, the Stabian Gate, just 750m away; a considerable difference in level, which the engineers had to take carefully into account when designing a watertight system.[55] The building, of trapezoidal shape, encloses a circular domed chamber, 5.7m in diameter and 4.3m high, into which the *specus* of the aqueduct flowed (figs 577, 578, 579). The water

passed through a grille on entering the settling tank, which was bordered on each side by a service walkway. A second grille, probably a finer one, went across the middle of the basin. At the outflow the water was held back by a lead plate, approximately 25cm high. The water flowed over this into three conduits, connected in the wall to three lead pipes (two 25cm and one 30cm in diameter)[56] forming the three principal branches of the urban

575 One of the compartments of the 'Cento Camarelle', the cistern complex at *Misenum* supplying a large coastal villa built in the first century BC. Width: 2m; height: 4m. Excavation identified a tunnel, 55m long, divided into four chambers cut at right angles by two other tunnels measuring 40 and 55m respectively. At a higher level a large cistern with four chambers was added, built in the course of the first century.

576 One of the five chambers of the large cistern of Albano, called 'il Cisternone', built in the Severan period and still in service today supplying the town. Capacity: $10,132\,m^3$.

577 The *castellum aquae* of Pompeii near the Vesuvius Gate, the highest point of the city.

577

distribution system.[57] Despite being of comparable size (a basin 5.5m in diameter, but 1m deep), the *castellum* of Nîmes, presumed to be Augustan, distributed a much larger volume of water into 10 pipes, 40cm in diameter, and had three outlets for emptying (figs 580, 581).

The most efficient supply pipes were of course made of lead, originally sheets rolled round a template, the edges of which were bent round and soldered again with lead, or simply placed together and lined with two string courses of clay between which

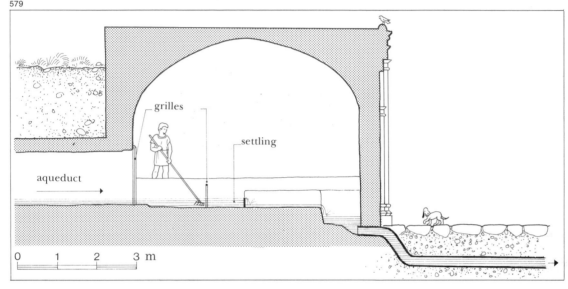

578 Division of the water into three channels in the *castellum aquae* at Pompeii. In front of the triple divider is the housing of the lead plate which once formed a dam for the water to settle and which was taken away to be reused after the eruption of 79.

579 Cross-section of the main *castellum aquae* at Pompeii.

580 The *castellum divisorium* at Nîmes. (P. Varène.)

lead was poured (fig.582).[58] The junctions along the length were reinforced by a short collar into which the two ends of the sections fitted and the joint was soldered with lead. The malleability and the low fusion temperature of this metal made it adaptable to all shapes and so allowed the distribution of water over the most complex routes, in any part of a building, within the limits imposed by the pressure (figs 583, 584).

The calibre of the different pipes had, at least by the Augustan period, been standardized. According to Vitruvius (VIII,6), this was based on the width and the weight of the lead sheet used to make a tube before it was rolled; the width, of course, determined the diameter. These specifications, which were too imprecise owing to variations caused by the bending of the junction, were standardized in the time of Frontinus into diameters expressed in quarter fingers, *quadrantes*, and fingers, *digiti*.

1 Small lead pipes, calibrated by diameter:[59]

Type	Diameter		
	quadrantes	*digiti*	mm
quinaria	5	1.25	23
senaria	6	1.5	27.6
octogenaria	8	2	36.8
denaria	10	2.5	46
duodenaria	12	3	55.2
quinum denum	15	3.75	69
vicenaria	20	5	92

2 Large pipes, calibrated by section surface (figs 585, 586):

Type	Section	Diameter	
	square fingers	fingers	mm
tricenaria	30	6.2	114
quadragenaria	40	7.2	132.4
quinquagenaria	50	8	147.2
sexagenaria	60	8.8	162
septuagenaria	70	9.4	173
octogenaria	80	10.1	186
nonagenaria	90	10.7	197
centenaria	100	11.3	208
centonum viconum	120	12.4	228

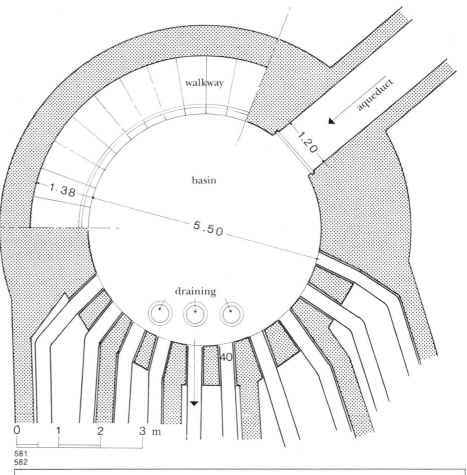

581
582

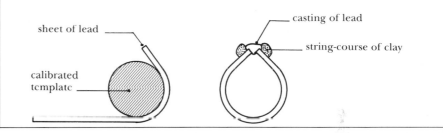

583

584

581 Diagram of the water-distribution chamber at Nîmes.

582 Manufacture of lead pipes by soldering, with a sealing of molten metal constituting an axial ridge.

583 Detail of a lead pipe supplying the baths of Julia Felix at Pompeii. The lengthways soldering can be seen, which seals the cylinder made of a rolled-up sheet of lead, and the circular soldering (left) which bonded it to the next pipe.

585 Two sections of lead pipes with a large diameter, in the Museo Nazionale delle Terme in Rome. Two of them are complete and have preserved a part of the soldered rim connecting them to their neighbours. Length: 2.6m; vertical diameter: 25cm; horizontal diameter: 22cm. From Castel Porziano.

585

586 Stamp of Marcus Aurelius (139-61) on a pipe.

587 Pipes made of terracotta tubes jointed and sealed with lime mortar at Ephesus.

586

587

Just like ceramic products, lead pipes, particularly those with a large diameter, could be given a stamp indicating the monument they were intended for, the owner, the manufacturer and, in the case of the aqueducts of Rome, the name of the emperor: *Imp(eratoris)* *Caes(aris) Traj(ani) Hadriani Aug(usti) sub cura Petronii Surae proc(uratoris), Martialis ser(vus) fe(cit)*.[60] It is curious to see here, running contrary to the segregation of slavery, that equality was re-established in a manufacturing mark which brought together the name of the all-powerful emperor, that of the aedile and that of the slave-manufacturer of the product. Lead pipes of the urban water system at Pompeii were more simple and carried a mark showing where they belonged: *(usibis) publ(icis) Pompe(ianorum)*.

Lead had only one disadvantage, but one which was particularly restrictive for modest provincial municipalities – its rather high cost. The raw material itself was difficult to obtain[61] and its preparation required a highly-skilled workforce; this is why it was replaced by other materials, principally ceramic pipes. These tubes had a constriction at one end for fitting into one another; they usually had a large diameter, 13 to 20cm, and were 45 to 70cm long. The connections were made watertight by lime mortar, which Vitruvius recommended should be kneaded with oil to increase its impermeability (VIII,6) (fig.587). The author of the *Ten Books* was also distrustful of lead piping, which he accused of poisoning the water (wrongly in fact),[62] confusing it with white lead (*cerussa*), a carbonate of lead used as a white pigment, which is in fact a dangerous poison.[63]

In wooded areas it was still more economical to use wood to make pipes. Not only could channels be carved from half-logs, but proper pipes were made by hollowing out straight trunks using drills with a very long bit, in all probability identical to those used by 'well-sinkers' of mountainous regions right up until the twentieth century. The junctions between two wooden pipes were made by leather collars or metal pieces, the whole thing possibly being contained in a drilled block of stone and enclosed in a guttering lined with clay. An installation of this type has been found in the supply to the monumental fountain at Argentomagus (St-Marcel, Indre)[64] (fig.588).

Returning now to Pompeii to follow the progress of the piping: from the main water distribution centre pipes radiated out, buried approximately 60cm under the pavements, then entered a series of secondary water towers intended to break the pressure caused by the significant change in level (figs 589, 590, 591). The principle adopted was that of stepped siphons, i.e. the same as that of the levels created to break the impetus of the torrents. The need to keep the water in watertight pipes forced the hydraulic engineers to install a series of masonry columns along the course of each branch emanating from the water distribution centre. These contained rising and falling pipes and supported a lead tank, the *castellum plumbeum*, at the top, in which the water lost its pressure before being distributed into the urban supply. The first column, placed 139m from the front of the *castellum*, was already 7m lower, and the builders, who were not very accurate in their levelling, built it to more or less the same height; probably realizing their

588

mistake, they gave a greater discharge to the other pillars. Thirteen of them[65] have been found distributed over the whole city, each one having a height such that the water arrived at its base at a pressure between 1.5 to 2 kg/cm^2. In order to allow maintenance of the system, taps, above the distribution points, made it possible to interrupt the current, while the different basins, reservoirs and fountains were provided with a means of drainage.

In view of the division into three of the *castellum* at Pompeii, it is tempting to presume a distribution of water conforming to the recommendation made

589

588 The monumental fountain at Argentomagus (St-Marcel, Indre). The four pillars in the basin supported a roof. The supply, at least in its final state, arrived via a wooden pipe under the steps.

589 A secondary water-tower of the supply network at Pompeii (VI,16) (height: 7m). At the top of the masonry pillar was a lead tank with a lid, supplied by pipes housed in a groove on the upstream side; the outflow pipes were located in the groove downstream (visible in the photo) and then went under the pavement; one of them supplied the fountain.

590 The Arch of Caligula at one end of the via di Mercurio at Pompeii. The structure served as a secondary water-tower, the lead pipes being housed in conduits made in the masonry piers. Two fountains, demolished in 62, were located at the foot of it.

591 Secondary water-tower in the Forum Baths at Pompeii, incorporated into the external wall of the building in the course of the developments in the Julio-Claudian period.

590

591

592 The communal latrines were constant consumers of water and formed part of the developments of public spaces, as at the *forica* of the Forum Baths at Ostia. A flow of water circulated under the seats at the bottom of the peripheral ditch. A fountain on the right-hand wall catered for ablutions and allowed a flow of water to run into the gutters of the paving.

593 Fountain of a *domus*, with a mosaic and shell decoration at the House of the Large Fountain, Pompeii (VI,8,22). These small structures were connected to the public main.

594 The large nymphaeum of the villa of the Quintilii, on the *via Appia* between Rome and Bovillae, built in the third century AD. The large apse containing the basin was covered over with a half-dome. The right-hand part of the structure is concealed by a medieval construction; a special aqueduct, as at the Villa dei Sette Bassi, supplied the building.

595 A public fountain at Pompeii, decorated with a head of Mercury. The supply pipe came out of the figure's mouth. The overflow channel is visible on the top of the rim, and, at a lower level, the outflow of the drainage hole VI,8.

596 Cross-section and plan of a public fountain at Pompeii (via di Stabia, VII,1).

by Vitruvius (VIII,6). He advocated, for fairness, dividing the *castellum* into three basins situated at different levels (or one single basin with pipes staggered in height coming out of it), with three destinations: *1* A level that was permanently supplied, even in the dry season, providing water for the domestic use of private individuals (fountains and houses). *2* A middle level supplying public monuments (baths). *3* An upper level, the first to be cut off in the event of a lowering of water level, leading to fountains or basins and to water spouts

(*lacus et salientes*)[66] (figs 592, 593, 594).

This automatic distribution, itself varying with changes of level, could have been replaced by a sluice-gate system maintained by the municipality, but it is possible that the reliability of the supply did not make such a precaution necessary and there is no conclusive evidence surviving to be certain whether Pompeii did or did not ration its supply.

Whatever the case, it was the public fountains that got the largest share of the water from the urban supply since forty have been found, almost all intact, over the uncovered three-fifths of the city. They were distributed as evenly as possible so that they were a distance of 70 to 80m apart; the people of the neighbourhood thus always had access to water less than 40m from their homes. The appearance of these fountains does not vary very much: a rectangular trough built half across the pavement, half across the roadway, made up of four dressed slabs, almost always lava[67] held together by iron cramps sealed with lead (figs 595, 596).

The water came through a lead pipe rising from inside a stone placed on the pavement side, and ran into the trough through a sculpted motif. These motifs always differed from one fountain to another (fig.597). Vertical water-proofing was ensured by a fixed string-course of pink mortar, poured into a channel dug into the joint between each slab (fig.598).

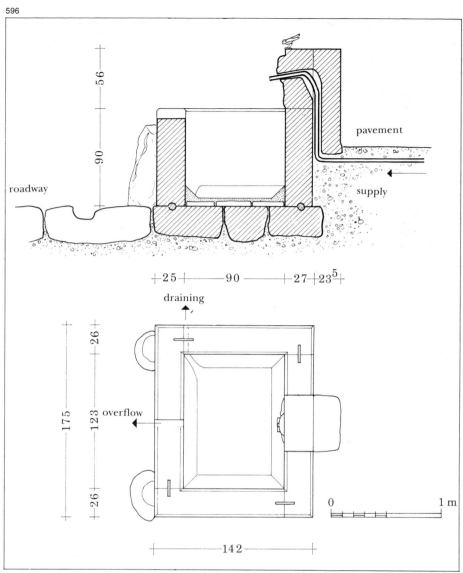

597 Pompeii: a fountain on the Via dell'Abbondanza (VII, 14). As the back edge stone has disappeared, the hole through which the supply pipe passed is visible.

598 Detail of the jointing of two dressed stone slabs in the trough of a public fountain at Pompeii, showing the channel into which was poured the string-course of mortar for waterproofing and the sealant for an iron clamp (IX,9)

599 Basin of a public fountain at Pompeii (at the crossroads of the via dell'Abbondanza and the via di Stabia) showing the lining covering the bottom, placed on bricks, and the watertight edging round the sides.

The bottom of the trough was covered with ceramic tiles (flat bricks or *tegulae*) placed on a layer of mortar and care- fully lined, while there was a watertight flange up against the walls (fig.599). A hole for emptying, normally stopped by

600

602

600 Limestone slabs forming the bottom of the basin of a public fountain at Bavay (Nord). The housing of the slabs has a channel cut down the middle designed to take mortar for waterproofing, identical to that found in the surfaces of joints.

601 A public fountain at Thugga. The enormous basin is edged with slabs fitted into grooved pillars; the joints were then filled in with mortar, here partially preserved.

602 The basin of a triangular fountain, cut out of a single limestone block – an ideal solution to the problem of waterproofing. Forum of Palmyra.

a wooden bung, opened on the bottom level, making it possible to empty the trough for maintenance, while in the upper part the ridge of one slab had an overflow channel cut into it, allowing water to flow on to the roadway.

The waterproofing of the troughs, whether a small utilitarian fountain or an enormous *natatio*, almost always followed the same principle of fixing string-courses of mortar mixed with broken tiles to bond the vertical slabs and the bottom slabs, when the bottom was covered with them[68] (fig.600). In North Africa, however, there is a different arrangement for fixing the slabs: they are socketed into grooves cut into small intermediate pillars, an arrangement completed by jointing with mortar to prevent any water getting through (fig.601). Finally there exists a more radical solution, consisting of carving the basin out of one huge piece of stone, rather like a sarcophagus with the addition of a drainage hole (fig.602).

An additional precaution could be carried out underneath large basins to prevent the risk of seepage. This consisted of lining the hollow ,dug to house the basin with clay, which could be continued up the walls to ground level. This is how the large fish trough at Mercin-et-Vaux (Aisne) was built, constructed in sandy soil and made not with slabs but with rendered masonry[69] (figs 603, 604).

Finally, to protect the fountains, one or two large blocks of lava were propped against the slabs on the street side, in case of knocks from carts.

The very marked wearing of the slab on the pavement side, on both sides of the month of the fountain shows

601

clearly the side from which the water was drawn. The consumers consistently took their water from under the outflow so as to have it fresh and pure.

The network of fountains at Pompeii clearly represents the most complete system, but other cities show that such public works tended always to have the same form, as at Herculaneum, Paestum, Ostia and even sites as distant as St Romain-en-Gal or Bavay.[70]

The fate of the water supply at Pompeii after the earthquake of 62 is very interesting. The system itself was in fact seriously damaged and the supply interrupted. At first the citizens of Pompeii made do with rainwater collected in the cisterns, in the absence of water from the fountains. Since the majority of houses had never been joined up to the main, the cisterns had been kept in order.

However, the considerable number of artisans who were large consumers, particularly the fullers and dyers, and the need to put the baths back into service, prompted the aediles to restore the water supply. Thus, while trenches were being opened up to put down and renew the damaged pipes,[71] temporary piping was put in place, running along the pavements and along the fronts of buildings, roughly protected by junction covers or small flanges of masonry (fig.605). Some archaeologists doubt the nature of this installation, considering it to be the remains of an early water-supply system on the grounds that it is interrupted in many places and that there are no filtering systems or distribution pipes at all in the water works. These objections, arising from observations of an extant system, can be countered, however, by the following arguments:

1 The disappearance of metal pieces from the water works can be perfectly well explained (cf. above) by both the pillaging and the systematic reuse of material carried out after 79. An opera-

603

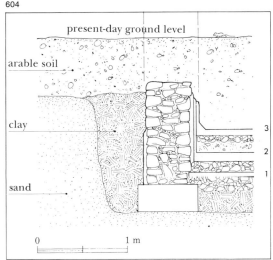

604

present-day ground level

arable soil

clay

sand

0   1 m

605

603   A section of the basin at Mercin-et-Vaux (Oise) showing the waterproofing. The foundation trench underneath and around the masonry walls was filled with a layer of clay with a maximum thickness of 50cm, forming a totally watertight lining.

604   Mercin-et-Vaux. Cross-section of one of the ends of the basin.

605   Lead piping from the temporary water supply network installed at Pompeii after 62. (VII,12,23.)

tion to save material and to help the survivors was undertaken at the behest of Titus,[72] using wells sunk into the lapilli. In the same way all the statues

606 Temporary water supply network at Pompeii in December 1980.

607 A vertical lead pipe in a house at Pompeii (IX,1). The collapse of the upper floor means that it is not possible to say whether it is a fall-pipe for waste water or a rising main. If the latter, it would be the only example discovered of an upper floor supplied with running water.

of the forum, the lead tanks and the piping of the towers and a number of works of art surviving in the houses were collected up. Apart from the disappearance of the metal parts, the *castellum* was in perfect working order, as was the surviving section of aqueduct and without doubt it was capable of once more providing the city with water by 79.

2 The depth at which the original pipes were buried (65cm) shows clearly that the Roman engineers would never have been negligent enough to install a permanent network on the surface, so protected in such a basic way. By way of comparison it is interesting to note that after the earthquake of 23 November 1980, the municipality of modern Pompeii repaired the water supply, just as the aediles of Pompeii had done after 62, and, quite naturally, while work was going on in the trenches, a temporary supply pipe was installed on the surface, roughly protected. (fig.606).

3 The disappearance of the majority of the pipes can be explained, not only by redeployment in ancient times but much more by the total disregard with which the excavations were carried out up to the twentieth century. It is known, in fact, that in the Bourbon period all movable and immovable objects of any value were dismantled and taken to be stored in the museum (at first in the royal collections of Portici and then in the Naples Museum). Among these objects were all the bronze taps from the water installations thrown together in a big heap without any indication of where they came from.[73] As for the lead pipes and the tanks, only a few examples were picked out; the rest were left in place, mostly hidden. Thus, when the Stabian Baths were first being uncovered in 1853, all the pipes were found intact and were recorded by the Niccolini brothers;[74] they then disappeared, buried in the museum stores or hidden from view.

4 Several establishments that were large consumers of water were indisputably in operation in 79; among these are the private baths of the House of Julia Felix, (II,4)[75] east of the *via dell'Abbondanza*. The baths had been open to the public in order to meet the demand while the great public baths were being repaired. An enticing advertisement, freshly painted on the façade, listed the services offered by the establishment: *In praedis Iuliae Sp. Felicis locantur balneum venerium et nongentum, tabernae, pergulae, caenacula ex idibus Aug(ustis) in idus Aug(ustas) sextas, annos continuos quinque. S(i) Q(uinquennium) D(ecurrerit) L(ocatio) E(rit) N(udo) C(onsensu)*[76] .'in the property of Julia Felix, one rents a bath (fit for?) Venus and persons of quality,[77] shops, pergolas,[78] apartments, from 1 August next until 1 August of the sixth year, for five years, with expiry of the lease at the end of the fifth.'

Also in the *via dell'Abbondanza*, the premises belonging to a fuller, the *fullonica* of Stephanus[79] (I,6,7) have been found in perfect working order, including the material press installed in the shop giving on to the street. Its vats were supplied by a pressure pipe joined up to the main under the pavement in front of the building. The establishment functioned so well that in the shop the proprietor of the establishment or his manager was found clutching the (quite high) receipt for a sum of 1089 sesterces in gold, silver and bronze coins.

The men's section of the Forum Baths had also been repaired, and its new decoration was finished[80] (the destruction visible today is attributable to the eruption and to the abandonment of the monument after its clearance); the women's section of the Stabian Baths[81] and a number of private houses' internal installations had also been repaired.

d Water disposal

Water, carefully collected and channelled at great expense, had also to be disposed of when it was in excess or when it was polluted by use.

As noted in reference to the cisterns of Pompeii, the overflow water ran out on to the roadway, and this was also true of waste water including that from the latrines[82] which ended up in the same place. Whereas the water off the roofs was as far as possible channelled into the cistern, the numerous latrines on the upper floors were evacuated via large pipes made of terracotta, some of them leading to a ditch, others joining up with the roadway (figs 607, 608, 609, 610). Pompeii, in fact, despite the relative wealth of its inhabitants, was in 79 still without an overall drainage system; only the area around the forum had such an arrangement, and it was the paved roadways, being impermeable, that fulfilled this role. The installation of the water-supply system and the introduction of public fountains resolved this delicate public health problem: by flowing day and night from the fountains, the water poured constantly over all the thoroughfares of the city, which fortunately were built on a sloping surface, and provided efficient cleansing comparable and even superior to that of the gutters in modern towns. Following the natural incline of the streets, the water left the city through the wall in the vicinity of the gates, via outlets made at the base of the wall (fig.611). The disadvantage lay in the permanent presence of water in the streets, forcing the municipality to place at regular intervals, and particularly at cross-roads, large stones allowing pedestrians to cross without getting their feet wet.

If Pompeii had survived much longer, it is quite likely that the city would have been provided with a system of underground sewers. It is understandable, however, that in such an old city, that had evolved gradually with solutions peculiar to it, the complete tearing apart of the roads represented a considerable amount of work and a serious disturbance to the activities of normal urban life; whereas in towns that originated in conquest, the laying out of the drainage system formed part of the town plan. And so the more 'modern' installations are found in modest Gallo-Roman settlements rather than in the ancient cities of Campania.

The problem of carrying out large-scale urban construction work is well illustrated by the restoration of Pompeii following the earthquake of 62. In fact, apart from the Temple of Isis, reconstructed thanks to the generosity of a donor, in 79 – that is, seventeen years after the catastrophe – no public building in course of reconstruction had been finished,[83] and the water supply, as just noted, was still limited to a temporary system.

The drains in towns that had them naturally follow the line of the streets, and their discovery in modern cities makes it possible to trace the course of the ancient roads (figs 612, 613, 614). Where the land surface permitted, it was usual to attempt to make a coherent network of secondary pipes flowing into a main sewer, which carried the waste water out of the town. The water drainage of Rome was organized in this way, its conduits ending at the *Cloaca Maxima*, which itself led into the Tiber.

A city such as Timgad (Thamugadi),[84] founded in 100 with a regular grid plan, was given at the beginning (and has preserved) a system of drains laid out under the course of each street in the form of tunnels 0.4m wide and from 0.8 to 1m high. These were accessible through inspection holes and flowed at right angles into the main sewer of the *Cardo*.

The structural appearance of the drainage tunnels varies little and every-

608 Drainpipes made of terracotta were protected by being sunk into a vertical groove so that they did not project from the wall. Pompeii, I,3,1.

609 Down-pipe from an upstairs latrine in a modern farm at Pompeii.

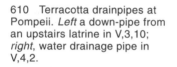

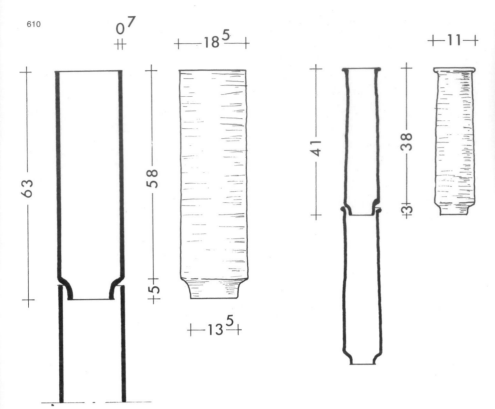

610 Terracotta drainpipes at Pompeii. *Left* a down-pipe from an upstairs latrine in V,3,10; *right*, water drainage pipe in V,4,2.

611 The outflow through the walls of Pompeii at the Nola Gate. The water running off the roadway would drain out of the city.

612 The mouth of a drain in the underground network at Pompeii.

613 The mouth of a drain on a street at Ephesus.

614 The mouth of a drain in the floor of the Forum Baths at Ostia.

where dimensions similar to those at Timgad can be found. The roofing consists of a barrel vault, corbelling, or a gable roof of two *tegulae* or two slabs, or else one flat slab (figs 615, 616).

Buildings constructed on slopes form obstacles that can sometimes turn into dams, stopping the water running away. When it was a house without a cellar, a brick channel, made along the side upstream, carried the water off sideways, whereas if the structure was not used for living in, like a town wall or a theatre, terracotta drains going through the walls carried the water straight downstream (fig.617). Buried

615 Section through a drain at Ostia with a gabled cover made of slabs.

616 The outflow from the Baths of Velia. The bricks or tiles serve as corbelled centring in the masonry.

617 A drain for runoff water, Hadrian's Wall.

618 A tunnel separating the retaining wall, *left*, from the wall of the building, *right*, at the *cryptoporticus* of Bavay (Nord).

619 The *cryptoporticus* of Bavay (Nord) and the corridor separating its walls.

620 The narrow corridor, 4.83m high and 0.54m wide, separating the retaining wall from the building wall built at the foot of the hill of *Avaricum* (Bourges). (Second century.)

features or retaining walls called for more stringent precautions, particularly when the walls were rendered and decorated. As Vitruvius recommends (VII,4), these were based on the creation of a cavity between the wall retaining the earth and the wall of the room or of the underground tunnel. Thus there is a narrow ventilated passage, into which water seepage can flow, while the visible wall, aired all the way up, is perfectly protected from the damp.

Cryptoportici represent particularly vulnerable installations due to their large cellar development, so they were arranged in this way and sanitary tunnels have been found behind their walls at Bavay (figs 618, 619) and at Reims.[85] Backing on to the bottom of the upper town of Bourges (*Avaricum*), a decorated wall, lined behind by a portico, had itself been separated from the true retaining wall by a cavity designed to protect the stucco of the facing (fig.620).

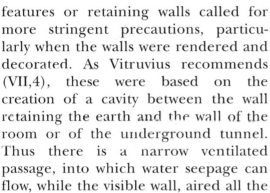

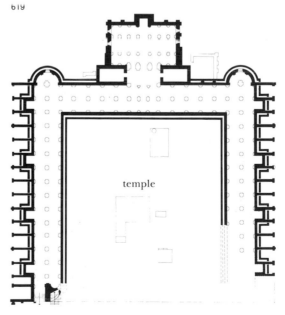

temple

2 Heating and baths

a Techniques of heating

The early Roman dwelling had no means of heating other than that in use in all early societies – a single hearth, in the *atrium*. This was probably kept going permanently to provide heating and for cooking food. The appearance, in the fourth or third century BC, of the kitchen moved the domestic hearth, or rather did away with it, by giving the fire a more specialized function.

In the kitchen the fire was situated on a raised work area, supported on a masonry block, on which the receptacles to be heated were placed on tripods. The smoke and cooking odours escaped through one or more roof openings made of tiles in the form of an oculus or a hood (see the section on roofing materials). This isolation of the fire necessarily led to the use of other means of heating during the cold season, in the form of movable braziers in which glowing coals were kept (fig.621). As there were no chimneys and as, at least during the night, openings were covered, the risk of carbon monoxide poisoning, added to the problem of smoke, meant that the Romans used only very dry wood or better still charcoal (*ligna coctilia*). The efficiency of such heating remained poor, but it was, nonetheless, the method used in the vast majority of dwellings. It was certainly the only form of heating that could be installed on upper floors, particularly in *insulae* of large towns where it was probably responsible for a great number of outbreaks of fire.

There is evidence of this from the earthquake at Pompeii, which took place in the middle of the winter, 5 February 62.[86] Apart from the damage caused by the collapse and disturbance to masonry, the tremor also resulted in many fires caused by braziers overturning or inflammable material falling on them.

Houses were not the only structures to be heated in this way, since the earliest bath-houses also had braziers, the size and number of which were adapted to the size of the rooms. The Forum Baths at Pompeii have preserved an impressive and richly decorated brazier made of bronze, given by a patron by the name of M. Nigidius Vaccula (fig.622). In a discreet allusion to his name, a bovine adorns the front of the object, while two accompanying bronze seats come with cows' feet.

The question must be asked why the Romans, who were so practical and ingenious, did not think of using fires with chimneys to heat their houses, especially as such a method of heating was in fact known to them, as is proved by the chimneys of hypocausts and bakers' ovens (fig.623). This question remains unanswered and even today, on some farms in Campania, the heating is still supplied by copper braziers, often decorated, burning charcoal which has been bought from bakers and lime-burners.

It is perhaps in more northerly regions, where there was more need for heating, that the chimney duct made its appearance. There are at least hints of this at the sites of Selongey ('Côte d'Or) and Alesia ('cellar' 59), in the form of fireplaces laid out in small

621 Brazier from the House of the Ephebe at Pompeii.

621

apses, which have the appearance of the lower part of chimneys. Unfortunately, the surviving height of the walls means that it is not possible to say whether these open hearths continued in the same way up to a hole in the wall or the ceiling, or if *tubuli*, or an enclosed flue, turned them into proper chimneys. Whatever the case, it is not until the sixth century that chimneys definitely form a part of architecture.

The true innovation, as much in the technical domain as in that of comfort, came about at the end of the second or the beginning of the first century BC, with the appearance of heating on a *hypocaust* ('heating underneath'). The name points to a Greek origin, even if the Romans attributed it to a certain C. Sergius Orata, a contemporary of Sulla.[87] In fact, there are underground heating ducts dating to 300BC at the baths of Gortys, Olympia and Syracuse. The earliest hypocaust heating systems at Pompeii are found in both private houses and baths, which suggests that the method did not change much over the centuries.

Though the Stabian Baths at Pompeii were built in the course of the second century BC, the initial system was modified at the beginning of the following century, when the warm rooms and the hot rooms were fitted with hypocausts, just like the Forum Baths, erected after the setting up of the colony in 80BC. It is not, however, out of the question that some private systems, such as that in the House of the Centenary (IX,8,6), the House of Trebius Valens (III,2,1) or the House of the Labyrinth (VI,11,10) were laid out in the second half of the second century BC.

The basis of any heating system is, of course, a fire, the heat of which is made use of either by direct radiation or through the mediation of a containment or heated partition. This latter solution is the one adopted in the principle of hypocaust heating, which made it possible to distribute dry, healthy

622 A large bronze brazier, presented to the Forum Baths at Pompeii by M. Nigidius Vaccula, to warm the *tepidarium*.

623 A baker's oven at Pompeii (VI,2,6). The chimney has a terracotta flue buried in the masonry; this arrangement could clearly also be used for heating, although that purpose is not found here.

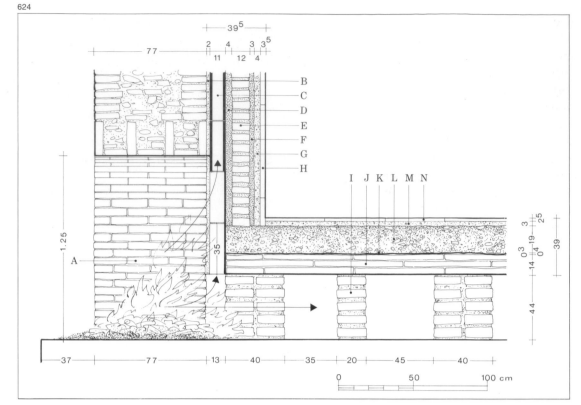

624

624 The Forum Baths at Ostia: a cross-section of the hypocaust of the *caldarium*, below the pool:

A furnace or *praefurnium*
B grey mortar
C *tubuli*
D mortar of broken tile fragments (*opus signinum*)
E bricks
F mortar of broken tile fragments
G grey mortar
H slabs of marble
I small column of bricks (below the pool, alternately single and double)
J *bipedales* bricks in three courses
K waterproof sheet of lead
L cement of coarse fragments of broken tiles
M grey mortar
N marble slabs.

625 Pool of the *caldarium* of the Forum Baths at Ostia (*c.*160). The furnace opened directly underneath it so that the tank received the greatest heat.

626 The kitchen of the Villa of Diomedes at Pompeii. On the right is the working surface where the fires were lit, with a small oven at the back. In the back wall is the mouth of the *praefurnium* heating the *caldarium* of the baths located just behind.

627 Small terracotta columns in the *caldarium* of the baths of the House of the Faun.

628 Hypocaust of a *caldarium* of the Baths of Baia (first century). The small columns were made up of terracotta elements, extended with bricks 20cm square. Height of the hypocaust cavity: 74cm; thickness of the floor: 14cm.

and efficient heating while resolving the problem of smoke and toxic gases.

The furnace, or *praefurnium* (Vitruvius V,10), was located under the floor in a ventilated service room designed for storing fuel (charcoal). It consisted of a simple opening in the wall, the width of which was dependent on the size of the hypocaust in service, with a metal door with a ventilation valve and usually an area in front on which the raked ashes could be piled up periodically (figs 624, 625). In large baths, these service rooms were laid out on the back or side façade and were provided with a tunnel to the outside for ease of supply (for instance, the Forum Baths and Baths of Neptune at Ostia, the Central Baths at Pompeii). In private houses the furnace was located, in most cases, in the kitchen (at Pompeii the villa of Diomedes [fig.626], House of Trebius Valens, House of the Faun), where both the fuel was stored and the fire kept. In some houses a bread oven was even built below the bath house and this was what heated the hypocaust (House of the Menander, I,10,4 and House of the Centenary, IX,8,6).

The heat from the *praefurnium* penetrated into the space occupying the entire basement of the room to be heated, the hypocaust (*hypocausis*), before going out through vertical ducts. The area of the hypocaust was not a single vaulted space, in the manner of an oven, but a space covered with a 'suspended' floor, the *suspensura*, supported on a large number of small columns, almost always made of square bricks approximately 20cm each side,

625

the axes of which are approximately 60cm apart, so that they could support large bricks measuring 2 feet square: *supraque laterculis bessalibus, pilae struantur: ita dispositae, uti bipedales tegulae possint supra esse conlocatae altitudinem autem pilae habeant pedes duo*: 'On top, small columns should be built made of bricks measuring two-thirds of a foot in such a way that bricks measuring two feet can be placed on them. These small columns should have a height of two feet' (Vitruvius V,10).[88]

The dimensions given in the *Ten Books* indeed correspond to those that have been recorded in systems using columns of square bricks; their height, however, ranges between 40 and 75cm. A variation sometimes occurs, taking the form of small cylindrical columns made by building up small circular bricks, finished off by one or more square bricks to hold the large covering bricks better.

In the old installations at Pompeii the small columns were made of ceramic elements, moulded in a single piece, forming hollow pillars with a footing at each end (baths of the House of the Faun, and of the House of Fabius Rufus). This had the advantage of providing standardization of hypocaust construction[89] (figs 627, 628). This method may have been discarded both because of decreased resistance to collapse, particularly

626

underneath large tanks where the small columns were usually doubled, and because of the greater ease of manufacture of small square bricks which could be put to multiple uses (fig.629).

Finally, there is the use, albeit more

627

628

629

629 A section through the hypocaust of the men's *tepidarium* in the Stabian Baths at Pompeii, with small columns of square bricks and thick mortar joints. The cavity wall is achieved by *tegulae mammatae*.
Height of the columns: 80cm; section: 20 x 20cm. Bricks of the *suspensura*: 60 x 60 x 5cm. Total thickness of the floor: 24cm. *Tegulae mammatae*: 53 x 53 x

630

crude, of columns made of small mono-liths cut in a heat-resistant stone; a spontaneous technique, with no geographical limits since small stone columns are found in south-west Gaul, at Vaison-la-Romaine, or at *Thuburbo Majus*.

Equally simple was the solution of replacing a hypocaust on small columns with heat ducts circulating under the floor from the furnace. Such arrangements, which have been found at the villa of Montmaurin[90] and

particularly at the villa of Lalonquette,[91] adopted a radiating design which distributed hot air most effectively, or alternatively made a random circuit from one room to another.

The surface for walking on, or *suspensura*, had a composite structure similar to that of all floors, the only difference being that it rested on the columns through the intermediary of one or more thicknesses of large bricks, two feet square, which acted as a base. There was a first layer of concrete made with fragments of broken tiles 15 to 20cm thick, then a thin layer of mortar on which was placed marble tiling or a mosaic. The total thickness of the *suspensura* ranged from 30 to 40cm, which, added to the small columns of 50cm, gave an average height to the whole thing of 80 to 90cm.

The plunge-pool in the hot rooms, situated in an exedra or totally occupying the end of a room, was always located over the opening of the furnace for maximum heat. Water-proofing, crucial in this situation, was sometimes reinforced, as at the Forum Baths at Ostia (*c*.160), by a sheet of lead the size of the tank, inserted between the large bricks of the base and the first layer of concrete.

The release of hot air and smoke was made use of to provide heating for the rooms through the walls; this is why,

631

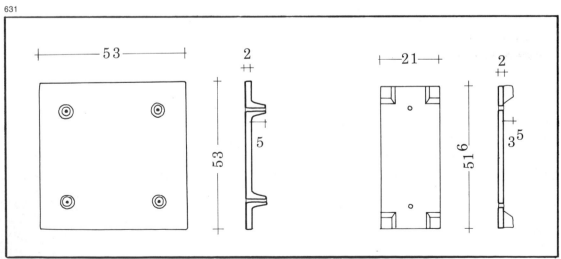

instead of putting in a chimney duct on the side against the furnace, even in the first systems, an empty space was left between the supporting wall and the facing. This space went up to the roof and sometimes went round the vaults; there were openings in it leading to the outside.

To ensure the maintenance of the external skin, the Romans came up with the idea of flat bricks, square or rectangular, with bosses in fours or fives, for this reason called *tegulae mammatae* (nippled tiles) (figs 630, 631). It is possible that these were first invented as insulation for painted walls in buildings subject to creeping damp, but this may perhaps be only a secondary usage. Whatever the case, such tiles were used in this way in the House of the Faun. In basement rooms in the House of Livy and the *domus Tiberiana* on the Palatine, double walls made with *tegulae mammatae*, without hypocausts, have been discovered, which therefore acted only as insulation.[92] This is also the use recommended by Vitruvius in his chapter devoted to the insulation of facings in damp places (VII,4,13).

However, the small projection of the bosses (approximately 5cm) and the fact that the cavity between the two walls was total did not favour a good draught of air, instead producing the effect well known in chimney-construction – the formation of turbulence preventing the hot air from rising, sometimes even causing it to reverse. To offset this disadvantage, *tubuli* were invented in the course of the first century AD. These are terracotta tubes of varying rectangular section (sections recorded: 8.5 × 13 to 14 × 24cm), that were joined together to form a flue. Some types of *tubuli* had lateral openings, to allow the passage of hot air from one set of tubing to another (fig.632). Placed against the length of the walls at the side of the first row of *bipedales* over the small columns, the

tubuli were attached to the wall by a layer of mortar and often anchored using metal T-cramps holding them in twos (figs 633, 634). They were then concealed by a layer of rendering, to which stucco, painting or marble veneer was applied. At one or more points of the vault or the upper part of the wall, were flue-openings providing a draught and allowing smoke and hot air to escape (fig.635).

630 Hollow wall designed to heat the *caldarium* in the House of Julia Felix at Pompeii (II,4) made up of *tegulae mammatae*, creating a cavity 7.5 to 8cm wide.

631 Two types of *tegulae mammatae* used in the Stabian Baths at Pompeii.

632 Heating *tubuli* at the Musée du Berry at Bourges. The grooves on the front were to aid the bonding of the mortar. The holes in the sides, found in many Gallo-Roman *tubuli*, if they were aligned, helped to channel smoke towards the exhaust ducts. This may also have improved the heating of the walls.

633 A wall faced entirely with *tubuli* at the Forum Baths in Ostia. Part of the facing also survives, showing the thickness of the rendering, which, like the floor of the *suspensura*, would have retained the heat.

634

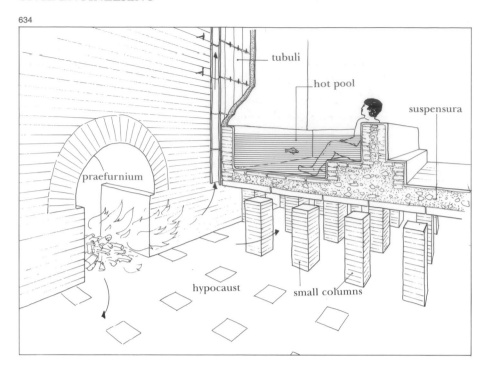

634   Heating system of the *caldarium* at the Central Baths at Pompeii.

635   A chimney to remove smoke, linking the cavity of the double wall with an opening at the spring of the vault. Another chimney opened symmetrically in the opposite wall. *Caldarium* at the House of Julia Felix, Pompeii, II,4.

The precise period in which *tubuli* appeared is difficult to establish, as the surviving heating systems, dating usually to the Imperial period, use only this method. At Pompeii, the Forum Baths and the Stabian Baths had been given their hypocaust heating at the beginning of the first century BC; however, though the first building is provided with *tegulae mammatae*, proving, like the

635

baths in private houses, that this method was then in use, the Stabian Baths have preserved *mammatae* in the men's *tepidarium* but have *tubuli* in the *caldarium*, repaired after 62. In the same way, the new Central Baths, unfinished in 79, are exclusively fitted out with *tubuli*. It is therefore possible to conclude that, as Vitruvius does not mention them,[93] the *tubuli* made their appearance in the first half of the first century.

Apart from heating rooms in houses and the hot rooms of baths, furnaces also provided a means of heating the water in these latter establishments. At the Stabian Baths, the *praefurnium* was installed in a space situated between the two sections – the men's and women's – in such a way as to form a direct supply to the *caldarium* of each part. In addition, above the furnace was a large metal tank, accompanied by two others indirectly exposed to the fire,[94] from which water flowed into the pools of the hot and warm rooms. Likewise, at the *villa rustica* of Boscoreale called 'la Pisanella', a cylindrical boiler made of lead and with a copper bottom was found in place above the hearth; it was connected by pipes with bronze taps to the water-tank and to the points where hot water was provided.

Whereas in southern towns such as Pompeii heating by hypocaust was limited to private and public baths, in more inclement climes like Gaul, the system formed an essential part of domestic comfort and could extend to the ground-floor dwelling rooms.

b   Bath construction projects

There is not the space here for establishing a chronological or geographical classification of bathing establishments, the development of their layout through time and the scale of the projects. Such an endeavour would be more appropriate in a work devoted to architectural theory and would divert attention away from this simple consideration of the techniques used. The authors of the publication on the Imperial Baths at Trier have partially accomplished the former task by comparing monuments not only in the Rhineland but also in Italy, North Africa and Gaul. Here discussion will be confined to the layout of the different parts which form the majority of these buildings, and their uses, with the help of some examples taken from ancient texts.

Even if practically nothing is left of the 170 baths in Rome, recorded in 33BC by Agrippa, this number alone is sufficient to illustrate how popular these establishments were by the first century AD. Agrippa himself was so aware of this that he first took control of the payment for public baths, then had built, between 25 and 19BC, the first large-scale baths that bore his name.[96] By the fourth century the number of baths had risen to about a thousand.[97]

It is noticeable that, although the arrangement of their facilities is logical, the baths built up to the first century AD still have a rather haphazard layout, without the slightest regard for a regular composition, either linear or symmetrical. The Baths of Pompeii, like those at Herculaneum, juxtapose rooms of different sizes which have often been converted without any attempt at achieving unity, either in the general design or in the façade (fig.636).

It was apparently in creating the Baths of Nero, in the reign of that emperor, that architects planned the first large-scale baths intentionally based on a symmetrical axis[98]; the foundations of these baths have been discovered between the Pantheon and the stadium of Domitian (Piazza Navona). The symmetrical plan was continued in the construction of the Baths of Titus, built on the remains of the Domus Aurea and completed in 80; the layout of these baths is known only from a survey by Palladio. The Baths of Trajan

covered those of Titus, and their considerable ruins confirm the existence of a trend that was to become standard – the rigidly geometric design of large-scale baths. However, although the new Central Baths at Pompeii, built after 62, display some innovations, such as enormous openings, the use of *tubuli* and alternating rectangular and semicircular exedrae in the *caldarium*, they still have a very free design, close to that of earlier buildings, without the least attempt at symmetry.

It seems, therefore, that the age of Vespasian was still, in the design of the baths, a transitional phase and that the stamp of Imperial building projects issued from Rome was not imposed uniformly until Trajan. From then on it is often sufficient to know only half a bath's building in relation to its axis to be able to work out the complete layout. Even if the general design differs each time, the compulsory balance, when

636 Plan of the Stabian Baths.
Men's baths:
1 *palaestra*
2 *apodyterium* - changing room for the *natatio*
3 small foot-washing basin
4 *natatio* - large, open-air cold pool
5 *apodyterium*
6 *frigidarium* - installed in the former dry sweating room
7 *tepidarium*
8 *caldarium*
9 *praefurnium* below the hot water pools, supplying both sections
10 office of the management of the establishment
11 latrines
12 secondary entrance and individual baths
13 well of the original establishment; water was extracted using a waterwheel.

Women's baths:
I entrance
II *apodyterium* with cold water tank
III *tepidarium*
IV *caldarium*
V-VI corridor and service room for storing goods and fuel. (After H. Eschebach.)

comparing layouts, produces a marked similarity, so that from the Baths of Trajan to the Imperial Baths of Trier in the fourth century there was little imagination at work (figs 637–638), even if the establishments in Ostia form a pleasant diversion.

It is necessary, however, to make a distinction between large official buildings, in which axiality is predominant, and more modest buildings such as the Central Baths at Pompeii, mentioned above. In the latter the composition remained less rigorous and a route is more noticeable than a geometric discipline; this consisted of access from one room to another following the principle: *apodyterium–frigidarium–tepidarium–caldarium*, and a return to the *apodyterium* following the same route (for instance, the Baths of Neptune at Ostia, Hadrianic).[99] This type is known, incorrectly, as the 'Pompeian type' because it conforms with the baths of that city, which is not necessarily its origin.

When Pliny,[100] a few years before the destruction of Pompeii, described the route the bathers took, he followed the traditional order, just as it was described before him by Martial;[101] and this was also the way the bathers of the Satyricon went.[102] In the large baths of the Imperial period the rooms not only followed on one after the other but also multiple access points (as at the Antonine Forum Baths, Ostia) meant the bathers did not have to retrace their steps; or, thanks to the symmetrical multiplication of the spaces, they could return to the *frigidarium* or the *apodyterium* via connecting rooms arranged around the central core.[103]

A description of, or a visit to, the Stabian Baths at Pompeii gives a clear idea of how a bathing establishment would have functioned. This one was already very ancient as it had been built in the second century BC, but had been reconditioned several times, notably shortly after 80 BC, and, of course, after the earthquake of AD 62.[104] The modest size of this establishment, the division into two and the specialized construction techniques, are perfectly representative of what baths in small towns were like.

The building is divided into two parts, men's and women's. The second, more modest, section had its entrance in a side street, via a relatively discreet door carrying on its lintel the word *Mulier* written in black (this was visible at the time of the discovery but has now disappeared). The main entrance, opening on to the *via Stabiana* at its widest section, gave access to the men's

637 The Great Southern Baths at Cuicul (Djemila, Algeria). The layout is rigidly symmetrical on an east – west axis; the *frigidarium* and *caldarium*, arranged on either side of the *tepidarium*, both have three surrounding pools. Second century. (After Krencker.)

637

0   10   20 m

cald.

c.   c.

tep.

c.   c.

frig.

latr.

ground floor

638 A symmetrical
arrangement: the Baths of Cluny
at Lutèce. (H = hot; C = cold;
c = courtyard; F = furnace.)

0   10   20 m

basement

639

639 The pool of the *frigidarium* in the public baths at the House of Julia Felix at Pompeii (II,4). There was in addition an enormous open-air *natatio* in the garden.

640 Stuccoed vault with light well in the *caldarium* of the men's baths in the Forum Baths at Pompeii.

641 Western façade of the Central Baths at Pompeii. Begun after 62, these baths with their numerous large openings would have been well lit, in great contrast to the previous establishments which were enclosed and dark. This included the *caldarium* (the three windows on the right). This structure remained unfinished, but it would have had glass panels.

642 *Caldarium* of the Baths of Buticosus at Ostia. The opening of the *praefurnium* can be seen at the back of the pool, which has lost its *tubuli* and its facing. The mosaic has a marine subject.

643 Cold pool (*natatio*) of the baths at Villards-d'Héria (Jura).

baths, arranged around a *palaestra*, an open space lined with porticoes, intended for sports and exercises (Vitruvius, V,11). These, or rather some of them, are briefly enumerated by Martial in an epigram addressed to a friend whom he accuses of physical laziness:[105] 'One never sees you preparing for the hot baths by playing tennis, or ball-games or rustic pelota, nor do you hit against a tree trunk with a blunt sword and you never leap around after the powdery ball'.[106] Wrestling, running and weight-training could be added to this list.

It is worth recalling that, while the Greeks considered sport to be, like the theatre, a healthy leisure activity practised for its own sake, with bathing being only secondary, in the case of the Romans the secondary was to become the main thing and sport nothing but an optional extra to the pleasures of the bath. The stadium was therefore always an exceptional building, that of Domitian in Rome being due to the personal taste of that emperor for the Olympic games. It was in the *palaestra* of the baths that the Romans could, if they so desired, move about a little and perspire in a different way from in the sweating room. At Pompeii, however, admittedly in a region that was more imbued with Hellenistic influence than Latium, two separate areas of the baths (the second having an enormous cold pool) were devoted to physical exercises:[107] the Samnite *Palaestra* and the Great *Palaestra* of the West. These two areas were in fact reserved for certain Pompeian youth groups who did various sports there, perhaps linked to paramilitary training.[108]

The *palaestra* of the Stabian Baths was lined on three sides by a portico, the fourth having a cold plunge pool in the middle, the *natatio*. In front of this was a changing room and a shallow basin for washing feet.

The bath building proper was entered on the opposite side, via an enormous hallway opening on to a large changing room, the *apodyterium*, where clothes were placed in small niches in the wall or given to a slave to look after, who took them into an adjoining waiting room. The visitor could then go into the dry sweating room, the *laconicum*, a small circular vaulted room heated to a high temperature by a special fire or, in earlier versions of the *laconicum*, by a brazier. After 80 the sweating room of the Stabian Baths was done away with and turned into a cold pool; by contrast, a *laconicum* (unfinished) was provided in the new Central Baths.

The temperature was certainly very considerable in the *laconicum* and could be regulated, if Vitruvius is to be believed, by an oculus opening at the top of the dome. This could be closed to a greater or lesser degree by an adjustable bronze disc.

The two main, large rooms were occupied by a warm bath room, the *tepidarium*, and a hot bath room, the *caldarium*, accessible by passing from one to the other. The second room had a basin of cold water, the *labrum*, for refreshing hands and face. In the *tepidarium* and the *caldarium* were one or more bathing pools (*alveus*) (one only at the Stabian Baths, two at the Central Baths) with steps inside and a bench for comfort (figs 639, 640, 641, 642).

640

641

642

Heat control depended on the proximity to, or the number of, furnaces which communicated with the hypocausts. In the simplest layout, the *praefurnium* opened under the *caldarium*. The hot air circulated under this, then passed through heating ducts from there to the hypocaust of the *tepidarium*, by which stage it had lost some of its heat. This is the system adopted at the Stabian Baths, with, in addition, a small furnace heating the tank in the warm room.

In the enormous Imperial baths there are a large number of rooms, sometimes on an upper floor. These have no special fittings and could only have been service rooms; they were probably used for related functions, such as massage, gymnastics, possibly dancing, music or reading, such as at the Baths of Caracalla where two libraries, alongside the tiers of the stadium on the south-west side, have been found, identifiable by the presence of a large number of niches.

Spas were developed around hot springs, the virtues of which were at first attributed by superstition to the high temperature, but were later defined more specifically. These had arrangements similar to those of ordinary baths, the only difference being that the water, instead of being carried by an aqueduct and heated artificially, was captured on the spot (as can still be seen at Vichy, *Aquae Calidae*) and used at its natural temperature. In

Gaul the Romans simply created monuments out of a number of sites, known already to the Gauls who regarded them as temples with prophylactic and curative properties, a double function that was to be maintained throughout the period of the Empire[109] (fig.643). It is almost certain that nearly all the spas known today were frequented in the Roman period.[110]

643

3 Roads and public works

a Road structure

The *via Appia* has the reputation, not unfounded, of being the oldest Roman road with an organized and systematic layout. In fact, though it was in effect laid out and built on the initiative of the Censor Appius Claudius after 312BC,[111] other routes had preceded it, such as the *via Salaria*[112] or the *via Tiberina*, both of which followed the valley of the Tiber.

However, unlike these two roads, whose winding routes mark the stages in the occupation of Latium, the *via Appia* truly represents, practically, politically and technically, the prototype for the vast Roman road network in the Imperial period (fig.644).

Politically, there is no doubt that Rome, by linking the city to Campania, wished to have at its disposal a permanent access road that bad weather would not put out of use, in order to convey troops as directly as possible to the south, which had a tendency to independence but was rich, well-populated and near to the Greek world. The declaration of the second Samnite War in 326BC[113] (the fighting

continued until 304) made it clear to Appius Claudius Caecus that it was indispensable to create this link which would usher in, not an alliance with a Romano-Capuan state, but the materialization of a Roman state embodying Latin dominance over the peoples of the territory crossed: Aequi, Volsci, Auronci, Osci and Samnites.

The strategic role of roads was rapidly eclipsed within the peninsula itself but persisted in the areas of Imperial conquest, where roads acquired a key economic importance. This developed to such a degree that a number of roads were laid out by the legions themselves, starting with the roads of Gaul, planned under the supervision of Agrippa between 16 and 13BC. In addition, the army in the colonies not only planned the roads and provided for their construction, but also plotted the centuriations (see Chapter 1).

Outside the periods and the territories of conquest, Rome had at its disposal an administration that, as Cicero informs us, was placed under the responsibility of the *Censores*,[114] but in the Imperial period, particularly after Domitian, it was the emperor who made the decisions about the building of roads and large public works.

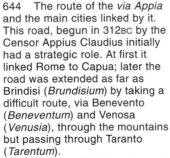

644   The route of the *via Appia* and the main cities linked by it. This road, begun in 312BC by the Censor Appius Claudius initially had a strategic role. At first it linked Rome to Capua; later the road was extended as far as Brindisi (*Brundisium*) by taking a difficult route, via Benevento (*Beneventum*) and Venosa (*Venusia*), through the mountains but passing through Taranto (*Tarentum*).

In the time of Trajan a second, flatter route was laid out from Benevento to the Adriatic coast, making it possible to shorten slightly the time taken for the journey.

644

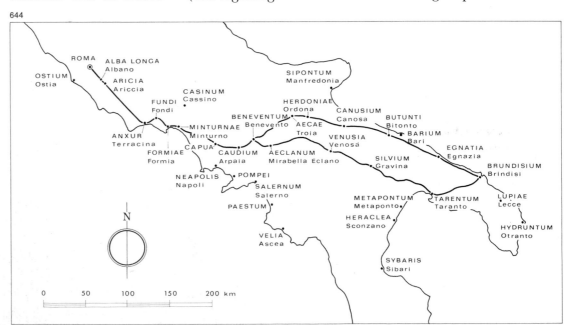

Depending on their importance, that is the route covered, the roads, just as today, were classified in an order that is known through an administrative document of the first century, drawn up by the geometer Siculus Flaccus:[115]

1 Public roads, *viae publicae*, built at the expense of the State and bearing the name of the builder.
2 Strategic roads, *viae militares*, built by and at the expense of the army; they became public roads.
3 Local roads, *actus*, built and maintained by the *pagi*.
4 Private roads, *privatae*, built and maintained by owners within their land.

The picture, so familiar and romantic, of the *via Appia* leaving Rome lined with tombs, shaded by pines and cypresses and with the roadway paved with broad lava flagstones, should not be viewed as typical of all Roman roads, nor even of the whole length of that most celebrated route (fig.645). The structure of the roadway, even though it was always carefully made, was not necessarily finished with that impressive paving that is particularly suitable for city streets. The sections laid down by the Romans generally have the following structure:

– on natural ground that had been levelled or dug in a wide trench, was placed a layer of stones laid on end, in rows. This solidified the base while aiding drainage. This is the *statumen*, suitable for the foundations of any wall or floor;
– this was followed by a thick layer of sand, or gravel and sand, sometimes mixed with clay, that can be incorporated into the *rudus*;
– a surface, usually made up of compacted pebbles, but sometimes slabs of hard stone, was laid in a curved profile. The total thickness of the roadway and its prepared base could reach 1 to 1.5m;

– at the sides, the roads were often defined by kerb stones and lined with ditches collecting rainwater running off the roadway and preventing water streaming on to it.[116]

Lime mortar has not been mentioned in the constitution of these different layers and its use is only very rarely in evidence.[117] It is therefore necessary to forget the images that have been in circulation for far too long, arising from a misinterpretation of Vitruvius and likening roadways to the floor surfaces described by that author. The passage that A. Léger devotes to the building of Roman roads and the pictures illustrating it,[118] one of the sources of this error, must be firmly dismissed.

In 1913 public works carried out in the Pontine region necessitated cutting a section through the *via Appia* to a considerable depth. The engineer in charge of the work, Scaccia, had the bright idea of drawing and describing

645 The *via Appia* leaving Rome, near the Villa of the Quintilii.

645

the structure of the ancient road thus exposed.[119] He distinguished a first layer, 1m thick, of earth and gravel, originating from the neighbouring mountain region, its width defined along the edges by two lines of large stones. On top of this was a thinner layer of gravel and crushed limestone, its width likewise defined by two rows, this time closer together, of large stones, which formed the original roadway of Appius Claudius. On top of this can be seen several layers of resurfacing of the same type, corresponding to the successive repairs carried out up to the third century.

Three recent trial sections[120] have confirmed the use of compacted added material and the absence of lime mortar in the substructure of roads.

1 Between 38 and 39km along the *via Flamina*, a section revealed a compact layer, 20cm thick, of clay and pebbles, rammed into the natural ground that had been levelled. On top of this was another layer, also 20cm thick, of pebbles and stones mixed with clay, then the surface of paving stones.

2 On the *via Appia*, 4.5km before Itri (between Fondi and Formia), a first layer of sand was covered with a thickness of crushed limestone into which slabs of lava 25 to 40cm were fixed.

3 On the *via Aurelia*, near Civitavecchia, the first layer was made up of a stratum of compacted pieces of tufa 40cm thick; next came a layer of stones and gravel also 40cm thick, and then slabs of lava.

Surfacing with paving stones does not seem to have been in use before the beginning of the second century BC. In the absence of archaeological evidence (test pits under the roads are disappointingly unproductive as regards datable material) a text of Livy[121] gives precise information that in 174BC roads had to be paved in towns but simply surfaced with sand or pebbles on country sections. The oldest paving known is that of the *via Appia* laid in 296BC, between the Porta Capena and the Temple of Mars (just beyond the Aurelian Wall) – a very short stretch (1 Roman mile).[122] The paving was extended at the beginning of the second century BC as far as Bovillae,[123] but this surfacing still had to be completed by the time of Nerva, then Trajan, and, even later; a milestone from southern Latium, shows that in the time of Caracalla (212-17) paving was laid on the section from Terracina to Formia. Among this work must have been simple repairs to the roadway, replacing a worn or displaced surface, but it is not certain that the whole length of the *via Appia* (Rome–Terracina–Capua–Benevento–Brindisi), completed in the period of the Gracchi (131-121BC), was ever systematically paved.

When building the *via Appia* through the Pontine region the Roman engineers were forced to place the roadway on a large embankment, repaired on several occasions, called *limes* or *agger*, terms also used in connection with earthwork defences. When such a solution was not feasible, due to lack of materials, the Romans, perhaps following local practice, based the roadway on a wooden structure, forming a 'causeway'. On this they placed stone slabs bonded with clay and then a layer of compressed gravel and pebbles.

646 The structure of the *via Mansuerisca* where it crosses the marshy area of the Hautes-Fagnes (Belgium). Two parallel rows of timbers, approximately 2m apart, were laid on regularly-spaced cross-pieces, 'nailed' into the ground with stakes. These supported a roadway made up of poles, limestone slabs, then gravel and compressed pebbles. (After J. Mertens, *Industrie*, Oct. 1955, p.39.)

646
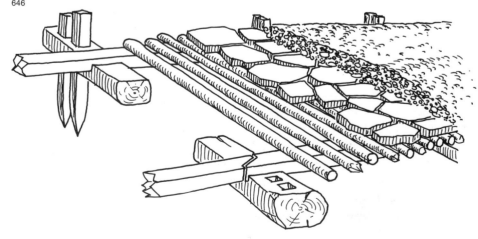

Arrangements of this type have been discovered on the *via Mansuerisca*[124] where it crosses the marshes of Haute-Fagne (fig.646), in the Rhine valley near Kembs and in the marshes of the Ems and the Hunse.

The ruts visible in the paving of the streets and roads correspond to the tracks of cart wheels and their distance apart (measured from axle to axle) may give an idea of the standardization of the distances between wheels. However, although an average of roughly 1.3m has been arrived at, the wide variations mean that a precise typology cannot be established. While it is evident that in the streets and on flat ground the ruts were formed naturally by the repeated passage of carts, it seems likely that in mountainous and coastal stretches, they were cut deliberately, to guide the vehicles and prevent them leaving the road (fig.647).

The width of a roadway varied according to its importance and the nature of the terrain; though it is not possible to distinguish standard sizes laid down by official prescriptions. The minimum dimensions, for secondary roads, had to allow for the passage of a chariot, or, better still, the passing of two vehicles, of which the minimum size can be estimated at 1.5m. It is probable, however, that some mountain roads were too narrow (less than 3m) and had slopes too steep (over 15 per cent) for carts and were only used by beasts of burden.

The following table giving some widths recorded in Italy illustrates the diversity:

Diversion of the *via Appia*[125]
   at Ponte di Mele 2.4m
Lanuvina Ardeatina near
   Lanuvio 2.6m
Via Aurelia from Pisa to Vada 2.8m
Via Tiburtina at Casale dei
   Cavallari 3.5m
Via Flaminia at Carsulae 3.8m
Via Cassia at Ponte Nicolao 4m

647

Coast road at Sperlonga 4m
Via Labicana at Tor Pignattara ... 4m
Via Praenestina at Gabii 4.3m
Via Bovillae before Bovillae 4.5m
Via Labicana after Tor
   Pignattara 4.7m
Via Flaminia near Treia 5.2m
Via Salaria at Antrodoco 7.5m

In towns, the width of the streets similarly varied, although there was some standardization when the town planning conformed to a systematic layout (fig.648).

At Pompeii the main roads have an approximately uniform carriageway width (4m) and distance from wall to wall (8m), as can be seen on the via dell'Abbondanza, the via di Stabia, the via di Nola and the via della Fortuna (with variations of around 20cm). The remaining 4m is divided, generally unequally, between the two pavements, *margines* or *crepidines*. This width is

647 The road, surfaced with limestone paving stones, climbing the hill at *Ambrussum*, near Gallargues (Gard). The wheel-ruts have worn deep into the surface of the road without dislodging it, despite the small size of the paving stones – proof of the quality of the laying. First century.

648

649

increased in the via di Mercurio, which is 9m wide in total, 4.5m for the roadway; and the widening of the via dell'Abbondanza in front of the Stabian Baths reaches 13m in total, with 9m of roadway. For secondary roads and alleys, some of which are not paved, the total widths vary between 2 and 4m (figs 649, 650, 651, 652).

At Paestum, comparable dimensions can be found at the crossroads near the forum, with a road width for the *cardo* of 5.3m and for the passage at right-angles with it, 4.8m, the pavements being between 2 and 2.6m. The roadways vary between 4 and 5m wide at Ostia, at Vaison (4.5m), at Timgad (5m) and in Rome on the via Biberatica. This seems to be an approximate unit, at least for commercial streets and principal arteries, corresponding to traffic requirements. The width from wall to wall is more subject to variation, due to expropriation for buildings and whether or not there is a portico on to the pavement, but is basically between 8 and 9m (in the main streets), with simple pavements, and can reach or exceed 12m where there is a portico (Vaison, Timgad, Tipasa).

b Public works

Parallels can easily be drawn between the civil engineering of roads and that of aqueducts, the aim being to overcome the same natural obstacles – both cross valleys and tunnel under mountains. A road, however, does not have to keep to a gentle incline and can cross a wide valley without a viaduct or siphon; and an average hill does not necessarily present an obstruction to be tunnelled through or bypassed. The Roman engineers always endeavoured to use the simplest and most economical means, while departing as little as possible from a straight line.

650

648 The via Biberatica in Rome, paved with lava, lined with pavements and shops, with commercial premises above, forming the Markets of Trajan.

649 A main commercial street at Pompeii, the via dell'Abbondanza, looking east.

650 Reconstruction of the via dell'Abbondanza from the same position as fig.649.

651 Back street without shops at Pompeii, region VII.

652 Detail of the via della Fortuna at Pompeii. The main streets of the city were paved with lava and edged by pavements. The lack of a sewer network to drain rainwater, household water and the water from fountains from the streets, meant that they could only be used by beasts of burden or draught animals and necessitated the placing of stepping stones across the road for pedestrians. There was room on this commercial street, 3.8m wide, for two vehicles to pass one another, as indicated by the worn furrows, partioularly noticeable between the three stones.

651

652

653

653 A particularly difficult stretch of the *via Flacca* at Punta di Trepani near Sperlonga (southern Latium), along a sea cliff. The retaining wall (*c.*200BC) is made of Cyclopean stone blocks. The entrance to the tunnel is visible in the rock wall at the back.

series of markers in feet, the last being CXX. Further south the coast road from Sperlonga to Formia, called the *via Flacca*,[127] overhangs the sea in a landscape of tortuous cliffs and cuts its way along faces that are almost vertical (fig.653).

The work is no less spectacular in crossing mountains, for instance the stretch of the *via Salaria* in the gorges of Antrodoco, at the start of the Abruzzi, or the Donnaz cutting in the Val d'Aosta.

Sometimes, instead of going round or tunnelling through an obstacle, a cutting is made, particularly if the rock is soft, as for example the tufa of Latium. Examples can be seen at Santa Maria di Cavamonte (near Palestrina) or on the *via Consolare Campana* at the place called 'Cupa Orlando'.

The tunnel is the ultimate solution when the above cannot be used, and tunnels can be found in succession on the same stretch of road. The *via Flacca*, for example, collides with a sudden rocky spur at the place called 'Punta da Trepani'. This is traversed by a tunnel roughly 40m long and 3m wide at its narrowest point; its height and original profile have, however, been distorted by rock falls.[128]

Better preserved and still in use, the tunnel of Furbo on the *via Flaminia*, between Cagli and Fossombrone, also begins by cutting into the rock face and then penetrates the rock for a length of 38m. An inscription provides the information that Vespasian had the work carried out, completed in 76.

Also the 'grottoes' of the Phlegrean area to the north of Naples should be mentioned, among which the best-known is the large tunnel that was dug through the hill of Vomero which cut Naples off from Pozzuoli, known as the *crypta Neapolitana*. It was Cocceius, one of Augustus' architects,[129] who, according to Strabo, was the creator of this impressive tunnel, 705m long, on average 4m wide and 5m high, and

The most basic way of overcoming an obstacle, though not always the easiest, is to cut a passage through the rock for the route. This is the work most often carried out in mountainous regions or steep coasts. As far as possible, the rock was cut into on one side only, so forming a corniche. One of the most impressive works of this kind is at the southern exit of Terracina, where the *via Appia* goes along the foot of a vertical wall that has been cut into for a height of 36m, on which can be read a

provided with light-wells.[130] Besides Strabo, Seneca also speaks of this tunnel in a letter to Lucilius,[131] in which he criticizes the formidable work:

Nothing longer than this tunnel, nothing gloomier than the torches one is offered [they were sold at the entrance to the tunnel], not because one can see by them in darkness, but because one can see the darkness by them. In any case, even if you have some light, the dust takes it away from you and this dust, troublesome enough outside, inside swirls upon itself, is trapped and falls on those who kicked it up.

This brief description illustrates that this road between two highly-populated ports, as Naples and Pozzuoli were by this time, and beyond them all the built-up areas adjoining these coastal towns, overcame an intimidating obstacle, an achievement which in itself justified the road's existence. The very uneven terrain of the coast between Naples and Cuma represented a sizeable obstacle to communications; fortunately, the soft nature of the volcanic tufa made it easy to bore other connecting tunnels, two of which go from Lake Averno: the 'Grotto of the Sibyl' and the 'Grotto of Cocceius'. The first linked the facilities of Lake Averno to those of Lake Lucrino, both connected to each other and to the sea (fig.654), while the second, nearly 1000m long, made it possible to shorten considerably journeys to Cuma.[132]

Corniche roads or those crossing small depressions, and those along a coast or leading up to a bridge, had a carriageway supported by an embankment held up on one or both sides by a retaining wall. This was a common type of road construction and several examples of different sizes can be found along the *via Appia*. The first encountered consists of a long embankment, of which 200m remain today in a good state of preservation. This fine

654

construction, called the 'viadotto di valle Ariccia', near the place of the same name,[133] is pierced by two arches to allow the passage of run-off water. It was probably erected in the period of the last great public works and repairs of the Gracchi, and was restored in the Augustan period. It is built of rectangular stone blocks with alternate courses of stretchers and headers (fig.655).

Further along, level with Lanuvio, the Appian Way is retained by a wall of stone blocks with buttresses, while another identical wall was built against the foot of the slope above the road. Between Terracina and Fondi, where the road descends the hillside, there is a strong retaining wall, built with rusticated blocks of stone, variously dressed – rectangular, polygonal or trapezoidal. By contrast, another embankment between Fondi and Itri has a retaining wall along one side of regular rectangular stone blocks which is in places preserved up to 4m high.

The *via Salaria*, where it crosses the gorges of Antrodoco, is not only cut into the rock but also embanked with a retaining wall of polygonal stone blocks. The coast road of Sperlonga,

654 The 'grotto of the Sibyl' – a tunnel dug into the volcanic tufa in the Augustan period, between Lake Lucrino and Lake Averno. This allowed a rapid passage for pedestrians and vehicles between the facilities at these two stretches of water, themselves connected with each other and with the sea by an enormous canal, now filled in. Length of the tunnel: 200m; width: 3.8 to 4m; height: 4 to 4.2m.

655   The viaduct of Valle Ariccia on the *via Appia*, at the foot of the Castelli Romani. In fact this does not cross a dip but is an embankment, 200m long, allowing the ascent of a hill with a steep incline. The imposing construction has now almost disappeared under the undergrowth. Second half of the second century BC.

656   An embankment on the *via Flaminia*, approaching a hill near Civita Castellana, known as the 'Muro del Peccato'. The work on this began in 220BC. This large construction, similar to the viaduct of Valle Ariccia, indicates a preference for a straight course rather than bends, which allow a gentler incline, because of the appreciable shortening of the distance covered.

655

for almost the whole of its uneven course, is built on a Cyclopean wall that accentuates the roughness of the natural environment and the finished work.

The great embankment of the *via Flaminia* near Civita Castellana ('il Muro del Peccato'), like the viaduct of the Valle Ariccia mentioned above, made it possible to ascend an abrupt slope by means of a large embankment and a roadway which follow the incline. The sizeable embankment is faced with rectangular stone blocks in alternate courses of stretchers and headers of the local tufa. Here, as on the *via Appia*, it is noticeable that the courses are not horizontal, but follow the line of the slope (fig.656).

Bridges, for roads as much as for aqueducts, represent the most spectacular construction works. They are also the most significant because of the place they occupy in a landscape or an urban environment and because many of those that have survived are still in use today.

The earliest bridges of wood, and indeed the numerous examples using this material of all ages, have survived only in two pictorial representations. The first, on Trajan's Column, shows the bridge on the Danube built by the legion in 104 (fig.657); the second is a mosaic of the Forum on the Piazzale della Corporazioni at Ostia, showing a boat bridge on the Rhône at Arles. Written references reveal the existence of some others, such as the *pons Sublicius* which the Romans, scrupulously respectful, rebuilt of wood on several occasions;[134] the *pons Aemilius*, the first stone bridge in Rome whose pillars, built in 179, had only a wooden superstructure until arches were built in 142; and the bridge on the Rhine created by Julius Caesar's legions.[135]

656

657

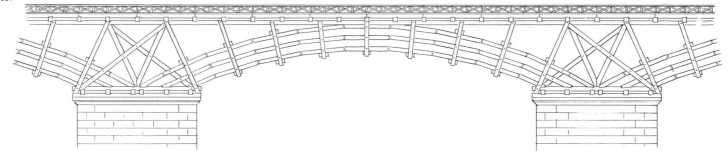

Fortunately, the numerous surviving stone bridges allow the technical aspects of these structures to be worked out. The construction of the foundations and the piers, as today, represented the most difficult task. In Mediterranean regions watercourses are often nearly or completely dry for several months, and so the work was identical to that on a land site. If the water level was always high, it was necessary to use a coffer-dam, that is, to put in place a watertight palisade cutting off the surface area needed to establish a pillar. It is again Vitruvius who supplies information on the method of installing such a dam to allow maritime or riverine construction work (V,12). He distinguishes two methods:

1 A coffer-dam constructed with wooden posts held together by clamps (the translation is uncertain but presumably the wooden pieces are either double thickness fitted together or are jointed and pegged). A cement bonded with mortar of pozzolana[136] is poured into the space thus made, until it forces out the water and reaches the top of the framework; this is allowed to dry and then the construction is continued upwards.

2 A caisson is constructed with a double wall of posts, with reed sacks containing clay piled up between the walls to make a watertight dam. Once this is finished, the water is emptied from the caisson using a lifting machine (X,4 and X,6) until the base is exposed, on which work can then begin. Depending on the nature of the base encountered, the builders could make do with simple coursing on the rock, or dig down to rock, or again drive in piles on which the bottom of the foundations could rest.

The Roman engineers were fully aware of the effects of erosion by the current, of the force it exerted on the pillars and the damage that tree trunks carried down by floods could cause, and they took three appropriate measures to combat these dangers.

1 In order to reduce the surface area exposed to the current, they tried to keep the number of piers, and thus the number of arches, as low as possible. This quickly led them to build quite large openings: 22m for the bridge of la porta Cappuccina at Ascoli Piceno; 24.5m for the Fabrician Bridge in Rome, in 62BC; 27.5m for the bridge of Alcantara in Spain, in AD 105; 32m for the bridge of Narni, in the Augustan period. Reducing the number of arches and the exclusive use of the semicircular arch involved a considerable height of superstructure. This sometimes required the provision of a hog's back outline or an embankment rising out of the bank.[137] This drawback disappeared over banked-up watercourses where a single arch was often all that was necessary. Examples include Ascoli Piceno, Ponte Amato (fig.658) on the Praenestina, the bridge of la Catena at Cori, the bridge of Vaison, and the 'Pondel' of Aymaville in the Val d'Aosta.

657 Reconstruction of the bridge over the Danube from the relief on Trajan's Column. (After A. Choisy.)

658

659

658 The Ponte Amato, on the *via Praenestina*, below Gallicano. On each side of this single-arched bridge is a large stone mass to avoid a fall in the level of the roadway.

659 The Pont Julien, over the Coulon, near Apt (Vaucluse); 68m long, it has preserved its three arches (here the central arch and the hog's back are visible); each pillar has a flood-opening through it. Augustan period.

2 To limit the direct force of the water on the lower part of a pillar, the pier had an upstream cut-water to reduce the power of the current and a downstream cut-water to counteract erosion by turbulence.

3 As the pier separating two arches was in danger of forming a dam against the flood waters, it had a small arch cut through it, depending on the estimated height of the water. This formed a safety outlet to prevent the construc-

tion being submerged or thrown down (fig.659).

Better than a list of examples, the Fabrician Bridge illustrates these various safety measures since all of them were used successfully in the struggle against the annual raging of the Tiber (fig.660).[138]

The straightforward crossing of a watercourse did not always satisfy the Romans. The engineers, to produce a prestigious piece of work as much as to make the route easier, did not hesitate to span a depression, sometimes an actual valley, so that the road, like the course of an aqueduct, remained on the same level. It is possible to see both the development in thinking and the appearance of new requirements in a bridge at a point where the *via Praenestina* just before Gabii crosses a small valley drained by quite a modest watercourse.[139] Here, a small bridge with a single arch built in the second century BC made it possible for the route to get over the obstacle at the bottom of the depression, and the roadway, on both sides, was quite steeply inclined in order to reach the construction. Around 100BC, a period of great development at the Temple of Praeneste, it was decided to modernize this route by spanning the obstacle completely, so that the road remained on the same level. This was achieved by the construction of a large viaduct with seven arches, the 'Ponte di Nona', 125m long and 16m high, over which the modern road still passes (fig.661).[140]

This construction, indisputably the oldest of the great Roman viaducts, was followed by other comparable structures that have fortunately survived. There are, for example: the Milvian Bridge with six arches, built in 109BC; the Augustan bridge on the *via Aemilia* at Rimini, whose five arches are separated by spandrels decorated with pediment niches; the bridge of Porto Torres in Sardinia (seven arches, 113m

long); the impressive bridge built in 106 by Trajan, the six arches of which span the Tagus at Alcantara in Spain to a length of 188m; or again the 'Pont-Ambroix' spanning the valley of the Vidourle at Ambrussum (Hérault) with at least nine arches, of which only one has survived the violent floods of the watercourse (the massive size of the pillars and the inadequate size of the flood-holes acted against the preservation of the construction[141]) (fig.662).

All these viaducts have a masonry mass faced with stone blocks, which is generally the case for this type of construction. However, the viaduct of Sessa Aurunca or 'Ponte degli Aurunci'[142], 170m long with 21 arches, has masonry carefully faced with brick.[143] An inscription, found at Sessa, mentions a road built by Hadrian for the Suessani and so this work, with its distinctive construction techniques, can be attributed to that emperor. The

660   The *Pons Fabricius* built in 62BC to connect the Isola Tiberina to the *Forum Boarium*. The arch openings are 24.5m wide.

661   The Ponte di Nona on the *via Praenestina* at the ninth mile after leaving Rome. Length: 125m; height: 16m; *c.*100BC.

662

663

662   The surviving arch of the beautiful bridge of *Ambrussum* crossing the Vidourle. On the sides of the arch the supporting corbels of the centring are visible, and, in the spandrels, the modest flood-openings. The force of the water defeated the construction, despite its mass and the cut-waters on the piers protecting the pillars. Julio-Claudian period.

663   A crossing of ways on two levels: the Arco Felice on the *via Domitiana*. To avoid a long detour of Monte Grillo, Domitian's engineers cut a deep trench through the hill (the 'Montagna spaccata'), allowing the rapid passage between Pozzuoli and Cuma on the new road. However, another road went along the crest of the hill, and so a short viaduct, 20m high, with a single arch and an upper level relieved by arches, was built to allow the route to continue. Opening: 6.2m wide; passage-way 17.65m long.

short viaduct of the Arco Felice was also built of masonry faced with brick; this carried a road across the *via Domitiana* near Cuma (fig.663).

The monumental nature of the bridges and the fact that they were obligatory points of passage, in the same way as the entrances to cities, meant that they were sometimes thought worth completing with one or more triumphal arches. This perhaps corresponded originally to the usual position of bridges at the entrance of towns situated on rivers.[144]

The Flavian Bridge near Saint-Chamas still has its two arches, positioned at the approaches, in line with the design found on the mosaic at Ostia already mentioned. At Alcantara an arch divides the bridge in the middle and at Saintes one formed a monumental entrance on the bank of the Charente.[145]

c Taverns and roadside facilities

Along with the road came also the necessity for services that were indispensable to travellers – the taverns, *tabernae*, where people could find food and drink and shelter for the night, for themselves and possibly for their mounts. These establishments tended to be set up everywhere where a stop or a rest was imposed by the topography, for instance at a ford, a pass, a watering-stop, the edge of a forest or of a deserted area, or the entrance to a town. The creation by Augustus of an official courier system, the *cursus publicus*,[146] intended to keep Rome informed of what was happening in each province, led to the formation of official roadside facilities, the *mansiones*, or inns, and the *mutationes*, for fresh mounts. The beneficiaries of these had to be bearers of the Imperial seal[147] or of tokens, the *tesserae hospitales* that served as payment for lodging.

These isolated buildings did not outlast the ravages of the early Middle Ages and have disappeared. Some were transformed into strongholds, such as the *castellum* of Jublains (Mayenne)[148] or else have become settlements. There are texts which give evidence for their existence, but without mentioning precisely how common they were – this must have varied considerably according to the nature of the country-side. Comparison with the distribution of the caravanserai in Turkey, or the coaching stops of the eighteenth and nineteenth centuries, suggests that the distance separating the ancient wayside facilities varied between 10 and 40km, depending on the topography. One of the most interesting statistical documents is the itinerary of a traveller, anonymous but conscientious, who travelled in 333 to Jerusalem and noted in his *Itinerarium Burdigalense sive Hierosolymitanum*, for the stretch from Bordeaux to Arles: 30 *mutationes*, 11 *mansiones* and 371 Roman miles covered (550km),[149] i.e. an average distance of approximately 18km between *mutationes*, on a relatively rough route.

It is worth remembering that the distances recorded on the road markers were counted in paces (*passus*) or in miles. The pace, in reality a double pace, was equivalent to 5 feet, or 1.48m and there were 1000 in a mile (hence its name), or 1480m. In Gaul, particularly in the north of Narbonensis, distances were counted in leagues, as the inscriptions of the milestones indicate and as mentioned in the 'Peutinger Table' and by Ammianus Marcellinus,[150] making it clear that this unit of distance took effect from Lyon: *usque hic leugas*.[151] The regional differences do not allow a strictly defined unit, despite Imperial planning, and the Gallic league varied between 2200 and 2475m.

One of the rare architectural remains of what was perhaps a roadside resthouse is visible at the western entrance to the village of Thésée (Loir-et-Cher), where there is a complex of buildings grouped around a courtyard. These are made up of service buildings (inn, stables?) and a large rectangular monument, 13.5 × 38m (already mentioned in relation to *opus spicatum*) perhaps used for commercial or judicial meetings, or simply as a store for wheat and fodder.

Finally, a chapter on Roman roads would not be complete without mentioning two sources, admittedly marginal to architecture but with some useful indications relating to it: the Antonine Itinerary and the 'Peutinger Table'.

The first, the *Itinerarium Antonini Augusti*, is a road guide, without maps, giving routes by a list of *mansiones* and their distances. It seems that the original document was drawn up in the period of Caracalla (M. Aurelius Antoninus, in power from 212 to 217) and completed at the end of the third century.

The second, more famous source, is a drawn document, not a map in the topographical sense of the term, but showing roads along which geographical references are given sequentially (fig.664). This document[152] is named after its oldest known owner, Conrad Peutinger, a citizen of Augsburg, who obtained it in 1508. It is a medieval copy on parchment (measuring 0.34 × 6.8m) of a document that was poorly dated owing to successive compilations and additions which, based on the original document or documents, resulted in the final design.[153] Thus there are references to Herculaneum, Pompeii and Stabiae, which disappeared in 79, and some towns are given their Latin place names from the Early Empire, such as *Avaricum*, which became Bourges in the Later Empire, taking the name of the people who lived there (the *Bituriges*) in line with a common nationalist reaction. Also, in the site of

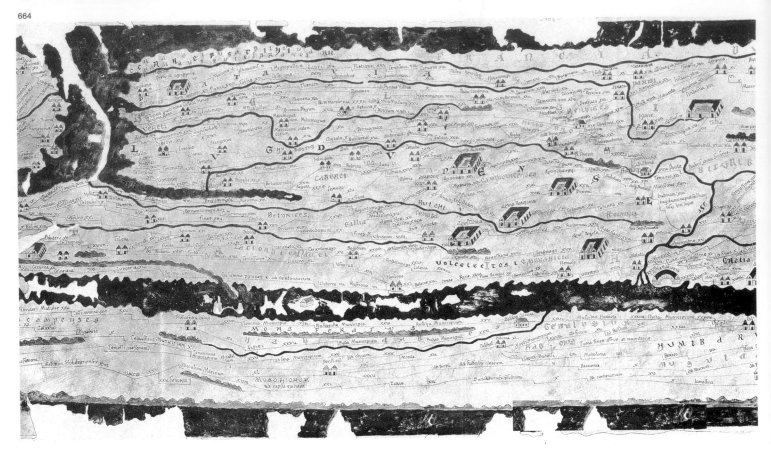

664   An extract from the 'Peutinger Table', showing Gaul.

Rome, there is an illustration showing St Peter's, Gaul is called Francia and Byzantium is called Constantinople.

On it are shown the names of towns,[154] the names of peoples, waterways, lakes, seas, some mountains, with individual illustrations indicating fortified towns, bathing places, temples, lighthouses, ports and perhaps *mansiones*. However, the typological attributions of A. and M. Levi should be treated with caution, as there are numerous possible explanations in relation to the archaeological reality (the 'turni towers' and the 'temples' could be attributed to many places).

11
DOMESTIC AND COMMERCIAL ARCHITECTURE

Although a chapter on building projects and architectural practice forms a diversion from the straightforward explanation of techniques, it seems useful to turn to the richest and liveliest architecture, in this case the buildings of everyday life, for the most numerous and varied applications of the categories previously covered.

The microcosmic design of the *domus*, managing to capture and re-create in the heart of towns (at least in Campania) practically everything that constitutes natural decoration and the monumental environment, but in miniature, provides examples of all the various construction types. It is not necessary to visit the enormous villas, that of Hadrian being the pinnacle, to become aware of this – the modest dwellings of Octavius Quartio and Trebius Valens at Pompeii amply illustrate this assertion.

As for artisans and traders, they often require very characteristic buildings (fullers, dyers, bakers) and the description of these should take account of the important position they occupied in towns.

1 The *domus* (Pompeian)

In provincial towns the urban family house, the *domus*, at times constituted the main domestic architecture. Such a situation cannot represent an especially privileged position when it is considered that the only towns where communal dwellings have been discovered are the cities of Rome and Ostia. However, the considerable expansion and modification of the towns of Europe over twenty centuries have meant that very little Roman domestic architecture survives except for cellars and ground floors – the upper parts are totally lost. The Campanian model is here absolutely dominant and, even though other Italian, Gaulish and North African towns have urban sites where houses are plentiful, apart from some local exceptions such as the underground dwellings of *Bulla Regia* (fig.665), the *domus pompeiana* displays such a wealth of information that it has come to represent the Roman urban house, from the Republican period up to the reign of Titus (fig.666).

The absence of large buildings within the walls of Pompeii is very noticeable – the highest remaining dwelling (in I,4,28) consists of two storeys above the ground floor, some-

665

665 House of the Hunt at *Bulla Regia*, Tunisia. A sunken *atrium* with underground rooms for the hot periods. Fifth century.

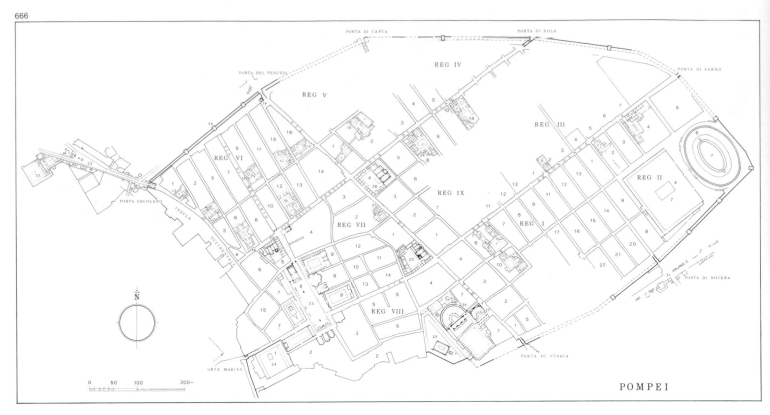

POMPEI

666 Pompeii. (After the general survey by H. Eschebach.)

thing of a peculiarity in this city (fig.667).[1] The reason for this is clear when it is noted that the *insulae* in the eastern part of the city are not built on but are simply occupied by enormous gardens. It is also in this area that the Great *Palaestra* and the amphitheatre were built – two sizeable complexes requiring large amounts of space. By 79 Pompeii had not filled the space within its walls, and so there was no need to go in for the high-rise development of the kind required by overpopulated and expanding cities.

The Pompeian house does not seem to have had its origins in a particular regional concept. The House of the Surgeon, the oldest suriving in the city, with a layout that had hardly changed from the fourth century BC, displays the usual arrangement of the Latin house (figs 668, 669). This is defined by and bound up with the *atrium*, a central space around which the living rooms are arranged. It was in the *atrium* that the domestic and communal activities of the family took place; it was a reminder of the single room of the

primitive hut. There the fire was kept going – thus the etymology of the word *atrium* has been traced to *ater*, black, as the smoke from the fire blackened the walls. Water was stored there in a *dolium* and meals were taken there.

In the earliest houses the *atrium* had only a narrow opening, serving both as chimney and skylight, and was called therefore an *atrium testudinatum* – this is how the House of the Surgeon originally looked. Later, this modest aperture became a proper light-well, the *compluvium*, lined up with a basin set into the floor, the *impluvium*, which collected rainwater for storage in an underground cistern.

The threshold of the Pompeian *domus*, usually framed by sober pilasters (figs 670, 671, 672) continued a little way into the house, forming a *vestibulum*. This was of very restricted size and unable to contain the benches for clients waiting to see the master of the house and so these were provided along the front of the building. Beyond the threshold were the door panels; the decoration of and even the system

667

668

669

Region VII
20 Stabian Baths
21 Bakery of Terentius Proculus
    (VII,2,3)
22 Forum Baths
23 Forum
24 Temple of Venus
Region VIII
25 Triangular Forum
26 Theatre
27 Odeon
Region IX
28 Central Baths (IX,4,5 and 18)
29 House of the Centenary
    (IX,8,6)
30 House of Obelius Firmus
    (IX,14,4)
Extra muros
31 Necropolis of the Nucerian
    Gate
32 Necropolis of the
    Herculaneum Gate or Street
    of the Tombs
33 Villa of Diomedes
34 Tower of Mercury

667   House of three storeys in
region I, with the floor levels
visible (I,4,28).

668   The House of the Surgeon,
built in the fourth century BC with
a frontage of limestone ashlar
(VI,1,10).

669   The *atrium* of the House of
the Surgeon. The basin of the
impluvium, made of tufa, was added
during the second century BC.

293

670

673

670   A door from the Samnite period (second century BC), with cubic capitals, in a frontage of *opus incertum* (I,9,5).

671   A door from the Samnite period (second century BC) with Corinthian capitals. House of the Faun (VI,12,2).

672   A door with brick columns and pediment, erected in the last construction period, between 62 and 79, at the House of Julia Felix (II,4,2).

673   Herculaneum, the House of the Black Salon. Imprint of a blocked-up door connecting a shop to the *atrium*. The remains of the nails hammered into the double doors can be seen.

671

672

674

of fastening these are known, thanks both to the exact imprints left in the ash from which casts have been made, and, even better, to the intact models from Herculaneum (figs 673, 674, 675, 676). Several doors in the via dell'Abbondanza still retain the large, sharply projecting bronze nails decorating the external surface of the panels, and numerous fastening bars, locks and iron keys have been discovered in the doorways (figs 677,678). The House of the Ephebus has the most complete surviving system. One of the doors of the house (since it consisted of two neighbouring buildings that had been connected there were several entrances) had been bolted at the time of the eruption, and it has been possible to make casts of the pieces holding the door closed. The two doors were secured by a metal lock, locked with a key, and made fast by a horizontal bar fixed into holes in the uprights. Additional security was provided by a prop wedged against the first door that opened inwards, and which rested in a small socket made in the passage floor (figs 679, 680).

675

676

674 Wooden double doors discovered intact in a house on the *decumanus maximus* at Herculaneum (no.19). Height: 2m; total width: 0.8m.

675 A door of a farm at Pompeii with a design identical to that found at Herculaneum.

676 A door with double lattice leaves at Herculaneum (Eastern *Insula* II). The left-hand door is modern.

The passage comprised the *fauces* (a word always used in the plural), or entrance corridor, which gave direct access to the *atrium*. Its floor was

677 Plaster-cast of a door at Pompeii that has preserved its decorative bronze nails. House of Octavius Quartio (II,2,2).

678 External elevation and cross-section of the entrance to a house at Pompeii, with a front door with bronze nails and an internal door with three leaves (I,6,15). (After Spinnazola, *Pompeii*, vol.I, p.265.)

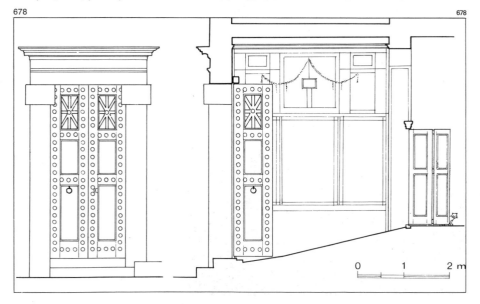

covered with mosaics with geometric or animal motifs, often used by archaeologists as identification – such as the House of the 'Bear' (VII,2,4), the House of the 'Boar' (VIII,3,8); or with a characteristic object – the House of the 'Anchor' (VI,10,7); with a maxim or greeting – *cave canem*, 'beware of the dog', the House of the Tragic Poet (VI,8,3); *salve lucro*, 'hail gain', the House of Siricus; or better still *lucrum gaudium*, 'gain is joy' (VI,14,39), or more simply *have* (possibly an abbreviation of *hospes ave*) at the door of the House of the Faun (VI,12,2).

In the *atrium*, where on summer days there was a contrast between the strong light coming through the *compluvium* and the surrounding shade, there was an almost unvarying arrangement. In line with the *fauces* and on the edge of the basin, the visitor could admire a small table, usually of marble, the *cartibulum*, a reminder of the table around which the family had formerly assembled for meals. Always richly decorated, these tables sometimes have a single leg, in the case of the oldest ones, and sometimes two legs in the form of griffons' feet. On the surface of the table, as later on the dressers of the great mansions, the best pieces of household crockery were placed. Also, beside the basin was the *puteal*, the well-head of terracotta or marble around the drawing-hole of the cistern (figs 681, 687).

In the Imperial period, when the city was provided with a town water supply distributed under pressure, rich owners had a small fountain built in the *impluvium*, whose jet fell either directly into the basin, sometimes through a statuette serving as an *emissarium*, or into a vessel from which it cascaded.

The household was placed under the protection of a large number of divinities, as everyone could gather under their roof the gods of their choice, but this role was essentially that of the Lares and the Penates, the former having given their name to the household shrine, the *lararium*, originally located in the *atrium*. The Lares, whom Ovid made into the twin sons of the nymph Lara and Mercury, had inherited protective powers from their father, the god of prosperity, which they ensured for the house in which they were venerated.[2] Unlike the Lares, the Penates remained invisible spirits, and consequently they are never found in any domestic representation. Besides, they do not have a particular mythology: it is known only that they had a temple in Rome where they were shown as two young men seated watching over the hearth.

In the course of the second Samnite period, with the enlargement of the *domus*, the *lararium* could be located in other places, such as the peristyle, the garden or the kitchen, thus following

680

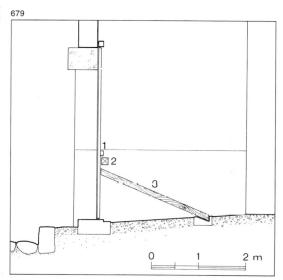

679

679 Triple bolting of a door at Pompeii (VII,2,51) with a key lock (1), a horizontal bar (2) and a prop (3).

680 Plaster-cast of a door and its bolting device, in the entrance *fauces* of the House of the Ephebe (I,6,10). Besides the lock, the two leaves are secured by a horizontal bar and a prop wedged against the floor.

681 *Atrium* of the House of the Wooden Partition at Herculaneum. On the right, on the entrance side, is the marble *cartibulum* and on the other side of the basin is the well of the cistern.

681

the hearth into its new position. The form and decoration of the *lararia* were so varied at Pompeii that they were distinct from one house to the next. In its simplest form the household shrine is just a niche, sometimes with a small pediment, at the back of which the Lares and the Genii were painted or where their statuettes could be placed (figs 683, 684). It could also project from the wall and, as at the House of the Menander (I,104) or that of the Gilded Cupids (Amorini Dorati) (VI,16,7), could be made up of a small building in the form of a temple (fig.685); it even furnished the pretext for a charming construction with access steps and small columns, laid out in the garden adjoining the *domus* (VIII,3,4). Generally, the two Lares are represented dressed in a short tunic,

holding in one hand a small receptacle for libations called the 'situla' and in the other the 'rhyton', a horn-shaped drinking vessel; they frame the family Genius,[3] shown officiating, pouring an offering on the altar (fig.682). These figures may be accompanied by one or two snakes, protective Genii of the household, and a number or an extremely variable selection of gods, among them Venus, the patroness of the city. Naturally, tradesmen tended to make their devotions to the divinity that was related to them, thus Vesta is found at the house of a baker (VII,2,11) and Epona at the house of a muleteer (IX,2,24).

The *lararium* can even be accompanied by a narrative representation, such as the one, already mentioned, of the banker L. Caecilius Jucundus,

682

682 The *lararium* of the House of the Vettii. The gods are shown as young men dancing and bearing libations; they stand on either side of the family *Genius* dressed in priestly robes.

showing the destruction of the forum during the earthquake in 62.

The roof over the *atrium* was held up by two massive timber beams, on which were two pieces at right angles, the whole acting as a support for roof timbers and sometimes ceiling coffers: in this form, by far the most common, the *atrium* or *cavaedium*, according to Vitruvius, was known as a Tuscan *atrium*[4] (fig.686). Later, the tetrastyle *atrium* relieved the roof-span by using four columns, placed one at each corner of the basin and borrowing from the three orders; very fine examples of

683 *Lararium* of the House of the Faun at Pompeii.

684 A small household shrine in the wall of a modern house at Ottaviano near Pompeii.

685 *Lararium* with small columns on a podium, Pompeii (VII,5,37).

686 *Compluvium* of the *atrium* in the House of the Vettii decorated with architectural terracotta (antefixes and water spouts).

687 Doric tetrastyle *atrium* in the House of the Ceii (I,6,15) with the well to the cistern and fountain basin.

688 Tetrastyle *atrium* with Ionic columns, with the *compluvium* covered by an iron grille (reconstructed), Pompeii (I,2,28).

689 A so-called Corinthian *atrium*, with 16 Doric columns in the House of Epidius Rufus (IX,1,20), from the second Samnite period.

690 House of the Centenary (IX,8,6), second century BC.
1 Main *atrium*
2 Secondary *atrium*
3 Peristyle
4 Nymphaeum
5 Cold pool (*frigidarium*)
6 Hot bath (*caldarium*)
7 Kitchen and *praefurnium*
8 Slaves' area, with a *lararium* with a representation of Vesuvius, its sides covered with vines, and protected by Bacchus.

At the front are shops. Around the two *atria* the relatively symmetrical arrangement of the rooms is noticeable, altered a little by successive developments. Along the western side there is a more random arrangement, attempting to fit into the space available.

687

688

689

this type can be found at the House of L. Ceius Secundus (I,6,15), the House of the Silver Wedding (V,2,1), the House of Obellius Firmus (IX,14,4) or the House of the Labyrinth (VI,11,10) (figs 687, 688). There are often iron rings towards the top of these columns, which made it possible to hang a cloth, a *velum*, across the opening of the *compluvium*, both to keep the house cool and to guard against prying eyes. From the adjoining floors it was in fact easy to see right into the household, and Plautus has one of his characters say: 'All my neighbours witness what is going on in my house by looking through my *impluvium*'.[5] Sometimes, a permanent arrangement was put in place at the level of the *compluvium*, and in two houses (I,2, 29 and IX,2,28) an iron grille has been found, which could not only support a *velum*, but also protected against burglars coming across the roofs.

Another type of *atrium* can be found at Pompeii, called a 'Corinthian' *atrium*, which has six or more columns and is therefore easily confused with a peristyle, distinguishable only because the second is slightly more extensive. It can be found on its own in the house and have the function of both these two elements. Thus, on the via dell'-Abbondanza (IX,1,20) the dwelling of Epidius Rufus is entered through a

Corinthian *atrium* with fine Doric columns made of tufa (fig.689).

Some large houses had two *atria*, such as the House of the Centenary (IX,8,6) (fig.690) and the House of the Faun, where this arrangement was necessitated by the scale of the building, requiring light and access for a large number of rooms. In most cases, however, as at the House of Siricus (VII,1,47 and 25), the existence of two *atria* was explained by the joining up of two neighbouring houses; this process was accelerated by the upheavals following the earthquake of 62, which also gave rise to division of houses (fig.691).

Facing the *fauces* and completely occupying one end of the *atrium* was almost always the *tablinum*,[6] a large, open room, serving as an office for the master of the house (fig.692); this space is a vestige of the recess in which, originally, the marital bed was situated, the *torus genialis*. The *tablinum* symbolized the owner's relations with the outside world; it is here that he received clients and suppliers and discussed business. Some examples still have the remains of a screen in the form of movable wooden panels, as can be seen in a remarkable state of preservation at the 'House of the Wooden Partition' at Herculaneum (figs 693, 694).

The *alae*, open exedrae like the *tablinum*, were arranged on both sides of the *atrium* and do not seem to have been intended for any particular purpose. They should perhaps be seen as a survival of alcoves for spare beds but this use was abandoned: sometimes remains of cupboards or storage shelving are found, sometimes a *lararium* or else dining-room couches, but most of the time there is no clear sign of any particular designation.

In some modest houses, the *alae* can be separate or mixed in with the *tablinum* when there is only one such room; conversely, at the beautiful House of the Vettii (VI,15,1) which has no *atrium*, it can be assumed that one of the *alae* took its place.

As the entrance *fauces* were almost always along the axis of the house, the rooms opening on the right and the left could be connected to it or be independent from it. In the main

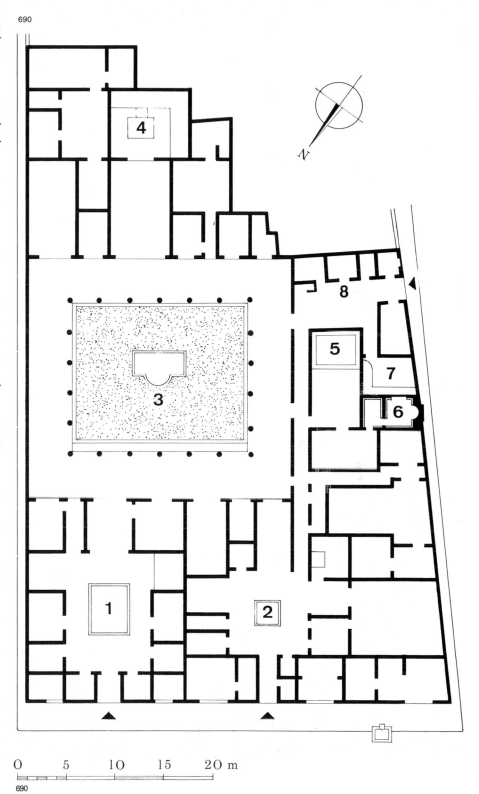

690

690

0   5   10   15   20 m

301

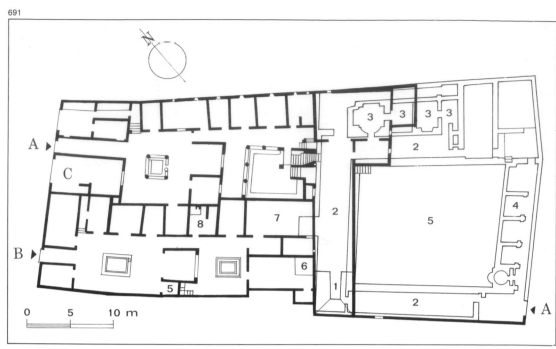

691

691 Example of a *domus* at Pompeii divided and rearranged after 62: the House of the *Cryptoporticus* (I,6, 2-3-4). This enormous residence was divided into three parts. The largest section kept the garden (4) and the *cryptoporticus* (1), in which a bath was installed (at the eastern end), and a slaves' area (3). The second dwelling is that of the Iliac Chapel in which there is a room decorated with giant pictures of elephants (5; at the bottom left). Finally, an enormous shop opened on to the via dell'Abbondanza between the two houses which belonged to the blacksmith-ironmonger Verus, and was where the *groma* was discovered. (After V. Spinnazola.)

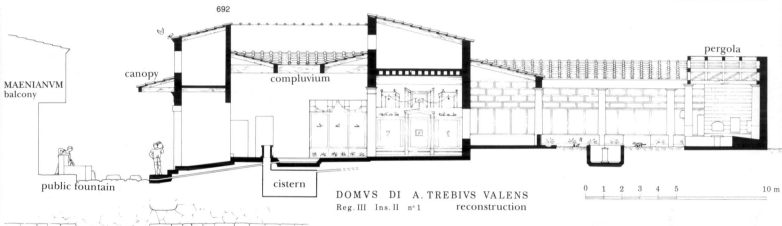

692

MAENIANVM
balcony

canopy

compluvium

pergola

public fountain

cistern

DOMVS DI A. TREBIVS VALENS
Reg. III Ins. II n° 1   reconstruction

0 1 2 3 4 5   10 m

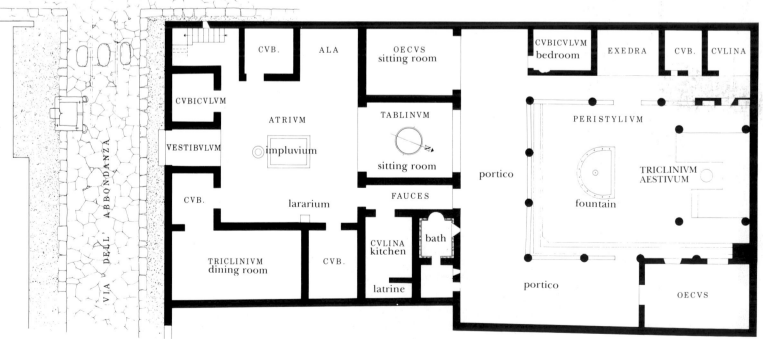

streets, the via dell'Abbondanza, via di Stabia and via di Nola, each house entrance, or almost all of them, was flanked with shops that were usually self-contained (figs 690, 691, 695, 696), and sometimes connected by a stairway to a living room on the first floor. By contrast, the houses whose front gave on to side streets where business was non-existent, integrated these rooms, each of them becoming a *cubiculum*, that is a bedroom (sometimes, but not very often, the more accurate term, *dormitorium*, is used). In the houses with staff, and conceivably this was most often the case in prosperous Pompeii, servants, slaves or freedmen were housed in these *cubicula* adjoining the entrance; the other occupants of

693
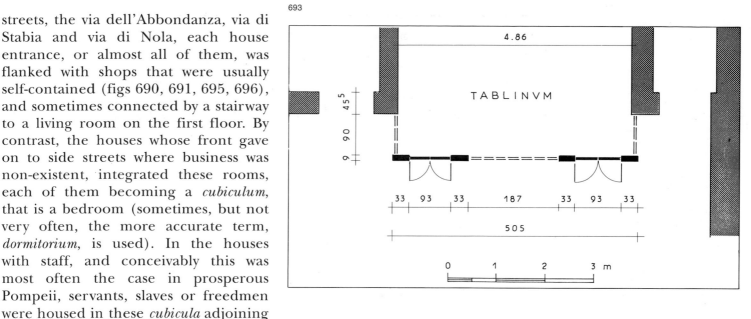

692 The House of Trebius Valens on the via dell'Abbondanza (III,2,1). This *domus* of modest size possesses all the elements typical of the urban residence and had in addition the advantage of a running water supply.

693 Plan of the shutter panels of the *tablinum* of the House of the Wooden Partition, Herculaneum.

694 The wooden partition separating the *atrium* from the *tablinum* in the House of the Wooden Partition, Herculaneum. The double panels on the right and the left are double doors; the middle section was unfortunately destroyed by an excavation pit.

695

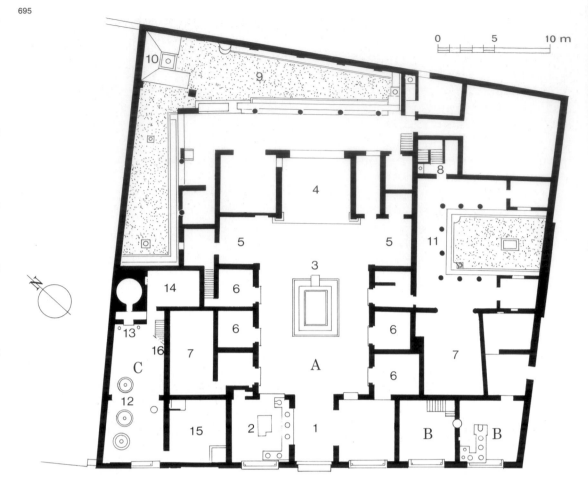

695 The fine large house called the House of Sallustius (VI,2,4). The original core, comprising the *atrium* and surrounding rooms, was built in the third century BC and is in every respect identical to the layout of the House of the Surgeon, its neighbour. Few alterations have been carried out apart from the openings on to the garden, at the back, and on to the peristyle on the right, added in the first century BC. After 62 the house was turned into an inn with a bar, a dining room and numerous rooms on the first floor.

1   Entrance *fauces*
2   Bar – *thermopolium*
3   *Atrium*
4   *Tablinum* – this was opened later on to give access to the garden. The two rooms adjoining it originally opened into the *atrium*.
5   *Alae*
6   *Cubicula*
7   Dining rooms. That on the left belonged to the inn. That on the right was private and opened on to the peristyle.
8   Kitchen
9   *Hortus*
10 Summer *triclinium*
11 Peristyle
B   Two separate shops with their living area on the first floor and at the back.
C   Separate bakery:
12 Milling area
13 Oven
14 Preparation area
15 Sales area
16 Access to the living area on the first floor.

696

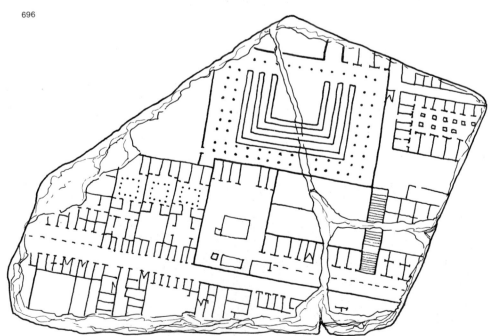

the house were distributed in the bedrooms opening on to the *atrium* or the peristyle.

The bed emplacement, which is obvious evidence of the room's use, is often marked in one of the walls by a slight recess that allowed it to be fitted in, thus giving a little extra room (fig.697). In some bedrooms a design in the mosaic floor indicates the position of the bed; sometimes there is an alcove (*alcova*) made in the wall and the ceiling.

The role played by the *compluvium* in lighting has already been mentioned; however limited it was, this vertical daylight was still more considerable than that inadequately provided by the windows, which, due to the narrowness of the slits and their height above ground for reasons of security, only let in a thin ray of light that had to be supplemented by the use of oil lamps (figs 698, 699, 700, 701, 702). Because of their small size, some of these window openings have retained the glass with which they were once filled.

698

697

699

701

696 Fragment of the *Forma urbis*, the ancient plan of Rome, engraved on marble around AD 200 and displayed in the library(?) of the Forum of Peace.
  Three particular houses can be made out. Each has a hallway opening on to the street, flanked by shops, which leads into the *atrium*, the peristyle occupying the back part. (Rome, Antiquarium Comunale.)

697 A small alcove for the head of a bed, in a *cubiculum* of modest dimensions, Pompeii (I,7,11).

698 Slit openings on the ground floor of the House of the Faun; only the upper floors had large-size windows.

699 A skylight of a ground-floor room looking out on to the street at Pompeii (VIII,3) viewed from the inside. For reasons of security and privacy, these lower-level openings were always placed high up.

700 An *oculus* of a ground-floor room looking out on to a street at Pompeii (VII,3).

701 When ground-floor windows were of some size they were barred with an iron grille. This example is on the *cardo* IV, *insula* 5, at Herculaneum.

702 A terracotta window grille, at the House of the Labyrinth (VI,11,10).

700

702

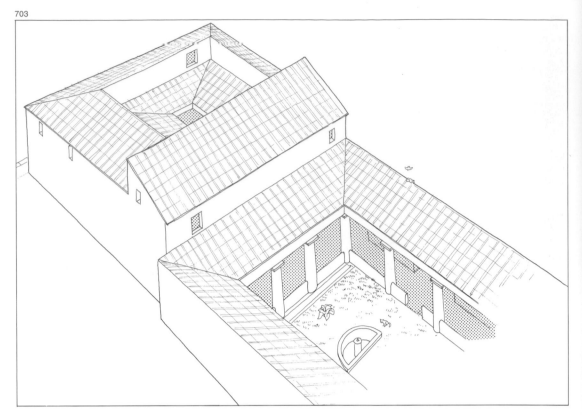

703

703 Aerial perspective of the House of Trebius Valens, showing the axial arrangement and the juxtaposition of the two closed elements, the *atrium* and the peristyle.

704 Peristyle in the House of Venus in the Shell (II,3). The lowest third of the stuccoed fluted columns is protected by a covering painted red (sometimes black) in which cabling is sometimes scored.

In the second Samnite period, the *domus* was enriched by an architectural element that was already found in fine Greek houses: the peristyle (*peristylum*). The Romans were to turn this space, closed off by a surrounding portico, into an inner garden. They developed garden designs to their own taste and embellished them with fountains and statues, so that they became the delightful, select focus of family life (figs 703, 704, 705, 706, 707). Depending on the importance attached to a floral environment, but also on the space available, the peristyle was surrounded by a variable number of rooms. At the House of Pansa (VI,6,1) the four sides are occupied by a total of 13 rooms, while at the House of the Faun, with a whole *insula* at its disposal, only 7 of some 40 rooms in this dwelling open on to the two large peristyles.

Around the peristyle, apart from the *cubicula*, were some rooms that did not exist in the original Italic house and whose appearance coincides with the enlargement of the *domus*. However, the distribution of rooms, perhaps because of the succession of occupants, was never fixed according to a stereotype and a considerable degree of freedom can be seen in the arrangement of layouts.

704

705

706

707

705 Peristyle in the House of the Amorini Dorati (VI,16,7). The arrangement of this enclosed green space is remarkable for successive rising levels, laid out like a stage set and perhaps sometimes used for that effect.

706 The so-called 'Rhodian' column, where two porticoes of different heights meet in the peristyle of the House of the Silver Wedding (V,2,1).

707 A peristyle with an upper floor in the House of the Lovers (I,10,11); a wooden balustrade linked the columns on the upper floor. The name of this *domus* comes from a charming gastronomic metaphor written on the eastern wall of the peristyle: 'lovers are like bees, they lead a life as sweet as honey'. Two mocking ducks watch over this saying.

Cooking and meals, formerly prepared and eaten in the *atrium*, were each given a special room. The hearth was installed in a *culina* or *coquina*, which, with rare exceptions, was a room of fairly modest proportions, furnished with a masonry platform covered with brick forming a working surface. On this one or more fires were maintained, over which the cooking containers were held by means of a tripod. A vaulted space, opening in the platform, was filled with a wood store or pots. Sometimes the layout was completed by a small oven, to bake bread for the household among other things (figs 708, 709) (VIII,2,30). The latrine was almost always located immediately next to the kitchen (an arrangement that is also often adopted in modern flats), and drained into a pit or sometimes, more simply, via a pipe into the street (fig.710).

708

709

710

708   A kitchen with an oven (VIII,2,30).

709   A kitchen installed in the basement at the House of the Centenary (IX,8,6); the bread oven also provided heating for the *caldarium*.

710   Latrine of a *domus* at Pompeii (VII,3,16).

711   The *triclinium*, with rendered masonry, in the House of the *Cryptoporticus* (I,6,2).

712   Couches faced with marble in the *triclinium* of the House of Julia Felix. A small fountain, supplied from two tanks, flowed into the basin in the middle.

Before becoming one of the main rooms opening on to the *atrium* or the peristyle, the dining room of the earliest houses of Latin type was often on the first floor and was called a *cenaculum*, a name that continued to be applied to upper rooms. Where there was no upper floor, meals were taken in the *tablinum*, a custom that was sometimes maintained in the smaller houses (VI,16,28). However, in the majority of cases, the houses had a large room reserved for meals, the *triclinium*,[7] the name deriving from the

711

712

713

three couches on which the guests reclined, following a custom borrowed from the Greeks (figs 711, 712).

Around a table, the *mensa*, were the three couches, each with room for three people in a particular order. On the couch placed on the left, the *lectus imus*, was the master of the house, with next to him his wife and one of his sons, or lacking them, his freedman; the middle couch or *lectus medius* was reserved for important guests and, in large houses, there was a place called the 'consulary place', next to that of the master of the house. Finally, on the right, there was the *lectus summus* intended for the other guests. Young children shared in the adults' meals, but were not seated on the couches; they ate sitting at a small table, a piece of furniture that was discovered in the *triclinium* of a *domus* behind the Central Baths (IX,5,11).[8]

When the room had only two couches it was called a *biclinium*; the couches were then arranged in a right angle, as can be seen in several smaller houses (I,2,20 and V,2,c). In the garden the citizens of Pompeii installed the summer dining-room, likewise in the form of a *biclinium*, shaded by a pergola or a trellis; between the couches ran water from a fountain. Two particularly elegant examples, where the delight attached to meal times is evident, can be found in V,3,11 and particularly at the House of Octavius Quartio (also called Loreius Tiburtinus; II, 2, 2) where the basin of a fountain leads into a channel running the whole length of the pergola that dominates the enormous garden. The painting decorating the supporting wall of this fountain is in addition the only one yet found to have the signature of its artist: *Lucius pinxit*.[9]

The couches of these summer dining-rooms are generally made of masonry, rendered and painted, and so they have often survived. The best examples can be seen at the House of Trebius Valens (III,2,1), where the summer *triclinium* is located under a pergola at the end of the peristyle (fig.713), at the House of the Moralist (III,4,2-3) and at the House of Julia Felix (II,4,2) where the couches are faced with marble. In indoor rooms the couches were of wood and nothing is left of them except bronze ornamentation and pieces of charred wood. Fortunately, in a house on the vicolo del Panettiere (the House of Caius Vibius, VII,2,8), the fine ash had made a relatively good imprint of the three beds, which could thus be reconstructed fairly accurately.

The *tablinum* and the *triclinium* can be identified either by their location within the house or by their furniture. There is sometimes also another room, which seems to have been for the reception of guests or for the gathering of the family – the living room of the house, known by the name *oecus* (from the Greek *oikos*: the house) – where meals were also taken when there were a lot of guests (figs 714, 715). However, the word *oecus*, as used and standardized by archaeologists,

713 The summer *triclinium*, sheltered under a light roof, in the House of Trebius Valens (III,2,1).

714

714 Corinthian *oecus* with pedestalled columns, following the definition by Vitruvius (VI,5,5–8), at the House of Meleager (VI,9,2).

appears to be somewhat inappropriate, given the rarity of its occurrence in Latin, though Vitruvius gives several definitions.[10]

The word *exedra*, or *exhedra*, applied to open rooms such as the *tablinum*, on the other hand, corresponds completely with their appearance. It is on the floor of the *exedra*, opening at the end of the first peristyle in the House of the Faun, that the mosaic of Alexander and Darius was found (now in the Museum of Naples), evidence of the luxurious decoration of these reception rooms.

As an element of comfort reserved for certain privileged people, the private bath appears in some dwellings at Pompeii some time before the Imperial period. The facilities, sometimes richly decorated, as at the House of the Labyrinth (VI,11,10), always retained their modest dimensions and it is conceivable that they could have been in use before the city was provided with a system of water supply under pressure. All that was needed, in fact, to supply the baths was a water reservoir. This could just be the cistern, from which the necessary water was drawn, or, more conveniently, a

roof tank filled by rainwater from which the water would flow by gravity by simply opening a sluice or a tap. This second type of arrangement is now difficult to discover since the roofs and upper floors have collapsed, but there is evidence that at the House of Julia Felix two tanks, fitted over a passageway, supplied a fountain in the *triclinium*. Other identical installations can be assumed to have existed in other houses, supplying, besides the baths, water to the occupants of the upstairs apartments without drudgery or transport.

In their simplest form, private baths consisted of two rooms: one used both as a changing room and a *tepidarium* (the warm room); and the second being the *caldarium* or hot room, in which there was the bath itself. The smallest of these installations is unquestionably that belonging to Trebius Valens, via dell'Abbondanza (II,2,1), where two tiny rooms, 1.7m wide and respectively 1.78m and 2m long, served as a *balneum*. In order to maintain a high temperature, these rooms were almost windowless, the only light being provided by a lamp or a small oculus, while the only access to the *caldarium* was through the *tepidarium*, each having a very narrow door (50cm at the House of Trebius Valens).

The House of the Faun, as a result of the destruction of the buildings, provides the best idea of how the heating system of these rooms worked. Almost always located next to the kitchen, the baths got their heat from an open fire in the wall that separated the *caldarium* from the kitchen. In the kitchen in the House of the Faun there was also a cistern well (this residence, however grand and luxurious, did not have running water) used as much for domestic use as for the bath. The floor of the two baths in this house was raised, while that of the kitchen was lower; thus the fire opening at the floor level of the latter comfortably heated the space made under the two neighbouring rooms.

Some houses, admittedly rare, had a more complete system, such as the House of the Cryptoporticus (I,6,2), where the baths, fitted out in the basement, had four rooms: a changing room, the *apodyterium*, a cold bath, a *tepidarium* and a *caldarium*. At the House of the Centenary (IX,8,6, so called because it was discovered in 1879, 1800 years after the eruption) and at the House of the Silver Wedding (V,2,1, discovered in 1893, the year of the silver wedding of the Italian king and queen), the *frigidarium* even had the benefit of a proper open-air pool, a *natatio*, comparable to those in public bathing establishments.

Houses with sufficient space could accommodate a peristyle of such dimensions that it gave the appearance of a vast garden, the *hortus*. At the House of the Faun (VI,12,2) the almost square area, opening in the middle of the second peristyle, measures approximately 30m each side. But often, in order to take advantage of the space, the garden extended as far as the perimeter walls without there being a portico: this is the case at many houses, including that of the Cryptoporticus (I,6,2), the *Insula Arriana Polliana* (VI,6,1), or the House of the Moralist (III,4,2 and 3); but one of the finest gardens discovered is that belonging to the House of Octavius Quartio (II,2,2) (figs 716, 717, 718).

Already referred to for its summer *biclinium*, this house possesses one of the most extensive and ornate gardens in Pompeii. It is also called that of Loreius Tiburtinus, due to the fact that these two names occur separately several times on the front of the house in election slogans. In fact, they were two different people without any immediate relation to the house, and it is the discovery in a room, to the left of the entrance, of a bronze seal marked with the name *D(ecimus) Octavi*

Quartionis that made it possible to identify the owner of the house.[11]

In the enormous garden, which occupies the whole of the area of the *insula* not built on, the owner had installed a canal, called a *euripus* after the channel separating Euboea from Greece. Here it was supplied by the fountain from the *biclinium* and passed under three small pergola constructions, adding to the floral scheme and garden plan elements of imaginative architecture of which the Romans were obviously very fond.

The emperor Hadrian had his vast Tivoli residence laid out in a similar spirit; in its parks were reproduced groups of monuments, evoking grandiose projects and wonders from all over the Empire.

Water which cascaded down in stages from a fountain and ran murmuring into a canal, in places interrupted by the noise of a small jet adding its water to a basin, charmed the Romans beyond measure. This pleasure, without equal in its refinement as well as its simplicity, is easily appreciated and shared by all those who live, or have lived, in regions of abundant sunshine.

715 Tetrastyle *oecus* with a large alcove at the House of the Silver Wedding (V,2,1).

The devotion of the people of the peninsula to the audial and visual pleasures of water has not altered over the centuries, as fountains remain one of the constants of decorative architecture and ornamentation.

Discovered during the excavations carried out by Spinazzola, the tree roots and bushes in the garden of Octavius Quartius showed that they were planted in parallel lines to the *euripus*, following the contour of the land, and provided shade, coolness, fruit and a refuge for birds, adding to the pleasure of the occupants of the house.

Indications of the types of smaller plants and trees that have now totally disappeared are found in a number of paintings at Pompeii whose subject is the garden. These include: acacia, oak, cypress, rose-laurel, plane-trees and numerous fruit trees including almond, cherry, chestnut, fig, pomegranate, walnut, olive, apple and pear. One tree, however, poses a puzzle that is particularly difficult to solve – the lemon. It is not attested in Italy in the first century, but there is perhaps a representation of it in the House of the Orchard (I,9,5).[12] Some elongated yellow fruits are depicted on a tree, but this is possibly a confusion between the lemon, the citron (another more primitive citrus fruit) and the quince.[13] The problem could only be definitively resolved by the discovery of a written reference or surviving pips among the food remains in one of the many houses that are still buried, as a number of uneaten meals and stores of food have been discovered in kitchens or on tables.

In the same way, the majority of trees, flowers and plants grown for pleasure and for cooking can be identified in the paintings. The list is still not exhaustive, but chance observations made at random during visits can be mentioned: the hollyhock decorating the walls with flowers; or asparagus, marrows, beans, figs, cherries, melons or pumpkins in still life paintings.

Minute excavation of the gardens has made it possible, particularly in the houses on the via dell'Abbondanza, to reconstruct the exact outline of the ancient land-surface. In this way, apart from the identification of a large number of plants, it was also possible to find evidence of the care taken by the gardeners of Pompeii over their gardens: each plant was surrounded by a small earth embankment, defining the prepared area and retaining water after watering. Certain more fragile flowers were planted out, after growing in a sheltered spot in terracotta pots carefully perforated with several holes so as not to prevent the further growth of the roots.

The designs of formal flower gardens have also been discovered, sometimes on the basis of the earth embankments mentioned above, and the furrows left by the horticulturalist, sometimes on the basis of brick borders dividing the ground into geometrical forms, creating beds of different colours (the garden at the House of Ariadne, VII,4,51).

A surprising discovery was made in the garden of Octavius Quartio by Spinazzola: a long row of 44 amphorae buried up to their necks extending along the east wall of the boundary.[14] Too close together to have contained sizeable plants and too large for small flowers, these amphorae had contained a liquid, wine or oil, kept cool in this way as the house had no cellar. Other similar finds, but with fewer containers, were made at several houses (IV,4,8 and VIII,4,2) confirming this method of preserving goods.

Cellars were not, in fact, in systematic use, though they could occur in two forms: the *cryptoporticus* and the proper cellar. The first were long tunnels laid out under the peristyle or the garden (House of the Cryptoporticus, I,6,2, Villa of Diomedes), sometimes even around the house (Villa of the Mysteries) and which could be used as an annex to the dwelling for their

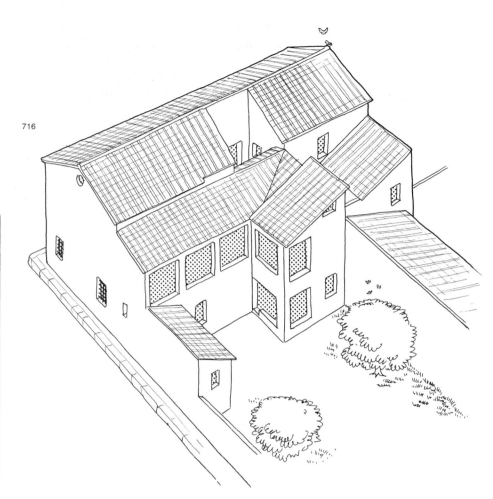

716 Perspective drawing of a *domus* which does not have the conventional arrangement entrance – *atrium* – peristyle, but in which, perhaps for this reason, there has been an exceptional attempt to provide openings on to the garden. Pompeii, House of the Moralist (III,4,2–3). (After Spinazzola.)

717 The reconstructed garden at the Villa of Diomedes, surrounded on four sides by a portico and centring on a basin with *exedrae* and fountains.

718 The garden of the House of Octavius Quartio (II,2,2), crossed by a *euripus* punctuated by aedicules in the form of a pergola or a canopy.

719

719 One of the tunnels of the *cryptoporticus* at the House of the *Cryptoporticus* at Pompeii (I,6,2).

720 Stairway made of masonry in V,2,d. The supporting piers were relieved by one or more vaults and used for storing various things.

721 First floor loggia with colonnade on the via dell'Abbondanza (IX,12,2).

coolness, or even to put rooms in (the House of the Cryptoporticus and numerous houses had them along their south-facing side) (fig.719).

The second type were vaulted recesses, lacking any sort of ornamentation and fulfilling the entirely utilitarian role of preserving food and, of course, wine: this is the *cella vinaria*, accessible via a stairway or sometimes a ramp. Their presence is revealed to the visitor by the ventilation shafts opening on to the street at pavement level (via Consulare, via degli Augustali, via della Regina) or, more discretely, on to the peristyle (I,2,3 or VIII,2,1).

Stairways made of masonry (fig.720) as well as of wood provided access to upper floors, but of the latter only wall timbers survive, the floors of Pompeii having all been destroyed. It is noticeable, nevertheless, that the upper rooms, unlike those on the ground floor, received plenty of light thanks to ample windows and sometimes even a gallery with a colonnade, such as the elegant loggia in the via dell'Abbondanza (IX,12,1-5) (fig.721). These windows often had a balcony in front or else opened on to corbelling that was usually made of timber framing. There are many such examples all over Pompeii, particularly in the eastern area that has been most recently uncovered.

These wall sections, which are very

unstable, are evidence of the presence of an upper level. In the absence of any masonry beyond the layer of lapilli, however, there are very rare examples of houses within the city in which the presence of three levels can be detected (one example, already mentioned, is quite well preserved in I,4,28).

On the other hand, houses built on the south-western edge of the city wall after its abandonment gained the space in the upper storeys that they lacked on the ground due to the sharp drop in level. These buildings, whose rooms were vaulted, are among the

best preserved so far discovered, and one of them, the House of Fabius Rufus, has revealed four levels (the entrance on the city side corresponding to the highest) and a number of rooms that make it the largest domestic house discovered at Pompeii.

It is interesting to note that some stairways went directly from pavement level, opening on to the latter via a special door. A good example of this can be seen in the via dell'Abbondanza, at VIII,3,10, where a Samnite door with elegant capitals provided access to a stairway made of tufa serving a private apartment situated on the first floor (fig.722)[15]. Such arrangements show that the houses at Pompeii were not always the property, or housing, of a single family, but that the notion of a communal building, even if not as it existed in Rome or Ostia, was already found in embryonic form at the level of a small provincial city with between 12 and 15,000 inhabitants.

2 Trade and commerce

a Wine and oil

It is the Greeks that the Romans had to thank for the basic methods of wine production, and their taste for wines produced in Greece was to remain considerable for quite a long time, despite their own large production from the Republican period on. The wines produced in the peninsula, although they were known to travellers from early on, are not recorded as having been distinguished and named until after 121BC.[16] From this time on, with the development of agricultural estates, Italy steadily increased its wine production, up to the territorial conquests of the Julio-Claudian period that were to bring about deep and ill-fated changes in Roman agriculture.[17] After this, imported wines, especially from

Gaul, were to compete very seriously with the agriculture of the peninsula, as was even more the case with imported wheat.[18]

The wine was made by the grower, who was also invariably the owner of the vineyards and who lived in an agricultural dwelling, the *villa rustica*, with his family and the slaves attached to the estate, the *familia rustica*. The wine-producing facilities formed the production quarter of the villa (but they may only have been a part, depending on the processing also of wheat and oil) and consisted of installations built into the structure. These have been well preserved in several villas in Campania.

722 Doorway made of tufa, from the second Samnite period, opening on to a stairway leading directly from the street to a living area on the first floor. It is curious to note that the builders, instead of laying their blocks in horizontal courses, followed the slope of the street (VIII,3,10).

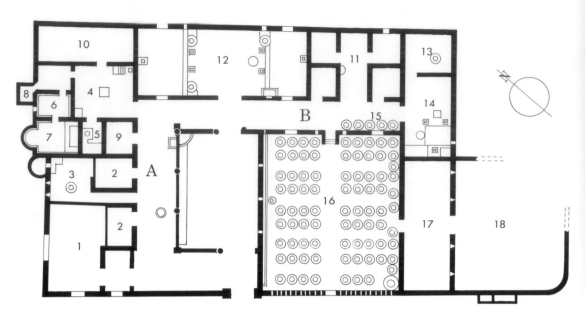

723

723   *Villa rustica* of La Pisanella
at Boscoreale near Pompeii:
A   *Pars urbana*:
1   Dining room
2   Bedrooms
3   Bakery with millstone and
     oven
4   Kitchen with stairway
5   *Tepidarium*
6   *Tepidarium*
7   *Caldarium*
8   Latrines.
B   *Pars rustica* (partly included
     in the above):
9   Tool store
10 Stable
11 Slaves' living quarters
12 Wine store with two grape
     presses, three *dolia* and a
     cistern.
13 Olive mill
14 Olive press
15 *Dolia* for oil
16 Open-air wine store with
     buried *dolia*
17 Granary
18 Threshing floor
(After Pasqui, *Monumenti dei
Lincei*, VII, 1897, p.398.)

Although, as with wine, a lot of olive oil was imported, this time from Spain[19] and North Africa,[20] the Romans always had a preference for their own oil, the most sought after being from Samnium.[21] The geographical area of olive cultivation was almost the same as today: all coastal regions and those not too high up were producers. Not surprisingly, many farms had equipment for both wine and oil production.

One villa has been particularly useful in explaining how this double production was divided and how it worked. The *villa rustica* of 'la Pisanella' at Boscoreale is situated a little more than a kilometre north of Pompeii (fig.723)[22] and forms a representative example for Campania in the second half of the first century. It is very instructive as it was designed in its entirety as an agricultural enterprise, with a living area called the *pars urbana* to distinguish it from the service and production area, the *pars rustica*, combining the slaves' quarters, the processing plant, the stables and the storage spaces[23].

The buildings of this villa extended along three sides of a space given over to wine and oil storage with a central courtyard. On the west side was the living area of the master or the manager, on the north was the production area and the servants' quarters, on the east a barn.[24]

The master's living area consisted, apart from bedrooms and a *triclinium*, of a kitchen (4 in fig.723), a milling area and a bread oven (3) for the community. Bread was the staple for the slaves and each received an amount in accordance with the work carried out. For example, in the time of Cato the allowance was 4 pounds of bread per day (1309g) for forced labourers and only 3 bushels (656g) for herdsmen and shepherds;[25] these allocations increased with time and in the time of Nero, Seneca recorded his slaves as receiving 5 bushels of wheat (1094g)[26] for domestic work. The master of the estate usually had baths (6 and 7), the fire for which was between them and the kitchen, while a stairway[27] provided access to the upper bedrooms. The slaves were housed in four rooms grouped together, adjoining the large room with the presses. These bedrooms were bare cells without any special fittings, just as in the *pars rustica* of the Villa of the Mysteries. All the archaeological remains point to the fact that living conditions of the rural slaves were certainly harder than those of urban slaves.[28] In the *domus*, the slaves participated in the life of the family; their duties were related to domestic service, the upkeep of the house, its decoration, the attendance on or even the supervision and education of the children and their medical care. Emancipation was common and numerous funerary in-scriptions illustrate mutual attachment between masters and their slaves.

In the rural environment, the slaves of the *familia rustica* worked the crops under the supervision of the *villici*, in conditions that grew harder in proportion to the size of the estate. On the great cereal-producing *latifundia* of Sicily, surely the worst in the Roman world, the slaves, mostly coming from oriental markets, were often not housed in the living quarters of the villa, but were literally farmed out in huts or troglodyte dwellings located near the work-place. It was also in Sicily that two of the three largest revolts experienced by the Roman state arose. The first broke out at Erma in 139BC, and plunged the island into seven years of bloodshed; the second lasted five years, from 104 to 99BC, and successfully rallied part of the Sicilian populace;[29] the third was that of Spartacus in 73BC. But none of these uprisings by desperate people, which set in motion uncontrollable forces, led to the slightest alleviation in the system of slavery. It was not until the Imperial period that humanitarian measures were introduced in favour of slaves, by the emperors themselves. From the *Lex Petronia* forbidding throwing them to the animals without trial, to punishment for their murder, Nero, Domitian and Hadrian decreed laws which, even if they did not end slavery, improved its conditions.[30]

The *villae rusticae* of Campania were nothing like the enormous Sicilian estates, and the slaves, considerably

fewer in number, lived in the establishment. Even so, their conditions were not necessarily as comfortable as in the towns and two *villae* have left proof of the penalties affecting punished slaves. At the villa with mosaic columns and at that of T. Siminius Stephanus[31] an *ergastulum* – a cell for locking up prisoners – was found, with iron shackles to hold the ankles; in each a skeleton remained.

To return to the villa at Boscoreale and its exceptionally complete layout,[32] flanking the slaves' quarters were a room containing grape presses and two rooms with olive presses. The grape presses consisted of a large wooden lever, the *prelum*, secured at one end, which pressed the grapes held in wickerwork containers as it was lowered, using a winch (*sucula*)[33] or a large vertical screw (*coclea*) (figs 724, 725). In earlier times the grapes would have been trodden in a vat, as a number of paintings and mosaics show, in order to

724 The grape or olive press (*torcular*).

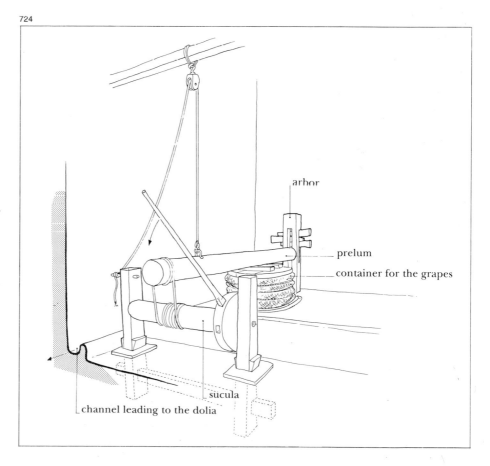

724

arbor

prelum

container for the grapes

sucula

channel leading to the dolia

725

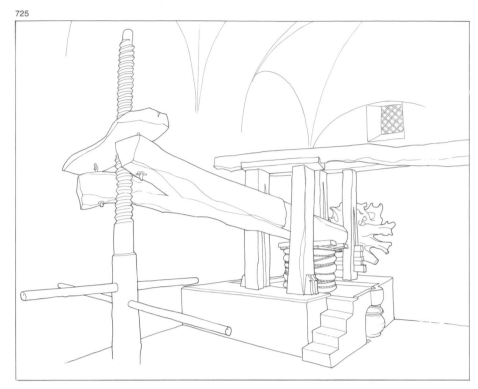

725 A traditional press at a farm at Pompeii. The beam is the trunk of an oak tree, with the roots left on to act as a counterbalance; the movement is provided here by a screw.

726 Ancient olive mill at Pompeii.

727 Cross-section of an olive mill. The turning millstones were suspended, by means of the *columella*, to allow the fruit to fall into the cavity of the *mortarium* and so be crushed.

726

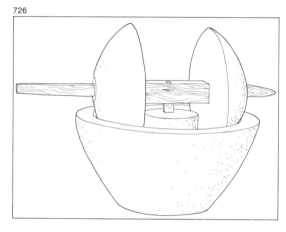

727

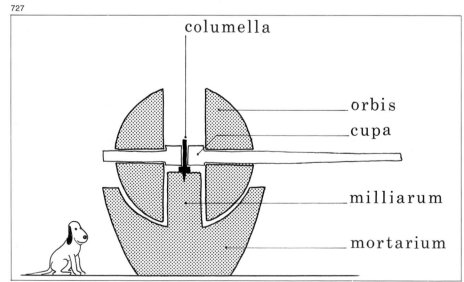

columella

orbis

cupa

milliarum

mortarium

reduce the volume of grapes to be contained in the baskets. The juice running out of the press was collected in an earthenware jar that was then emptied into a *dolium*, or was fed directly via a pipe with a movable end to the wine store (*cella vinaria*) where the *dolia* were set out. In the villa of la Pisanella, the *dolia*, 85 in all, were buried almost up to their necks in a courtyard, which had one wall pierced with numerous ventilation holes. Presumably a cloth could also have been used to reduce the heat of this area given over to the laying down and ageing of the wine. Other *dolia* still contained grain and oil.

Two rooms were used for processing oil (*olearia*), one of which contained an olive mill, the *trapetum*, in which the fruit was crushed by semicircular grinding stones (figs 726, 727). In the other was a press, identical to the grape presses but connected up to a decanting trough in which the oil was separated from its water before being put into earthenware jars (fig.728).[35]

An enormous room with a rendered floor still containing grains of oats must have been used as a granary, while horse skeletons have made it possible to identify the stable, in which the animals were still tethered; as for the wagons, they must have been kept in the courtyard around which were the various buildings.

A very similar arrangement has been revealed by excavations at the villa of Settefinestre near Cosa,[36] the production facilities of which consisted of three grape presses, an oil press and the corresponding storage areas. The preservation of this complex is admittedly nothing like that found around Vesuvius, but the care taken over its uncovering and the permanent marks made by the equipment allow it to be compared with the examples in Campania. On the basis of a detailed study of the rural economy archaeologists have been able to explain how the villa functioned – its social life, everyday existence and production – between the second quarter of the first century BC and the period of Antoninus, when it was abandoned.[37]

In contrast to these two examples, the famous Villa of the Mysteries at Pompeii (fig.729) was from the very beginning conceived as a luxury residence. It was built during the first half of the second century BC on a slope overlooking the shore and backing on to one of the two roads leading to the Herculaneum Gate.[38] Around 60BC the house was bordered on its eastern side by a rural area that was to be developed in the Augustan period, while the master's rooms were given the

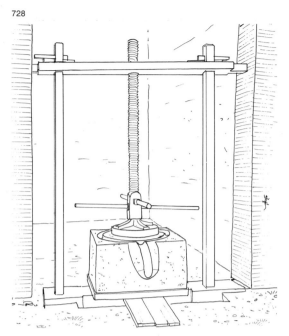

728

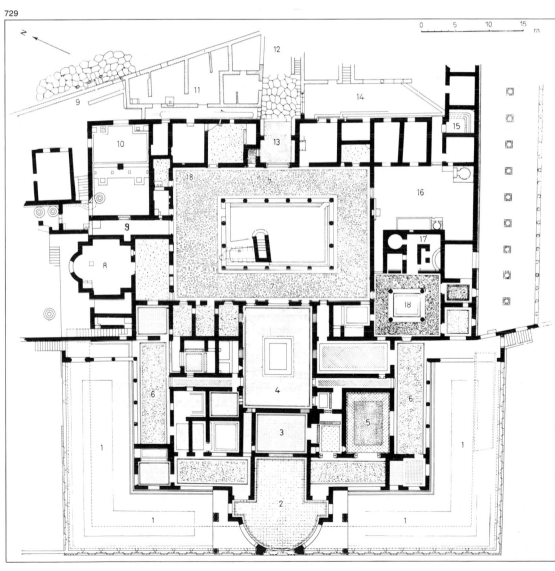

729

728 Olive press on the premises of an oil merchant at Pompeii (VII,4), via degli Augustali. This apparatus, in which the screw acted directly on the fruit, made it possible for an urban shopkeeper to sell to the citizens a product which was normally manufactured in the country.

729 Villa of the Mysteries:
1 Pleasure garden (*viridarium*)
2 *Exedra* (or *exhedra*).
3 *Tablinum*
4 *Atrium*
5 So-called room of the 'Dionysiac Mysteries'
6 Portico
7 Peristyle
8 Room with apse
9 Access to the press and the wine cellar
10 Press (*torcular*)
11 Slaves' quarters
12 Main access to the via delle Tombe
13 Entrance passage
14 Small courtyard belonging to the slaves' quarters
15 Latrines
16 Kitchen yard
17 Baths
18 Secondary tetrastyle atrium.
(After A. Maiuri, H.-J. Bejen, *Ercolano, Pompei e stili pompeiani*, Rome, 1965, p.56, fig.73.)

luxurious decoration in the Second Style that have made the building famous. After the earthquake of 62 new alterations increased the agricultural character of the house, with the extension of the peasant area taking over the rooms flanking the entrance, still on the eastern side.

The excavation concentrated mainly on uncovering the residential area and only partly exposed the production area for the manufacture of wine – the press, *torcularium* or *torcular* and the *pars fructaria*, in this case the wine-store, uncovered over a very small area and containing the buried *dolia* for the grape-juice.

The production of wine and oil was, of course, carried out on a large scale in all the regions bordering the Mediterranean,[39] but it was also obviously consumed on the spot, being offered on sale at the local markets which, like that at Pompeii, must have been very well provided for. The productive capacity of the Villa of the Mysteries cannot be assessed (it is not out of the question that oil presses too may be discovered there), but those of the villa of la Pisanella can be estimated on the basis of the storage space discovered in the *pars fructaria*. Of the 84 dolia, 72, buried up to their necks (*dolia defossa*), were reserved for storing wine; the others contained grain or oil; their capacity is 93,800 litres (liquids were measured in *culei*, each *culeus* being equivalent to 536 litres, so there were 175 *culei* at Boscoreale).[40] Oil production was smaller in volume, approximately 12,000 litres. Such quantities necessitated a processing plant in the middle of the growing areas; however, agricultural products were also pro-cessed by tradesmen based in town, since excavations at Pompeii have found olive mills and even a small screw press in a shop in the via di Augustali (fig.728).

b Shops and taverns

Premises used for trade and commerce have been referred to several times as occupying the street frontages of houses or the ground floor of buildings. They usually consist of a single room, largely open, sometimes with a small apartment behind or a stairway leading to an upper room. Apart from

730 Entrance to a shop at Pompeii (VII,12,11), showing the groove for fixing the shutter in front of the counter; note also the passage left for the door at one end.

731 Plaster cast of the shutter of a shop in the via dell'Abbondanza (IX,7,10). The vertical planks were secured by a horizontal iron bar with a padlock. The door is on the right.

731

these standard characteristics, shops are distinguishable by their method of closing up: as the merchandise was displayed on a counter occupying the whole width of the shopfront, except for an access passageway, at night the trader had to ensure the protection of his goods by putting up a detachable wooden shutter. Imprints of these have been preserved in the ash at the entrance to several shops at Pompeii in the via dell'Abbondanza. A shutter consisted of a series of vertical interlocking planks which were socketed into the floor by means of a groove made in the stone threshold. One door-leaf, turning in a socket, closed the passage and two long iron bars, inserted through rings fixed either on the inside or the outside of the planks and the door, held the whole thing solidly in position by means of a block fastened with a key (figs 730, 731).[41]

These arrangements are common to all shops and so do not identify the nature of the trade; this requires special installations, furniture, a sign or an inscription. In the absence of such clues on the actual sites where the activity was carried out, the trades and branches of commerce have to be sought on funerary reliefs where they are represented in the process of being carried out or are suggested by tools or materials.

The most easily recognizable shops at Pompeii, Herculaneum or Ostia (fig.732) are those with a masonry counter enclosing enormous earthenware jars up to their necks. These *tabernae*, a word referring to all types of shops, are often identified as being taverns;[42] in fact, even though the large receptacles often contained liquids, which might be wine or oil, they might equally have held grain or dried vegetables, as have been found at Herculaneum. The sale of drink, indeed sometimes located in one of these shops,[43] can be safely established by the presence, at one end of the counter or in a corner of the room, of a small fireplace above which was a cauldron; this meant that hot drinks or soup could be served, hence the name, *thermopolium*, given to these establishments (fig.733).[44] One example in the via di Mercurio (VI,10,1) is in addition decorated with paintings depicting tavern scenes: patrons are shown seated at table being served by a young boy, while over their heads various victuals, sausages, dried fruit and cheeses, hang from hooks. The painter has

732 Shop-front of a *thermopolium* in the street of the House of Diana at Ostia. The benches were for customers to sit outside.

733 *Thermopolium* at Pompeii (VI,3,19). The fire was in the open space at the nearest end of the counter.

taken concern for detail as far as showing his figures speaking: 'a little cold water,' one of them says; 'another glass of Setinum wine,' is ordered by the other one. In another establishment (VII,2,44), it is the hostess who announces 'Edonus tells you, here you can drink for one *as*, for two you can drink better, for four you will get Falernian wine.'[45]

c Bakeries

The second category of easily identifiable shops, even for the uninformed visitor, is the bakery. The bakeries, at least in Pompeii, were also mills (*pistrinum et panificium*), so their shop area included mills made of lava, an area for the preparation of the dough and an oven.

The millstones at Pompeii are all of the same type. Carved from hard lava, they are made up of three parts. First there was a fixed part, the *meta*, in the shape of a bell with elongated sides, which was encircled by a masonry pedestal for an annular metal trough to put the flour in. Above the *meta* was placed the *catillus*, a hollow moving piece in the shape of a double truncated cone; the upper part acted as a funnel for inserting the grain, the lower part performed the milling by rotation against the sides of the *meta* (total height: 1.4 to 1.7m). To enable the grain to filter between the two pieces and to prevent excessive friction blocking the movement, the *catillus* was kept slightly independent by means of a vertical axle connected to a wooden frame, the whole thing being harnessed to a beast of burden, usually a donkey, hence its name, *mola asinaria* (figs 734, 735). The area where millstones were installed was open to the air, on account of the animals (kept in a stable at night[46]), and so that they did not dig up the floor of beaten earth or *opus signinum,* a paved way was laid around each millstone. The brick oven, *furnus,* was often in the same outside area, sheltered under a simple lean-to, close to the preparation area and connected directly to it by means of a side window opening on to the platform built in front of the mouth of the oven (figs 736, 737).

When the geographical conditions were favourable the Roman millers could make use of water as a driving force, as attested by Pliny[47] and Vitruvius;[48] their texts have been given archaeological support by the identification of a multiple mill at Barbegal (Bouches-du-Rhône; published by F. Benoit[49]). This installation, in use

734

734 Relief showing two wheatmills in action, driven by a horse with blinkers. (Rome, Museo Nazionale.)

735 Cross-section of a wheatmill driven by animal power (*mola asinaria*).

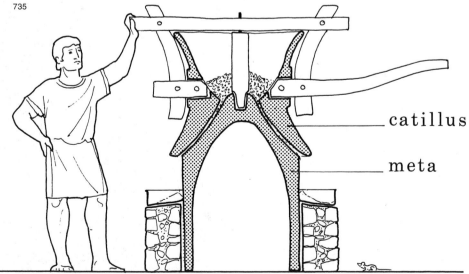

735

catillus

meta

736

736 The miller-baker's of Terentius Proculus at Pompeii (VII,2,3) located in a *domus* after 62.

737 Reconstruction of the bakery in fig.736.

737

between the third and the fifth centuries, consisted of a series of eight waterfalls, artificially arranged on the slope of a hill, each one supplying two vertical wheels; there were thus two millstones per level, 16 millstones in all. If the hourly production of each millstone is estimated at 15kg and taking a day as being 10 hours, daily production must have been 2400kg (fig.738).

Such a quantity, even if it is only an approximate estimate, is quite large, and far greater than that which the small urban mills could produce. These, however, were fairly numerous (about thirty at Pompeii), thus illustrating the importance of flour for the making of gruel, cakes and bread that were staple foods for manual workers, whether freedmen or slaves.[50]

The baking of bread in the bakeries of Pompeii is illustrated still today by the rural ovens in use in the region around Vesuvius. In such ovens, a leavened bread has been baked since

738

739

740

738 Reconstruction of the mechanism of one of the sixteen millstones of the water-mill at Barbegal (Bouches-du-Rhône). (Cf.Vitruvius X,5.)

739 Ancient bread loaf found intact at Herculaneum. House of the Wooden Partition.

740 Loaf of 'pane casareccio' (household bread) from the countryside of Pompeii (1980).

the Augustan period, often still in the shape of a circular cob with divisions, similar to the loaves dicovered at Pompeii and Herculaneum (figs 739, 740).[51]

The process is as follows:[52] a fire made of sticks from vine-shoots (the ideal fuel for Pompeii) is lit in the oven, the iron door of which is left open; the smoke escapes via the pipe placed in front of the door, the pipe sometimes ending in *tubuli* (VI,2,6). The fire is kept blazing until the bricks of the oven vault have become white; the time needed to heat a rural oven 2m in diameter is an hour and a half.[53] The dough, which has been left to stand in the kneading trough situated in the preparation room and covered with a cloth, is moulded into shape ready to be put into the oven quickly as soon as it is at the required temperature. When this point is reached, the ashes and the hot coals are taken out and stored in a *dolium* (nowadays an

enormous non-descript metal can) to be reused as charcoal; then the oven is cleaned out with a brushwood besom or rags soaked in a receptacle filled with water (an earthenware jar or a basin made of lava placed at the end of the oven). The bread is then put into the oven on a wooden shovel, or 'peel', and the oven is closed up by means of an iron door with a small shutter which makes it possible to gauge the temperature; after 30 to 45 minutes the bread is baked and it is taken out with an iron shovel.

d Laundries and dyers

Other tradesmen whose fitted equipment is still recognizable are the fullers, *fullones.* They are represented at Pompeii by four large workshops, the most complete and best preserved of which is the *fullonica* of Stephanus on the via dell'Abbondanza (I,6,7).[54]

The work of these artisans consisted of removing the grease from woollen material just woven[55] and cleaning cloth and clothing; the soap, following a custom now rare, was replaced by certain flowers or by urine. To obtain the latter, the fuller placed in front of his shop amphorae which the passer-by was invited to fill (discovered at the *fullonica* in IX,13,5, and at the entrance to the wool market on the forum), in the absence of which he would have to go and collect it from the *forica*, the public urinal, paying a duty imposed by Vespasian.[56]

The urine, in which the cloth was soaked, was placed in small vats which had sides lined with low walls on which the fuller leant while he trod the material. There are five of these vats, the *lacunae fullonicae*, in Stephanus' premises, located at the end of the building, on either side of three large washing tanks supplied with running water (figs 741, 742). The paintings of the fuller's in the via di Mercurio[57] (VI,8,20) show the artisans in the process of sorting and washing cloth in their small tubs, a scene that is depicted in great detail on a relief preserved at the Musée de Sens (fig.743).

After the grease had been removed with urine, the cloth was treated in the same way with 'fuller's earth' mixed with water. This product was simply clay selected for its cleansing properties; the supplies found at Pompeii, when analysed, were found to be from the island of Ponza (off Anzio).

After being rinsed several times, the cloth and garments were put out to dry; the woollen cloths were then combed and clipped (second panel of the Sens relief) (fig.744) and the white woollens, stretched over wicker cages, had sulphur burnt underneath them to bleach them, by means of a small burner. Another painting, also from the fuller's in the via di Mercurio, shows the method used for combing and also a launderer carrying the large

wicker frame, as well as a small brazier used either to speed up the drying process or for burning sulphur (fig.745). The last stage was ironing, using a large screw press, some parts of which were discovered in the workshop of Stephanus[58] and one of which was found intact in a *fullonica* at Herculaneum.

The wool laundry (*officina lanifricaria*) and the dyer's (*officina infectoria*) were linked both with the fullers and with the weavers. They have simpler installations, also easy to identify, consisting of large terracotta cauldrons which fitted into a masonry mass under which there was a hearth (fig.746). It is only possible to distinguish between the two establishments, whose functions

741 Plan of the *fullonica* of Stephanus, via dell'Abbondanza, Pompeii (I,6,7) (after Spinazzola):
1 *Atrium*
2 Peristyle
3 Treading bowls
4 Washing vats
5 Position of the press
6 Kitchen
7 Latrine.

742 The *fullonica* of Stephanus at Pompeii (I,6,7). On the left are three treading basins where the cloth was trodden in urine or water mixed with clay. In the middle there are three large washing vats; the running water flowed into the upper vat through a lead pipe to the right of it. The water then ran through an overflow into the two lower vats.

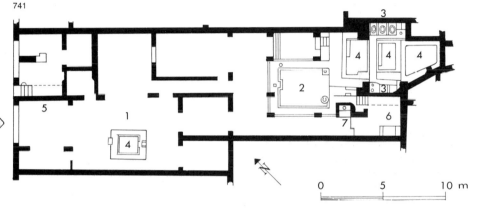

741

742

perhaps overlapped, as for example the wool laundry in the vicolo del Lupanar (VII,12,17), when either cleansing agents or dyes one found.

e Tanneries

However notorious for the unpleasant smells that it produced, the tannery, *officina coriariorum*, was also part of the town, at least at Pompeii. Here two of them have been identified, one near the forum, behind the wool market, the other one in a more outlying area, near the southern wall (*in* I,5,2). In

743 Relief of a Gallo-Roman fuller at work in his vat. (Musée de Sens.)

744 A Gallo-Roman cloth dyer. (Musée de Sens.)

745 A painting of the *fullonica* in the via di Mercurio at Pompeii (National Museum of Naples). The man on the right is carrying a wicker cage on which the clothing was stretched out to be bleached, using sulphur burnt in the brazier (which the man is holding in his hand and which was placed under the cage). The owl is the symbol of Minerva, patron of artisans. On the left, a man is combing a piece of wool stretched out on a line.

746 Furnaces and vats belonging to a dyer's installed in the peristyle of a *domus* after 62; Pompeii (VII,2,11).

743

744

746

745

one tannery the tables were found on which the skins were scraped, and the vats where they were put to soften by soaking between two layers of tanner's bark; in the second tannery, the tools, paring-knife and scraper were still in place.

f The potter

As the potter's kiln, and its workings, has already been described in relation to construction materials, it will not be returned to here, except as a reminder of the existence of this craft which, as a result of the amount of smoke it produces, is usually located outside inhabited areas. Even today, the places in Tunisia where potters and brick-makers operate using ovens of the ancient type, both in Nabeul and in Kairouan, are grouped together in a specific site some way from the nearest inhabited area.

The potter's quarter of Tasciaca (on the south bank of the Cher, near Thésée) is likewise set apart, near the river that acts as a means of distribution for the products. At Pompeii, a potter's kiln and his shop have been discovered on the via delle Tombe, outside the city limits but on an important highway (the road leading to Herculaneum).

g Miscellaneous trades and commerce

The finds of furniture within shops are often more certain pointers to identification than the architecture that has collapsed or been robbed of its identifying metal parts.

Among the most significant finds made at Pompeii is the studio belonging to a sculptor discovered near the Odeon (VIII,7,24), in which several statues were found, some broken, others unfinished, and about thirty tools – mallets, chisels, compasses of various types and even a saw still cutting into a block of marble. The shop of the *faber aerarius*, the blacksmith, in the via d'Abbondanza (I,6,3) should be mentioned, on whose premises the *groma* was found.

Finally, a large number of occupations are known by means of inscriptions or paintings, which might have been put up on or in the shop (a panel advertising the *officina quactilaria*, a manufacturer and dealer in felt, in IX,7,7); or else by electoral inscriptions (approximately 2800!) announcing the choice made by such and such a group or guild of artisans. The inscriptions of the last elections at Pompeii have in this way enabled a list to be made of more than fifty occupations.[59]

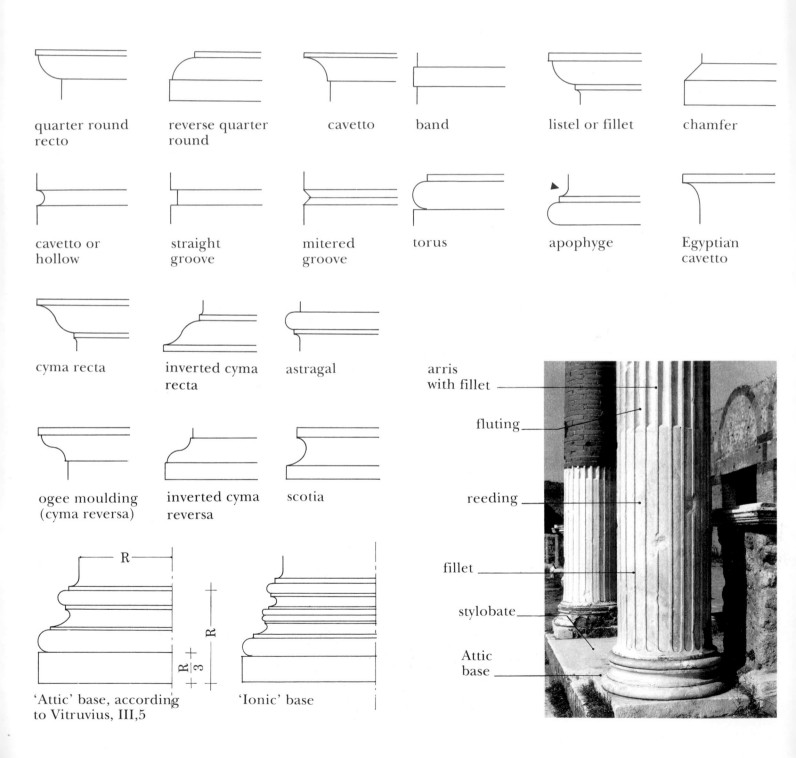

quarter round recto

reverse quarter round

cavetto

band

listel or fillet

chamfer

cavetto or hollow

straight groove

mitered groove

torus

apophyge

Egyptian cavetto

cyma recta

inverted cyma recta

astragal

arris with fillet

fluting

reeding

fillet

stylobate

Attic base

ogee moulding (cyma reversa)

inverted cyma reversa

scotia

'Attic' base, according to Vitruvius, III,5

'Ionic' base

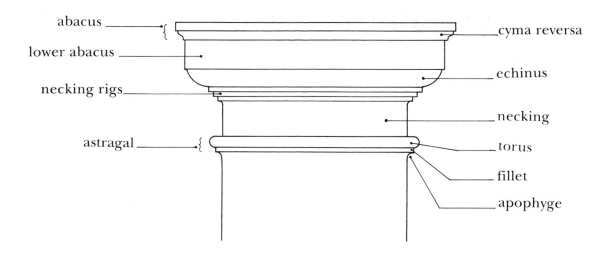

abacus

lower abacus

necking rigs

astragal

cyma reversa

echinus

necking

torus

fillet

apophyge

Doric capital

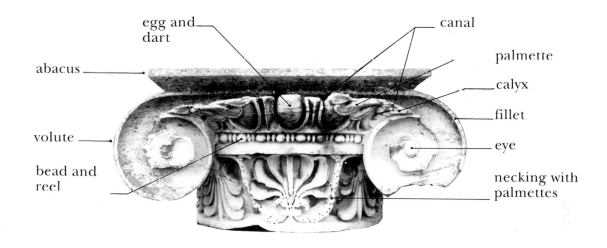

egg and dart

abacus

volute

bead and reel

canal

palmette

calyx

fillet

eye

necking with palmettes

abacus

volute

pulvinus

balteus

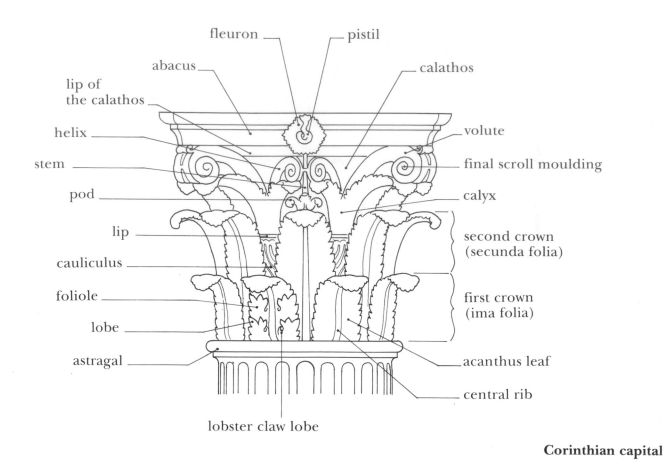

fleuron · pistil

abacus · calathos

lip of
the calathos

helix · volute

stem · final scroll moulding

pod · calyx

lip · second crown
(secunda folia)

cauliculus

foliole · first crown
(ima folia)

lobe

astragal · acanthus leaf

· central rib

lobster claw lobe

Corinthian capital

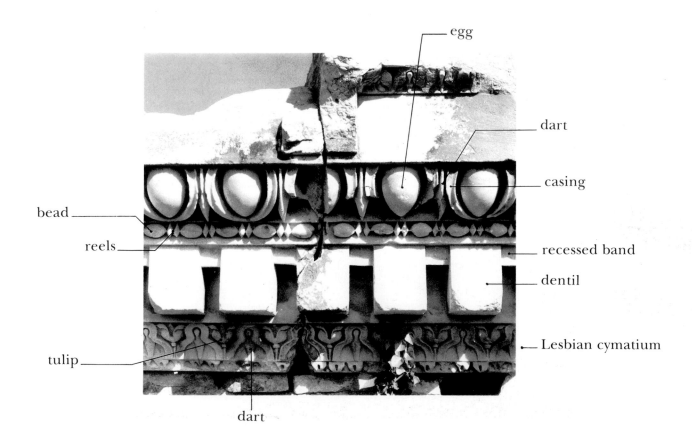

egg

dart

casing

bead

reels

recessed band

dentil

Lesbian cymatium

tulip

dart

Lesbian cymatium

corona

modillion with double volute (scroll modillion)

dentils

Lesbian cymatium

soffit with fleuron coffer

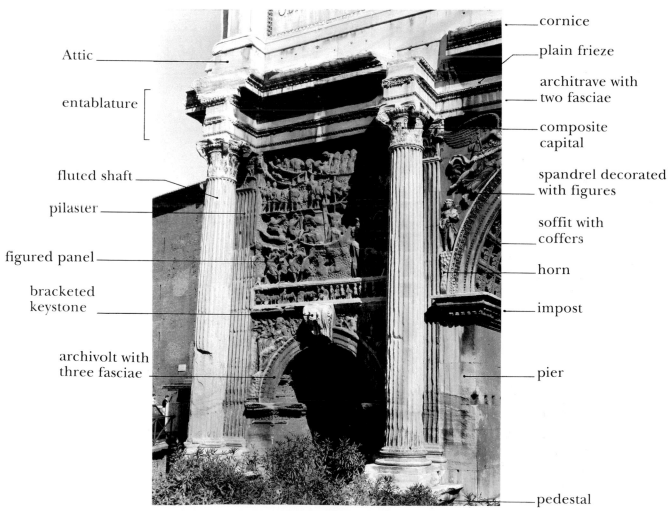

Attic

entablature

fluted shaft

pilaster

figured panel

bracketed keystone

archivolt with three fasciae

cornice

plain frieze

architrave with two fasciae

composite capital

spandrel decorated with figures

soffit with coffers

horn

impost

pier

pedestal

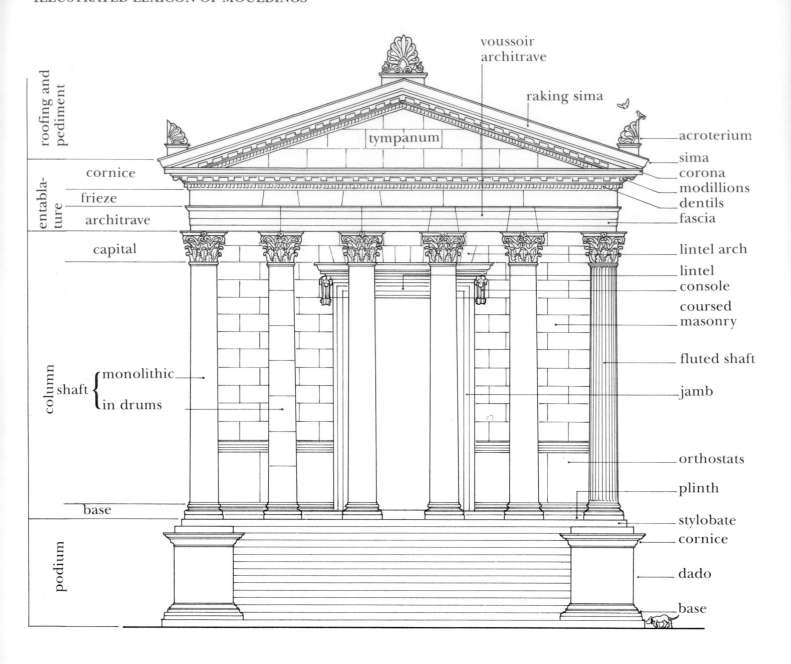

roofing and pediment

entablature

cornice
frieze
architrave

capital

column

shaft { monolithic
        in drums

base

podium

voussoir
architrave

raking sima

tympanum

acroterium
sima
corona
modillions
dentils
fascia

lintel arch
lintel
console
coursed
masonry

fluted shaft

jamb

orthostats

plinth

stylobate
cornice

dado

base

NOTES

Notes to Chapter 1:
Surveying

1 This systematic aspect could be defined, as opposed to spontaneous and arbitrary methods, as the use of alignments and right angles.

2 The functioning of the cadaster, *Khet* and the instrument, the knotted cord, *nouh* (a word also referring to the measure of 100 cubits), are mentioned at the time of the Old Kingdom, while very precise representations of surveying operations (the tomb of Menna) provide us with valuable information on the geometer's profession.

3 It may be recalled that it is the same for the techniques of construction, disciplines richly illustrated in Egypt and Rome, as much by the work of the stone-cutter and the sculptor as by the scenes of building sites or the representation of tools. By contrast, Greek art remains strangely reticent on the subject.

4 Derek de Solla Price, 'Gears from the Greeks, the Antikythera Mechanism, a Calendar Computer from c.80BC' in *Science History Publications* 1975. Discovered in 1902 in a Greek wreck of the first quarter of the first century BC, this bronze machine, probably originating in Rhodes, represents an accurate gear mechanism capable of giving an animated representation of the movements of the sun, moon and stars or groups of stars in the Zodiac. At present on display at the National Museum in Athens.

5 Hero of Alexandria, *On the dioptra*, especially chapter 6,30. The geometric formulas are to be found in his other treatise: *Metrica*. The interpretation of the works of Hero is to be found in: Heronis Alexandrini, *Opera*, ed. Teubner.

6 Hero, *Opera*, vol.III, ed. Teubner, p.193, fig.836.

7 The Arabic word *alidade*, the translation of [δίοπεα], gives its name to the modern functioning instrument following the same principle.

8 Aristophanes, *The Birds*, 993, 1009, quoted by R. Martin, *L'Urbanisme dans la Grèce Antique*, Paris, 1956, pp.16–17.

9 Ch. Mugler, article on Arpentage (Surveying) in *Dictionnaire archéologique des techniques*, Paris, 1963, vol.I, pp.87–8.

10 *Altertümer von Pergamon*, vol.I, pp.37–40.

11 Ch. Fabricius *Athenische Mitteilungen* vol.9, 1884, pp.159ff., and J.G. Landels, *Engineering in the Ancient World*, London, 1978, p.40. It is Herodotus (III,60) who gives us the name of Eupalinos, the architect responsible for this work of art under the reign of Polycrates (third quarter of the sixth century BC). Designed to enable the passage of water, this tunnel-aqueduct is 1100m long and passes under a hill 300m high. It has a square section varying between 1.7m and 2.4m. Everything points to the boring having been undertaken by starting at both ends, given the changes of direction and the difference of height visible at the presumed meeting place of the two galleries.

12 F. Blume, K. Lachmann and A. Rudorff (eds), *Gromatici veteres: Die Schriften der römischen Feldmesser*, Berlin, 1848. From this one learns that the surveyor is sometimes referred to as *gromaticus* or more simply *mensor*.

13 O. Dilke, *The Roman Land Surveyors: An Introduction to the Agrimensores*, Newton Abbot, 1971. On the boundary markings and the boundary texts, the article: 'Limitatio',

Toutain and Barthel in *Fabricius R.E.*, XIII, 1, 1926, coll.672–701, completed by the article 'Limitatio' in *Dizionario Epigrafico di Antichita Romane*, vol.IV, Rome, 1964, p.1383.

14 R. Chevallier and P. Gros have been kind enough to read through these pages and suggest some interesting references for which I am most grateful. My gratitude is also due to Prof Fausto Zevi who has allowed me to use an unpublished photo of the stele of Nicostratus.

15 The author, having used the masculine in an earlier article to refer to this instrument, now comes into line with the practice recommended by Matteo della Corte, i.e. *la groma* (cf. n.18), from B. Bruci and Pol Trousset, *Les Bornes du bled Sequi, nouveaux aperçus sur la centuriation romaine du Sud Tunisien*, *Antiquités Africaines*, 12, 1978, p.137 and n.2.

16 It is useful to distinguish cadastral laying-out, consisting of a definition of the *ager limitatus* by the orthogonal division of a territory in centuries, from the topographical plotting of any piece of land.

17 'Surveying' is in French 'arpentage'. The term has its root in *arapennis*, referring to a surface measurement used in Roman Gaul and maintained in usage until the complete adoption of the metric system. The common 'arpent' equalled 100 perches with a side of 20 feet, i.e. approximately 12,000 sq.m.

18 Frontinus, op.cit., pp.33–4, quoted by P. Trousset, op.cit., p.147.

19 Matteo della Corte, *groma*, *Monumenti Antichi della reale Accademia dei Lincei*, vol.

XXVIII, 1922 coll. 5–100 and *l'Eco degli Ingegneri e Periti agrimensori, Anno XXX*, 1924, no. 11, pp.81–126 and *Case ed abitanti di Pompei*, Naples, 1965 (3rd edition), p.291; a study taken up and completed by the reference to the *gromatici* by B. Bruci, *La groma pompeiana e il testo dei Gromatici Veteres, Bulletin du Cange*, vol. 1 1924–5, pp.98–101.

20 Identical layout to the one on the Ivrea stele.

21 Matteo della Corte, *Case ed abitanti di Pompei*, 3rd ed., Naples, 1965, p.291. Eleven weights of iron and bronze were found in the same shop (April 1912).

22 As the *groma* of Pompeii was broken by the collapse of the superstructure of the house, its exact height is unknown.

23 See the I.G.N. Photographic collection plotted on 1/50,000 scale maps in the *Atlas des centuriations romaines de Tunisie*, Paris, 1959. For Algeria where the topographical plan is quite different, consult the study by Jacqueline Soyer, *Les cadastres anciens de la région de Saint-Donat*, *Antiquités Africaines*, vol.7, 1973, pp.275–92.

24 J. Toutain, 'Le cadastre de l'Afrique romaine', *Mémoires de la Société nationale des antiquaires de France*, 7th series, vol.10, 1910, pp.79–103, a study carried out in numerous articles by the same author and considerably enriched by R. Chevallier, 'Essai de chronologie des centuriations romaines de Tunisie', *MEFRA*, vol.70, 1958, pp.96–105, following on from A. Caillemer and R. Chevallier, 'Les centurations romaines de Tunisie', *Annales E.S.C*, 1957, pp.276–86, Pol Trousset, op.cit.

25 On the terminology of the boundary stones, see O. Dilke, op. cit., pp.87–93 and E. de Ruggiero, op.cit., p.1383.

26 P. Trousset, op.cit., p.126 and n.3.

27 J. le Gall, 'Les Romains et l'orientation solaire', *MEFRA*, vol.87, 1975–1, pp.287–320.

28 J. le Gall, op.cit., p.310.

29 The *Gromatici* mentioning only the case of Hammaedara in Africa where the town and the centuriation share a common grid (*Gromatici*, vol. I, p.180).

30 Frontinus gives us his sources: *Limitum prima origo sicut Varro descripsit, a disciplina etrusca.* (J. le Gall, op.cit., p.303.)

31 Pol Trousset, op.cit., p.149. The author envisages a chronology of order based on four possible sightings, as many as the branches of the *groma*. This proposal that has the obvious advantage of covering all eventualities is in fact quite reasonable as it does not modify the cardinal and decumanal orientations, visible from the air, and at least makes it possible to decipher the indications given on the boundary stones.

32 The aerial photographs do not allow the value of the feet used to be assessed. The century 2400ft across must have measured, with a foot of 0.296m, 710.4m across. For the different values of the foot and their application to centuriation, see A. Piganiol, 'Les documents cadastraux de la colonie romaine d'Orange', XVI supplement to *Gallia*, Paris, 1962, p.42ff. (The cadastral fragments are presented in a special room in the Archaeological Museum of Orange.)

33 See the methods of interpreting the remains of centuriation and of the urban division of land by R. Chevallier in *Présence de l'architecture et de l'urbanisme romains*, *Caesarodunum*, 1981, supp. 38.

34 F. Salviat, 'Orientation, extension et chronologie des plans cadastraux d'Orange', *Revue Archéologique de Narbonnaise*, X, 1977, pp.107–18.

35 F. Salviat, op.cit., p.112, fig.3.

36 A. Piganiol, op.cit., pp.401–2, also came to the conclusion that there was a chronological difference.

37 These dimensions should not be considered as constants since the instrument is not a standard of measurement and only the ease of operation and the optimum efficiency of the stationing and sightings determine the choice.

38 As the site chosen was Vaison-la-Romaine, when the Mistral was blowing, the setting up was quite a problem. It seemed obvious therefore that the plumb lines had to be of such a weight as to withstand the effects of the wind.

39 The experimental operations using the *groma* and the *chorobates* were carried out in the area of la Villasse. The uneven terrain limited both of them to horizontal distances of the order of about 50m.

40 G. Carettoni, A. M. Colini, L. Cozza, G. Gatti, *La pianta marmorea di Roma antica, Forma urbis romae*, Rome, 1960 and more recently: E. Rodriguez-Almeida, 'Forma urbis marmorea, nuovi elementi di analisi e nuove ipotesi di lavoro', *MEFRA*, vol. 89, 1977: 1, pp.219–56, and *Forma Urbis Marmorea, aggiornamento generale* 1980, Rome, 1981. In this latest study, E. Rodriguez-Almeida makes the supposition (pp.46–7) that in view of the uneven topography the work of surveying the land at Rome could have required *dioptrae* working by means of arbitrary sightings, leading to the working out of triangles in the horizontal plane and in the vertical plane.

41 This approximation is equivalent to saying that, on the laying out of a square 10m across, one could have, in the most unfavourable case, a side of 9.9m or of 10.1m, an approximation that can easily be corrected by a direct cross-check measurement on the ground as well as in the

records. For the totality of angular values (the orientation of walls) and linear dimensions (the lengths of sightings and lengths of walls), the discrepancies with plotting by alidade go from 0 to 1.5% (see note 42). Certainly an alignment operation which is a direct sighting leads to a much more satisfactory accuracy. M. Legendre, 'Notes sur la cadastration romaine en Tunisie', *C.I.*, 1957, no.19–20, pp.135–66. This engineer carried out an interesting study relating to the accuracy of topographical layouts as regards direction (angular accuracy) and distance, and suggests with some justification the simultaneous use of several *groma(e)*.

42 For the *Forma urbis*, E. Rodriguez, op.cit., pp.220–2 and fig.1, p.221, notes an accuracy of measurement of 1 to 2.1% in comparison to modern surveys on and between the same monuments.

43 Today's surveyor follows an arbitrary interrupted line made possible by his theodolite and combines at each sighting distance meaurement, angle measurement and levelling.

44 CIL, VIII, 18122, text dated to the years 151–2.

45 Although this building work has not been the object of an exhaustive study, the history and the description of the town of Seleucia-in-Pieria figure in the article by Honigmann, *R.E.*, II, A. I, 1921, coll. 1184. The tunnel is described by R. Dussaud, P. Deschamps, H. Seyrig in *La Syrie antique et médiévale*, Paris, 1931, article 'Séleucie', p.65.

46 A.M. Colini, G.P. Sartorio, *Museo della Civiltà Romana, Catalogo*, Rome, 1982 ed., pp.310–12. Cleaned and improved in the reigns of Trajan and Hadrian, the *emissarium* outlet of Fucino remained in use until the sixth century, after which it was blocked up and the lake formed once again. The work was done again in 1870 and today a vast cultivated plain replaces the stretch of water; to the west of the plain there has developed the town of Avezzano.

47 H. Eschebach, 'Die städtebauliche Entwicklung des antiken Pompeji', *Römische Mitteilungen*, supp. 17, Heidelberg, 1970 and: 'Pompeji: Strassenbau in der Antike', *Antike Welt*, 9-4, 1978, pp.3ff. J. Ward-Perkins, *Note di topografia urbanistica, Pompei 79*, Naples, 1979, p.25ff.

48 The topographical names in Pompeii are the work of archaeologists, as is the numeration of the areas and blocks (*insulae*); however, one does know the name of the *porta Ercolano* (gate of Herculaneum): *Veru Sarinu* in the Oscan language and *Porta Saliniensis* in Latin (it opened on to the *via salina* the 'salt road', leading to the salt pans on the sea-shore, the *salinae Herculis*) and the name of the *Porta di Sarno: Veru Urubla(nu)* or *Porta Urbulana* (CIL IV, 7676).

49 This amphitheatre, the oldest that has survived practically intact (only the paintings of the podium visible at the time of the discovery have today disappeared), is referred to in the Pompeian inscriptions by the term *spectacula*; it seems that the word *amphiteatrum* only spread during the Augustan age; cf. M. Girosi, 'l'Anfiteatro di Pompei', *Memoria dell'Academia di Archeologia Lettere e Belle Arti di Napoli*, 5, 1936, pp.29ff.

50 A. Maiuri, *Scavo della Grande Palestra nel quartiere dell'-Anfiteatro, Notizie degli Scavi*, 1939, pp.165ff.

51 W. Jashemski, 'The Discovery of a Large Vineyard at Pompeii', *American Journal of Archaeology*, 77, 1973, pp.27ff.

52 A. Sogliano, 'Il Foro di Pompei', *Memorie dell' Academia dei Lincei*, 6-1, 1925, pp.221ff. A. Maiuri, *Saggi nell'area del Foro di Pompei, Notizie degli Scavi*, 1941, pp.371ff. and 1942, pp.253ff.

53 CIL X, 794 or: ILS 5538. The *Kvaisstur*, an Oscan word

referring in fact to the quaestor, is a magistrate introduced by Roman influence into Samnite Pompeii, a magistrate whose post was to disappear with the installation the Latin colony after 80.

54 Vitruvius, Book VIII, 5,1,2 and 3.

55 Except perhaps at Herculaneum, since the conditions of the devastation of the city, its burial under the flow of mud from Vesuvius, made possible the preservation of all the wooden material (beams, doors, furniture, small objects).

56 The graphic interpretation of Perrault (1673) was correct and it is found without modification in Choisy and also G. Cozzo, *Ingegneria romana*, pp.123–4, Rome, 1970 or F. Kretschmer, *La technique romaine*, p.12, Brussels, 1966.

57 One is also struck by the modest dimensions of the channel serving as a water level: only 5ft (less than 1.5m), whereas it is precisely this technique that would need a great length to counteract more effectively the effects of capillary attraction and molecular tension.

58 The *groma* and the *chorobates* presented here have been taken to Pompeii for identical demonstrations designed to illustrate the architectural techniques employed in that city.

59 The demonstrations of the use of the *groma* and the *chorobates* have been published for the most part already in: J.P. Adam, 'Groma et Chorobate, exercices de topographie antique', *MEFRA*, 94, 1982–2, pp.1003ff.

Notes to Chapter 2:
Materials

1 Two works, separated in time but complementing each other, have examined all the technical and economic problems relating to quarries: Ch. Dubois, *Étude sur l'administration et l'exploitation des carrières dans le monde romain*, Paris, 1908, J.B. Ward-Perkins, *Quarrying in Antiquity: Technology, Tradition and Social Change*, The British Academy, London, 1972.

2 The *Encyclopédie* of Diderot and d'Alembert, *Maçonnerie et parties relatives*, pl.V, pl.X and under *carrier-platrier*. In these articles the adjectives *quarré* and *quarrée* are found along with the words *carrier* and *carrière*.

3 Vitruvius, *II, VII*.

4 P.-M. Duval, 'Pour une enquête sur les carrières gallo-romaines', *Revue des Études Anciennes*, 1966, p.367.

5 For studies and inventories of types of marble, consult: F. Braemer, 'Les marbres des Alpes occidentales dans l'Antiquité', *Actes du 96° congrès national des sociétés savantes*, Toulouse, 1971, p.274ff.
  H. Blümner, *Technologie und Terminologie der Gewerbe und Künste bei Griechen und Römern*, Leipzig, ed. 1913, vol.III, pp.8ff. R. Cagnat, V. Chapot *Manuel d'Archéologie romaine*, Paris, 1916, vol.I, p.4ff.
  Ch. Daremberg, E. Saglio, E. Pottier, G. Lafaye, *Dictionnaire des Antiquités grecques et romaines*, article on *marmor*, vol.III, pp.1601ff.
  R. Gnoli, *Marmora romana*, Rome, 1971.
  Ch. Klapisch-Zuber, *Les maîtres du marbre, Carrare 1300–1600*, Paris, 1969.
  D. Monna, P. Pensabene, *Marmi dell'Asia Minore*, Rome, 1977. P. Pensabene, *Scavi di Ostia*, VII (devoted to imported marbles), Rome, 1973.
  J.P. Sodini, 'Aliki I, Les carrières de marbre à l'époque paléochrétienne', *Études Thasiennes*, 1980, pp.5ff.

6 F. Coarelli, *Guida archaeologica di Roma*, Rome, 1975, p.339.

7 J.-P. Adam, *Pompéi, Étude de dégradation, proposition de restitution*, CNRS, 1983, chap. *Les matériaux pompéiens*.

8 Vitruvius, op.cit., II,7.

9 The phenomena of the ageing and degradation of stones are known to have been already perfectly understood. On this point it is useful to consult the work published by the Caisse Nationale des Monuments Historiques: *La maladie de la pierre*, Paris, 1975.

10 Lacking the ancient terms, in the original French edition of this work the modern French technical vocabulary was used, in general that fixed at the time of the writing of the *Encyclopédie*, but which sometimes has numerous local variations. These French terms have been given in the text where thought helpful, with their nearest English equivalents.

11 In general it is beneficial to consult the work by Peter Noël, *Technologie de la pierre de taille*, Société des techniques du bâtiment et des travaux publics, Paris, 1965, and more particularly the articles *carrière* and *extraction*.

12 A typology of tools used in mines and quarries is given by A. Léger, *Les travaux publics, les mines et la métallurgie aux temps des Romains*, Paris, 1875, pp.65–71.

13 P. Noël, op.cit., p.162.

14 J.-P. Adam, *L'architecture militaire grecque*, Picard, Paris, 1981, pp.248ff.

15 V. Lassalle, 'Le Pont du Gard et l'aqueduc de Nîmes, Dossiers de l'archéologie', no.38, Oct./Nov. 1979, pp.57ff.

16 F. Mazauric, *Fouilles à Barutel*, Académie de Nîmes, 1909.

17 G. Monthel, M. Pinette, 'La carrière gallo-romaine de Saint-Boil', *Revue Archéologique de l'Est et du Centre-Est*, XXVIII, 1–2, 1977.

18 The first global study of Gallo-Roman quarries is the work of R. Bedon, *Les carrières et les carriers de la Gaule romaine*, Ph.D. thesis, University of Tours, 1981. The topographical information and bibliography are very useful. (Published by Picard, Paris, 1984.)

19 G. Lugli, *La tecnica edilizia romana*, Rome, 1957, vol.II, pls XXVII, XXVIII, XXIX.

20 J.P. Sodini, op.cit., pp.27, 28 and 32 and figs 46, 47 and 57.

21 A. Léger, *Les travaux publics, les mines et la métallurgie aux temps des Romains*, op.cit., p.704. This work, republished in 1979 by J. Laget, devotes only a small space to quarries.

22 G. Nenci, 'Le cave di Selinunte', *Annali della Scuola Superiore di Pisa, Classe di lettere e filosofia*, seria III, vol.IX-4, Pisa, 1979, pp.1417ff.

23 R. Bedon, op.cit., vol.I, pp.133–4, indicates the process carried out in the quarries of Kruft, where the workmen cut out two blocks, the width of the gallery, undercutting at an angle, thus reducing the back surface to be pulled out.

24 If the descriptions are sometimes in the past, sometimes in the present, it is because of the great similarities existing between ancient quarries and their modern counterparts, which sometimes retain the same working practices. This remark is equally true of

traditional stone- and wood-cutting techniques, until the appearance of mechanical tools.

25 F. Mazauric, op.cit., p.208.

26 J.P. Sodini, op.cit., p.23 and n.17.

27 A.K. Orlandos, *Les matériaux de construction et la technique architecturale des anciens grecs*, Athens, 1955, Paris, 1966–8, vol.II, pp.21–3, figs 6, 7 and 8.

28 Vitruvius, X,2.

29 A piece of graffiti, found on the bedding surface of a capital, gives the date as AD 60, making it possible to consider the temple a project carried out under the emperors Claudius and Nero. This estimation does not allow for the inclusion of the construction of the podium in the same period. As megalithic size had been a current form of expression in ancient Syria for several centuries, the possibility cannot be excluded of an earlier unfinished project. The term *trilithon*, referring to the back surface of the podium, does not appear before Michael the Syrian, IX, 16. Cf. E. Will, *Du trilithon de Baalbek et autres appareils colossaux, Mélanges offerts à K. Michalowski*, Warsaw, 1965.

30 J.-P. Adam, *A propos du trilithon de Baalbek, Syria*, LIV, 1977, 162, pp.31ff.

31 In fact horizontal, not vertical, draught force calling by definition for a greater force than the weight to be raised; with the help of a pulley a man cannot lift a weight greater than his own.

32 A.K. Orlandos, op.cit., vol.II, pp.25–8, figs 9 and 13.

33 J.-P. Adam and P. Varène, 'Une peinture romaine représentant une scène de chantier', *Revue Archéologique*, 2, 1980, pp.213ff.

34 The author was able to follow such an operation, still carried out entirely by hand, in a lava quarry on the slopes of Vesuvius.

35 Pliny, *Natural History*, XXXVI, 50–1.

36 J. Röder, 'Dokimion', *Jahrbuch des Deutschen archäologischen Instituts*, 86, 1971, fig.64, pp.303ff. R. Martin, *Manuel d'architecture grecque*, I, Paris, 1965, p.152, n.10, mentions a Roman stele, published in 1913 and unfortunately lost, showing stone-cutting with a saw.

37 A. Leroi-Gourhan, *L'Homme et la matière*, Paris, 1943, 2nd edition 1971, pp.47ff.

38 The medieval pictorial record relating to scenes of building sites is incredibly rich. Consult on this the selection made by P. du Colombier, *Les chantiers des cathédrales*, Picard, Paris, 1973.

39 P. Varene, *Sur la taille de la pierre antique, médiévale et moderne*, University of Dijon, Centre de recherche sur les techniques greco-romaines, 1974, pp.10, 48, 49, 50 and pl.1,2. The author here describes in minute detail each dressing operation of a section of moulding intended for the restoration of a historic monument and the tools relating to it.

40 Th. and J.-P. Adam, *Le tecniche costruttive a Pompei*, ICCD, Rome, 1981, p.102.

41 G. Lugli, op.cit., vol.II, pl.XXX-3.

42 The location of buildings at Pompeii is fixed by 'regions', 'insulae' and 'numbers'; the references are thus always in this order (one Roman numeral and two Arabic numerals); see the plan of Pompeii in the chapter on *domus*.

43 Cf. the collections at Saint-Germain-en-Laye.

44 Musée de Saint-Germain-en-Laye, Musée du Berry (Bourges), Pompeii.

45 Musée de Saint-Germain-en-Laye, Museum of Syracuse.

46 A.K. Orlandos, op.cit., vol.II, p.52, fig.41.

47 A journeyman's saying goes as follows: 'wood on wood, iron on iron'.

48 The *Antiquarium* of Pompeii.

49 The definition of these terms relating to the location of a stone in organized construction work will be given later.

50 *Notizie degli scavi di Ostia*, 1897, p.524, fig.6.

51 The latest one being that by A. Piganiol, in *Les documents cadastraux de la colonie romaine d'Orange*, op.cit., pp.42ff.

52 The origin of *actus versus* is the length of the furrow marking the pause before making another.

53 In the new southern area of the E.U.R.

54 J. Conneau, 'Une équerre-niveau gallo-romaine', *Bulletin archéologique* du Vexin, no.1, 1965, pp.79ff.

55 J. Conneau, op.cit., p.85, figs 4 and 5.

56 The Museum of Naples has two examples.

57 At least in this form of a drum motor; in reality, certain horizontal hand mills were operated with a vertical wooden dowel in an off-centre position which was moved with a turning handle.

58 G. Lugli, op.cit., vol.I, p.225, fig.39 and *Mitteilungen des deutschen archäologischen Instituts (Röm-Abt)*, II, 1949, p.23.

59 J.-P. Adam, P. Varene, op.cit., p.216, fig.2.

60 F. Kretschmer, *La technique romaine*, La Renaissance du livre, Brussels, 1966, pp.24, 25, 26. Model reconstructions of various lifting machines can be seen at the Rheinisches Landesmuseum in Bonn.

61 Its use was maintained on medieval building sites, as is proved by an abundance of pictorial representations, and even in stone quarries up to the beginning of the twentieth century, under the name of quarryman's wheel or quarryman's winch.

62 Relief offered by *Luccius Peculiaris* to three divinities: Minerva, Jupiter and Diana. G. Lugli, op.cit., vol.I, p.226, *Mostra Augustea della Romanità, Catalogo*, 5th edition, p.590.

63 Marble relief originating in the tomb of the family of the Haterii (period of Domitian) built on the *via Labicana*. It is preserved in the Lateran collections at the Vatican Museum. Cf. J.-P. Adam, *A propos du trilithon de Baalbek*, op.cit., pp.40–1, fig.5.

64 It is in fact the carpenter who places the bouquet or a flag, when the topping is complete. The same custom existed when the last sheaf of corn had been put on the cart on harvesting day.

65 E. Viollet-le-Duc, *Dictionnaire raisonné de l'Architecture française du XIe au XVIe s.*, Paris, 1875 edition, vol.V, pp.212–13.

66 A.K. Orlandos, op.cit., vol.II, pp.87ff. and R. Martin, *Manuel d'Architecture grecque*, I, Picard, Paris, 1965, pp.209ff.

67 *Monumenti Antichi dei Lincei*, XII, 1903, p.169, fig.8, G. Lugli, op.cit., vol.II, pl.XXX-2.

68 A.K. Orlandos, op.cit., vol.II, pp.99 and 100; R. Martin, op.cit., pp.114–99.

69 H. Seyrig, R. Amy, E. Will, *Le Temple de Bel à Palmyre*, Paris, 1975, vol.I, p.63, fig.33 and p.111, fig.57.

70 G. Lugli, op.cit., vol.I, p.201.

71 P. Gros, *Bolsena*, École française de Rome, 1981, pp.16–17, fig.1.

72 J. Röder, 'Quadermarken am Aquädukt von Karthago', *Mitteilungen des deutschen archäologischen Instituts, Römische Abteilung*, 81, 1974, fasc.1, pp.91–105.

73 The practice of marking the blocks still exists in a number of quarries both to keep a tally on the work and

to indicate the destination of the stones (cf. the chapter on quarries).

74 G. Lugli, op.cit., vol.I, pp.232–5.

75 R. Martin, op.cit., pp.241–7. A.K. Orlandos, op.cit., vol.II, pp.101–5.

76 Gismondi, *Scavi di Ostia*, I, p.191. G. Lugli, vol.I, op.cit., pp.236–7.

77 Primitive wooden dowels were retained quite late by the Greeks for the joins between column drums.

78 Durm, *Baukunst der Römer*, p.15, fig.9.

79 M.E. Blake, *Ancient Roman Constructions in Italy from the Prehistoric Period to Augustus*, Washington, 1947, p.134.

80 E.B. Van Deman, *The Building of the Roman Aqueducts*, Washington, 1934, p.127.

81 A. Von Gerkan, *Dura Europos, the fortifications*, 1939.

82 In recent times strong metal collars have had to be put around these abutment masses to support them, apparently confirming this hypothesis.

83 O. Aurenche, *Dictionnaire illustré multilingue de l'architecture du Proche-Orient ancien*, Lyon-Paris, 1977, pp.40–2; *Dictionnaire archéologique des techniques*, article *brique: Asie occidentale et Égypte*, vol.I, pp.169ff.

84 A. Orlandos, op.cit., vol.I, p.68 and n.2.

85 P. Mingazzini, *Velia, scavi della fornace di mattoni*, Atti della società Magna Grecia, 1954, pp.21ff. The Velia bricks, square (38 × 38cm) and 9.5cm thick or rectangular (56 × 30cm and 38 × 23cm), have one or two recesses in which the stamp is printed.

86 Walls with timber framing and filled with daub have been discovered in ancient houses in Amiens, cf. J.-L. Massy, *Samarobriva Ambianorum, une ville de la Gaule Belgique*, thesis, Amiens, 1977.

87 A. Danzat, J. Dubois, H. Mitterand, *Nouveau Dictionnaire étymologique et historique*, article *pisé*, Paris, 1964, p.570.

88 By contrast, he refers to them (V.10, *De balnearum dispositionibus et partibus*) for the construction of hypocausts.

89 Pompeii, the Basilica, the Odeon and the individual houses.

90 Pliny, *Natural History*, XXXV, 170.

91 A. Orlandos, op.cit., vol.I, pp.70–4, refers to some Greek tile kilns, from the fourth and third centuries at Corinth and Olympus, of rectangular and square shape. G.S. Weinberg, 'The Tile Factory', in *Ancient Corinth, A Guide to the Excavations*, 1954, pp.87ff. and H. Schleif, R. Eilmann, 'Bericht über die Ausgrabungen in Olympia', IV, Berlin, 1944, figs 11 and 19.

92 Lime kilns function in exactly the same way, as will be seen later.

93 H. Bloch, *I bolli laterizi e la storia edilizia di Roma*, Rome, 1947.

94 See the detailed commentaries by Dresseel in the CIL, XV and the chapter *Bolli Laterizi* by G. Lugli, op.cit., vol.I, pp.553ff.

95 CIL XII, p.683.

96 CIL VIII, p.2173.

97 A. Maiuri, *Saggi e ricerche intorno alla basilica, Notizie degli scavi*, 1951, pp.225ff.; E. La Rocca, M. de Vos, A. de Vos, *Guida archeologica di Pompei*, Rome, 1976, pp.107ff.

98 Philo of Byzantium, *Book V of Mechanical Syntax*, A, (1), (8) (11) and (20). The word used by Philo is ννψοδ (gypsos), but this word means both gypsum (i.e. plaster) and lime. The reference of Dura-Europos would tend towards the first use, but it was a custom specific to Syria and one cannot generalize from this.

99 From the Latin *aggregare*, to reunite, to gather together.

100 Depending on the region, the kiln can be narrower at the bottom or narrower at the top.

101 G.L. Flach, *Fours à chaux dans le Nord-Est de la France à l'époque Gallo-romaine*, Sarreguemines, 1981, p.3. The name *chamotte* is still today used to mean the ceramic fragments employed as a tempering agent in the manufacture of fire-proof bricks.

102 Local artisans have not been able to come up with the etymology of this word and it does not occur in the standard Italian vocabulary. The only *lamia* known in Latin was a female monster (mother of Scylla) pursuing children to eat them (hence the name, *lamna*, given to a dangerous type of shark).

103 Cato, *De agricultura*, XLIV, *De fornace calcaria*.

104 Some ancient lime kilns have been restored at the Museum of Iversheim-Eifel (near Münstereifel on Tolbiac's site) in Germany.

105 V. Spinazzola, *Pompei alla luce degli scavi nuovi*, Rome, 1953, vol.I, pp.446–7.

106 A phenomenon perfectly understood by the Romans: cf. Vitruvius, II,5.

107 The author was able to experiment with the preservation of rich lime by making a slaking pit on a site in Asia Minor, made necessary by construction work, and found the putty perfectly usable after a period of one year, as the pit was covered by 35 to 40cm of earth.

108 Pliny, *Natural History*, XXXVI,55.

109 See what was said on the subject of fat clay and lean clay.

110 M. Frizot, *Mortiers et enduits peints antiques*, Centre de recherche sur les techniques greco-romaines, University of Dijon, 1975.

111 Vitruvius makes a direct allusion to this in II,8: '. . . these walls are falling down because the joints are coming apart, the force of the mortar of which they are made having dissipated and evaporated in the process of drying . . .'.

112 J.-P. Adam, *La dégradation des sites antiques, l'exemple pompéien*, Centre Jean-Bernard, Naples, 1983. *Dégradation et restauration de l'architecture pompéienne*, CNRS, 1983.

113 References to mortar, depending on its composition and its usage, can be found in several places in the *Ten Books*: II,4, sand – II,5, manufacture of lime, composition of mortar – II,6, pozzolana – II,8, types of masonry, facings and fillings, use of mortar with broken tiles – V,12, foundations and masonry in water – VII,1, cement and mortar for flooring – VI,2, preparation of lime intended for rendering and stucco – VI,3, creation of stucco cornices – VI,3, creation of stucco cornices and vaults and ceilings – VI,6, preparation of stucco on marble – VIII,7, the masonry of cisterns.

114 The French word for 'mixing mortar', 'gâchage', comes from the Germanic 'waskon', to wet, containing the Indo-Germanic radical, 'was', meaning water.

115 Some of them have been recovered, still full of water, from several houses in Pompeii: House of the Beautiful Soffit, V,3,4 – or in VII,3,17.

116 This hoe is called in French a 'rabot', from the Central dialect word 'rabotte', a rabbit, because of the similarity between a wood plane (rabot) and the silhouette of this rodent when recumbent.

117 The French word for 'tempering', 'corroyage', is a synonym for preparation or treatment and also refers to the fine preparation of leather skins or the planing of wood; it is used here

because of the planing movement made by the 'rabot' (plane – see note above) in crushing the lumps.

118 The term refers only to construction with rubble stones or bricks bonded with mortar and never to the dressed stone used in stone block construction; likewise, the mason should not be con-fused with the stone-cutter.

119 A curious remark by Vitruvius, as it is the most common building technique; but perhaps the author wishes to allude to masonry of rural origin decorated with dry stones whose in-filling was bonded with clay. It is, however, justified to note how much this author's academic mind, somewhat set in its way of looking back to Greek architecture, made him reject new techniques associated with the standardization of detailed masonry.

120 The French word for 'concrete', 'béton', comes from 'bitumen', meaning in fact the mixture of mortar and pebbles, then becoming a synonym for mortar or a bonding agent, the bitumen used as a glue for bricks and a waterproof rendering in eastern architecture.

121 Cato, *De agricultura*, XIV, I,5,15 – XVIII,7. This work is taken to have been written between 175 and 149 BC, the year of his death.

122 Varro, *De re rustica*, I,14,4, almost contemporary with Vitruvius; it would have been enormously interesting to possess this author's *Rerum humanorum et divinarum antiquitates*, a work of which only tiny fragments have survived but which no doubt contained precise information on the origins of Roman monumental techniques.

123 CIL, X, 1781, I,r,16–22, quoted by G. Lugli, op.cit., vol.I, p.363.

124 CIL, III, 633, I,r,11.

125 *Codex Theodosianus*, XIV, VI, the work of Theodosius II.

126 R.C. Carrinton, 'Notes on the Building Materials of Pompeii', *Journal of Roman Studies*, 23, 1933, p.130.

127 A. Maiuri, *Notizie degli scavi*, 1942, pp.285ff.

128 F. Coarelli, 'Public Building in Rome between the Second Punic War and Sulla', *Papers of the British School of Rome*, XLV, 1977, p.1ff. The author presents (p.23) a table of masonry monuments, their identifications and dates, from the Temple of Magna Mater to the Theatre at Pompeii.

129 P. Romanelli, *Lo scavi del Tempio della Magna Mater sul Palatino, Monum Lincei*, XLVI, 1963, col.202-330.

130 Livy, XXXV,10,12 and XLI,27,8, quoted by G. Catti, in the *Bollettino della commissione Archeologica comunale di Roma*, LXXII, 1934, pp.134ff, whose reconstruction perspective has been taken up by A. Boethius and J.-B. Ward-Perkins, *Etruscan and Roman Architecture*, Harmondsworth, 1970, p.107, fig.62.

131 The Temple of Apollo at Didyma, 118m long and 60m wide, is one of the great Greek temples comparable in size and decoration to the Temple of the Ephesian Artemis or the Heraion of Samos. The perfection of its stonework is total; an optical correction curve can be verified starting from the peristyle and reverberating in the height of the naos, with a central rise of only 10cm.

132 The stamps on the bricks and a biographical note on Hadrian make possible this precision; cf. F. Coarelli, *Guida archéologica di Roma*, Rome, 1974, pp.258ff. and H. Bloch, *Bolli laterizi*, p.102.

133 G. Lugli, *I monumenti antichi di Roma e suburbio*, 4 vol., Rome, 1930–1938–1940, I, pp.414ff.

134 A word that has remained for catafalque, the raised platform supporting a coffin.

135 Traditionally referring to the theatre stage made up of beams or cross-beams (in French 'traverses' from vulgar Latin *trastellum*) and resting on legs and supporting a floor.

136 This tomb, now in the urban area, is not visible, but a reproduction is on display at the Museo della Civiltà Romana, room LII.

137 Medieval pictorial representations confirm the later very frequent use of this type of scaffolding.

138 A. Choisy, *L'Art de bâtir chez les romains*, Paris, 1873, pp.23–6.

139 See below for the typology of masonry.

140 Vitruvius, II,9.

141 Up to the beginning of the twentieth century, the word for 'felling or cutting down' in French, 'abattage', was spelled with one t: 'abatage'; this peculiarity has now dropped out of use in keeping with the Latin etymology *battuere, battere*, to beat.

142 The word that gives the French word for 'fir', *sappinea*, is applied by Vitruvius only to the lower part of the trunk.

143 Average density, with 15 per cent humidity, of wood dried in the open air. For the complete data, consult: E. Barberot, *Traité pratique de charpente*, Béranger, Paris, 1952, pp.561ff.

144 G. Giordano, *Tecnologia del legno, dalla foresta ai vari impieghi*, Hoepli, Milan, 1956, see particularly ch.II, *abattimento*, pp.13ff. and *Ferri ed attrezzi*, pp.58ff. This work, one of the most complete in existence at present, gives illustrations with the profiles of axes and saws in traditional use in most countries in the world.

145 The French word for cleaver, 'merlin', probably comes from *marculus*, a hammer.

146 The French word for saw, 'scie', comes from the Latin *secare*, to cut (cf. secateur) and was originally spelled *sie*.

147 The French word for log is 'grume'. It seems there has been a shift of meaning from the Latin *gluma*, skin, to *gruma*, bark (cf. grumeau, grumeleux) coming to mean any felled log still with its bark which is the characteristic of a log.

148 Shown in a plaster-cast at the Museo della Civiltà Romana, room III, no.3417; published at the beginning of the century by H. Gummerus, in the *Jahrbuch des deutschen archäologischen Instituts*, 28, 1913, p.101, fig.20.

149 Several are preserved in the Musée de Saint-Germain-en-Laye in a cabinet of 'agricultural instruments'.

150 There is a whole host of local names for wood tools in France; the 'hache d'équarrissage', squaring axe, is also known as 'épaule de mouton', 'bigeoir' or 'hache à peler'.

151 It is sometimes worth reflecting on the fact that only seventy-five generations have gone by since the reign of Trajan. A skill passed on by such a small number of people with the same means at their disposal had little chance of being radically modified.

152 J.L. Goodman, *The History* of *Woodworking Tools*, London, 1976, pp.110ff.

153 Pliny, Natural History, XVII,23. Vitruvius, X,V, F. Benoît, 'L'usine de meunerie hydraulique de Barbegal', *Revue archéologique*, janv-mars 1940, pp.19–80.

154 This admirable piece of evidence is preserved in the Archaeological Directorate of the city of Rome on the Capitoline but a copy can be seen in the Museo della Civiltà Romana, room LII.

155 The English and French words 'carpenter' and 'carpentry', 'charpentier' and 'charpente', derive from

carpentum, meaning the covered wagon of the Gauls.

156 The French word for wood plane, 'rabot', has the same etymology as the tempering plane (= hoe), i.e. 'rabotte', old French for rabbit, relating in fact to the similarity of the wood plane's shape to a recumbent rabbit.

157 W. L. Goodman, op.cit., pp.43ff.

158 National Museum of the Baths and the Museum of Syracuse. The Syracuse plane is shown in a restoration, using the blade wedging, in W. Gaitzsch, 'Eiserne römische Werkzeuge', *B.A.R. Inter-national Series,* 78, Oxford, 1980, vol.II, pl.26. The author shows three other planes (pls 59, 63) and the picture of a joiner using this tool (pl.73).

159 Two are preserved at Saint-Germain-en-Laye, one from Abbeville, the other from Compiègne.

160 The screw-shaped drill appears to be of Gaulish origin; perhaps it is the *terebra gallica* that Pliny speaks about (XVII,15).

161 W.L. Goodman, op.cit., pp.165ff.

162 *Triclinium* in the House of the *Vettii,* a painting of the workshop of Daedalus.

163 Side face of the funerary cippus, already referred to, also showing a wood plane.

164 Ch. Frémont, *Origine et évolution des outils,* Paris, 1913, pp.50–83.

165 E. Barberot, op.cit., pp.7ff.

166 The subject of trusses will be dealt with later.

167 The architect Jean-Marie Gassend, attached to the Ancient Architecture Service of the CNRS, Aix office, has specialized in this field and has considerably helped to enrich our knowledge of ancient naval architecture.

168 Wood joints are set out in professional works intended for the use of carpenters and architects; the most complete are at present: E. Barberot, *Traité pratique de charpente,* Paris, 1952, *joints,* pp.7–41. Y. Gasc and R. Delporte, *Les charpentes en bois,* Paris, 1965, *Les assemblages,* pp.199–232 (the most current work but mainly devoted to modern woodworking). L. Mazerolle, *Traité théorique et pratique de charpente,* Paris, 1866, republished by the Compagnons charpentiers des devoirs du Tour de France, *Assemblages,* vol.I, pl.14, a work of considerable value particularly devoted to the marking out of timber work.

Notes to Chapter 3:
Construction using large stone blocks

1 Originally *Italia* was *Bruttium,* the extreme south of the peninsula (the heel and toe of the boot) but, between the end of the fourth century BC and the beginning of the third, the meaning was extended to include Gaul on the Roman side of the Alps which was itself integrated in 42BC. Besides Greek and Etruscan, around a dozen languages were spoken there until the fourth century BC. Rome managed to impose Latin, even though Oscan was still spoken in Campania at the beginning of the first century BC, and Greek in Sicily. Etymologically, the word *Italia* comes from the eponymous hero *Italos,* the legendary king of *Bruttium.*

2 J.-P. Adam, *L'Architecture militaire grecque,* Picard, Paris, 1981, p.23.

3 G. Lugli, op.cit., vol.I, pp.55ff.

4 G. Lugli, op.cit., vol.II, pl.IV.

5 G. Lugli distinguishes four types of construction with polygonal stone blocks, op.cit., vol.I, pp.65ff.; in fact the distinctions are not as clear as this author seems to indicate in his thoroughly admirable wish to set up a typology, for one has to take into account the thickness of the stone work, the treatment of the facings or the horizontality of the courses and one ends up with as many categories as there are examples.

6 *Forma Italiae, Anxur-Terracina,* zona III, fig.8.

7 It is also not possible to deny the fact that archaeological research has tended to concentrate on the most recent periods and the richest in monuments.

8 For details and historical documentation, the reader is referred to R. Bloch, *Les origines de Rome,* P.U.F., seven editions between 1946 and 1978, and L. Homo, *Nouvelle histoire romaine,* Paris, 1941, revised edition and publication by Ch. Pietri, Marabout Université, 1979.

9 P.-C. Jonta, *Storia di Segni,* Cavignano, 1982.

10 *Forma Italiae, Circeii,* zona I, Rome, 1928.

11 G. Gullini, 'I monumenti dell'acropoli di Ferentino', *Archeologia Classica,* 1954, pp.185ff.

12 Appian, *Roman History, The Civil Wars,* I, 94. The historian describes in succession the taking of Praeneste, then the resistance and capture of Norba by treachery, and the voluntary burning of the town by its inhabitants.

13 *Forma Italiae, Anxur-Terracina,* Rome, 1926, zona III, figs 4 to 16.

14 Appian, op.cit., *Hannibal,* 39, and Livy X,I,I and XXVI,II,II. Results of the Belgian excavations: J. Delaet, J. Merteus, F. de Ruyt and F. de Visscher in *Antiquité classique* since 1951.

15 G. Lugli, op.cit., vol.I, *Aletrium,* pp.131ff.

16 Franck E. Brown, E.-R. Richardson, 'Cosa I, History and Topography', *Memoirs of the American Academy of Rome,* XX, 1951, pp.12ff. and XXVI, 1960.

17 X. Lafon, 'La voie Littorale Sperlonga–Gaeta–Formia', *MEFRA,* vol.91, 1979-81, pp.399ff.

18 No mention can be made here of the huts on the Palatine, belonging to the seventh-century village corresponding to the legendary village of Romulus. The excavations were published by S.M. Puglisi, *Gli abitatori primitivi del Palatino, Monumenti antichi dei Lincei,* 1951.

19 See the commentary by R. Bloch, *Les origines de Rome,* P.U.F., 1978, p.52.

20 A.M. Colini, 'Il Campidoglio nell'antichita', *Capitolium,* 40, 4, 1965, pp.175ff.; F. Coarelli, 'Le tyrannoctone du Capitole et la mort de Tiberius Gracchus', *MEFRA,* 81, 1969, pp.137ff. The systematic evolution of the planning of Rome is very clearly described by Sylvia Pressouyre, in *Rome au fil du temps,* J. Cuenot, Paris, 1973.

21 The sixth king of Rome (578-535).

22 *Roma Medio Repubblicana, Catalogo della Mostra,* Rome, 1973, pp.7ff. Another interesting indication of chronology is given by the material of which it is largely constructed, tufa of Grotta Oscura from Veii, an Etruscan town conquered by the Roman army under Camillus in 396BC.

23 F. Rakob, W.-D. Heilmeyer, 'Der Rundtempel am Tiber in Rom', *Deutsch. Arch. Inst., Sonderschriften* 2, Mainz, 1973, pp. 9 and 20.

24 This initial precaution in all

works of construction, however obvious it may seem, has not always been followed with equal care, as is proved by numerous médieval buildings, particularly in the Romanesque period, literally placed on the ground.

25 In French 'bousin', rock that is powdered or split up.

26 The combination of different techniques of Roman construction here shows the difficulty (and a similar situation runs all through the literature) that arises when one wishes to establish a strict sequence of techniques, appearances and stages of architecture starting with the Later Republican period.

27 On the recent discoveries of pile foundations, see: P. Debord, M. Gauthier, *Bordeaux, Saint Christoly, sauvetage archéologique et histoire urbaine*, Bordeaux, 1982, pp.50ff., figs 42-58.

28 A word that one must be careful not to confuse with *ager*, meaning a domain or territory, particularly used to refer to the public domain, the *ager publicus* gained by conquest.

29 E. La Rocca, M. and E. de Vos, *Guida archeologica di Pompei*, Rome, 1976, pp.33ff.

30 R. Amy, P. Gros, *La Maison Carrée de Nîmes*, XXXVIII supplement *Gallia*, Paris, 1979, vol.II, pl.12.

31 The terms column and pillar have been chosen as defining respectively supports of circular section and supports of square section. A pier is considered to be a more massive piece of work of no matter what section.

32 The details of mouldings belonging to the orders will be given in the illustrations on decoration.

33 Below will be shown that they can even be made out of masonry.

34 A Doric temple built in 480BC after the victory of Himera.

35 P. Gros, *Aurea Templa, Ecole Française de Rome*, 321, 1976, pp.119-20.

36 The Greeks rarely attempted it and then in a curious and excessive manner as at the Temple of the Giants at Agrigentum (end of the sixth century, beginning of the fifth century BC), with engaged Doric columns 4m in diameter and 17m high, or on the delicate monument of Lysicrates in Athens (334BC) whose six small Corinthian columns are supported on a tholos 1.8m in diameter.

37. Which is not the case when they are made of masonry.

Notes to Chapter 4:
Structures of mixed construction

1 This heading draws attention to the difficulties of terminology that sometimes occur in defining those arrangements of material that do not belong to the basic models; in this case caused by the possible confusion with *opus mixtum*, the term used for the mixtures of materials in concrete masonry.

2 To this observation can be added the simple disappearance, beginning in antiquity, of numerous buildings judged to be unsound and pulled down to make room for other constructions.

3 P. Gros, *Les éléments architecturaux, les murs en damier*, in: A. Balland, A. Barbet, P. Gros, G. Hallier, 'Bolsena II, les architectures', coll. de l'École Française de Rome, 1962-67, pp.69-75, and 'Bolsena', *MEFRA*, supp.6, Rome, 1981, p.59.

4 The excavators at Velia proposed to define it as *opus velinum*, but such a name is an excessive appropriation, given the geographical area concerned; a building of the Dipylon in Athens has a well-preserved example of it.

5 P. Gros, op.cit., p.18 and n.78.

6 E. Greco has pointed out a wall of undated 'chequer-work' on the site of the Castella near Croton.

7 The same question can be asked about the chequer-work walls at Velia, a coastal town of Lucania in the zone of exclusive Greek influence, and those at Bolsena at the heart of Etruria.

8 This is clearly seen in the case of conquest architecture in the peninsula as in the Greek and Oriental world.

9 A. Beschaouch, R. Hanoune, Y. Thebert, *Guide archéologique de Bulla Regia*, De Boccard, Paris, 1977, pp.18-21, figs 9, 10, 11.

10 This construction technique is also called 'colombages' in French, probably because of the similarity it displays to a colonnade when it has not yet been filled in; each post used to have the name 'colombe' (dove) by a shift from *columna* to *columba*.

11 The origin of the term in French, 'sablière', according to timber-working tradition, comes from the fact that the horizontal pieces of wood, the whole length of which was supported by the top of a wall, in fact rested on the sand filling a cavity made in the wall-ridge, so that compression of the weight (timber-framing or roof timbers) is distributed in a completely even way.

12 It is chiefly at Herculaneum that wood has survived; as for doubts about the antiquity of certain constructions at Pompeii, they are justified by a certain number of restorations carried out in the Western sector of the site in the course of the nineteenth century and which, because of ageing, now look original.

Notes to Chapter 5:
Masonry Construction

1 The Latin terminology used is that suggested by G. Lugli in his *Tecnica edizia romana*, vol.I, pp.40ff.: *Terminologia degli antichi sistemi costruttivi*. The author there makes a synthesis of the Latin sources and the terms most traditionally used by archaeologists.

2 It must be remembered that ancient authors used the words *opus* and *structura* interchangeably to refer to the characteristics of a wall, masonry or a vertical or horizontal facing; the term *opus* has been chosen as it has passed into the Italian language in the form *opera*, with its most usual meaning.

3 F. Coarelli, 'Public Building in Rome between the Second Punic War and Sulla', *P.B.S.R.*, XLV, 1977, appendix 2, p.23.

4 Above the Piazza della Consolazione.

5 Livy XXXVIII, 28,3; F. Coarelli, op.cit., p.13 and fig.b, pl.I; G. Lugli, op.cit., vol.II, pl.CVIII, fig.3.

6 F. Coarelli, op.cit., appendix 2, p.23 and figs c and d, pl.I.

7 F. Coarelli, op.cit., p.14,

8 G. Lugli, op.cit., vol.II, pl.CXXVI, fig.4; C. Morselli, E. Tortorici, *Ardea Forma Italiae*, I, 16, Florence, 1982.

9 G. Lugli, op.cit., vol.II, pl.CXX, fig.4 and pl.CXVII, fig.1; F. Coarelli, op.cit., p.255.

10 G. Lugli, op.cit., vol.II, pl.CXXI, figs 2 and 3; *Formia*, collective publication, Formia, 1977.

11 G. Lugli, op.cit., vol.II, pl.CXX, fig.3.

12 G. Lugli, *Anxur-Terracina, Forma Italiae*, I, 1, Rome, 1926; B. Conticello, *Terracina*, Itri, 1976.

13 P. Gros, op.cit., pp. 79 and 80, fig.37.

14 The presence of bricks in the piers and the lintels encourages the attribution of a later date going up to the Flavian period, but we know Campania was more advanced in the use of terracotta than the rest of the peninsula.

15 This 'standardization' does not imply a unity of size; even when they are very close they remain peculiar to each centre of production.

16 A. Maiuri, *L'ultima fase edilizia di Pompei*, Rome, 1942; R.C. Carrington, op.cit., pp.135-6.

17 From *reticulum*, a net.

18 F. Coarelli, *Public Buildings*, p.16, appendix 2, p.23 and pl.II.

19 The poverty of remains from Republican Rome is explained by the immense destruction caused by fires, particularly the one in 64 and the many reconstructions that followed.

20 F. Coarelli, op.cit., p.23.

21 F. Zevi, *MEFRA*, LXXXV, 1973, pp.555ff.

22 G.F. Carettoni, *Cassino, esplorazione del teatro. Notizie degli scavi*, 1939, pp.99ff.; G. Lugli, op.cit., vol.II, pl.CLIII.

23 This defence work that could be taken to be contemporary with the civil war is in fact well dated by an Augustan inscription: CIL IX, 2443.

24 *Scavi di Ostia*, I, pl.II, fig.I.

25 B. Conticello, *Terracina*, 2nd ed., Itri, 1976; F. Coarelli, *Lazio*, pp.316-17.

26 G. Lugli, op.cit., vol.I, p.494; M. Torelli, *Innovazioni nelle tecniche edilizie romane tra il I sec. a.C. e il I sec. d.C.*, Technologia, Economia e Societa nel mondo Romano, Como, 1980, p.142.

27 M. Torelli, op.cit., p.147.

28 V.P. Meloni, *La Sardegna romana*, Sassari, 1975, pp.154ff.

29 M. Torelli, op.cit., p.154.

30 *Guide archéologique de Bulla Regia*, pp.18-20, figs 9, 10 and 11.

31 M. Torelli, op.cit., p.154 and n.90.

32 G. Lugli, op.cit., vol.II, pl.LXXXVIII,4.

33 C. Giuliani, P. Verduchi, 'Ricerche sull'architettura di Villa Adriana', *Quaderni dell'Istituto di Topografia Romana*, VIII, 1975.

34 From *vitta*, meaning a band or a ribbon.

35 The *Fanum Fortunae* where Vitruvius built a basilica.

36 This small settlement on Mount Subasio, near Assisi, has preserved from its transformation from *Hispellum* into *Colonia Julia* perhaps the most complete example of an Augustan wall. G. Lugli, op.cit., vol.I, p.634 and vol.II, pl.CLXXXIII, 2-3.

37 W.O. Moeller, 'The Building of Eumachia, a Reconsideration', *American Journal of Archaeology*, LXXVI, 1972, pp.323ff. It is useful to note that the façade of the forum, destroyed by the earthquake of 62, was reconstructed in brick.

38 Essentially, it is true, in the form of infill of *opus africanum*.

39 However, there are bricks in the arches of the amphitheatre that was built around the end of the century, producing a chronological peculiarity explicable by the proximity of Italy; it probably also had exterior facings of stone block construction and marble. Cf. the copious bibliography of A. Donnadieu and J. Formigé quoted by A. Grenier in his *Manuel d'Archéologie Gallo-romaine*, 3rd part, I, 1958, pp.99ff.

40 With the presence, however, of stone block construction in the framing of the openings and for the mouldings.

41 It must be remembered that the Herculaneum Gate, whose central arch was destroyed by the earthquake in 62, was not reconstructed after the catastrophe but simply tidied up, cf. H. Thédanat, *Pompéi*, II, p.15. A. Mauri, Pompéi, Roma–Novara, 1929, p.12. M. de Vos *Pompéi, Ercolano, Stabia*, Laterza, Rome, 1982, p.229.

42 R.C. Carrington, op.cit., p.134.

43 L. Cozza, *Notizie degli scavi*, 1952, pp.257ff.

44 M. Torelli, op.cit., pp.139ff.

45 V. Ciotti, *San Gemini e Carsulae*, Milan, Rome, 1976.

46 M. Torelli, op.cit., p.147.

47 F. Coarelli, *Lazio, guide archeologiche*, Laterza, Rome, 1982, p.95.

48 N. Lupu, *La villa dei Sette Bassi sulla via Latina, Ephemeris Daco-romana*, VII, 1937, pp.117ff.

49 F. Coarelli, *Dintorni de Roma*, Rome, 1981, pp.55ff.

50 E. Greco, D. Thedorescu, *Poseidonia-Paestum*, I, Rome, pp.35ff.

51 G. Lugli, op.cit., vol.I, p.653.

52 G. Pisani Sartorio, R. Calza, *La villa di Massenzio sulla via Appia*, Rome, 1976; F. Coarelli, op.cit., pp.30ff.

53 J. Richmond, *The City Wall of Imperial Rome*, Oxford, 1930.

54 The presence of brick already mentioned in the arches of the amphitheatre of Fréjus, the construction of which goes back at the most to the period of Vespasian, might be a local peculiarity due to the proximity of Italy.

55 The find of a coin of Trajan in the foundations of the Tour de Vésone establishes the maximum possible age of this monument, but we must wait for the publication of the Bureau d'Architecture Antique du Sud-Ouest for more precise conclusions.

56 Arcisse de Caumont, whose particularly clear and analytical pioneering work is still outstanding, describes this unique monument as early in his *Abécédaire d'archéologie, ère gallo-romaine*, Paris, 1862, pp. 47-8.

57 I.A. Richmond, 'Augustan Gates at Torino and Spello': *Papers of the British School at Rome*, XII, 1932, pp.52ff.

58 Vitruvius uses the name *lateres* (II,3) for unbaked bricks intended for the construction of walls. He takes up the term again in the diminutive form *laterculis* to refer to the material making up the small hypocaust piles and he applies *tegulae* (V,10) to the square bricks used in tiling and also to roof tiles.

59 The square hypocaust bricks of the Stabian Baths at Pompeii have diagonal incisions made before baking, making it possible for the user to break them up as required.

60 The bricks intended for columns will be dealt with below.

61 H. Kammerer-Grothaus, 'Der Deus Rediculus im Triopion des Herodes Atticus', *Römische Mitteilungen*, LXXXI, 1974, pp.131ff.

62 To get to the 'Temple of Rediculus', which is not easy to find, one must follow the *via Appia* out of Rome until one reaches the crossroads of the church *Domine quo Vadis*, separating the *via Ardeatina*

341

(on the right) from the *via Appia* (on the left) facing an access road to the catacombs. Take the *Appia* and almost immediately fork to the left along a small lane, the via *della Caffarella* (circular hut at the fork) that turns into a path leading to the valley of the same name. The funerary monument is 2km further on the left.

63 The event has been analysed for its architectural and economic consequences, in particular by two authors:
– A. Maiuri, *L'ultima fase edilizia di Pompei*, Rome, 1942;
– J. Andreau, *Histoire des séismes et histoire économique, le tremblement de terre de Pompéi*, Annales économie, société et civilisation, Paris, 1973, pp.369ff.

64 Seneca, *Quaest. Nat.*, VI,I,1-2.

65 Tacitus, *Annals*, XV,22.

66 It must be remembered that on the 23 November 1980 Pompeii was once more a victim of an earthquake that ravaged the Basilicata and Campania. Cf. J.-P. Adam, *Dégradation et restauration de l'architecture pompéienne*, éditions du C.N.R.S., Paris, 1983.

67 It was in fact the father of the donor who took on the reconstruction but, as a simple freedman, he could not claim this honour in his own name. Cf. H. Thédanat, *Pompéi*, vol.II, Paris, 1906, pp.70ff.

68 One of them, that of the Vesuvius Gate, was unfortunately stolen in 1977.

69 A. Maiuri, op.cit., pp.174ff.

70 J.-P. Adam, *Observations techniques sur les suites du séisme de 62 Pompéi. Eruptions volcaniques et tremblements de terre dans la Campanie antique*, Centre Jean-Berard, Naples, 1983.

71 A. Maiuri, *Saggi e ricerche intorno alla basilica*, Notizie, 1951, pp.225ff.

Notes to Chapter 6:
Arches and vaults

1 Or rather the re-inventors, since in the third millennium Mesopotamia and Egypt were able to span spaces with arches and vaults of unbaked brick; see also the article by G. Lugli, *L'origine dell'arco a conci radiali*, Palladio, 1952, pp.9ff.

2 This question has already been dealt with in an earlier publication: J.-P. Adam, *L'architecture militaire grecque, Les portes et l'origine des arcs clavés*, pp.99ff.

3 E. Bertaux, Rome, Paris, 1936, p.9 and F. Coarelli, *Guida archeologica di Roma*, Rome, 1974, pp.52, 61, 280.

4 See the discussion by G. Lugli, *La tecnica edilizia romana*, vol.I, pp.338ff. and more recently the article by Pol Defosse, 'Les remparts de Pérouse, contribution l'Histoire de l'urbanisme pré-romain', *MEFRA*, 92, 1980, 2, pp.725ff.

5 The site of *Falerii Novi* was abandoned very early on. In the twelfth century the Romanesque abbey of Santa Maria di Falerii was built on it. The ruins of this today are given over to agricultural use. In contrast, the population returned in the Middle Ages to the heights of ancient *Falerii Veteres*, now Civita Castellana.

6 For the architecture of Etruscan tombs, see the bibliography provided by A. Boëthius and J.-B. Ward-Perkins, *Etruscan and Roman Architecture*, The Pelican History of Art, 1970, pp.590-1, and those in the *Guide archeologiche Laterza: Etruria* by M. Torelli and *Umbria, Marche* by M. Gaggiotti.

7 Seneca, *Epist.*, 90,32.

8 F. Kraus, *Paestum*, Berlin, 1943; H. Riemann, article *Paestum, Real Encyclopedie*, vol.XXII, 1953, col.123ff.

9 P. Fabrizio, following M. Napoli, *Velia, Salerno*, 1978, pp.20-1, figs 1, 2, 3. E. Greco, *Magna Graecia, Guide archéologiche Laterza*, Rome-Bari, 1981, pp.40-8.

10 J.-P. Adam, op.cit., pp.100ff.

11 A. Orlandos, op.cit., vol.II, pp.253ff.

12 The brick facing between the arches is the result of later restorations.

13 It is sufficient just to compare the outline of the Fabrician Bridge with that of similar structure from any period. Two other surviving structures can be mentioned, the Pont du Gard, whose central arches have an opening of 24.52m, and the Bridge of Alcantara erected in 105, with a central arch of 27.4m

14 The reader is strongly recommended to consult the excellent analytical articles by E. Viollet-le-Duc: *Construction* and *Voûte*, in his *Dictionnaire raisonné de l'architecture*.

15 From *corvus*, a raven, a name referring to any corbelled keystone, also called a 'corbin' in French, by analogy with the bird perched on top of the wall.

16 'Clavage' in French, from *clavis*, a key, the part 'closing' an arch (but perhaps as likely to be from *clavus*, a nail).

17 Once more we are here talking about crossing a space with split material. When wood cannot be used, a stone lintel resolves all the problems, but its use over a large span remains limited to a few exceptional materials (Greek marble, Egyptian hard limestone), never having made it possible to span more than 6.5m in Greece (Propylea) and 8m in Egypt (Karnak).

18 It must be remembered that the simple picture of the 'key' holding the whole arch corresponds to one way of looking at the construction; as this stone is the topmost, it is of course put into position last in the centring, but it is evident that all the archstones have exactly the same function.

19 It is necessary to be aware that only the span of an arch enters into consideration; its length is a matter of total indifference. The calculation is thus done following a transversal section, i.e. the shape of an arc.

20 The author has been able to check the efficiency of this method by applying calculation to it, based on the study of a Byzantine arch, cf. J.-P. Adam, 'La basilique byzantine de Kadyna', *Revue Archéologique*, 1977, I, pp.53ff.

21 It is to be noted that we are just as ignorant as to how the domes of Florence and St Peter's were built.

22 E. Viollet-le-Duc, *Dictionnaire*, 1875 ed., vol.IX, voûte, pp.472ff.

23 Head of the Dijon office of the Service d'Architecture antique of the CNRS since 1967; experiment published in A. Olivier, S. Storz, 'Analyse et restitution d'un procédé de construction antique: réalisation d'une voûte d'arête sur coffrage perdu en tubes de terre cuite', in *Recherches archéologiques franco-tunisiennes: Bulla Regia, Miscellanea*, 1, coll. de l'École française de Rome, 1982.

24 L. Crema, *Enciclopedia classica*, vol.XII, vol.I, *L'architettura romana*, Turin, 1959, p.571 and fig.755.

25 A. Choisy, *L'Art de bâtir chez les Romains*, Paris, 1873, see in particular chapter II and the relevant plates: *Constructions des voûtes en maçonnerie*. Despite its age, this work remains irreplaceable for the quality of its technical observations and illustrations.

26 A. Choisy, op.cit., pl.XI.

27 F. Coarelli, *Dintorni di Roma*, pp.162ff.

28 F.-W. Deichmann, A. Tschira, 'Das Mausoleum der Kaiserin Helena und die Basilika der Heiligen Marcellinus und Petrus', *Jahrbuch des Instituts*, LXXII, 1957, pp.44ff.

29 G. Lugli, *I monumenti antichi di Roma e Suburbio*, Rome, 1930- 38, vol.III, pp.105ff. G. Cozzo, *Ingegneria romana*, Rome, 1958, new ed. 1970, pp.286ff, pls XCVI to CXVII. K. de Fine Licht, *The Rotunda in Rome*, Copenhagen, 1968.

30 A. Choisy, op.cit. shows the drawing by Piranesi, p.88, fig.49.

31 As was the case for example for the domes of Santa Sophia, St Peter's in Rome or the Panthéon in Paris.

32 Ch. Hülsen, *Die Thermen des Agrippa*, Rome, 1910.

33 *Bolletino d'Arte*, X, 1930, I, pp.241ff.

34 G. Giovannoni, 'La cupola della Domus Aurea neroniana in Roma', *Atti del 1o convegno nazionale di Storia dell'-Architettura*, Rome, 1936, pp.3ff.

35 H. Finsen, 'La résidence de Domitien sur le Palatin', *Analecta Romana, Istituti Danici*, 5, supp. 1969.

36 A. Barattolo, 'Nuove ricerche sull'architettura del tempio di Venere e Roma in età adrianea', *Römische Mitteilungen*, 80, 1973, pp.243ff.

37 H. Kähler, *Hadrian und seine Villa bei Tivoli*, Deutsches Archäologisches Institut, Berlin, 1950. In it the author carries out a retrospective study of the dome and its place in the composition of monuments.

38 It is astonishing to see the size of the monumental projects in the area of Pozzuoli–Baia–Miseno when compared to the smaller scale of the architecture of Pompeii which is thus revealed to be a small com-mercial town with quite modest ambitions.

39 At present lost in the gardens and separated from the archaeological area of the baths by a railway and a narrow alley.

40 Despite being known for a long time and appearing on engravings of the eighteenth century, with an impressive height underlining the size of their underground depth, this collection of monuments have only been identified, cleared and studied in recent times. Apart from A. Maiuri, consult: I. Sgobbo, *I nuclei monumentali delle Terme romane di Baia per la prima volta riconosciuti, Atti del III congresso di Studi Romani, Bologna*, 1934. P. E. Auberson, 'Études sur les thermes de Vénus Baia, Rendconti dell'Accademia d'Archeologia', *Lettere e Belle Arti di Napoli*, XXXIX, 1964, pp.167ff. For a visit to this hardly known but very rich archaeological area, use the work by S. de Caro, A. Greco, Campania, *Guide archeologiche Laterza*, Rome, 1981, pp.53ff.

41 Lake Averno is at present private property but an un-made path makes it possible to approach the group of monuments which is fenced off. Close inspection of them is not at all recommended because of frequent falls of stone, set off by movements of the ground and general displacement of the masonry. The architect of the Centre Jean-Bérard in Naples, J. Rougelet started making plans of this monument in 1983 with a view to their publication.

42 A. Orlandos, op.cit., vol.II, pp.250-1, figs 345, 346.

43 P. Coupel, E. Frezouls, *Le théatre de Philoppopolis en Arabie*, Paris, 1956, p.77, pl.IX-1, pl.XXIX-4.

44 L. Crema, op.cit., pp.340-1, fig.394.

Notes to Chapter 7:
Carpentry

1 The remains, which have now disappeared, had been preserved thanks to the permanent humidity of the subsoil into which it was sunk.

2 In French 'solives', a metaphorical derivation from *solea*, a sandal.

3 The term parquet is reserved for boards jointed together by tongues and grooves.

4 In French 'poutre', a word deriving via animal metaphor from the vulgar Latin *pullitra*, 'mare'.

5 From *suffigere*, to suspend, a generic term referring to ceilings and the whole inner surface of a construction.

6 Vitruvius makes only one mention of stairways (preface to L,X) to recommend putting them in a Pythagorean triangle, 3 being the height, 4 the base and 5 the incline.

7 E. Barberot, op.cit., pp.464-5.

This author refers to the antiquity of such a method of working in wooded regions but has the steps resting not on a string but on one another.

8 E. Barberot, op.cit., pp.508-9.

9 F. Mielke, op.cit., p.45.

10 The whole of the building has been quoted as an example for comparison by James E. Packer in: 'The Insulae of Imperial Ostia', *Memoirs of the American Academy in Rome*, vol.XXXI, p.57 and pl.CVI, figs 303 and 304.

11 The description of this house is found in A. and M. de Vos, *Pompei, Ercolano, Stabia, Guide archeologiche Laterza*, Rome-Bari, 1982, pp.160-4.

12 A. Maiuri, *Herculaneum*, Istituto Poligrafico dello Stato, Rome, 1968 (6th ed.), p.60. F. Mielke, op.cit., p.44.

13 V. Spinazzola, *Pompei alla luce degli scavi nuovi di Via dell'Abbondanza*, Rome, 1953, pp.435-593, and 869-970.

14 The timbers recovered at Herculaneum and Pompeii are all of modest size, cf. the illustrations.

15 C.I.L. 577, A. Choisy gives this text as a supplement to his translation of Vitruvius, vol.I, p.291.

16 M. Torelli, *Etruria, Guide archeologiche Laterza*, Rome, 1982, p.71ff.

17 In French 'appentis', a deformation of the past participle simply meaning sloping ('pentu').

18 In French 'chevron' from 'chèvre', a goat, because of the shape of a goat's croup made by the rafters of a double-sided roof.

19 In his reconstruction, V. Spinazzola placed rafters the width of a tile apart so the latter could rest directly on them; this solution cannot be dismissed, but it called for very careful positioning of the timbers.

20 The only work exclusively devoted to Greek roof timbers is the one by A.T. Hodge, *The Woodwork of Greek Roofs*, Cambridge, 1960.

21 In French, 'ferme', simple contraction of 'fermée', from the Latin *fermus*.

22 By way of comparison, some spans of Gothic timbers, roofing central naves: Reims, 12m; Paris, 13m; Beauvais, 14m.

23 In French 'moises', perhaps from *mensa*, a table. The name *moises* is used for two pieces which enclose a third.

24 The oldest triangulated timbers known, datable to the sixth century by means of an inscription, are those of the monastery of St Catherine on Mount Sinai. Cf. Forsyth and Weitzmann, *The Monastery of St Catherine at Mt Sinai*, The University of Michigan, 1979.

25 J. Rondelet, *Traité théorique et pratique de l'Art de bâtir*, Paris, 1814, vol.III, pp.200-1 and pls LXXV and LXXVI. The author who saw the basilica before the fire of 1823 gives a cross-section of the monument, allowing it to be compared with the basilica of St Peter's.

26 A. Choisy studied this document in conjunction with the estimate for repairs to the Long Walls, Paris, 1883.

27 Pillaged by the Vandals of Genseric, then in the seventh century by Constantine II, who had the bronze tiles taken off the roof.

28 A. Palladio, *I quattro libri dell'architettura*, 1570, *libro quarto*, XX, pp.73-4, and pl.77, new edition Milan, 1968.

29 Place-name distinction based on the regions where these two products were originally produced. Cf. A. Orlandos op.cit., vol.I, p.82.

30 In the reconstruction of Pompeii, after 62, the masons were to include at random a large number of antefixes in their facings.

31 V. Spinazzola, op.cit., vol.I, pp.35ff., figs 52 and 53 and vol.II, pp.715-16.

32 P. Coupel, P. Demargen, *Fouille de Xanthos III, le Monument des Néreides*, Paris, 1969, vol.II, pls LXXX to LXXXVII.

33 A. Olivier, 'Les couvertures en dalles sciées', *Dossiers de l'Archéologie*, no.25, Nov.–Dec. 1977, pp.100ff., and *Les couvertures dalles sciées de Glanum, opus pavonaceum?*, *Revue Archéologie de Narbonnaise*, 1982.

34 Carl Blümlein, *Bilder aus den Römisch-Germanischen Kulturen*, Munich, Berlin, 1918,p.48.

Notes to Chapter 8:
Wall covering

1 Studies by the Istituto centrale per il Restauro, Rome, of the renderings on the House of Livia.

2 Excluding, naturally, the many cases where decoration was overlaid in reponse to a change in fashion.

3 To gain an insight into the problem of the composition, see the series of tests of mortar rendering carried out by M. Frizot, *Mortiers et enduits peints antiques, Étude technique et archéologique*, Centre des Recherches sur les techniques gréco-romaines, Dijon, 1977, and more generally on the mortar at Pompeii, J.-P. Adam, M. Frizot, *Pompéi, étude de dégradation, proposition de restauration* CNRS, Paris, 1983.

4 A. Barbet, C. Allag, 'Technique de préparation des parois dans la peinture murale romaine', *Mélanges de l'École Française de Rome, Antiquité*, 84, 1972, pp.935ff.

5 From the Italian *a fresco*, fresh. The contraction of the word only arrived in France (and England) in the eighteenth century.

6 S. Augusti, 'Sui colori degli antichi: la chrysocolla', *Rendiconti dell'Academia di Archeologia Lettere e Belle Arti di Napoli*, 34, Naples, 1960, pp.7ff, and *I colori pompeiani*, Rome, 1972.

7 F. Guidobaldi, '*Analysis of Organic Substances*' in Ancient Mural Painting, Istituto di fisica, Vernice, CNR, Rome, 1972.

8 The easel painter who painted on wood or canvas, considered a superior sort of artist, is not referred to here but it is not out of the question that the same artists could have carried out all types of painting.

9 H. Thédanat, *Pompéi*, Paris, 1927, p.13, fig.6.

10 A.-M. Uffler, 'Fresquistes gallo-romains, le bas-relief du Musée de Sens', *Revue Archéologique de l'Est*, 22, 3–4, 1971, pp.393ff.

11 V. Spinazzola, op.cit., vol. I, p.404, fig.460.

12 C.-L. Ragghianti, 'Personalità di pittori a Pompei', *Critica d'Arte nuova*, 3, 1954, pp.202ff. *Pittori di Pompei*, Milan, 1963.

13 A. Mau, *Geschichte der dekorativen Wandmalerei in Pompeji*, Leipzig, 1882.

14 H.-G. Beyen, *Über Stilleben aus Pompeji und Herculaneum*, The Hague, 1928. *Die Pompejanische Wanddekoration vom zweiten bis zum vierten Stil, I–II*, The Hague, 1938, new edition, 1960.

15 M. Borda, *La pittura romana*, Milan, 1958.

16 K. Schefold, *Die Wände Pompejis, topographisches Verzeichnis der Bildmotive*, Berlin, 1957, and *Vergessenes Pompeji*, Bern, 1962.

17 A. Barbet, 'Les bordures ajourées dans le IVe style de Pompéi', *essai de typologie, Mélanges de l'École Française de Rome, Antiquité*, 93, 1981–1982, pp.917ff.
F.-L. Bastet, M. de Vos, *Proposta per une classificazione del terzo stile pompeiano*, The Hague, 1977.
I. Brigantini, *Tra il III il IV stile: ipotesi per l'identificazione di una fase della pittura pompeiana*, ICCD, Rome, 1981.
A. Barbet, *La peinture murale romaine, les programmes décoratifs*, Picard, CNRS, 1984.

18 M. Frizot, *Stucs de Gaule et des provinces romaines, Motifs et techniques*. Centre de Recherche sur les techniques gréco-romaines, Uni-versité de Dijon, 7, 1977. Note that Vitruvius does not use a special word for stucco, which consists for him of *tectoria* in relief.

19 A. Maiuri, *Herculaneum*, Rome, 1968, pp.68–71, pl.XL, fig.72.

Notes to Chapter 9:
Floors

1 A first flooring of tufa paving has been found about 40cm below the level of the limestone.

2 G. Lugli, op.cit., vol.I, p.538 and fig.109.

3 From the town in *Latium*, Signia, an important centre for the manufacture of tiles; any broken bits were recovered for the manufacture of mortar. Cf. R. Cagnat and V. Chapot, op.cit., vol.II, p.35.

4 From the Greek τεσσαρα (four) referring to the square fragments.

5 Ph. Bruneau, *Exploration archéologique de Delos, vol. XXIX, les mosaïques*, Paris, 1972. For Sicily see: M. von Boeselager, *Antike Mosaiken in Sizilien*, 1983.

6 See the word *Musivum opus*, in the *Dictionnaire des Antiquités grecques et romaines* by Ch. Daremberg, E. Saglio.

7 See this word in P. Grimal, *Dictionnaire de la Mythologie grecque et romaine*, Paris, 1969, p.211.

8 See the bibliography on mosaics.

9 In keeping with the fortune of the occupier of the place, the owner of the largest house found at Pompeii.

10 Consult the documentation and the vocabulary given in *Dossiers de l'Archéologie*, no.15, *Mosaïques, décors de sols*, Dijon, March–April 1976 and no.31, *Mosaïque romaine, l'âge d'or de l'École d'Afrique*, Dijon, November–December, 1978.

Notes to Chapter 10:
Civil engineering

1 It must be remembered that 2/5 of the city are still to be excavated. See A. Mauri, *Pozzi e condotture d'acqua nell'antica citta di Pompei*, *Notizie degli scavi di Pompei*, 1931, pp.546ff.

2 Vitruvius, VIII,7.

3 See the model displayed at the Musées Royaux d'Art et Histoire in Brussels, Department of Romano-Belgian archaeology.

4 C. Blümlein, op.cit., p.39ff., figs 95-6.

5 D. Raines, 'A Roman Timber-lined Well at Skeldergate', *Archaeology of York*, 1973–4, p.9, fig.5.

6 G. Ph. Stevens, *Corinth: Result of Excavations*, American School of Classical Studies, 1933.

7 H. Rolland, *Fouilles de Glanum 1947–1956*, Xth supplement to *Gallia*, 1958, pp.89–98.

8 This exceptional testimony to Greek monumental art in Gaul was unfortunately damaged in 1980 during a repair job on its facing, carried out by an architect from Monuments Historiques.

9 H. Roland, *Fouilles de Glanum*, supplement I to *Gallia*, 1946, p.45.

10 Technical studies of Roman dams are summarized in two works: N. Schnitter, *A Short History of Dam Engineering*, *Water Power*, London, 1967 and N. Smith, *A History of Dams*, London, 1971. However, for North Africa there is the irreplaceable Gsell, *Enquête administrative sur les travaux hydroliques anciens en Algérie*, Paris, 1912.

11 Hence the modern name of Subiaco, from *sublaqueum*, 'under the lake'. Cf. M. de Rossi, 'Note topografiche sulla villa di Nerone a Subiaco', in *Lazio ieri e oggi*, 9, 1973, pp.286ff.

12 The most complete work on the study of the aqueducts of Rome is that by R. Lanciani, *Le acque e gli acquedotti di Roma antica*, Rome, 1881, reissued 1975. This study was continued and completed by Th. Ashby, *The Aqueducts of Ancient Rome*, Oxford, 1935.

13 Ph. Leveau, J.-L. Paillet, *L'alimentation en eau de Caesarea de Maurétanie et l'acqueduc de Cherchell*, Paris, 1976. The authors, besides an archaeological and technical study of the layout and construction of a large acqueduct, illustrate the political prestige of such a project, linked to the importance of the city and its organization, sometimes to the detriment of the benefits it could bring to the rural economy.

14 G. Downey, 'The Water Supply of Antioch' in *The Orontes in Antiquity*, *Annales archéologiques de Syrie*, I, 2, 1951.

15 A. Triou, 'Les aqueducs gallo-romains de Saintes', *Gallia*, XXVI. 1968, pp.119ff.

16 Abbé Baccrabère, 'L'aqueduc de la Reine Pédauque à Toulouse', *Mémoires de la Société archéologique du Midi de la France*, Toulouse, 1964.

17 'The Aqueduct of Minturnae', *American Journal of Archaeo-logy*, 5, 1901, pp.187ff.

18 Desguines, *Au sujet de l'aqueduc romain de Lutèce, dit d'Arcueil-Cachan*, Paris, 1948. See the chapter devoted to this subject in: P.-M. Duval, *Paris antique*, Paris, 1961, pp.171ff. and the plan by F.G. de Pachtere, in *Paris à l'époque gallo-romaine*, Paris, 1912, pp.80–4 and pl.VII.

19 R. Lanciani, op.cit., pp.246–54.

20 A. Grenier, Manuel, vol.IV, pp.71ff.

21 R. Lanciani, op.cit., pp.295–8.

22 M. Toussaint, *Metz à l'époque Gallo-Romaine*, Metz, 1948, pp.168ff. and A. Grenier *Manuel*, vol.IV, pp.199ff.

23 R. Lanciani, op.cit., pp.380-9.

24 See 'l'inscription de Lambèse', CIL VII, 2728, referred to in the chapter on surveying, concerning the aqueduct of Saldae and the digging of a tunnel.

25 C. Germain de Montauzan, *Les aqueducs antiques de Lyon, Étude comparée d'archéologie romaine*, Paris, 1908, pp.63-80.

26 Germain de Montauzan, op.cit., pp.50–62.

27 Ph. Leveau, 'La construction des aqueducs', *Dossiers de l'Archéologie*, no.38, Dijon, Oct.-Nov. 1979, p.11.

28 Ph. Leveau, J.-L. Paillet, op.cit.

29 A. Grenier, *Manuel*, vol.IV, pp.41ff. and bibliography p.43.

30 Ph. Leveau, J.-L. Paillet, op.cit.

31 A. Grenier, *Manuel*, vol.IV, pp.88ff.

32 R. Lanciani, op.cit., pp.255–69.

33 Germain de Montauzan, op.cit., pp.81–93.

34 R. Lanciani, op.cit., pp.345–49.

35 Germain de Montauzan, op.cit., pp.81–135. For a revised dating of this construction see: Divier Lavrut, 'La datation de l'aqueduc du Gier', *Cahiers de l'Histoire*, XXXIX, 1, 1984, pp.47–58.

36 E. Samesrenther, *Bericht der Röm. German. Kommission*, 26, Frankfurt, 1936, pp,.24ff.

37 R. Lanciani, op.cit., pp.345–64.

38 R. Lanciani, op.cit., pp.270–87.

39 I. Sgobbo, 'L'acquedotto romano della Campania: "Fontis Augustei Aquaeductus"', *Notizie degli scavi, Ac. Naz. Linc.*, 1938, XVI, pp.75ff.

40 F. Rakob, 'Das Quellenheiligtum in Zaghouan und die römische Wasserleitung nach Karthago', *Mitteilungen des Deutschen Archäologischen In-stituts, Römische Abteilung*, 81, 1974, no.1, pp.41ff.

41 On an intact underground section of the aqueduct of Traslay leading to Bourges, the author was able to verify the existence of a horizontal level of 50m.

42 See the section models of these two constructions at the Museo della Civiltà Romana, room XXVIII.

43 These last two remarkable constructions in addition pose an archaeological problem that is unresolved: that of their dating. Roman history claims that the *emissarium* of Albano was tunnelled during the siege of Veies in 396BC, and that of Nemi slightly earlier. However, the presence of keyed arches made of stone blocks would seem to question the history of this technique, if these arches dated from the beginning of the fourth century. But they may well be later work.

44 A. Léger, *Les travaux publics aux temps des Romains*, op.cit., pp.601ff., at the end of the last century established an interesting comparison be-tween the characteristics of Roman aqueducts and those constructed in his time.

45 These pipes are five in number, of which there are two complete sections 2.6m long, bearing stamps from the period of Marcus Aurelius (139–61). Cf. M. Bailhache, 'Étude de l'évolution du débit des aqueducs gallo-romains', *in Journeés*

d'études sur les aqueducs romains, (Lyon, 26–28 May 1977), Paris, 1983, pp.19–49.

46 No piece has ever been found, only the perforated cubes of stone holding the pipes. By contrast, on the sections of less incline, thousands of ceramic pipes are still in place. See: Günther Garbrecht, 'Die Wasserversorgung des antiken Pergamon', in: *Die Wasserversorgung antiker Städte*, Ph. von Zabern, Mainz am Rhein, 1987.

47 The aqueduct siphons of Lyon were 8 in number: 4 on the aqueduct of Gier, 2 on the aqueduct of Mont d'Or, 1 on the aqueduct of Brévenne. The quantity of lead needed to make them is estimated at between 12,000 and 15,000 tonnes.

48 G. de Montauzan, op.cit., p.118.

49 F. Rakob, op.cit., pl.35–7.

50 Document studied by P. Grimal, in the *Collection des Universités de France, Les Belles Lettres*, Paris, 1961.

51 H. Boriello, A. D'Ambrosio, *Baiae, Misenum, Forma Italiae*, Regio I,XIV, Florence, 1979, La piscina Mirabile.

52 To give an idea of its size, it is worth remembering that the two largest Roman halls, that of the Basilica of Maxentius on the Roman Forum measures 58 × 80m and that of the Basilica Julia 49 × 101m.

53 This enormous complex, where Domitian liked to reside, still has not been the subject of an exhaustive literature, but the records provided by the excavations have been published by G. Lugli, *La villa di Domiziano sui colli Albani, Bulletino communale*, XLV, 1917, pp.29ff. – XLVI, 1918, pp.3ff. – XLVII, 1919, pp.153ff. – XLVIII, 1920, pp.3ff.

54 G. Lugli, *La Domus Aurea e le Terme di Traiano*, Rome, 1969, pp.41–2.

55 In fact, with a 10m fall the water acquires a pressure of

1kg f./sq. cm, or 1 bar. It was therefore out of the question to let it rush down 34m without a means of breaking the pressure.

56 L. Jacono, 'La misura delle antiche fistole plumbee', *Rivista di studi pompeiani*, Naples, 1935, pp.102ff.

57 When the building was excavated, the grilles, the lead plate with surviving attachments, and the beginnings of the pipes had been concealed during the search for material to reuse in antiquity, which after the eruption of 79 involved digging wells in the lapilli, as was done in several places in the city, wherever the highest buildings came above the ground forming points of reference.

The hypothesis of A. Maiuri, *L'ultima fase edilizia di Pompei*, pp.92–3, seeking to locate a fountain in front of the façade of the *castellum*, does not hold good because of the level of the water exit which would have required an underground fountain. Cf. 'Wasser-castellum in Pompeji', *Jahrbuch des Deutschen Archäologischen Instituts und Archäologischer Anzeiger*, 19, 1904, F. 115–16. – Bassel, 'Die Wasserleitung von Pompeji', *Deutsche Kunst- und Denk-malpflege, Jahrg.* 23, 1921, no.4, pp.34–6.

58 J. Marechal, 'Métallurgie, techniques métallurgiques', *Dic. archéologique des techniques*, Paris, 1964, vol.II, p.672.

59 F. Kretschmer, op.cit., p.55.

60 CIL XV, 7309.

61 The principal deposits were in Spain, Sardinia, Gaul (in the Massif Central) and England.

62 In fact, only very harsh water is capable of causing a partial dissolution of lead in water, making it noxious when the presence of this metal exceeds 0.1mg per litre.

63 Ceruse (white lead) is an extremely toxic carbonate of

lead, the use of which has been banned in France since the beginning of the century.

64 G. Ch. Picard, 'Informations archéologiques de la circonscription du Centre', *Gallia*, vol.30, fasc.II, 1975, pp.267–8. C. Bourgeois, 'La fontaine d'Argentomagus, les problèmes de l'architecture', *Bulletin de la Société des Antiquaires de France*, 1972, pp.61ff.

65 H. Eschebach, 'Die Gebrauchswasserversorgung des antiken Pompeji', *Antike Welt*, 10–2, 1979, pp.3ff. The highest column, via di Nola in VI,16, is preserved to a height of 6.75m. The smallest, via dell'Abbondanza in II,2 measures only 1.6m; it is the only one found in the twentieth century with its lead tank in place, measuring 56 × 65 × 65cm, made of soldered iron sheeting 6mm thick, its inlet and outlet pipes regulated by a bronze tap. The largest of the secondary tanks is none other than the Triumphal Arch of the via di Mercurio, used to supply the forum area. A large quantity of pipes, taps, collars and tanks were taken down in the course of the nineteenth century and transported in bulk to the *antiquarium* without any indication of where they came from.

66 See the technical study by F. Kretschmer, *La technique romaine*, op.cit., pp.47ff.

67 They break down as follows: 32 fountains made of lava, three fountains made of volcanic tufa, three fountains made of white limestone (of which 1 is semicircular), one fountain made of marble (the Fountain of the Cock) and a curious fountain made of brick masonry and small stones (near the forum in VIII).

68 Verifiable on the tanks of Villards d'Heria: L. Lerat, *Gallia*, vol.24, fasc.2, 1966, pp.365ff.; of Besançon, J.-P. Morel, *Gallia*, vol.32, fasc.2, 1974, pp.401ff; on the

natatio of the Baths of Glanum: F. Salviat, Glanum, *Caisse Nationale des Monuments Historiques*, 1977, p.15.

69 A. Barbet, 'Mercin et Vaux, un établissement gallo-romain à bassin en forme de T.', *Revue du Nord*, vol. LIII, 211, 1971, pp.631ff.

70 J.-P. Adam, 'Une fontaine publique à Bavay', *Revue du Nord*, LXI, 243, 1979, pp.823ff.

71 A. Maiuri, *L'Ultima fase*, p.93. One of these trenches was discovered at the top of the via di Stabia filled with lapilli from the eruption and was therefore in use in 79. At the bottom lay two sections of piping in the process of being replaced.

72 H. Thédanat, *Pompéi*, vol.I, pp.30–1. Suetonius, *Titus*, VIII,9.

73 See the complaints of the French architects working on the site in the nineteenth century, published in the catalogue of the exhibition: *Pompéi, École Nationale Supérieure des Beaux-Arts*, Paris, January-March 1981.

74 See the plan and the description of the Stabian Baths in F. and F. Niccolini, *Le case ed i monumenti di Pompei disegnati e descritti*, Naples, 1854, 1896, 4 vols.

75 Exposed and partly excavated between 1755 and 1757, then buried again, this house was again uncovered under the direction of A. Maiuri between 1936 and 1953 and published as it progressed in the *Notizie degli scavi*.

76 Matteo della Corte, *Case ed abitanti di Pompei*, Naples, 1965, article 'Julia Felix', p.391, inscription 821.

77 The translation of *Venerium et nongentum* remains problematic; it is not known whether the establishment is reserved for one particular social group (an association or 'club') or whether quite simply, and this is my opinion, it was to flatter the potential customers.

78 A word meaning both a garden pergola (in the modern sense) and a room under the roof, the sense in which it is to be understood here.

79 V. Spinazzola, op.cit., vol.II, pp.763ff.

80 A. Maiuri, *L'Ultima fase*, pp.73ff.

81 H. Eschebach, 'Die Stabianer Thermen in Pompeji', *Denkmäler Antiker Architektur*, 13, Berlin, 1979.

82 In the houses provided with running water, a common waste channel served the kitchen, the latrines and the bath-house. In addition, the latrines flowed directly into a cesspool or ditch with an inspection hole for draining.

83 Only the three buildings of the Curia had their major works finished, but the application of decoration had not yet begun. Cf. A. Maiuri, *L'Ultima fase*, pp.35ff.

84 The city was excavated by A. Ballu, and described by him in three publications, *Les ruines de Timgad*, Paris, 1897, 1903 and 1911. More recently, a summary has been provided by C. Courtois, *Timgad, antique Thamugadi*, Algiers, 1951.

85 E. Will, *Le cryptoportique de Bavay, Revue du Nord*, 40, 1958, pp.493ff.; ibid., 42, 1960, pp.403ff.; ibid., 46, 1964, pp.207ff.
F. Frezouls, *Le cryptoportique de Reims, les cryptoportiques dans l'architecture romaine*, École Française de Rome, no.14, 1974, pp.293ff.
J.-P. Adam, Cl. Bourgeois, 'Un ensemble monumental gallo-romain enterré dans le sous-sol de Bourges', *Gallia*, vol.35, 1977, 1, pp.115ff.

86 G.-O. Onorato, *La data del terremoto di Pompei, 5 Febraio 62, Rendiconti, Atti della Accademia Nazionale dei Lincei*, ser. VIII, vol.IV, 1949, pp.644ff.

87 Pliny, *Nat.Hist.*, IX,168.

88 The author also recommends that one give the

brick floor of the hypocaust an incline down in the direction of the *praefurnium* so as to facilitate the circulation of hot air, an efficient precaution but one rarely kept to in reality.

89 It is not unusual to find different types of small columns in one and the same building. Cf. G. Fouet, *La villa gallo-romaine de Montmaurin*, XXth suppl. to *Gallia*, Paris, 1969, pp.138–40.

90 G. Fouet, op.cit., Paris, 1969, p.57, fig.26, pl.VIII, pl.X.

91 J. Lauffray, J. Schreyeck, N. Dupré, 'Les établissements et les villas gallo-romains de Lalonquette', *Gallia*, vol.31, 1973, fasc.1, pp.138ff., pl.11 and folder.

92 G. Lugli, op.cit., vol.I, p.550.

93 But nor does he speak of masonry of baked brick despite its existence.

94 See the description of the three water tanks by Vitruvius (V,10).

95 D. Krencker, E. Krüger, H. Lehmann, H. Wachtler, *Die Trierer Kaiserthermen, Ausgrabungsbericht und grundstatzliche Untersuchungen römischer Thermen*, Augsburg, 1929.

96 Ch. Hülsen, *Die Thermen des Agrippa*, Rome, 1910.

97 J. Carcopino, *Daily Life in Ancient Rome*.

98 The idea of this type of composition is not, however, new, as the Forum of Augustus is already a spectacular example of it and, long before that, the Temple of Fortune at Palestrina or, on another level, the Villa of the Mysteries at Pompeii.

99 F. K. Yegül, 'The Small City Bath in Classical Antiquity', *Archeologia Classica*, XXXI, 1979, pp.108ff.

100 Pliny, XXXVIII,55.

101 Martial VI,42.

102 Petronius, S 28.

103 F. K. Yegül, op.cit. The author here analyses the

bath projects of the Imperial period through the description given by Lucian, about 160, of the baths belonging to a person called Hippias.

104 H. Eschebach, 'Die Stabianer Thermen in Pompeji', *Denkmäler Antiker Architektur*, 13, Berlin, 1979. A. and M. de Vos, op.cit., pp.194ff.

105 Martial, VII,32. It is in the reign of Nero that Martial composed this epigram, written, as with all of his works (15 books) in a sharp descriptive style full of everyday detail.

106 This is the *harpasta*, a ball filled with sand or flour.

107 We leave out of the category *palestrae* reserved for the training of gladiators, whose sporting contests involving much spilling of blood can hardly be considered conducive to physical and moral well-being.

108 Starting with Augustus, the regional associations bringing together young people from noble or patrician families were organized in *collegia iuvenum*, in which sports for military training were combined with the cult of the emperor.

109 See the work by P.-M. Duval, *Les dieux de la Gaule*, P.U.F., Paris, 1957. It is worth noting that it is the Gallic god of watering places, Borvo, whose name was the origin of the family name of 'Bour-bonne' and 'Bourbon', the main French royal dynasty.

110 Some place-names, despite being contracted, still betray their origin: *Aquae Sextiae*: Aix (en-Provence); *Aquae gratianae*: Aix (les-Bains); *Aquae Tarbellicae*: Dax; *Borvo* (the god already mentioned): Bourbonne-le Bains;Bourbon-l'Archambault;Bourbon-Lancy.

111 Livy, IX,29; it is one of the few roads whose construction is mentioned. See in: R. Chevallier, *Roman Roads*, London, 1976, p.17, and F. Castagnoli, A.-M. Colini, G.

Macchia, *La via Appia*, Rome, 1972.

112 It entered Rome in the area of the *Salinae*, the salt pans, where the salt from the coast was sold; cf. S. Quilici Gigli, *La via Salaria da Roma a Passo Corese*, Rome, 1977.

113 It is in the course of this conflict that Pompeii enters into history, with the reference to a naval raid organized by Marcus Decius on the mouth of the river Sarno in 310BC, a raid victoriously repulsed by the citizens of Pompeii and Nuceria.

114 Cicero, *De Legibus* III,3,7.

115 R. Chevallier, op.cit., p.65 and n.1. Siculus Flaccus must not be confused with the Censor Lucius Valerius Flaccus who, in 184, had a coastal road constructed in the region of Formia, wrongly identified with the road works called the *via Flacca*, near Sperlonga, that has already been mentioned and will be referred to again later.

116 R. Agache, 'Présence de fossés parallèles à certaines voies romaines', *Bulletin de la Société des Antiquaires de Picardie*, 3rd term, 1968, pp.258ff.

117 R. Chevallier, op.cit., pp.86ff. The author records an observation made by P. Broise on the road leading to Annecy, whose *rudus* was in places bonded with a thin mortar.

118 A. Léger, *Les travaux publics*, op.cit., pp.157–8, pl.III.

119 D. Sterpos, F. Castagnoli, 'La strada romana', *Quaderni di Autostrade*, 17, Rome, 1970, pp.28–9, fig.28.

120 D. Sterpos, op.cit., pp.25–6.

121 Livy XLI,32.

122 Livy X,23,12.

123 Livy X,47,4.

124 J. Mertens, *Industrie*, 10 October 1955, pp.38ff. Documents presented to the Romano-Belgian Department of the Musées Royaux d'Art et d'Histoire in Brussels. M. H. Corbiau, 'La 'Via

Mansuerisca', voie antique des Hautes Fagnes belges', and J. Mertens, 'Quelques aspects chronologiques du réseau routier romain en Belgique', in *Actes du colloque: Les voies anciennes en Gaule,* Université de Tours, 1982, pp.323ff. and pp.329ff.

125 D. Sterpos, op.cit., pp. 26, 27 and 36 also for the other dimensions.

126 M. Sordi, 'La via Aurelia da Vada a Pisa nell'antichità, Athenaum', 39, 1971, p.308.

127 X. Lafon, 'La voie littorale, Sperlonga-Gaeta-Formia', *MEFRA*, 91, 1979, 1, pp.24ff.

128 D. Sterpos, op.cit., pp.102–3 with 3 photographs of the tunnel.

129 D. Sterpos, op.cit., pp.94–7. S. de Caro, A. Greco.

130 The tunnel, whose entrance at the Naples end abuts 'Virgil's Tomb' behind the church of Piedigrotta, some metres from the entrance to the modern road tunnel, has been made dangerous by numerous rock falls and cannot be visited any more. Campania, op.cit., p.34.

131 *Letter to Lucilius*, VI,5.

132 Though the 'grotto of the Sibyll' can be visited (turn left on arrival at Lake Averno), the 'grotto of Cocceius', from the Augustan period, like its neighbour, was unfortunately turned into a munitions depot during the

1939–45 War and seriously damaged: its access has therefore been blocked up.

133 G. Lugli, op.cit., vol.II, pl.XLVII,1. To admire this construction, it is worth going down the valley below the built-up area and taking the narrow road following the course of the *Appia Antica*, then leave this at the start of the incline and go into the orchards from where the imposing embankment can be seen.

134 The construction date of the first bridge at this spot is not known, but it certainly goes back to the period of the kings. It is because Horatius Cocles defended it alone against the army of Porsenna that the Romans made it into a national monument and were careful to rebuild it with pegged wood with no nails, until the fourth century.

135 *Gallic Wars*, IV,17.

136 It was indicated earlier that the addition of pozzolana gave hydraulic advantages to the mortar allowing it to set under water.

137 Noticeable at the Milvian Bridge, the Fabrician Bridge and, even more so, at the Pont Julien.

138 More successful than its neighbour, the Emilian Bridge, which became the Ponte Rotto, since a flood carried it away in 1598. Visitors to Rome who have been able to admire the

height above the water of the Fabrician Bridge, should be aware that the flood waters of the Tiber are capable of coming almost up to the level of its keystones.

139 At the IXth mile of the *via Praenestina* out of Rome, hence the name 'Ponte di Nona' given to the viaduct.

140 G. Lugli, op.cit., vol.II, pl.LXXII,1. L. Quilici, *La via Prenestina i suoi monumenti, i suoi paesaggi*, Rome, 1977. The old bridge has been preserved under the central arch of the new viaduct.

141 J.-L. Fiches, *L'oppidum d'Ambrussum, le pont romain, le quartier bas*, Association pour la Recherche Archéologique en Languedoc Oriental, Caveirac, 1982.

142 Not far from Formia, this viaduct carried a branch of the *via Appia* leading to the town of Suessa (Sessa).

143 D. Sterpos, op.cit., pp.68–70.

144 In this layout, which was to become a normal part of urban design, the arch is placed both at the town entrances and at the ends of bridges or entrances to the forum, characteristics that are combined in the Porta Flumentana in Rome, built on the Emilian Bridge at the entrance to the Forum Boarium.

145 The Arch of Germanicus was taken down at the time of Louis-Philippe and re-

erected some distance away when the old Roman bridge was pulled down and replaced.

146 Suetonius, *Lives of the Twelve Caesars, Augustus*, XLIX ('Distribution of military forces and organization of information').

147 R. Chevallier, op.cit.

148 Jublains, *Armée Romaine et provinces*, I, *École Normale Supérieure*, 1977, pp.11ff.

149 C. Jullian, *Inscriptions de Bordeaux*, II, pp.203ff.

150 Ammianus Marcellinus XV,II,17.

151 R. Chevallier, op.cit., p.41 and n.90.

152 The 'Peutinger Table', broken up into eleven segments of parchment, is preserved at the National Library of Vienna (Austria).

153 A detailed study of the document has been carried out by, amongst others, A. and M. Levi, *Itineraria picta, contributo allo studio della Tabula Peutingeraria*, L'Erma di Bretschneider, Rome, 1967.

154 Everyone can imagine the energy and pride with which excavators search through the Peutinger Table to find the real or presumed presence of the site on which they are working, as this authority would seem to be a guarantee of a site's importance.

Notes to Chapter 11:
Domestic and Commercial Architecture

1 The suburban houses belonging to the southern and eastern sectors, built on the slope leading down to the sea, are particular cases of the pursuit of a privileged view outside the city. The aforementioned house is, by contrast, built on a flat piece of land.

2 R. Cagnat, op.cit., vol.I, pp.388–90. P. Grimal, *Dictionnaire de la mythologie grecque et*

romaine, Paris, 1969, p.253.

3 Originally the Genius watched over all beings; in early representations he has the form of a snake, then he takes on human form. In fact at Pompeii the two appearances exist side by side.

4 Vitruvius, VI,3 *De cavis aedium, sive atriis.*

5 H. Théandat, op.cit., vol.I, p.64.

6 The Romans derived the name of this room from the *tabulae*, the tablets on which were writ-ten the documents forming the archive of the family and the master of the house; however, the presence of a partition with double doors at the 'House of the Wooden Partition' at Herculaneum points to an etymology rela-ting to this shutter (the *tabula*).

7 From *klinai*, the Greek for couches.

8 H. Thédanat, op.cit., vol.I, p.89.

9 V. Spinazzola, op.cit., vol.I, pp.402–4, figs 458–60.

10 Vitruvius, VI,5.

11 V. Spinazzola, op.cit., vol.I, p.369, fig.414.

12 The gardens of Pompeii and their vegetation have been

studied by W. Jashemski, *The Gardens of Pompeii, Herculaneum and the Villas Destroyed by Vesuvius*, New York, 1979; the painted representations of gardens have been the subject of numerous studies, among which it is worth referring to those by H. Sichtermann, 'Gemalte Gärten in Pompejanischen Zimmern', *Antike Welt*, 5-3, 1974, pp.41ff. and D. Michel, *Pompejanische Garten-malereien*, *Tainia*, Mainz, 1980, pp.373ff.

13 The citron, *citrum*, is known from Virgil as an exotic fruit, but it is still not known which citrus fruits were cultivated first, and when, in Italy.

14 V. Spinazzola, op.cit., vol.I, p.413, fig.474.

15 See the section on staircases in chapter 7.

16 J. André, *L'alimentation et la cuisine à Rome*, Paris, *Les Belles Lettres*, 1981, p.165 and see the same author's commentaries on Book 14 of Pliny, 1958.

17 R. Remondon, *La crise de l'Empire romain*, Paris, P.U.F., 1970.

18 Even though, in the Republican period, wheat was assured of a lively home market, from the first century AD its production was limited to rural consumption, as the towns were supplied with imported wheat from North Africa, Egypt, Gaul, Sardinia and Sicily (cf. Pliny, XVIII 63,66,79).

19 Martial, XII, 63,1.

20 J. André, op.cit., p.182. A. Sirago, *L'Italia agraria sotto Trajano*, Louvain, 1958, pp.211ff.

21 Pliny, XV,8. Strabo, V,3,10.

22 This villa, which is justifiably important, must not be confused with the famous villa of P. Fannius Synistor, where the paintings belonging to the Second Style, are frequently referred to and were dispersed at the beginning of the century to museums in Amsterdam, Brussels, New York, Paris and

a small number in Naples. Up to now, 37 villas or remains of agricultural buildings have been identified within a radius of 4km around Pompeii, stretching from Torre Annunziata in the west to Scafati in the east, describing an arc northwards (towards Vesuvius) passing through Boscoreale. Cf. A. and M. de Vos, *Pompéii, Ercolano, Stabia, Guide archeologiche Laterza*, Rome, 1982, pp.238ff. A. Casali, A. Bianco, 'Primo contributo alla topografia del suburbio pompeiano', *Pompei 79*, suppl. *Antiqua* 4, Rome, 1979, pp.27ff. In 1983, S. de Caro, director of excavations at Pompeii, was carrying out the excavation of the villa de la Regina, discovered at Boscoreale, the layout of which is similar to that of La Pisanella.

23 The layout of the villa forms part of the recommendations of the authors of treatises on agriculture and architecture: Cato, *De agricultura*, III and IV. Columella, *De re rustica*, I,4,2 to 13. Varro, *De re rustica*, 1,4 and I,11. Vitruvius, VI,7 and VI,8.

24 The description of the villa of La Pisanella, discovered in 1894, was published by A. Pasqui, 'La villa pompeiana della Pisanella presso Boscoreale', *Monumenti Antichi dell'-Accademia dei Lincei*, 7, 1897, col. 397–554. Shortly afterwards R. Cagnat gave an imaginative version of the last moments of this dwelling, then of its excavation and the discovery of the hoard of silver, in an article entitled: 'Une ville endormie sous les cendres', *Lecture pour tous*, Oct. 1899, p.26.

25 J. André, op.cit., pp.69–73.

26 Cato, *De agr.*, 56.

27 J. André, op.cit., pp.71–2.

28 P. Veyne, 'Vie de Trimalcion', *Annales ESC*, March–April, 1961, pp.213ff. M.I. Finley, *Ancient Slavery and Modern Ideology*, Cambridge, 1979.

29 M. Andrieux, *La Sicile*, Paris, 1965, pp.157–8.

30 J. Carcopino, op.cit.

31 A. Casale, A. Bianco, 'Primo contributo alla topografia del suburbio pompeiano', *Pompei 79*, suppl. *Antiqua*, 4, Rome, 1979, pp.27ff. A. and M. de Vos, *Pompeii, Ercolano, Stabia, Rome*, 1982, p.243.

32 The site, unfortunately abandoned and buried once again, can no longer be visited. A model of the villa is displayed at the Museo della Civiltà Romana, in the room on agricultural labour.

33 The Cupids working on the vintage in the House of the Vettii clearly illustrate the instrument (re-constructed at the Villa of the Mysteries) and its use.

34 Cato, *De re rustica*; the detailed installation of the press is given in Chapter XXI: *Torcularium si aedificare voles*: 'If you wish to construct a press'.

35 Cato, XIV, XV, XVI, XXIII, XXIV, XXV.

36 A. Carandini, S. Settis, *Schiavi e padroni nell'Etruria romana, La villa di Settefinestre dallo scavo alla mostra*, Rome, 1979.

37 A. Carandini, S. Settis, op.cit., pp.89–93.

38 The most complete description is found in A. Mauri, *La villa dei Misteri*, Rome, 1931, new ed. 1947, but more recently other authors have come up with a clear synthesis: R. Étienne, *La vie quotidienne à Pompéi*, Paris, 1974, pp.264ff. A. and M. de Vos, op.cit., pp.245ff.

39 C. Picard, J. Rougé, *Textes et documents relatifs à la vie économique et sociale dans l'Empire romain*, Paris, Sedes, 1069.

40 R. Étienne, op.cit., p.179.

41 Via dell'Abbondanza I,6,7 and IX,7,7. The metal pieces, bars, rings, lock, have remained in place and were able to be preserved by using a plaster cast. Cf. V. Spinazzola, op.cit., vol.II, pp.768–9, figs 749j-51.

42 It is, in addition, curious to note that the word has

become French 'taverne' and the English 'tavern' meaning only a bar.

43 As Pompeii was, from the end of the Republican period, a large wine-producing area, it is unsurprising to find numerous drink outlets there, both for consumption on the premises and to take away. Nowadays, it produces the famous 'Lacrima Cristi', a very sweet aperitif, and a great variety of white wines bearing the names of the villages where they are produced (Terzigno, Boscotrecase, Ottaviano, etc.). These often slightly sparkling wines (spumante) must be drunk young; as for the local red wine, delicate palates should stay clear.

44 T. Kleberg, *Hôtels, restaurants et cabarets dans l'Antiquité romaine*, Uppsala, 1957. J. André, op.cit., p.385.

45 Falernian wine was a highly regarded product of the region situated between Formia and Capua; still today, around Mondragone they make a fruity white wine that is particularly tasty, so it is worth taking the coast road from Rome to Naples to call there.

46 The bakery in VI,3,37, had a large stable, 8 x 5m, with a manger made of masonry; as it had only 4 millstones, it can be presumed that they hired out animals, or else they accommodated those belonging to other owners.

47 Pliny, XVII,23.

48 Vitruvius, X,5.

49 F. Benoit, 'L'usine de meunerie hydraulique de Barbegal', *Revue archéologique*, Jan–March 1940, pp.19ff. Recently, H.-P. Eydoux has given a summary résumé of this publication in: 'La meunerie de Barbegal', S.F.A., *Congrès archéologique de France*, 134th session, 1976, pp.165ff.

50 J. André, op.cit., pp.50ff.

51 A baking of 81 loaves was discovered in an oven in the

via degli Augustali by G. Fiorelli.

52 Besides their archaeological value, these explanations can be of use to those fortunate enough to have a house in the country with a bread oven.

53 The largest oven recorded at Pompeii, that in the bakery of Terentius Proculus (VII,2,3), measures 2.65m in diameter and 1.82m high.

54 Excavated and described in detail by V. Spinazzola, op.cit., vol.II, pp.763–85.

55 A weaver has been identified, in IX,2,1, thanks to an inscription on an interior wall of his shop, detailing the timetable for the making of a weft.

56 Suetonius, *Vespasian*, XXIII, 'as his son Titus reproached him for having the idea of imposing a tax even on urine, he put under his nose the first sum of money acquired from this tax, asking him whether he was shocked by the smell and when Titus replied in the negative, he concluded: "it is nevertheless produced from urine".'

57 V. Spinazzola, op.cit., vol.II, p.771, fig.755.

58 V. Spinazzola, op.cit., vol.II, pp.765ff.

59 H. Thédanat, Pompéi, vol.I, pp.10–11. R. Étienne, *La vie quotidienne à Pompéi*, Paris, 1977, pp.129–31. The bibliography of these innumerable inscriptions appears in the bibliographical corpus of Pompeii established by H. Van der Poel, *Corpus topographicum pompeianum*, *IV*, Bibliography, Rome, 1977, a considerable work that is, unfortunately, difficult to consult.

BIBLIOGRAPHY

Some useful works on Roman construction originally appeared during the 18th and 19th centuries; happily, a number of them are available in modern editions.

GENERAL WORKS, TERMINOLOGY, ETYMOLOGY

AURENCHE O., *Dictionnaire illustré multilingue de l'architecture du Proche-Orient ancien*, coll. de la Maison de l'Orient méditerranéen ancien, n° 3, Lyon-Paris, 1977.

Bautechnik der Antike, actes du colloque, Berlin, 1990.

BENOIT F., *Manuels d'Histoire de l'Art, l'Architecture, Antiquité*, Paris, 1911.

BIANCHI-BANDINELLI R., *Rome, le centre du pouvoir et Rome, la fin de l'art antique*, Paris, Gallimard, 1969, 1970.

BIANCHI-BANDINELLI R., M. TORELLI, *L'arte dell' antichità classica, II, Etruria e Roma*, Turin, 1976.

BLAKE M. E., *Ancient roman construction in Italy*, Washington, I, 1947, II, 1959 *and* III, 1973.

BOETHIUS A., J.-B. WARD-PERKINGS, *Etruscan and Roman Architecture*, Harmondsworth, 1970.

CAGNAT R., V. CHAPOT, *Manuel d'Archéologie romaine*, 2t., Picard, Paris, 1920.

CALLEBAT L., *Livre X*, Belles Lettres, Paris, 1986.

CARCOPINO J., *La vie quotidienne à Rome à l'apogée de l'Empire*, Paris, 1939 (nombreuses rééditions,.

CHABAT P., *Dictionnaire de construction*, 3t., Paris, 1875.

CHOISY A., *L'art de bâtir chez les Romains*, Paris, Ducher, 1873.

COLINI A.-M., G.-O. GIGLIONI, G. PISANI-SARTORIO, *Museo della Civiltà Romana, catalogo*, Rome, 1982.

COZZO G., *Ingegneria Romana*, Rome, 1928 (1970).

CREMA L., *Architettura Romana, Enciclopedia classica*, XII, 3, 1, Turin, 1959.

DAREMBERG C., E. SAGLIO, E. POTIER, *Dictionnaire des antiquités grecques et romaines*, Paris, 1877-1919.

DAUZAT A., J. DUBOIS, H. MITTERAND, *Nouveau dictionnaire étymologique des techniques*, 2nd edition Larousse, Paris, 1964.

Dictionnaire archéologique des techniques, 2 vol., Accueil, Paris, 1963.

Dictionnaire d'art et d'archéologie, Paris, Larousse, 1930.

DIDEROT et D'ALEMBERT, *L'Encyclopédie*, Paris, 1751–1772, (1965).

DURM J., *Die Baukunst der Etrusker. Die Baukunst der Römer, Handbuch der Architektur*, II, 2 vol. Stuttgart, 1905.

DUVAL P.-M., *La vie quotidienne en Gaule pendant la paix romaine*, Paris, Hachette, 1953.

FLETCHER'S BANISTER, J.-C. PALMES, *A History of Architecture*, 18th edition, London, 1975.

FLEURY Ph., *La mécanique de Vitruve*, Presses Universitaires de Caen, 1993.

GINOUVES R. et al., *Dictionnaire méthodique de l'architecture grecque et romaine*, EFA-EFR, De Boccard, Paris, vol I, vol II 1992.

GROS P., *Livre III*, Belles Lettres, Paris, 1990.

GIOVANNONI G., *La tecnica della costruzione presso i Romani*, Rome, 1925, (1969).

GRENIER A., *Manuel d'Archéologie gallo-romaine, 3ᵉ partie, l'architecture, l'urbanisme, les monuments*, Paris, Picard, 1958.

GRIMAL P., *La civilisation romaine*, Paris, Arthaud, 1968.

Histoire gémérale des techniques, I, Les origines de la civilisation technique, Paris, P.U.F. 1962.

GROS P., *La France gallo-romaine*, Nathan, Paris 1991.

GROS P., TORELLI M., *Storia dell'urbanistica. Il mondo romano*, Laterza, Rome-Bari, 1988.

KRETZSCHMER F., *La technique romaine*, Brussels, La renaissance du Livre, 1966.

LANDELS J.-G., *Engineering in the Ancient world*, London, 1978.

LUGLI G., *La tecnica edilizia romana*, Rome, 1957.

MAC DONALD W., *The architecture of the Roman Empire*, New Haven and London, Yale University Press, vol. I, 1982. vol. II, 1986.

ORLANDOS A. K., *Les matériaux de construction et la technique architecturale des anciens Grecs*, Athens. 1955; Paris. 1966.

PÉROUSE DE MONTCLOS J.-M. et autres, *Vocabulaire de l'architecture*, 2 t., Paris, Imprimerie Nationale, 1972.

RACHET G., *Dictionnaire de l'archéologie*, Paris, R. Laffont, 1983.

ROMANELLI P. *Topografia e archeologia dell'Africa Romana, Enciclopedia classica*, III, 10, 7, Turin, 1970.

RONDELET J., *Traité théorique et pratique de l'art de bâtir*, 6 vol., Paris, 1802–1817.

SOUBIRAN J., *Livre IX*, Belles Lettres, Paris, 1969.

VITRUVIUS, *Les dix livres d'architecture*. Translations and commentaries:

> CALLEBAT L., *Livre VIII, monuments des eaux*, coll. Guillaume Budé, Paris, Belles Lettres, 1973.
>
> CHOISY A., *Traduction commentée et illustrée des dix livres*, Paris, 1909 (Nobele, Paris, 1971).
>
> FENSTERBUSCH C., *Vitruv Zehn Bücher über Architektur*, Darmstadt, 1964.
>
> FERRI S., *Vitruvio* (books I to VII), Rome, 1960.
>
> PERRAULT Cl., V*itruve, les dix livres d'architecture*, illustrated translation of the 1673 edition, without commentaries, Paris, Les Libraires Associés, 1965.
>
> SOUBIRAN J., *Livre IX, l'astronomie*, coll. Guillaume Budé, Paris, Belles Lettres, 1969.
>
> WARD-PERKINS J., *Taste, tradition and technology: some aspects of the late Republican and Early Imperial Central Italy, Studies in classical Art and Archaeology*, New York, 1979, p. 197 ff.

1. — SURVEYING

ADAM J.-P., 'Groma et chorobate, exercices de topographie antique', *MEFRA*, 94, 1982-2, P. 1003 to 1029.

CAILLEMER A., R. CHEVALLIER, 'Les centuriations romaines de Tunisie', *annales E.S.C.*, 1957, p. 276 ff.

CHEVALLIER R., 'Essai de chronologie des centuriations romaines de Tunisie', *MEFRA*, 1958, p. 61 FF.

CHOUQUER G., FAVORY F., *Les arpenteurs romains*, Errance, Paris, 1992.

DILKE O. A. W., *Gli agrimensori di Roma antica*, Bologna , 1971.

DILKE O. A. W., *The Roman Land Surveyors, An introduction to the Agrimensores*, Newton Abbott, 1971.

LE GALL J., '*Les Romains et l'orientation solaire*', *MEFRA*, 87, 1975–1, p. 287 ff.

Collection of sources on *agrimensores* in: K. LACHMAN, A. RUDORFF, *Gromatici veteres*, Berlin, 1848.

PIGANIOL A., 'Les documents cadastraux de la colonie romaine d'Orange, sup. to *Gallia* XVI, 1962.

SALVIAT F., 'Orientation, extension et chronologie des plans cadatraux d'Orange', *Revue Archéologique de Narbonnaise*, X, Paris, 1977, p. 107 ff.

Tabula Peutingeriana, Table de Peutinger, Graz, 1976 (colour facsimile).

TROUSSET P., 'Les bornes du Bled Segui, Nouveaux aperçus sur la centuriation romaine du Sud tunisien', *Antiquités Africaines,* 12, 1978, p. 125 ff.

ULRIX F., 'Recherches sur la méthode de traçage des routes romaines', *Latomus*, XXII, 1963, p. 157 ff.

WARD-PERKINS J. B., '*Note di topografia urbanistica,*' in POMPEI 79, Naples, 1979, p. 25 ff.

2. — MATERIALS

ADAM J.-P., 'Observations techniques sur les suites du séisme de 62 à Pompéi', dans *Éruptions volcaniques et tremblements de terre dans la Campanie Antique, Centre Jean-Bérard*, Naples, 1986.

ADAM Th. and J.-P., *Le tecniche costruttive* a Pompei, *Pompei, i tempi della documentazione*, ICCD, Rome, 1981.

ADAM J.-P., P. VARENÈ, 'Une peinture romaine représentant une scène de chantier' *Revue Archéologique*, 1980–1982, p. 213 ff.

ADAM J.-P., P. VARÈNE, 'Fours à chaux artisanaux dans le bassin méditerranéen' from the symposium *Histoire des techniques et des sources documentaires*. Aix-en-Provence, October 1982.

ADAM J.-P., *L'edilizia storica in zona sismica: vulnerabilità e consolidamento*. Storia Geofisica Ambiante, Bologna, 1989.

ALADENISE V., *Technologie de la taille de pierre*. Paris, 1983.

AMY R., P.-M. DUVAL, J. FORMIGÉ, J.-J. HATT, A. PIGANIOL. CH. PICARD, G.-CH. PICARD, *L'arc d'Orange*, 2 vol. supplement XV à *Gallia*, Paris, 1962; see R. Amy's chapter on building.

AUDIN A., Y. BURNAND, 'Le marché lyonnais de la pierre sous le Haut-Empire romain', *Actes du 98ᵉ congrès national des Sociétés savantes*, St-Etienne, 1973; Paris 1975, p. 157 ff.

BACCINI P., 'I marmi di cava rinvenuti a Ostia', *Scavi di Ostia*, IX, Rome, 1979.

BADEI GIGLIONI G., *Lavori pubblici e occupazione nell'antichita classica*, Bologna, 1974.

BARADEZ J., 'Nouvelles fouilles à Tipasa, les fours à chaux des constructeurs de l'enceinte', *Libyca*, V, Autumn 1957, p. 277 ff.

BEDON R., *Les carrières et les carriers de la Gaule romaine, Université de Tours*, 2 t. 1981; Paris, Picard, 1984.

BESSAC J.-C., J.-L. FICHES, 'Étude des matériaux en pierre découverts à Ambrussum (Hérault)', *Archéologie en Languedoc*, 2, 1972, p. 127 et suiv.

BISTON M., *Manuel théorique et pratique du chaufournier*, coll. des manuels Roret, Paris, 186 (Paris, Léonce Laget, 1981).

BLOCH H., 'I bolli laterizi di Ostia', *Bulletino Comunale di Roma*, Rome, 1936, p. 141 ff.; 1937, p. 83 ff.; 1938, p. 61 ff.

BLÜMNER H., *Technologie und Terminologie der Gewerbe und Künste bei Greichen und Römern*, 1879 to 1912.

Le bois dans la Gaule romaine, Actes du colloque, *Caesarodunum*, Errance, Paris 1985.

BROISE P., 'Recherches sur les carriéres antiques de Savoie, essai de méthode', *Caesarodunum*, 12, Université de Tours, fasc. 2, 1977, p. 404 ff.

CHAMPION P., *Outils en fer du Musée de Saint-Germain en Laye, Revue Archéologique*, 3, 1916, p. 211 ff.

CHEVALLIER R., 'Pour un inventair des carrières antiques de la Gaule, problématique de l'étude' *Caesarodunum*, IX, Université de Tours, 1974. p. 184 ff.

CISNEROS CUNCHILLOS M., *Marmoles hispanos: su empleo en la España romana*, Saragossa, 1990.

DOLCI E., *Carrara, Cave antiche*, Carrara, 1980.

DROUOT E., 'La carriére romaine de Barutel', *Mémoires de l'Académie de Nîmes*, 7th series, t. LIX, 1977.

DURVIN P., *Les ateliers des tailleurs de pierre de Saint-Leu-d'Esserent*, Amiens, 1971.

FELLER P., F. TOURNET, *L'outil*, Paris, 1970.

FONTANA D., edited by P. PORTOGHESI, *Della trasportazionne dell'obelisco vaticano*, Rome 1590; Naples, 1604.

FORBES R. J., *Studies in ancient technology*, t. VII, *Ancient geology, mining and quarrying technics*, Leyden, 1963.

FRIZOT M., *Mortiers et enduits peints antiques, étude technique et archéologique*, Centre d'Études gréco-romaines, Université de Dijon, 1975.

FURLAN V., P. BISSEGER, 'Les mortiers ancients, Histoire et essai d'analyse scientifique'. *Zeitschrift für schweizerische Archäologie und Kunstgeschichte*, 32, 1975, p. 166 ff.

GAITZSCH W., *Eiserne römische Werkzeuge, BAR, international series*, Oxford, 1980, 2 volumes (tools for working stone, wood and concrete).

GIORDANO G., *Tecnologia del legno, II, il legno dalla foresta ai vari impieghi*, Hoepli, Milan, 1956.

GOODMAN W. L., *The History of woodworking tools*, London, 1964.

GOSE E., B. MEYER-PLATH, J. STEINHAUSEN, E. ZAHN, *Die Porta Nigra, Trierer grabungen und Forschungen*, IV, Berlin, 1969.

GROS P., 'Architecture et société à Rome et en Italie centroméridionale aux deux derniers siècles de la République' *Latomus*, 156, Bruxelles, 1978, p. 17 ff.

HELEN T., 'Organization of Roman Brick Production' *Acta, Inst. Rom. Finl.* IX, 1, p. 21 ff.

KAMMERER-CROTHAUS H., 'Der Detus Rediculus im Triopion des Herodes Atticus', *Mitteilungen des Deutschen Archaeologischen Instituts, Roemische abteilung*, 81, 1974, fasc. 2, p. 131.

KORRES M. *Vom Penteli zum Parthenon*, Munich, 1992.

LAMPRECHT H. O., *Opus caementicium*, Düsseldorf, 1968.

LEGER A., *Les travaux publics, les mines et la métallurgie au tempes des Romains*, Paris, 1875 (Jacques Laget, Nogent-le-Roi, 1979.)

MONTHEL G., M. PINETTE, 'La carriére gallo-romaine de St-Boil' *Revue Archéologique de l'Est et du Centre Est*, XXVIII, 1977. 1–2, p. 37 ff.

NOËL M., BOCQUET A., *Les hommes et le bois*, Paris, 1978.

NOËL P., *Technologie de la pierre de taille*, SDRBTP, Paris, 1965.

PESCHLOW-BINDOKAT A., *Die steinbrüche von Selinunte*, Mayence, 1990.

RICHMOND I. A., 'Augustan Gates at Torino and Spello', *Papers of the British school of Rome* XII, 1932, p. 52 ff.

RÖDER J., 'Quadermaken am aquaedukt von Karthago' *Mitt. des Deutschen archaeologischen Instituts, Roemische abteilung*, 81, 1974-1, p. 91 ff.

ROMANELLI P., 'Lo scavo al tempio della Magna Mater sul Palatino e nelle sue adiacenze', *Monumenti Antichi dei Lincei*, 46, 1963, col. 201 ff.

SODINI J.-P., A. LAMBRAKI, 'Les carrières de marbre d'Aliki à l'époque paléochrétienne', *Études thasiennes IXI*, École française d'Athènes, 1980.

VARENE P., *Sur la taille de la pierre antique médiévale et moderne*, Centre de Recherches sur les techniques gréco-romaines, Université de Dijon, 3rd revised edition, 1983.

WARD-PERKINS J.-B., 'Tripolitania and the Marble Trade', *Journal of Roman Studies*, XLI, 1951, p. 89 ff.

3. — LARGE STONE BLOCK CONSTRUCTION

ADAM J.-P., 'A propos du trilithon de Baalbeck, Le transport et la mise en œuvre des mégalithes' *Syria*, ILIV, 1977, pp. 31 to 63.

ASHBY Th., *The Aqueducts of Ancient Rome*, Oxford, 1935.

BERANGER G. M., 'Nuovi contributi per la conoscenza della cinta muraria di Arpino', *Antiqua*, II, 5, 1977, pp. 39 to 46.

CIANCIO-ROSSETTO P., 'Contributo alla conoscenza delle mura di Alatri' *Bolletino di Storia e di Arte del Lazio Meridionale*, 8, 1975, p 5 to p 20.

CONTA HALLER G., *Ricerche su alcuni centri fortificati in opera poligonale in area campano-sannitica*, Naples, 1978.

CROS P., 'Les premières générations d'architectes hellénistiques à Rome', *Mélanges à J. Heurgon*, Rome, 1976, p. 387 ff.

GULLINI G., 'I monumenti dell'Acropoli di Ferentino', *Archeologia classica*, 6, 1954, pp. 470 to 506.

MAIURI A., 'Studi e ricerche sulle fortificazioni di Pompei,' *Monumenti Antichi dell'Academia dei Lincei*, 33, 1929, col. 120 ff.

MAIURI A., 'Isolamento della cinta murale fra Porta vesuvio e Porta Ercolano', *Notizie degli scavi*, 1943, p. 275 ff.

VAN DEMAN E.B., *The building of the Roman Aqueducts*, Washington, 1934.

4. — STRUCTURES OF MIXED CONSTRUCTION

GROS P., 'Les éléments architecturaux, les murs en damier', in A. BALLAND, A. BARBET, P. GROS, G. HALLIER, *Bolsena II, Les architectures*, coll. de l'École française de Rome, 1962–1967, pp. 69–75.

'Chequer-work' walls in:

HALLIER G., M. HUMBERT, P. POMEY, *Bolsena VI, Les abords du forum*, coll. de l'École française de Rome, 1982.

LEZINE A., *Architecture punique, Recueil de documents*, Université de Tunis, 1961.

LEZINE A., *Architecture romaine d'Afrique, recherches et mises au point*, Université de Tunis, 1963.

5. – MASONRY CONSTRUCTION

CARRINGTON R., 'Notes on the building materials of Pompeii', *Journal of Roman Studies*, 23, 1933, p. 125 ff.

COARELLI F., 'Public building in Rome between the second Punic war and Sulla', *Papers of the British school at Rome*, vol. XLV, 1977, p. 1 ff.

HALLIER G., M. HUMBERT, P. POMEY, 'Bolsena VI, Les abords du forum', coll. de l'École française de Rome, 1982.

MAIURI A., *I nuovi scavi di Ercolano*, Rome, 1958.

MAIURI A., *L'ultima fase edilizia di Pompei*, Rome, 1942.

MARTIN R., P. VARÈNE, *Le monument d'Ucuetis à Alesia*, supplement XXVI to *Gallia*, Paris, 1973.

TORELLI M., *Innovazioni nelle tecniche edilizie romane tra il I sec. a. c. e il I sec. d. C., Tecnologia economia e societa nel mondo romano*, Como, 1980, p. 139 ff.

6. — ARCHES AND VAULTS

BRIGGS C. R., 'The Pantheon of Ostia' *Memoirs of the American Academy*, Rome, 8, 1930, p. 161 ff.

DEFOSSE P., 'Les remparts de Pérouse' *MEFRA*, 2, 1980 2, p. 725 ff.

DE FINE LIGHT K., *The Rotunda in Rome*, Copenhagen, 1968.

KÄHLER H., *Hadrian und seine villa bei Tivoli*, Berlin, 1950.

LEZINE A., 'Les voûtes romaines à tubes emboîtés et les croisés d'ogives de Bulla Regia', *Karthago*, 5, 1954.

LUGLI G., *Porte di città antiche ad ordini di archisovrapposti, Archeologia classica*, Rome, 1965, p. 182 ff.

NAPOLI M., 'Scavi di Velia' *Atti del IV convegno di studi sulla Magna Grecia*, Naples 1965, p. 119 ff., id. 1966, p. 209 ff.

OLIVIER A., 'Sommiers de plates bandes appareillées et armées à Conimbriga et à la villa d'Hadrien à Tivoli' *MEFRA*, 1983, II, p. 937 ff.

OLIVIER A., S. STORZ, 'Analyse et restitution d'un procédé de construction antique: réalisation d'une voûte d'arêtes sur coffrage perdu en tubes de terre cuite', in *Recherches archéologiques franco-tunisiennes à Bulla Regia*, I, Miscellanea, 1, coll. de l'École française de Rome. 1982.

ZANDER G., *Nuovi studi e ricerche sulla Domus Aurea, Palladio*, N.S. 15, 1965, p. 157 ff.

Les cryptoportiques dans l'architecture romaine, Actes du colloque, coll. de l'École française de Rome, 1978.

7. — CARPENTRY

AMY R., P. GROS, *La Maison carrée de Nîmes*, supplement XXXVII to *Gallia*, Paris, 1979.

BARBEROT E., *Traité pratique de charpente*, Béranger, Paris, 1952.

Encyclopédie des métiers: La charpente, Association ouvrière des Compagnons du Devoir, Paris, 1990.

JOUSSE M., *L'art de charpenterie*, Paris 1702 (Paris, Léonce Laget, 1978) The oldest fully illustrated treatise on carpentry.

MUROLO M., 'Il cosiddetto « Odeo » di Pompei ed il problema della sua copertura' *Rendiconti accademia di Archeologia, Lettere e Belle Arti di Napoli*, Nuova Serie 34, 1959, p. 89 ff.

RIVAL M., *La charpenterie navale romaine*, CNRS, Paris, 1991.

SPINAZZOLA V., *Pompei alla luce degli scavi Nuovi di Via dell'Abbondanza*, Rome, 1953.

VALLERY-RADOT N., *Les toits dans le paysage*, La Maison de Marie-Claire, Paris, 1977.

8. — WALL COVERING

RARBET A., 'Les bordures ajourées dans le IVe style de Pompei, Essai de typologie', *MEFRA*, 93, 1981, p. 917 ff.

BARBET A., 'Les décors à matériaux mixtes à l'époque romaine' *Revue archéologique*, 1981, p. 67 ff.

BARBET A., C. ALLAG, 'Technique de préparation des parois de la peinture romaine', *MEFRA*, 84, 1972–2, P. 935 ff.

BARBET A., *La peinture murale romaine en Italie, les styles décoratifs*, Paris, Picard, 1984.

BASTET F., M. DE VOS, 'Proposta per una classificazione del terzo stile pompeiano', *Archeologische Studiën van het Nederlands Instituut te Rome*, 4, The Hague, 1979.

BRAGANTINI I., M. DE VOS, F. PARISE BADONI, *Pitture e pavimenti di Pompei*, I *Repertorio delle fotografie del Gabinetto Fotografico Nazionale*, Roma, 1981.

BORDA M., *La pittura romana*, Milan, 1958.

Bulletin de liaison du Centre d'Étude des peintures murales romaines, Six editions in 1983.

FRIZOT M., 'L'analyse des pigments de peintures murales antiques' *Revue d'Archéométrie*, 6, 1982, p. 47 ff.

FRIZOT M., *Stucs de Gaule et des provinces romaines, Motifs et techniques*, Centre d'études des techniques grecoromaines, Université de Dijon, 1977.

GIAMBATTISTA PAOLA DI, MONIQUE REICHLEN-POMEY, FRANCA ZAVATTI, 'Note technique sur la dépose et la restauration de la peinture murale des latrines du forum de Bolsena' *coll. de l'École française de Rome*, Bolsena VI, Rome, 1982, p. 133 ff.

MAU A., *Geschichte der dekorativen Wandmalerei in Pompei*, Leipzig, 1882.

MORA P., 'Proposte sulla tecnica della pittura murale romana' *Bollettino dell'Istituto del Restauro*, 1967, p. 63 ff.

MORA P. and L., P. PHILIPPOT, *La conservation des peintures murales*, Bologna, 1977.

9. — FLOORS

BECATTI G., *Scavi di Ostia, IV, I mosaici e pavimenti marmorei*, Rome, 1961.

BECATTI G. et al, *Mosaici antichi in Italia Regio VII*, Baccano, Rome, 1970.

BLAKE M. E., 'The pavements of the Roman buildings of the Republic, and the early Empire', *Memoirs of the American Academy in Rome*, VIII, 1930.

BLAKE M. E., *Roman mosaics of the Second Century in Italy*, XIII, 1936.

BLAKE M. E., *Roman mosaics of the Third Century after Christ*, XVII, 1940.

D. VON BOESELAGER, *Antike mosaiken in Sizilien*, 1983.

GENTILI G. V., *La villa Erculia di Piazza Armerina, I mosaici figuratti*, Rome-Milan, 1959.

MORRICONE MATINI M. L., *Mosaici antichi in Italia regio X, Roma, Palatium*, Rome, 1968.

MORRICONE MATINI M. L., *Pavimenti di signino repubblicani di Roma e dintorni*, Rome, 1971.

PICARD G. CH., E. KITZINGER, K. KÜRBEL, *Mosaico, Enciclopedia universale dell'arte*, IX, Venice-Rome, 1960.

STERN H., 'Mosaïque', in *Enciclopaedia Universalis*, II, 1971.

General works on Mosaics in Gaul:

STERN H., I, *Province de Belgique*, vol. 1, *Belgique de l'ouest*, 1957 (1979); vol. 2, *Belgique de l'est*, 1960; vol 3, *Belgique du sud*, 1963.

STERN H., II, *Province de Lyonnaise*, vol. 1, Lyon, 1967.

STERN H. et MICHÈLE BLANCHARD-LEMÉE, II, *Province de Lyonnaise*, vol. 2, south-east region, 1975.

DARMON J.-P. and H. LAVAGNE, II, *Province de Lyonnaise*, vol. 3, central region, 1977.

LAVAGNE H., III, *Province de Narbonnaise*, vol. 1, central region, 1979.

BALMELLE C., *Aquitaine*, vol. 1, 1980.

10. — CIVIL ENGINEERING

ADAM J.-P., 'Une fontaine publique à Bavay', *Revue du Nord*, 61, 1979, pp. 823 to 826.

AGACHE R., 'Présence de fossés parallèles à certaines voies romaines', *Bull. soc. des Antiquaires de Picardie*, third quarter 1968, p. 258 ff.

ASHBY Th., R. A. L. FELL, 'The Via Flaminia', *Journal of Roman studies*, XI, 1921, p. 125 ff.

AUPERT P., 'Le nymphée de Tipasa', *coll. del'École française de Rome*, 1974.

BALLANCE M. H., 'The Roman Bridges of the Via Flaminia', *Papers of the British school at Rome*, XIX, 1051, p. 78 ff.

BARRUOL G., 'Le pont romain de Ganagobie', *Gallia*, XXI, 1963-2, p. 314 ff.

BERNARDELLI R., 'Il tripartitore d'acqua di Porta Vesuvio a Pompei, studi urbinati di storia', *Filosofia e Litteratura*, n° 45, Urbino, 1971.

BROISE H., THÉBERT Y., *Recherches archéologiques franco-tunisiennes à Bulla-Regia. Les thermes Memmiens*, EFR, Rome 1993.

BUNDGARD J.-A., 'Caesar's Bridges over the Rhine', *A. Arch.* XXXVI, 1965–66, p. 87 ff.

BUTLER H., 'The aqueduct of Minturnae', *American Journal of Archeology*, 5, 1901, p. 187 to 192.

CARETTONI G., 'Le gallerie ipogee del Foro Romano e i ludi gladiatori forensi', *Bulletino della commissione archeologica comunale di Roma*, 76, 1956–58, p. 23 ff.

CASTAGNOLI F., *Via Appia*, Milan, 1956.

CASTAGNOLI F., M. Colini, G. Macchia, *La via Appia*, Rome, 1972.

CHEVALLIER R., *Les voies romaines*, Paris, A. Colin, 1972.

CHEVALLIER R., A. CLOS ARCEDUC, J. SOYER, 'Essai de reconstitution du réseau routier gallo-romain. Caractères et méthode' *Revue archéologique*, 1962, I, p. 1 ff.

CLOS ARCEDUC A., 'La métrique des voies gallo-romaines', *Actes du colloque int. d'archéologie aérienne*, Paris, 1964, p. 213 ff.

DEGBOMONT J.-M., *Le chauffage par hypocauste dans l'habitat privé*, Etudes et Recherches Archéologiques de l'Université de Liège, 2nd ed., 1984.

DUVAL P.-M., 'La construction d'une voie romaine d'après les textes antiques' *Bull. de la Soc. des Antiquaires de France*, 1959, p. 176 ff.

ESCHEBACH H., 'Die gebrauchswasserversorgung des antiken Pompeji', *Antike Welt*, 10-2, 1979, p. 3 ff.

ESCHEBACH H., 'Die stabianer Thermen in Pompeji', *Denkmäler antiker Architektur*, 13, Berlin, 1979.

FABRE G., PAILLET J.-L., *Le pont du Gard*, CNRS, Paris, 1992.

FICHES J.-L., *L'Oppidum d'Ambrussum, le pont romain, le quartier bas*, A.R.A.L.O. Caveirac, 1982.

FUSTIER P., 'Notes sur la construction des voies romaines en Italie', *Revue des études anciennes*, 1960, p. 95 ff.; 1961, p. 276 ff.

GAZZOLA P., *Ponti romani*, Florence, 1963.

GERMAIN DE MONTAUZAN C., *Les aqueducs antiques de la ville de Lyon*, Paris, 1909.

GINOUVES R., *Balaneutikè, recherches sur le bain dans l'Antiquité grecque*. Bibliothèque des Écoles françaises d'Athènes et de Rome, 1962.

Journées d'études sur les aqueducs romaines, Actes du colloque de Lyon, des 26–28 mai 1977, Paris, Belles Lettres, 1983.

JULLIAN C., 'La Gaule dans la Table de Peutinger', *Revue des études anciennes*, XIV, 1, 1912, p. 60 ff.

KRENCKER D., E. KRÜGER, H. LEHMANN, H. WACHTLER, *Die Trierer Kaiserthermen, Ausgrabungsbericht und grundsätzliche Untersuchungen römischer Thermen*, Augsbourg, 1929.

LAFON X., 'La voie littorale Sperlonga-Gaeta-Formia', *MEFRA*, 91, 1979-1, p. 399 ff.

LANCIANI R., *Le acque e gli acquedotti di Roma antica*, Rome, 1881 (1975).

LEVEAU P., J.-L. PAILLET, *L'alimentation en eau de Caesarea de Mauritanie et l'aqueduc de Cherchell*, Paris, L'Harmattan, 1976.

LEVI A. and M., *Itineraria Pieta, Contributo allo studio della Tabula Peutingeriana*, Rome, 1967.

MERTENS J., 'Les voies romaines de la Belgique' *Industrie*, IX, 1955, no 10, p. 673 ff.

MONKEWITZ K., 'Der Pont Julien, ein römische Bauwerk im Herzen der Provence', *Antike Welt* 1982, 13, p. 29 to 36.

NEUERBRUG F., 'L'architettura delle fontane e dei ninfei nell' Italia antica', *Memorie Accademia di Archeologia, Lettere e Belle Arti di Napoli*, 5, 1965.

PERSICHETTI N., *La via Salaria nel circondario di Ascoli Piceno*, Rome, 1904, p. 299 ff.

QUILICI L., in the series *Italia nostra*:
— *La via Appia da Roma a Boville*, Rome, 1977. — *La via Prenestina: i suoi monumenti, i suoi paesaggi*, Rome, 1977. — *La via Latina da Roma a Castel Savelli*, Rome, 1978.

QUILICI L., G. M. DE ROSSI, P. G. DI DOMENICO,' La via Aurelia da Roma a Civitavecchia' *Quaderni dell'Instituto di topografia dell'Universita di Roma*, IV, 1968, p. 13 ff.

QUILICI GIGLI S., *La via Salaria da Roma a Passo Corese*, Rome, 1977.

RAKOB F., 'Das Quellenheiligtum in Zaghouan und die Römische wasserleitung nach Karthago', *Mitt. des Deutschen Archaelogischen Instituts, Roemische abteilung*, 81, 1974-1, p. 41 ff.

SALANEA P., *Les voies romaines de l'Afrique du Nord*, Algiers, 1951 (map).

STERPOS D., 'La strada romana in Italia' *Autostrada* 17, Rome, 1970.

VAN DEMAN E. B., *The building of the Roman Aqueducts*, Washington, 1934.

YEGÜL F. K., 'The small city bath in classical antiquity', *Archeologia classica*, XXXI, 1979, p. 108 ff.

Dossier de l'archéologie, no 38, *Aqueducs romains*, Dijon, Oct.–Nov. 1979.

Étude technique sur un texte de l'empereur Julien relatif à la constitution des voies romaines', *R.E.A.*, LXI, 1963, 1–2 p. 114 ff.

For hydrological construction mentioned by Vitruvius, see the annotated translation by L. CALLEBAT, du Livre VIII, *coll. Guillaume Budé*, Paris, Belles Lettres, 1973.

'Les voies anciennes en Gaule', *Caesarodunum*, XVIII, Université de Tours, 1983.

11. — DOMESTIC AND COMMERCIAL ARCHITECTURE

ADAM J.-P., *La costruzione romana privata in una zona sismica: Pompei e l'agro pompeiano*, Storia Geofisica Ambiante, Bologne, 1989.

ANDRÉ J., *L'alimentation et la cuisine à Rome*, Paris, Belles Lettres, 1981.

ANDREAU J., 'Les affaires de Monsieur Jucundus', *coll. de l'École française de Rome*, 19, 1974 and 'Histoire des séismes et histoire, économique, le tremblement de terre de Pompei (62 ap. J.-C.)', *Annales Économies, sociétés, civilisations*, 28, 1093, p. 369 ff.

BEDON R., CHEVALLIER R., PINON P., *Architecture et urbanisme en Gaule romaine*, Errance, Paris, 1988.

BLANC N., NERCESSIAN A., *La cuisine romaine antique*, Glénat-Faton, Grenoble, 1992.

BOETHIUS A., 'Appunti sul carattere razionale e sull'importanza dell'architettura domestica in Roma Imperiale', *Scritti in onore di Bartolomeo Nogara*, Rome, 1937.

CARANDI A., S. SETTIS, *Schiavi e padroni nell'Etruria Romana, La villa di Settefinestre dallo scavo alla mostra*, Bari, 1979.

CARANDINI A., 'La villa del Casale a Piazza Armerina, problemi suggi stratigrafici ed altre ricerche', *M.E.F.R.A.*, 83, 1971.

CERULLI-IRELLI G., 'La casa del colonnato tuscanico, ad Ercolano', *Memorie di Archeologia, Lettere e Belle Arti di Napoli*, 7, 1974.

CERULLI-IRELLI G., 'Officina di lucerne fittili a Pompei', in *L'instrumentum domesticum di Ercolano e Pompei nella prima età imperiale. Quaderni di cultura materiale. 1*, Rome, 1977, p. 53 to 72.

BIBLIOGRAPHY

CURTIS ROBERT I., 'The garum shop of Pompei (I, 12, 8)' *Cronache Pompeiane*, V. 1979, p. 5 ff.

DALMASSO L., V. USSANI, *Guida allo studio della civilta romana antica*, Naples, 1952.

FABBRICOTTI E., 'I bagni nelle prime ville romane', *Cronache pompeiane* II, 1976, p. 29 ff.

FOUET G., *La villa gallo-romaine de Montmaurin* (Haute-Garonne), supplement XX to *Gallia*, Paris, 1969.

FELLETTI MAJ B. M., 'La casa delle volte dipinte' *Bolletino d'Arte*, 45, 1960, p. 45 ff.

FERDIÉRE A., *Les campagnes en Gaule romaine*, Paris 1988.

FRANCISCIS A. DE, *La villa romana di Oplontis, La parola del passato*, 28, 1973, p. 453 ff.

FRANCISCIS A. DE, *La villa romana di Oplontis, Neue Forschungen in Pompeji*, Reklinghausen 1975, p. 9 ff.

FRAYN J.-M., 'Home-baking in Roman Italy', *Antiquity*, LII, 1978, p. 28 ff.

LE GALL J., 'Le Tibre, fleuve de Rome', in *l'Antiquité*, Paris, 1953.

GHISLANZANI E., *La villa romana in Desenzano*, Milan, 1962.

GRIMAL P., *Les jardins romains*, Paris, 2nd ed., 1969.

HOFFMANN A., 'Ein Rekonstruktionsproblem der Casa del Fauno,' *Bericht Koldewey-Gesellschaft*, 1978, p. 35 to 41.

JASHEMSKI W., 'The discovery of a large Vineyard at Pompeii' *American Journal of Archaeology*, 77, 1973, p. 27 to 41.

JASHEMSKI W., *Ancient roman gardens*, Dumbarton Oaks, 1981.

KOCKEL V., *Archäologische funde und forschungen in den Vesuvstädten*, Deutsches Archäologisches Institut, Berlin 1985.

KOCKELL V., WEBER B. F., 'Die villa delle colonne a mosaico in Pompeii', *Mitteilungen des Deutschen Archaologischen Instituts*, R. A. 90, 1983, p. 51 to 89.

MAIURI A., *La casa del Menandro e il suo tesoro di argenteria*, Rome, 1933.

MAIURI A., *La Villa dei Misteri*, Rome, 1931–1947.

MANACORDA D., *Il frantoio della villa dei Volusii a Lucus Feroniae, I volusii Saturnini, Archeologia, Materiali e Problemi*, 6, Bari, 1982, p. 55 ff.

MIELSCH Hararld, *Die römische Villa, Architektur und Lebensform*, Munich, 1987.

MORETTI M., 'La villa dei saturnini a Lucus Feroniae', *Autosdrade* X, 8, 1968.

PACKER J. E., 'The domus of Cupid and Psyche in Ancient Ostia', *American Journal of Archaeology*, 71, 1967, p. 123 ff.

PAILLET J.-L., *Belo III. Le Macellum*, Casa de Velasquez, Archaeology Series no 5, Madrid 1986.

PAOLI U. E., *Vita romana*, Vincenza, Mondadori, 1976.

PASQUI A., 'La villa pompeiana della Pisanella presso Boscoreale', *Monumenti Antichi dell'Accademia dei Lincei*, 7, 1897, col. 397. ff.

PAVOLINI E., *Ostia Vita Quotidiana*, Rome, 1978.

PIETROGRANDE A. L., *Le fulloniche ostiensi, scavi di Ostia VIII*, Rome, 1976.

ROBERT J.-N., *La vie à la campagne dans l'antiquité romaine*, Les Belles Lettres, Paris, 1985.

DE RUYT C., *Macellum, marché alimentaire des Romains*. Louvain-la-Neuve, 1983.

SABRIÉ M. and R., *La maison à portiques du Clos de la Lombarde à Narbonne*, Supplement 16 to *Revue Archéologique de Narbonnaise*, Paris 1987.

SARTORIO G., *Il sistema agro-alimentare a Roma attraverso i secoli*. Museo della civiltà Romana, 1982.

SIRAGO A., *L'Italia agraria sotto Trajano*, Louvain, 1958.

SPINAZZOLA V., *Pompei alla luce degli Scavi Nuovi di Via dell'Abbondanza*, Rome, 1953.

TCHERNIA A., *Le vin de I'Italie romaine*, EFR, 1986.

TCHERNIA A., *Il vino: produzione e commercio, Pompei 79*, Naples 1979, p. 87 ff.

TCHERNIA A., F. ZEVI, *Amphores vinaires de Campanie et de Tarraconaise à Ostie, Recherches sur les amphores romaines*, Rome, 1972, p. 35 ff.

THÉBERT Y., 'L'utilisation de l'eau dans la maison de la pêche à Bulla Regia' *Cahiers de Tunisie*, 19, 1971.

For the development of agricultural products as described by Pliny, see the annotated translation of PLINY THE ELDER, *Historie naturelle*, Paris, Belles Lettres, 1950–81, particularly Books XIV (wine) and XV (oil) with notes by J. ANDRÉ.

SITES AND MONUMENTS
(select list of works containing technical information)

ADAM J.-P., DEYTS S., SAULNIER-PERNUIT L., *La façade des thermes de Sens*, 7th supplement to *Revue Archéologique de l'Est*, Dijon 1987.

ADAM J.-P., BLANC N., *Les Sept Merveilles du Monde*, Librairie Académique Perrin, Paris, 1989.

AUPERT P., *Sanxay*, Imprimerie Nationale, Paris, 1992.

AURIGEMMA S., *La villa Adriana*, Rome, 1961.

BALLU A., *Les Ruines de Timgad: sept années de découvertes*, Paris, 1911.

BALTY J.-Ch., *Guide d'Apamée*, Bruxelles, 1981.

BESCHAOUACH A., R. HANOUNE, Y. THÉBERT, *Les ruines de Bulla Regia*, coll. de l'École française de Rome, 1977.

BIRLEY E., *Research on Hadrian's wall*, Kendal, 1961.

BORRIELLO M. ET A. D'AMBROSIO, *Baiae-Misenum, Forma Italiae, Regio I*, ...

BROISE H., SCHEID J., *Le balneum des frères Arvales*, EFR, Rome, 1987.

CALZA G. et al, *Scair di Ostia, I, Topografia generale*, Rome, 1953.

CARO S. DE, A. GRECO, *Campania, Guide archaeologiche Laterza*, Bari, Rome, 1981.

CARO S. DE, *Saggi nell' area del tempio di Apollo a Pompei*, Istituto universitario orientale, Naples, 1986.

CASTAGNOLI F., *Topografia e urbanistica di Roma antica*, Bologna, 1969.

CERULLI-IRELLI G., *Ercolano*, Cava dei Tirreni, 1969.

COARELLI F., *Guida archeologica di Roma*, Mondadori, Verona, 1974.

COARELLI F., *Dintorni di Roma, Guide archeologiche Laterza*, Bari-Rome, 1981.

COARELLI F., *Lazio, Guide archeologiche Laterza*, Bari, Rome, 1982.

COARELLI F., *Il foro Romano II, Periodo republicano e augusteo*, Rome, 1985.

COARELLI F., *Il foro Romano, periodo arcaico*, Rome, 1983.

COURTOIS C., *Timgad: antique Thamugadi*, Alger, 1951.

COZZA L., *Tempio di Adriano*, Rome 1982.

DELLA CORTE M., *Case ed abitanti di Pompei*, Naples, 1965.

DOREAU J., J.-C. GOLVIN, L. MAURIN, *L'amphithéâtre gallo-romain de Saintes*, C.N.R.S., Bordeaux, 1982.

DURET L. and J.-P. NERAUDAU, *Urbanisme et métamorphose de la Rome antique*, Les Belles Lettres, Paris, 1983.

DUVAL M.-M., *Paris antique des origines au IIIe s.*, Paris, 1961.

ESCHEBACH H., *Die Städtebauliche Entwicklung des antiken Pompeji, Römische Mitteilungen*, supplement 17, Heidelberg, 1970.

ÉTIENNE R., *La vie quotidienne à Pompei*, Paris, Hachette, 1965–1974.

FERRARO S., *Stabiae, Le ville e l'Antiquarium*, Castellamare di Stabia, 1980.

FINSEN H., 'La résidence de Domitien sur le Palatin', *Analecta Romana Instituti Danici*, 5, sup. 1969.

FRANCISCIS A. DE, *Ercolano e Stabia*, Novara, 1974.

GAGGIOTTI M., D. MANCONI, L. MERCANDO, M. VERZAR, *Umbria, Marche, Guide archeologiche Laterza*, Bari-Rome, 1981.

GIULANI C. F., *Tibur 1, forma Italiae*, I, 7, Rome, 1970.

GIULIANI C., P. VERDUCHI, 'Ricerche sull'architecttura di Villa Adriana,' in *Quaderni dell'Istituto di topografia Romana*, VIII, 1975.

GOLVIN J.-C., *L'amphithéâtre romain*, De Boccard, Paris, 1988.

GOUDINEAU C., de KISCH Y., *Errance*, Paris, 1991.

GRANT M., *Le forum romain*, Paris, Hachette, 1970.

GRANT M., *Cités du Vésuve*, Paris, Hachette, 1972.

GRECO E., *Magna Grecia, Guide archeologiche*, Laterza, 1981.

GRECO E., D. THEODORESCU, *Poseidonia-Paestum* I, ICCD, École française de Rome, 1980; II, 1984; III, 1987.

GRELL CH., *Herculanum et Pompei dans les récits des voyageurs français du XVIIIe s.* Bibliothèque de l'Institut français de Naples, 3e série, vol. II, Centre Jean Bérard. Naples, 1982.

GROS P., *Bolsena, guide de fouilles*, collection de l'École française de Rome, 1981.

KRAUSE Cl. et al, *Domus Tiberiana, move ricerche studi di restauro*, Rome, Zurich, 1985.

LANCIANI R., *L'antica Roma*, Bari, Laterza, 1981.

LANCIANI R., *Rovine e scavi di Roma antica*, Rome, 1985.

LEZINE A., *Carthage, Utique, études d'architecture et d'urbanisme*, C.N.R.S., Paris, 1968.

LUGLI G., *Roma antica, Il centro monumentale*, Rome, 1946.

MAIURI A., *Ercolano, I nuovi scavi (1927–1958)*, I, Rome, 1958.

MAIURI A., *Pompei ed Ercolano fra case ed abitanti*, Milan, 1959

MAU A., *Pompeji in Leben und Kunst*, Leipzig, 1908.

MEIGGS R., *Roman Ostia*, Oxford, 1960.

NAPOLI M., *Napoli greco-romana*, Naples, 1959.

OLESON J.-P., *Greek and Roman Mechanical Water-Lifting Devices: The History of a Technology*, University of Toronto, 1984.

PAVOLINI C., *Ostia, guide archeologiche Laterza*, Rome-Bari, 1983.

PENSABENE P., *Tempio di Saturno, architettura e decorazione*, Rome 1984.

POINSSOT C., *Les Ruines de Dougga*, Tunis, 1958.

Puteoli (Pouzzoles), various authors, *Studi di storia antica* I-II, Naples, 1977–1978.

RICHMOND I. A., *Roman Britain*, London, 1967.

LA ROCCA E., M. and A. DE VOS, *Guida archeologica di Pompei*, Milan, 1976–1981.

ROLLAND H., *Fouilles de Glanum*, 1946, supplement I to *Gallia*, Paris, 1946.

EL-SAGHIR M., GOLVIN J.-Cl., REDDÉ M., HEGAZY E., WAGNER G., *Le camp romain de Louqsor*, Institut Français d'Archéologie Orientale, Le Caire, 1986.

SOLIER Y., *Narbonne*, Guides archéologiques de la France, Paris 1986.

SOMMELLA P., *Forma e urbanistica di Pozzuoli Romana, Puteoli, studi di storia antica*, II, Naples, 1980.

STARCKY J., *Palmyre*, Paris, 1952.

TALIAFERRO-BOATWRIGHT M., *Hadrian and the city of Rome*, Princeton University Press, 1987.

THEDENAT H., *Pompei*, Paris, 1906–1927.

TORELLI M., *Etruria, Guide archeologiche*, Laterza, Rome-Bari, 1982.

VARÉNE P., *L'enceinte gallo-romaine de Nîmes. Les murs et les tours*, 53rd supplement to *Gallia*, CNRS, Paris 1992; 'L'apport de l'ethno-archéologie à la connaissance des techniques antiques de construction: deux exemples tirés de la reconstruction partielle d'un temple à Glanum', *JRA*, 6, 1993, p. 193 to 204.

DE VOS A. and M., *Pompei, Ercolano, Stabia, Guide archeologiche Laterza*, Bari-Rome, 1982.

WAELE F.-J. DE, *Corinthe*, Paris, 1961.

WALTER H., *La Porte Noire de Besançon*, Centre de Recherches d'Histoire Ancienne, vol. 65, Besançon, 1986.

WISEMAN F.-J., *Roman Spain: an introduction to the Roman antiquities of Spain and Portugal*, London, 1956.

ZEVI F., *Il santuario della Fortuna Primigenia a Palestrina*, ivi, 16, 1979, p. 2 to 22.

Various 'I campi flegrei nell'archeologia e nella storia', in *Atti del Convegno dei Lincei, Rome, 4–7 mai 1976*, Rome, 1977.

Les enceintes augustéennes dans l'Occident romain, Actes du colloque international de Nîmes des 9–12 Oct 1985, Nîmes, 1987.

INDEX

The index does not give words used in headings or proper names relating to Pompeii, Rome and Vitruvisu that come up regularly.